The Study of Real Skills
Volume 2

Compliance
and
Excellence

The Study of Real Skills

Series Editor: W. T. Singleton, *Applied Psychology Department,*
University of Aston in Birmingham

The Study of Real Skills
Volume 2

Compliance
and
Excellence

Edited by
W. T. Singleton MA DSc
Professor of Applied Psychology
University of Aston in Birmingham

MTPPRESS LIMITED
International Medical Publishers

Published by
MTP Press Limited
Falcon House
Lancaster, England

Copyright © 1979 MTP Press Limited

British Library Cataloguing in Publication Data

Compliance and excellence – (The study of real skills; vol. 2).
1. Ability
I. Title   II. Singleton, William Thomas
153.9   BF431

ISBN 0–85200–090–1

Typeset, printed and bound
in Great Britain by
BLACKBURN TIMES PRESS
Northgate, Blackburn
Lancs. BB2 1AB

Contents

Contributors

A. Baddeley
MRC Applied Psychology Unit, 15 Chaucer Road, Cambridge CB2 2EF

P. Branton
22 Kings Gardens, West End Lane, London NW6 4PU

W. G. Brown
Department of Applied Psychology, University of Aston in Birmingham, Gosta Green, Birmingham B4 7ET

A. J. Cochran
Interdisciplinary Higher Degrees Scheme Office, University of Aston in Birmingham, Gosta Green, Birmingham B4 7ET

H. Drasdo
The Tower, Capel Curig, Betws-y-Coed, Gwynedd LL24 0DR

E. Edwards
Department of Applied Psychology, University of Aston in Birmingham, Gosta Green, Birmingham B4 7ET

D. Godden
University of Aberdeen, Institutes of Environmental and Off-shore Medicine, Foresthill, Aberdeen AB9 2ZD

A. Hedge
Department of Applied Psychology, University of Aston in Birmingham, Gosta Green, Birmingham B4 7ET

J. G. Kyle
School of Education Research Unit, University of Bristol, Lyndale House, 19 Berkley Square, Bristol BS8 1HF

B. R. Lawson
Department of Architecture, University of Sheffield, Sheffield S10 2TN

T. Nettelbeck
Department of Psychology, The University of Adelaide, Box 498, G.P.O., Adelaide, South Australia 5001

W. T. Singleton
Department of Applied Psychology, University of Aston in Birmingham, Gosta Green, Birmingham B4 7ET

P. Spurgeon
Department of Applied Psychology, University of Aston in Birmingham, Gosta Green, Birmingham B4 7ET

M. Thomson
Department of Applied Psychology, University of Aston in Birmingham, Gosta Green, Birmingham B4 7ET

A. T. Welford
Slaughting Cottage, 187A High Street, Aldeburgh, Suffolk IP15 5AL

J. Wirstad
Ergonomrad, Skattkarr, Box 10032, S-650 10 Karlstad, Sweden

Introduction

W. T. SINGLETON

THE PRECEDING BOOK

The present book is the second in a series devoted to the study of real skills. The purposes of the first book were to describe the concept of skill, to review knowledge about skilled performance which has emerged from experimental psychology and to illustrate, by studies of particular jobs, the ways in which real skills have been investigated. The jobs described and analysed in terms of skill as understood by the particular author are illustrated in Table 0.1.

Table 0.1   Case studies in *Study of Real Skills 1*

Industrial classification	Author	Job
Primary	B. Pettersson	The forester
	J. Matthews	The farm worker
Secondary	R. G. Taylor	The metal-working machine tool operator
	W. T. Singleton	The sewing machinist
	L. Bainbridge	The process controller
Tertiary	B. A. Lacy	The tea blender
	J. D. Eccles	The dentist
	P. Branton	The train driver
	R. G. Thorne and G. W. F. Charles	The pilot
Quaternary	D. Whitfield and R. B. Stammers	The air traffic controller
	R. B. Miller	The information system designer
	B. R. Lawson	The architect as a designer
	J. T. Reason	The passenger

It will be noted that they cover the range of human work as classified by economists into primary, secondary, tertiary and quarternary industries. They may also be categorized in terms of technological support. For *the forester* and *the farm worker* the most evident support is the provision of mechanical power to reinforce the traditional muscle power. This relieves the worker of the need for excessive energy expenditure and incidentally results in a modification of the required skills; these have become more manipulative and require tracking-type behaviour instead of the direct application of forces. The same trends are apparent for *the sewing machinist, the machine tool operator* and *the train driver*, where there is ample power available and skill is required in the controlled release of this power on the basis of sensory data. For the two latter these sensory data are supplemented by instrumentation. Instrumentation becomes highly significant, even dominant, for *the pilot*, whose task is perhaps the most typical of those where the man is 'in the control loop' and his skill is expressed by the matching and phasing of outputs to inputs from instruments. For *the process controller* and *the air traffic controller* the interpretation of data provided by instruments becomes the most demanding part of the tasks and outputs are secondary. *The dentist* has no routine instrumentation beyond a mirror but his skills change under the impact of technology as a consequence of improved tools and materials. *The architect as a designer* and *the information system designer* depend for their success on more central cognitive activity rather than peripheral perceptual and motor skills. The computer is beginning to provide some support for these tasks but this impact is not yet strong enough to result in obvious changes in the required skills. There is a cybernetic aspect in that studies of ways of providing computer assistance help to increase our understanding of high level activity: this is also true for *the tea blender*. *The passenger* is not a worker in the sense that he has a desired positive output but there is skilled activity in maintaining integrity in an artificial environment.

Skill so far

In the first volume skill was introduced as learned behaviour, inevitably highly variable within and between individuals and difficult to analyse because of its essential continuity. It is integrated in space and time and there is always a purpose, objective or goal providing meaning to the activity.

It is possible to structure the field in a very general way by separating input, output and cognitive skills or alternatively perceptual and motor skills but these taxonomies have elements of uncertainty and obscurity which may be an inevitable consequence of the completely integrated nature of skilled activity on the part of an individual. Skills are certainly hierarchical in the sense that complex skills are made up of simpler skills and also in the different sense that, at any level, skills can be described in terms of input, processing and output aspects while, at a lower level, each of these aspects can itself be analysed into input, processing and output aspects. This distinction is illustrated in Figure 0.1. In passing it is interesting to recall that the original meaning of hierarchy was not merely a graded organization but graded sets of trios, three divisions of angels each subdividing into three orders of angels.

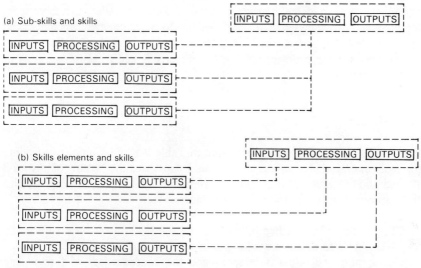

Figure 0.1 Different skill hierarchies

Methodologically the study of human skill seems to progress by sensitive observation of the real situation supported when possible by laboratory experiments. The experiment remains the ancillary supporting technique rather than the pioneering one; experimental data are used to reject hypotheses rather than to generate them.

Almost all the jobs studied involved the human operator coping with the physical world and achieving his particular objective through the help of hardware. Within these situations the man–machine relationship is a partnership where the machine provides the power and sometimes the precision while the man provides the sequencing and timing. The term 'partnership' describes adequately the complementary and closely integrated functions of man and machine but it disguises the dominance of the man who provides knowledge of the context, a term which can cover everything from the ambient environment to the objectives. It is significant that even for the least sophisticated jobs the skills of the man involve assessment and judgement. These higher level functions occur not only in relation to the external world but also in relation to the man's own performance. The skilled man is always a monitor of his own achievements. Information theory provides useful insights into the sequential and iterative nature of human performance but the theory does not readily extend to highlight the importance of continuity in space and time, nor does it encourage the consideration of individual differences which appear not only in level of achievement but also in learning and fatigue.

The way in which the skilled operator comprehends and controls the total situation seems to be best described by the concept of *models of reality*. These vary from *enactive models* which are extended body images, unvisualized and inaccessible to logical reasoning, through *spatial models* which have some topological correspondence to the real world with changes in space and time, to *symbolic models* which vary from iconic to completely abstract and which are used for problem solving not directly linked to sensory inputs or muscular outputs.

Skill appraisal

Each of the different investigators listed in Table 0.1 had a unique procedure for skill appraisal depending on personal expertise, the nature of the skill studied and the reasons for studying it. Nevertheless it is possible to generalize their approach into the following sequence:

1. Observation of the skilled activity in the normal context on a sufficiently long-term basis to detect any changes in rhythm, possibly over days or even weeks, to note individual differences and the consequences of fatigue and learning
2. Clarification and unification of hypotheses developed during observation using protocol methods, good/poor contrast, critical incident techniques and so on
3. Study of the development of the skill during the training phase with examination of the reasons for particular training practices and assessment procedures
4. Analysis of the structure of the skill: the dimensions of perceptual activity, decision making and action strategies
5. Checking of hypotheses by specific experiments or field performance measurement
6. Validation of the success of any innovations in system design, training or work design introduced as a result of the appraisal.

The coherence of skilled activity appears to pose insurmountable problems for the skills analyst. If the essence of skill is in the interrelatedness of the activity then the attempt to analyse would seem to be self-defeating. Nevertheless attempts continue since understanding or even description in scientific terms traditionally requires that a search be made for the elements from which the topic of study has been composed or at least that the topic be structured in some meaningful way. Structure in turn requires that some relevant dimensions be identified which are preferably orthogonal and along which it should be possible to construct scales of measurement. This is the orthodox conceptual approach and it is reinforced by operational demands in that the current technology of training and of work design is based on the assumption that job specifications and task descriptions are available. Behind the various kinds of specifications and descriptions there is again the need for, or the assumed existence of, methods for analysing the skills which are required to perform the tasks.

It is desirable at this stage to be as definitive as possible about these various terms. A *job* is an activity carried out for gain by an individual; it may be a collection of tasks or a part of a task. A *task* is that part of a system activity which is carried out by human operators, it may be less than a job for one person or it may require more than one person. Thus *task* is a system- or operation-oriented term while *job* is a person- or operator-oriented term. Since human activity always changes by learning through training and experience, skills are involved in jobs and tasks. Unfortunately, although the above convention about the difference between tasks and jobs is now reasonably established, there is, as yet, no corresponding convention about the meaning of the term *skill*. The Oxford Dictionary defines *skill* as expertness, practised ability, facility for doing something, dexterity, tact and discernment; it involves adroitness and ingenuity. This would seem acceptable within skill psychology but it is broad enough to contain considerable ambiguity. It can be applied equally readily to persons, to jobs or to tasks. This gives rise to various confusions: between job analysis, task analysis and skills analysis, between the level parameter and the learning parameter and between the entity and the manifestation. Accepting that there is no sign of consensus in the literature it would be premature to try to impose an arbitrary convention. At this stage unless the context removes this ambiguity it is desirable when using the noun to add some qualifying epithet or alternatively to use the adjective to qualify a particular noun, namely perceptual skill, motor skill, cognitive skill, skill level, skill acquisition, skilled performance and skilled operator. However it is sometimes convenient and apposite to use the term alone meaning the entity which has been acquired by learning and which is manifested in performance.

The interrelated nature of all skilled activity does not inevitably result in the complete homogeneity of space and time dimensions. This does occur at the level of a controlled movement where the mass of the moving system provides the constant linking together space and time as expressed in Newtonian equations of motion. The observable smoothness is a natural consequence of minimized energy expenditure achieved by a control system which must be using data looking forwards and backwards. That is, the activity at any instant is clearly a function of what has happened just previously and what is going to happen next, all in the context of progression towards an objective. Although such controlled activity can be described reasonably precisely in the mathematics of control theory it is much less easy to encompass verbally and it cannot be represented diagrammatically. Taking a more molar view of behaviour; time and timing in the form of order and sequencing become dominant in output behaviour where the completion of one segment of activity is the trigger for the initiation of the next and the structure in space is less basic than the structure in time. The opposite, however, seems to be true of input activities which are dominated by the visual channel and here order is not necessarily of great consequence because of the flexibility with which the eyes can scan the spatial environment. Order is, of course, a fundamental characteristic of auditory inputs but since these are normally used to supplement and confirm visual information it remains reasonable to generalize to the point of postulating that time is the key dimension in outputs but spatial array is the corresponding key set of dimensions in inputs. At the more central cognitive level one can only speculate that both modes of operation are possible although perhaps not simultaneously. This might be called the contexture of behaviour. That is, whether the controlling programme of the particular behaviour is integrated into a sequence (not necessarily linked to real time) or whether it is integrated into a spatial array or picture with sequence of little or no significance. Beyond these procedures are the symbolic types of thinking which need be neither spatial nor temporal but in which integration is provided by the rules of the particular symbolic system or language. Hence the importance of grammar and syntax. This is another way of looking at enactive, pictorial and symbolic skills respectively. Unfortunately the only easily observable part of any human activity is effector functions which cannot be other than sequentially ordered. Thus skills analysis always depends on creative reconstruction of what is probably happening behind the appearance of sequential outputs.

A further source of complexity is that the skilled man is not restricted to a unitary stream of activity at any level higher than the physical output. The effector actions necessarily develop from previous effector actions within one dimension of performance but there may be several kinds of performance (that is, performance related to several different objectives) proceeding in parallel or intermittently in succession. The operator keeps track of what is happening including what he is doing from his record of all the previous relevant effector actions which are stored as a developing chain in which each successive action modifies the total stored model. This is what Head and Bartlett meant by developing schemata.

The whole business of motor skills is based on the facilitation of these models and their separation so that particular incoming information is allocated to the relevant schema. The operator must categorize to keep the whole operation in order and tidily articulated. The inputs of a skilled man are similarly complex and are controlled in an analogous manner. That is, there are separate schemata developing to do with the different outputs, actual or potential, and information is allocated according to the relevance to possible outputs. This is one reason why it is so difficult to distinguish clearly between motor skills and perceptual skills. Motor skills are organized by criteria of *inputs* and perceptual skills by criteria of *outputs*. This is an extraordinarily ingenious control system design which ensures that the two kinds of skill mesh together into total performance in an almost inseparable fashion. Among other implications it follows that, in dynamic behaviour with continuous streams of inputs and outputs, the decision or choice element vanishes as a separate mechanism. For the skilled man decisions are essentially off-line rather than on-line; they are partly predetermined and wholly governed by the relationship to the overall purpose. There are always higher level mechanisms which monitor the relative success in relation to purpose. It is such mechanisms which Bartlett had in mind when he coined the memorable phrase "turning round on one's own schemata". He was discussing how memory functions, but the same mechanism operates in decision making. The decision is made by the complex interaction of receptor and effector mechanisms at the central level, but the operator must 'turn round on it' using higher level mechanisms to find out what it is.

This speculative model throws some light also on the significance of context. Just as within prose the meaning of a word or phrase can only be traced by examining the preceding and succeeding parts of the passage and sometimes the passage as a whole, so also the meaning of an element of behaviour depends on its position within the more general purposive activity in which it is embedded. This applies correspondingly to the understanding of decision making based on the interpretation and combination of separate clues. The skilled diagnostician or decision maker relies on the context of the apparently isolated items of information which he puts together so that his strategy or course of action is selected. He can check what it is afterwards if he wishes to.

All this goes some way towards explaining why skills analysis is such a difficult and essentially creative business and also why it cannot be done in vacuo. The skills analyst, himself a diagnostician and decision maker, needs a purpose. It also follows that he cannot avoid the field study of the skilled operator as the fundamental approach to the understanding of skilled behaviour. This is not to underrate the importance of laboratory experiments in tidying up the fine detail and in providing the evidence to reject what may seem to be attractive hypotheses in the untidy field situation. The snag about experiments is the extraordinary difficulty of devising a laboratory situation which accurately reflects rather than disguises the intricacy of skilled behaviour. Thus, both contextural and contextual aspects of behaviour reinforce the view that skills appraisal, and analysis in so far as it is possible, must begin with and continue to depend upon the study of real skills.

This is the justification for the method adopted in these skills books. Particular studies of particular skills are described as examples of what can and has been achieved and collectively as the foundation for some generalizations about human skill.

THE PRESENT BOOK

The previous book began with a description of the activities of human–experimental psychologists; this book begins with the description of the activities of skills analysts. The origins of these techniques are in attempts to improve industrial productivity. Practitioners have always been in close contact with the real situation but for a long time there was no theoretical support, so that time study and method study became rather static in methodology in spite of very widespread utilization. A new impetus was provided by the Second World War with operational problems such as the design of training schemes or the evolving design of equipment with technological advances. In more recent times skills analysts have sometimes been concerned with both in that, as participants in systems design, any greater understanding of the behaviour of the human operators in the system can in principle contribute to both training and work design or even to the allocation of problem solutions between these two areas. Because the number of experienced practitioners is small compared with experimental psychology the state of the art is inevitably less mature and it cannot be presented within an established systematic structure. Nevertheless a great deal of effort and ingenuity has been devoted to these studies and they are worthy of description and discussion at the methodological level.

After this first chapter the succeeding studies are by different authors, each of whom has a special interest in a particular kind of skilled activity. Some of these studies focus on the practice of particular skills within jobs and tasks (diving, climbing, golfing, piloting, music playing and research) while others focus on skills required by particular kinds of persons which are not specific to particular jobs (occupational disability, mental retardation, hearing impairment, aging, institutionalization, safety, visual detection and creative thinking). The aim is to illustrate the variety of skilled activity supporting human aspirations and yet to demonstrate that there are principles of skill which are general across this vast range of behaviour. As in the first book each chapter was written especially for the book and although the aim and content was discussed no author saw any other contribution before he wrote his own. So far as I am aware the only exception to this is that I wrote three chapters in the order in which they appear and obviously, for example, I knew what was in Chapter 1 when I wrote Chapter 2. This is not to suggest that there was any desire or attempt to impose any secrecy, and inevitably authors would know the work of other authors from previous publications. Nevertheless the independence of authorship does marginally strengthen the case for any generalization which can be made by comparisons between chapters. If two or more different investigators of different topics have used the same method or reached the same conclusion then we can feel that much more secure in accepting it.

The invitations to authors were made within the structure that there should be a few chapters about jobs where the context was hostile to the point that compliance was a reasonable strategy, and a few chapters about jobs or tasks where there do seem to be people who can perform at a level of excellence well above that to which the average person could expect to rise. Thus the range of behaviour under discussion has been extended in two directions from the average skilled performance of the individual with normal endowments characteristic of the first book. This book concentrates on the extremes of compliance and excellence. Compliance is appropriate when the performance of the individual is restricted either because he is unfortunate enough to have some peculiar limitation of his capacities (occupational disability, mental retardation, hearing impairment, old age) or because the system is imposing peculiar demands (safety, institutionalization, diving). Excellence seems to be the appropriate description when the operator is well beyond the average skilled performance and is deliberately seeking achievements to which most people do not aspire (the rock-climber, the golfer, the expert pilot, the musician, the research worker) or which demand the higher levels of human activity (visual detection, creative thinking). The aim is to encompass the total range of human achievement rather than the normal range covered in the first book. This is itself a particular method of skills analysis frequently mentioned in the first book, namely the method of contrasts. One tries to identify some characteristics of skilled performance by contrasting the extremes: trained and untrained, expert and novice, good and poor, fast and slow, and in this case compliance and excellence.

1
Skills Analysis

W. T. SINGLETON

INTRODUCTION

We wish to examine a situation involving two skilled individuals; one is an operator engaged in some activity, the other is an investigator who wishes to understand and describe this activity. To state that they are skilled implies that whatever is being done by either individual requires intelligence, effort, sensitivity, training, experience and a purpose. To state that they are individuals implies that the focus of the whole business is persons rather than tasks and that any generality achieved will require some simplification of the unique behaviour of particular individuals at a given time. This last point is worth emphasising because there is a natural tendency to aspire towards skills analysis, skill descriptions and skill specifications which are pure in the sense that they are logical, unemotional and carried out by routine formulae agreed by and acceptable to the relevant scientific establishment. This is not the case and even in principle can never be the case because we are studying human beings and there are always differences between and within individuals. We may attempt to encompass these individual differences within some averaging statistics but such summaries inevitably involve a loss of information. On the other hand although the particular operator is the main source of data it does not follow that the investigator is primarily interested in individuals. His purpose may be to design a workspace for a particular job or to design a training scheme for all entrants to a particular occupation. In these cases generalization is a necessary part of his analysis and its implementation through some design process.

Continuous reference to the purpose of the activity is one of the main anchors for the understanding of what is happening for both the investigator and the operator who is the subject of analysis. To regularly remind oneself why any activity is being carried out is an inherent part of understanding how it is carried out. The emphasis and direction of a skills analysis depends on the purpose of the particular analysis.

The inevitable fuzziness of procedures and results is not a good excuse for avoidable untidiness of approach. Unfortunately the literature is somewhat untidy in that there are considerable ambiguities of terminology. In this chapter the distinction between jobs, tasks and skills already established will be maintained as far as possible. A *job* is usually a collection of tasks carried out by an individual, a *task* is defined by a particular system-type objective and a *skill* is a person-referenced attribute involved in carrying out tasks and jobs. There is a correspondingly arbitrary distinction between analysis, description and specification. *Analysis* means the process of acquiring and collating evidence, *description* means the output of this process in input–output terms and a *specification* is the result of an analysis in more detailed functional terms (Singleton, 1974).

The ambiguities are due not only to interchangeability of terminology but also to the necessary flexibility of approach and the overlapping procedures between different kinds of analysis. For example, an investigator may consider that he is carrying out a skills analysis because he wishes to understand what has been acquired by a skilled operator through learning and experience so as to design a training scheme which will facilitate a corresponding acquisition by novices, but he might start the procedure by a job analysis or a task analysis. Similarly he may decide to employ a particular technique such as good/poor performance comparison, but this same technique might contribute to understanding at the job, the task or the skill level. There is another terminological distinction in the hierarchy of ways of considering what the investigator is doing. Again somewhat arbitrarily the hierarchy assumed in this chapter is in the order: philosophy, method, procedure and technique. A *technique* is a specific way of acquiring evidence, e.g. the critical incident technique. Unfortunately the literature generally contains the phrases critical incident method, critical incident procedure and critical incident technique with no detectable consensus in favour of any one of these. A *procedure* is a more generalized way of tackling a particular kind of analysis and may involve a series, a matrix or a set of techniques. (Just to clarify this sentence a *series* is a one-dimensional array, a *matrix* is a multidimensional array and a *set* is a collection which may have no attributes which readily suggest dimensions.) A *method* is a style of investigation which rests on a competence in particular scientific disciplines or combinations of disciplines e.g. a physiological method, or it may transcend particular disciplines e.g. an experimental method. Behind each method or set of methods there is a *philosophy* which can be appealed to if there is some obscurity about the validity or reliability of the use of the method in a particular context.

One final cause of confusion is worth mentioning; most of the terminology used in analysis is also used outside the context of analysis, e.g. there are training methods as well as analytical methods. Analysis itself is often used to describe a particular statistical technique which is required during a skills analysis, e.g. cluster analysis.

HISTORY OF ACTIVITY ANALYSIS

There have always been investigators interested in describing and analysing the activity of individuals. The origin, no doubt, is in the perpetual aspiration to improve performance in athletics, games and war. In terms of work or industrial performance, and restricting the backward view to this century, the pioneers were undoubtedly Taylor (1911) and Gilbreth (1911), the founders respectively of Time Study and Motion Study. Taylor was concerned with heavy physical work in the steel industry and he not unreasonably concentrated on optimizing time utilization by allocation of rest-pauses and provision of incentives; his objective was improved productivity. He is worthy of mention and respect because he did attempt to approach the problem systematically, to measure what could be measured at reasonable cost and thus to generate hypotheses which could be tried out in practice immediately. He called this approach "Scientific Management", and if his contribution has been underrated it is because his successors made excessive claims for the validity of the approach, pushed it unreasonably beyond the state of the measurement arts and generally created suspicions of charlatanism and paternalism. This is a fate which overtakes pioneers in the study of work with depressing regularity. Gilbreth seems to have had a wider industrial experience and a greater interest in a more microscopic view of human activity particularly manual manipulation. He understood that any kind of analysis must be based on a sensitive taxonomy of kinds of activity and developed the very detailed therblig system ('Gilbreth' backwards, more or less; see Table 1.3) for classifying movements. His aim was to improve working efficiency.

It will be noted that these investigators were concentrating on the prevalent kinds of work in the early years of this century and that their success depended not only on their creative scientific effort but also on their compatibility with the attitudes of workers and management in that era. Their approach reflected the social climate of the time as well as the real problems found in human work.

This characteristic has been sustained through to the present times and the present problems. Because a skills analyst is so close to the real world his approach is bound to be a function not only of the styles of work which are of interest and importance but also of more elusive but equally influential factors such as the attitudes of management, workers and the many kinds of relevant institutions such as trade unions and professional associations. Behind these attitudes is the general ethos of the society of which both the analyst and his subject of study are members.

Taylor and Gilbreth both continued to work under the title Scientific Management during World War I. The need was accentuated by the importance of greater productivity and reduction of waste for both materials and human labour. The psychologists at this time were making their main contribution through the development of selection tests for the military, although there was some involvement in industrial work. In the UK the Industrial Fatigue Research Board was founded in 1916; their studies were mainly to do with conditions of work – climate, hours, fatigue, accidents and so on – rather than with the activities of operators engaged in particular jobs. In the USA the two Gilbreths, husband and wife, developed at this time Fatigue study as the complement of Motion study (Gilbreths, 1916) covering the same field as that studied by the Industrial Fatigue Research Board. During the period between the wars Time and Motion Study was practised as a method of improving industrial productivity, but the emphasis was more on time taken than on actions carried out so that the analysis technique was simplified to the measurement of cycle time with a stop-watch and the adding of various allowances for perceived degree of skill and effort and for expected deterioration over time which could be compensated for by adding fatigue allowances (see Figure 1.1). During World War II there was a return to interest in method study. This arose from the introduction of a new and fundamental concept about training, quite different from theory and practice either in the industrial world of apprenticeships and imitation learning or the educational world of formal theory and rote learning. The innovation was simply to examine what skilled practitioners within a particular job actually did as a basis for the design of training for those who wish to learn how to do that job. The idea emerged on a large scale in industry with the "Training within Industry" (TWI) movement in the USA and the Process Analysis (PA) training in the UK (Seymour, 1968). Study of real working methods resulted not only in the design of more effective training schemes based on the progressive acquisition of new skills but also in the complementary design process of modifying the work space and procedure for more effective operation. The refinement of method study techniques resulting from this extensive practice is described in Barnes (1949) and Shaw (1952). Since the 1950s, Time and Motion Study, rechristened Work Study, has flourished on a vast scale in industry but conceptually has made little or no advance. The few academics and other intellectuals who had industrial interests mostly operated through newer subjects such as Operational Research and Ergonomics.

For military equipment after World War II, the increasing complexity of technological support for human activity resulted in a further change of emphasis from manual exertion and direct material manipulation to information processing and decision making. There were extensive new skill requirements in maintenance as well as on-line operation of equipment and this led to the study of better ways of training maintenance engineers in fault location and repair. This movement was another reaction against the educational principle that sound indoctrination in basic theory was the best preparation for such diagnostic skills. Once again it was necessary to find out what the skilled maintenance man did, and although there was an overt procedural aspect to this there was also a covert component of selective perception and weighting of evidence which, of course, proved more difficult to analyse. An excellent description of the results of these and other psychological activities in US military systems is contained in Gagne (1962). This was the specific origin of Task Analysis, partly as a research method but mainly as part of a system design process with emphasis on operator training for on-line operations and for maintenance. The corresponding automation movement in industrial systems led to studies of what came to be called the process control operator as distinct from the assembly operator. Again the skills involved are more difficult to analyse because they can only be inferred rather than directly observed, and verbal communication between operator and analyst becomes correspondingly more important (Edwards and Lees, 1974). Greater insight into these perceptual or cognitive skills was also encouraged by the development of teaching machines in the 1950s and 1960s. The necessary formality of programming these machines was a useful stimulant to more incisive thinking about learning processes leading to skills and the ways of analysing and classifying both the processes and the resultant skills (Glaser, 1965; Wallis et al., 1966). During the 1960s there was also increased emphasis on the Task Description as evidence in relation to equipment design and as a basic component of the system design process (Meister and Rabideau, 1965; Singleton et al., 1967).

The present position seems to be that Task Analysis is still seen as the broad term for the acquisition of evidence about human performance on real tasks, particularly with reference to the design of training schemes (de Greene, 1970; Annett et al., 1971). The term Skills Analysis is often used in the UK meaning an acquisition of evidence process in the design of training schemes which rely on a 'progressive part' method (Seymour, 1968; Singer and Ramsden, 1969). Task Analysis techniques are now spreading into education (Gagne, 1974).

The increased sophistication of Process Control Analysis continues with the emphasis on the greater involvement of computers not only as data banks and as parts of closed loop control systems but also as contributors to off-line decision making (Whitfield, 1976). The pursuit of more precise analysis of cognitive activities has resulted in increased emphasis on the taxonomic problems of describing high level human skills (Singleton and Spurgeon, 1975).

Although the techniques of analysis change continuously the objectives do not. These latter have always been productivity, safety, health and well-being. We improve in our ability to achieve these ends rather than the aspiration to do so. Taylor and Gilbreth wrote at length about the problem of ensuring that the worker was satisfied with his activities and his achievements.

Table 1.1 Historical development of analysis techniques

	Society	Technology	Labour Supply	Typical Worker	Analysis
1900		Beginning of mass production	Shortage	Heavy physical work	Time Study
					Motion Study
				Rapid manipulative work	
1910	World War I		Shortage		Fatigue Study
1920		Mechanization		Machine feeding	Work Measurement
1930	Economic depressions		Excessive		
1940	World War II		Shortage		Industrial Skills Analysis
1950	Cold War	Automation		Machine maintenance	Task Analysis
1960	Rapid economic advance		Shortage		Factorial Task Analysis
1970		Computerization		System monitoring	Error Analysis
	Environmentalism		Excessive		Process Control Analysis
	Energy limits				
1980					

The techniques and their utilization are influenced mainly by changing economic conditions such as labour supply/demand and changing technology as shown in Table 1.1.

TIME STUDY

F. W. Taylor (*op. cit.*) working in the 1880s correctly identified one fundamental problem of management, namely how to discover "what really constitutes a proper day's work for a workman". He also identified with considerable prescience two major scientific principles, one physiological and one psychological: what we would call static versus dynamic physical work which he described as "a man who stands still under load is exerting no horse-power whatever and this accounts for the fact that no constant relation can be traced between . . . energy exerted and the tiring effect of the work on the man", and what we would call a problem of feedback and knowledge of results which he stated as "a reward, if it is to be effective in stimulating men to do their best work, must come soon after the work has been done." He relied extensively on the use of the stop-watch not only to measure cycle times but also to ensure that the total time was optimally divided between work and rest. He considered that "the workman and the management" had the joint task of specifying "not only what is to be done but how it is to be done and the exact time allowed for doing it". Successful completion of this joint task should result in an addition of from 30 to 100% to ordinary wages.

This is probably the origin of the basic principle of Time Study or Work Measurement, which is that a piece-work effort is 33% greater than a day-work effort, enshrined in the three bench mark systems for day-work and piece-work known as the 60 : 80 scale, the 75 : 100 scale and the 100 : 133 scale. The former, known as the Bedaux system, assumes that a 'normal pace' of work as in day-work results in 60 'standard minutes' of work per hour, whereas when 'normal incentives' are applied as in piece-work then 80 'standard minutes' of work per hour will result. This becomes an axiom on the basis of which operator effort can be 'rated' by the assumption of the 60/80 bench marks, and the time study engineer estimates his effort by asking himself whether the work being observed is at an ordinary day-work pace in which case he will rate it as 60, or an ordinary piece-work pace which he will rate as 80, or between or outside these fixed points of the scale.

There are other, much less commonly used systems for rating; see Barnes (1949). Effort rating can be regarded as a method of using a skilled observer to compensate and correct for small samples and for distortions due to effects on working tempo of awareness of being observed. These latter can be in either direction: an observed worker may speed up as a matter of pride if he knows he is being watched or he may slow down if he suspects that the time obtained from the observation is going to determine his piece-work rate of pay. There can also be distortions from the observer side, for example, if he wishes markedly to increase productivity or cut earnings he may deliberately underrate the observed performance.

Having obtained a corrected time for the work cycle there is another problem of how much of the total time is expected to be devoted to the work. Clearly the operator requires time for personal needs, for rest and for some margin of slowing down as he gets tired during a shift. These are called Fatigue Allowances or Rest Allowances; some vary with the kind of

work and some are independent. The problem is usually resolved by the use
of tubular data as shown in Table 1.2. These allowances also are susceptible
to distortion by political issues; they may become a topic of negotiation
between management and unions and they may be deliberately tightened or
loosened by some higher management policy decision.

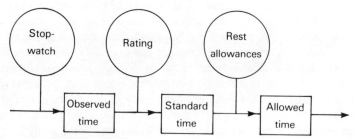

Figure 1.1 Work Measurement procedure

Table 1.2 Typical fatigue or rest allowances used in time study

	Maximum allowance
High energy output	50%
Difficult posture	10%
Excessive movement	15%
Visual fatigue	8%
Personal needs	4%
Thermal conditions	100%
Atmospheric conditions	20%
Total allowance usually about 20%	

   The vulnerability to criticism of the time study technique and the ease with
which one can quote misuses of the system are essentially products of the
enormous use which has been made of the technique in practice in every
industrially based country. No other way of observing and measuring human
performance has had anything approaching the practical impact of time

study. The basic methodology is difficult to argue with, namely measure what can be measured and try to obtain the best possible estimates of unmeasurable factors by relying on experienced human judgement and the use of bench marks (Figure 1.1).

The study of rating accuracy reveals that there are three separable problems (Gregory, 1961); the correct concept of a 'normal' performance, the tendency to 'flatness', i.e. underestimation of high rates of work, and consistency or reliability. Research findings are scattered and difficult to collate but it does seem likely that teams of work study practitioners can establish an agreed concept of normal performance, although this may differ between teams and almost certainly will differ between teams in different industries. Flatness is a universal tendency but probably not to the extent that it causes serious operational problems. One well-organized study of consistency (Rodgers and Hammersley, 1954), involving three simulated industrial tasks and twenty-four experienced practitioners as subjects, concluded that "time study is fourteen times as inaccurate as it is commonly supposed to be". The overall variation was 21% (standard deviation) and this was contrasted with the common belief that time study is accurate to about 3%. Acceptable research studies have not been extensive or conclusive because it is so difficult to agree simple systems-relevant criteria. The problem is that time study is used so widely in very different contexts with very different degrees of expertise, and anyway the numbers arrived at by specific observation and rating are rarely treated as sacrosanct and may even be only a minor dividend within the total effect of the time study. Within a small organization time study data are one relatively clear bit of evidence with which to initiate the dialogue between management and workers – about production times and payment rates. Within a medium-sized organization the continuous presence of work study observers on the factory floor provides an invaluable link between the production workers and the management which serves all kinds of purposes beyond the mere time study which is the ostensible reason for their presence. In the large organization work study experience will be part of the expertise of both lower management and trade union representatives and the time study data becomes a vehicle which may do little more than trigger negotiations. Nevertheless the dubious level of accuracy and the dominance of bargaining procedures has resulted in a considerable diminution in the use of time study in the context of wage negotiations over the past decade. The problem of cycle time estimation remains important for machine allocation, line balancing and other production planning purposes.

It is possible to arrive at some estimates of time allocation without using stop-watches at all. The most widely used method is that involving "Predetermined Motion Time Systems" (PMTS). The assumption is that if a task is analysed into sufficiently small elements, these elements will be definable independently of the particular task and will take a standard time which also is not dependent on the particular task. There are many systems of this kind;

the two most commonly used are "Methods Time Measurement" (MTM) and "Work Factor" (WF). The structure of the systems is usually that a task involves hand movements such as 'reach', grasp' and 'move' with various additions for more complex manipulations and for non-manual activity such as eye movements and postural changes. Analysing a task into such elements is tedious rather than difficult because the elements are precisely defined but very small. Gershoni (1972) has shown that differences in working method are much more readily detected by observers using such an analysis than those using stop-watch time study. The assumption of independence and additivity of element times has often been challenged by psychologists. In particular Smith and Sussman (1969) have conducted extensive experiments demonstrating that a hand movement time varies with learning, direction and with what happens at the end of it, although the latter point is taken into account within, for example, the MTM system and performance is assumed to be asymptotic in terms of the learning curve.

Sanfleber (1966) has investigated the "effect of the motion gestalt" on element times and concluded that there are effects of extensive individual differences as well as task differences on element times, but that these effects although statistically significant are of little practical importance. Moores (1968) compared task times arrived at using PMTS with those arrived at by time study using more than a hundred work study officers and six very different tasks from bricklaying to charging out library books. He concluded that the differences were less than 10%. Thus, although some assumptions behind PMTS are not theoretically tenable, the result in practice is an estimate of cycle time and an analysis of overt movements which is sufficiently valid to be of considerable practical use.

Another method of arriving at time estimates without using a stop-watch is that pioneered by Tippet (1934) and called ratio-delay, snap reading or work sampling. In essence the method depends on the inference that, for example, if at any instant 10% of the workers are not at their work-space then the best estimate of the situation from this datum is that a worker is at the work-space for 90% of the time. The method can be elaborated with orthodox statistical rules concerning the accuracy of the inference with different sample sizes and variations, numbers of classes of events observed and so on; see for example Zacks (1962). It is frequently used in association with time-lapse photography where a frame of film is taken at regular intervals but much less frequently than normal cine-filming.

This time study situation has been explored in detail, not because there is much to be learned theoretically from the vast experience in this field, but because it illustrates the untidiness of the real situation and the complexity of interacting factors which increase so rapidly with the potential practical relevance of an observational technique. It seems that a technique remains pure and unambiguous only as long as it remains operationally useless. The fact that use of the system has declined rapidly in the last few years is not so much because of the weakness of the system but reflects rather the changing nature of industry as technology advances. Manual tasks have been replaced by cognitive tasks which are much less accessible to direct observation, and cycle times have become much more a function of machine characteristics rather than of direct human effort. The interaction effects between processes and people have also increased so that jobs are less readily treated in isolation.

MOTION STUDY

F. B. Gilbreth (*op. cit.*) was a contemporary of Taylor; he was person-centred rather than productivity-centred and he was much more sensitive to the need for classification systems as the precursor to any measurement (Gilbreth, 1973). His therblig classification of hand movements is well known but he also approached the disablement problem by a preliminary classification. He indentified the most difficult class as those who were restricted by injury to mental work although by experience, capability and inclination they were confined to physical work. His study of bricklayers incorporated a five-way classification of skill level from the labourers to those capable of ornamental and exterior face brick. He divided intermediate management into the planners and the performers, an assumption which is still commonly accepted although it probably ought to have been abandoned by this time. From this background Motion Study had an excellent start and the two classification schemes, the ASME symbols for process charts and to a lesser extent the therbligs for micro-motion charts, have survived with little change because the elements or classes have just about the right degree of precision/imprecision of definition, the right level of detail and the right time length for their respective purposes. The various symbol systems are illustrated in Table 1.3; for details of their application see Shaw (1952). The ASME symbols are still widely used but during the past twenty years the therbligs have been superseded by the classifications associated with predetermined motion time systems (PMTS). These are similar in detail and in definition to the therbligs but have as described earlier, the added advantage of standard times associated with each element. There are not many publications about the particular systems, no doubt because they are part of the expertise of specialist management consultants and are provided on a confidential basis for particular companies as clients.

The simple motion chart of an activity is not sufficiently respected as the preliminary to any kind of more detailed analysis. The main advantage is that the observer is forced to observe. He cannot prepare even a two-handed process chart without looking in detail at exactly what the two hands of the operator actually do and how their activities are phased together. Even experienced observers find it difficult to prepare a SIMO chart (abbreviation

Table 1.3   Motion study symbols

ASME	Therblig	PMTS*
☐ Inspection	⟨⊙⟩ search	
	⊙ find	E eye movement
	◊ inspect	
○ Operation	∩ grasp	G grasp
	⊙ position	P position
	# assemble	
	∪ use	T manipulate
	⊬ disassemble	
	႘ preposition	
	∩ release load	
⇨ transport	→ select	
	∪ transport loaded	M move
	∪ transport empty	R reach
▽ storage	⌓ hold	
	႖ rest	
	⌒ unavoidable delay	
	⌐o avoidable delay	
	႖ plan	
D delay		

*Symbols and categories in this column are typical of those used in the various PMTS systems. There are many sub-categories within each category so that a standard time can be allocated, e.g. the time for a Reach in the MTM system varies with the distance moved (about 20 sub-categories) and with what happens after the reach (four sub-categories) of Simultaneous Motion, coined by Gilbreth) using therbligs or PMTS symbols without the aid of a film of the operation which can be stopped, started, played in slow motion, played backwards and so on, thus providing a check on exactly what is happening. When such charts have been prepared they become a permanent record of the operation. Such a record has many uses from a check on the way production methods change over time and with increasing skill to a comparison of different styles of work and procedures of workers.

The actual analysis of the record with the objective of improving the working method turns out in practice to be rather less important. The observational and intellectual effort required actually to produce the chart generates a familiarity and awareness of the operation concerned which provides a sufficient basis for any deliberation about training design or method changes. There are the so-called "principles of motion economy" which provide some guidelines. These are rather simplistic − "motions must be simultaneous, symmetrical, natural, rhythmical and habitual" but they are broadly in line with the adaptive economy of movement which emerges as the basis of manual skill. Motion Study has been patronisingly described as "a set of procedures which enables people who are not very bright to think reasonably rationally". This is accurate and in fact complimentary in that it pinpoints the value of these procedures as an aid to incisive and creative thinking which can be readily understood and practised by individuals of no more than average intellectual achievement.

One interesting point worth exploring is why they work so well in practice. Why is it that operators will carry out a job for years by a method, which, when investigated systematically, proves to be readily and simply capable of improvement? Given such extensive experience coupled with the incentive of piece-work why did these operators not learn? What happened to the assumed universal improvement of skill with practice? There is no simple answer; there must be many contributing factors. For example there is no short-term incentive for an operator on piece-work to work faster if this might lead to a cut in piece-work rates; there is in fact every incentive to maintain the status quo. More fundamentally motion study has its greatest dividends for operations which are of short cycle time and which demand manipulative rather than cognitive activity. Such an operation becomes virtually automatic in that it is performed without conscious attention. After this delegation to low level control has occurred there will be no improvement resulting from drastic change of method without the intervention of an outsider. In addition, the questioning of management decisions by operators is a recent development and even now is not common. If a machine is provided with controls in non-optimal positions or if a bench has been perhaps accidentally laid out with components in the wrong places very few operators will question these decisions, and it is usually these apparently fixed points of an operational cycle where changes are required to improve the working method.

It will be clear that method study and also time study are best suited for jobs where the cycle time is short (minutes or even seconds) from which it follows that the activity is highly repetitive, where the activity is mostly overt and therefore visually traceable and where the limitation on performance is a physical one of sequences and patterns of hand movements. Press operations and assembly operations typify this kind of job. Because of the supremely versatile limbs with which human operators are endowed many of these operations are difficult to automate and they remain common even in advanced industries based on electronics.

There is a continuum from the automatic manipulation which can be carried out almost entirely by control via touch and kinaesthesis, through the operations which are visually demanding such as miniature assemblies, to operations which continuously require decisions based on accumulated data from dials or from the real scene. The utility of motion study diminishes along this continuum but never vanishes. Almost all jobs involve some kind of locomotor effort which may not limit the performance but is still susceptible to improvement following motion study. Research on anatomy and biomechanics and particularly its application to athletics has resulted in the rapid development of knowledge of human motion, this is now available to establish motion economy on more fundamental physiological rather than logical principles (e.g. Wells *et al.,* 1976; Hollingshead, 1976).

INDUSTRIAL SKILLS ANALYSIS

W. D. Seymour (1954) has been the British pioneer of the extension of motion study into jobs requiring activity more complex than automatic manipulation. His primary interest has been in the design of training schemes based on the progressive-part method. This is an optimal intermediate between whole methods which have the advantage of incorporating all the necessary integration of skills or elements of skill, and part methods which have the advantage of providing intensive practice and direct knowledge of results for the separate skills. In the progressive part method the parts are learned separately thus retaining the part training advantages but they are combined progressively during the training thus incorporating the advantage of linking skills together systematically. Such training assumes of course that a job can be analysed into skills which require separate training and this process is called skills analysis. The terminology is somewhat loose in that the analysis proceeds through a motion study type set of elements together with details of sensory inputs such as vision, hearing and touch and direction of attention. Thus an analysis chart looks very much a process chart with details of what the hands are doing but with the addition of a column indicating related attentional activity or sensory activity. Incidentally it is emphasised that training must cover not only the observable skills but also related knowledge of the job and of the factory and its products including quality standards and their assessment (Seymour, 1968).

The change of emphasis from movements to attentional activity is justified in relation to training by Seymour's (1966) research on a variety of jobs, some in factories and some in the laboratory, where he was able to show that differences in speed of 'performance can be traced to more marked changes in times for perceptually loaded elements such as 'grasp' and 'position'. Other elements such as 'reach' and 'move' show relatively little change as overall speed of performance changes.

Crossman (1956), working with Seymour, devised another extension of the process chart based on the concept that control activity in relation to any task element can be divided into five sequential phases: plan, initiate, control, end and check. He devised a symbol for each of these and added columns to the process chart for the sense modalities including touch and kinaesthesis. Thus the analyst must hypothesize from his observation and other sources of knowledge of a task which sense modality or which combination of modalities the operator uses to transmit information in relation to particular control activities. This is an ingenious idea but one which seems to have been rarely used in practice because of the strong inferential element and, probably more important, it is not clear what one does with such data having recorded it. However, the general approach to this kind of skills analysis with its crude but still critical emphasis on perceptual activity does seem to have made a significant contribution as a tool for the designer of training schemes (Singer and Ramsden, 1969).

Similar techniques have been used as an aid to appraisal of machine controls rather than training design. Again the basic model is the human information processing one of sensory, central and action processes linked to a machine through an interface of displays and controls. In the case of many working systems the displays are real, that is the operator gains his information from the world itself as in lathes (Singleton, 1964) vehicles (Singleton, 1966) and tractors (Singleton et al., 1973). For these systems identification of specific inputs is almost impossible and the analysis is based on the output, that is the operation of controls. The first purpose of the analysis is to assess priorities of what is worth considering for redesign, and here the criteria are frequency of use and criticality (that is, consequences of improper or inadequate control operation). All this can emerge from a link-design chart which is based on the assumption that every control actuation must have a purpose, a trigger, an action and a check. The purpose is the reason for doing something such as providing power, the trigger is the stimulus actuating the particular response which may be the previous check or some external event, the action is the response and the check is the evaluation of the result of the response against the purpose. By direct observation coupled with some enlightened guesswork it is possible to complete a chart called a link-design chart which has these four column headings and one line, for each action in the sequence used by a skilled operator. Such a chart forms the basis for the analysis of what can be done to improve the method of work and the design of the controls (Singleton, 1964). The justification for and check of the inferential component in this analysis may come from the evaluation of new procedures or designs which have emerged, but since this is somewhat indirect it is often desirable to devise experiments which may be conducted in the laboratory. Some of the subjects can be skilled operators whose performance may be contrasted with unskilled operators, the controls are those used in practice and some form of artificial display is provided to generate a reasonably realistic but completely programmed task from which relatively unambiguous performance measurements can be obtained. Thus Singleton (1964) used a task involving a capstan star wheel actuating a light. He also devised a task in which a sewing-machine generates responses on a 'stitching display' to evaluate control changes (Singleton, 1960) and to study the skills of the operator (Singleton, 1957).

There is inevitably a close link between the task of the operator and the technological aids which he uses to achieve his purpose. Since the technological aids are readily identifiable and their use is easily measured (by comparison with the problems of understanding what is going on inside the operator), Singleton (1972a) suggested that these aids might be used as the basis of the description of the task. This provides a taxonomy for a task description. The operator can in principle have aids to support his outputs, his inputs and his control or monitoring activities in addition to aids to protect him from the environment such as clothing or ambient protection. Thus it is possible to describe a task under the four headings: environment aids, output aids, input aids and decision aids. Such a description is valuable in pinpointing the changes in the task required of an operator as technology advances. In itself it does not lead directly to the solution of personnel problems such as training but to this end it can be related to the complementary job descriptions. A job description is different from both a task description and a skill description; it involves some statement not only of required skills but also of required capacities, relevant knowledge and appropriate disposition. Such a job description is a necessary basis for personnel decisions such as selection and placement as well as for training.

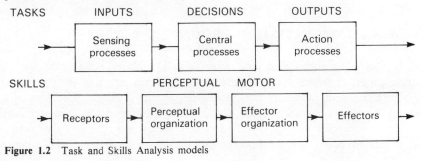

Figure 1.2 Task and Skills Analysis models

A job is a set, of which skills are one sub-set; this set is essentially person-oriented and is thus qualitatively different from the task concept which is essentially system-oriented. A task could usually in principle be carried out by a machine rather than a man but this is inconceivable for either a job or a skill, terms from a different domain. Nevertheless it is possible to formulate the distinction between tasks and skills in terms of the common language of communication theory as shown in Figure 1.2 (Singleton, 1967). Thus a task analysis requires the identification of inputs, decisions and outputs although the output may be trivial (speaking into a microphone or pressing a button) and the important process may be that of selecting between alternative courses of action (i.e., decision making). The analysis begins by the identification of the range of these choices and goes on to the definition of the information inputs required to select rationally between the alternatives. The required inputs need not be immediate or on-line; they can be off-line and more remote in time. These latter particularly set the context for the decision and aid the weighting of particular cues. For example my decision whether or not to read the domestic mail before going to work will be determined partly by an on-line input in the form of a scan of the envelopes but also by previous off-line inputs from which I know whether or not I am expecting an important letter; there are other context influences such as the time available.

By contrast a skills analysis requires a consideration of the abilities of the individual involved, in the form of native capacities supplemented by learning and experience into the various kinds of skills: perceptual and motor or receptor, cognitive and effector or enactive, spatial and symbolic or hierarchial input/output from just beyond the reflex to abstract thinking. However, it must be accepted that this apparently straightforward distinction between a task and a skill is not easily sustained in the current state of the art. This is partly because of the confusion just mentioned between available models of skill and partly because of inconsistencies in terminology between various authors. Thus, as described in this section, Seymour and others stretch the term skills analysis to include activities such as vision where there is either non-existent or very limited learning, and in the next section Miller and others use the term task when their focus and orientation is very much on skills manifested in activities susceptible to change by training.

TASK ANALYSIS IN SYSTEMS DESIGN

R. B. Miller has been called the "father of task analysis" (de Greene, 1970). Although his approach could be described as a development of the traditional job analysis such a description would disguise two distinct contributions. Firstly he was a member of the group which developed the man–machine systems philosophy (Gagne, 1962), and he therefore sees the task description as an integral part of the total problem of system design. Secondly his concise thinking about what can and cannot be achieved during and with a task analysis simultaneously tidied and revealed the complexity of the whole problem of describing real human behaviour.

In the systems context the description of tasks is seen as the identification of what men are actually doing within a particular system in terms of their interaction with the system and system environment. Such descriptions are the basis for all aspects of the development of the personnel sub-system, including particularly interface design and training. Since the man is functioning as a system component his functions can be described in terms of his contribution to the system objectives and his interactions through displays and controls with other system elements. Reference to system objectives and corresponding human objectives begins to integrate the analysis concept with the theory of human skill since understanding of objectives or purposes is fundamental to any skill psychology approach. Miller points out that it may be part of the operator's task to discover or at least understand his set of goal conditions and that this can be one of the creative elements in a task. The simplest way of describing an operator function is with a sequence of indication (stimulus), activation (response) and feedback.

Philosophically Miller takes a complex view of what can be expected from a task analyst. On the one hand he cannot be too rigorous in either his definitions or his procedures because such pursuit of rigour will be and ought to be defeated by the flexibility of human performance. Thus the approach must be heuristic and the appeal in case of doubt is to utility rather than to logic. On the other hand the requirements of utility are formidable: a task analyst should in principle be able to arrive at a solution which not only serves the whole personnel subsystem as described above but also does so by orientating the designer towards "applicable research findings and principles of training" (Miller, 1962). The task analyst should facilitate some prediction or anticipation particularly in the context of a system design. It would be too much to expect a quantitative prediction of performance level, but the work of the analyst should enable kinds of error to be more readily predictable and the point at which predictions become no better than random should be evident.

Miller also generated the idea that we might develop a taxonomy of the necessary functional dimensions of a human operator by considering what functions would be required in a robot which imitated human performance. In this way he arrived at the following set of classifying terms: concept of purpose, scanning function, identification of relevant cues function, interpretation of cues, short-term memory, long-term memory, decision making and problem solving and effector response. It is interesting to contrast this range of parameters with the motion study approach which concentrates almost entirely on the last item. Even this list is not sufficient; as Miller (op. cit.) points out these items form only one dimension of a classification matrix which has at least three dimensions, two others being individual differences in strategies and in degree of learning. Strategies incorporate items such as form of information storage (see also p.40) and handling of noise and uncertainty. It is known that degree of learning can change motor patterns, perceptual organization and mediating behaviour. He suggests that a complex multi-dimensional taxonomy of this kind will not be clarified or developed from orthodox synthetic laboratory tasks: "real life tasks have contingencies, options and choices that are fundamentally absent in rote learning". While pursuing in further detail the basic taxonomic problems Miller (1975) points out that the carrying out of a task analysis aimed at the designing of a training scheme involves much more than task characteristics; it involves the inter-action of these properties with learning or performance properties or particular training procedures.

In spite of the declared intention to take a system-wide view the Miller approach does focus mainly on the personnel problems. Task analysis involves finding out what kinds of abilities, skills and knowledge are required to carry out the specified tasks. It is seen as one vehicle for ensuring a consistency of objectives and criteria across selection, training and evaluation. The behaviour taxonomy behind the analysis need not be entirely rigorous; utility is regarded as the most important criterion although the principle of embedding the taxonomy in what we know about human behaviour is accepted. The training context cannot be avoided because methods of training for part-tasks will interact with the structure of the task taxonomy used for analysis. Similarly the required level of detail of analysis will be determined by the potential training dividend from further analysis. The close relationship between training and job performance comes not only from the directional effects of training on performance but opposite direction effects of perform-ance on training and analysis. Thus experience in a job moulds what is done in what order and may adjust the psychological task boundaries which the analyst is looking for. The organization of stimuli and mediating activities inevitably changes with practice. It is individual experience which results in the elements of behaviour coming together into integrated dynamic wholes (Miller, 1967). He is sensitive to all the 'levels' problems which confuse the business of analysis. Levels of the analysis itself, levels of performance after training along a dimension identified by the adjectives stereotyped, routinized, formatted, improvizational and inventive, and levels of description from para-graphs of descriptive prose to more concise categorization using block diagrams or the behavioural taxonomies mentioned above. He places relatively little emphasis on the form of the task description; presumably he would regard this as secondary to getting the total picture fitted to the problem triggering the analysis.

Annett et al. (1971) follow the principles enunciated by Miller but take a more specific view about the final form of the description. Again they empha-sise that task analysis is closely related to training aspects including course content, methods and criteria of success. The task is again defined in terms of objectives or end products and it follows that the analysis must be a process of diagnosing the appropriate plans needed to achieve the goal. The plan for the overall goal includes both sub-plans and sub-goals. Thus it is necessary to describe operations which incorporate not only what is done in the form of actions but also what is achieved in the form of objectives. In addition to the operations and sub-operations some conception of their structure is required. This is often best described in terms of priorities rather than sequences. Their criterion for required level of analysis incorporates two parameters, the cost to the system of failing to achieve a particular performance and the probability of this failure. Their experience is mainly in manufacturing industry which results in emphasis on the contextual influences such as the duration of a job, the turnover of workers, the working conditions, the quality of supervision and so on. Duncan (1975) explores further the question of appropriate levels of analysis and mentions a number of attempts to define the different potentially useful levels. These usually conclude with three or four defined by terms such as jobs, duties, tasks and elements (Smith, 1964). Duncan (*op. cit.*) develops the principle of progressive redescription until the training requirement is clear. There is a basic level of 'primitives'; these are unambiguous statements which need not be further refined.

Task Analysis techniques, like Skills Analysis techniques, have been developed to solve problems but in the context of what is known about the theory of human performance. The core problem has been training and more rarely selection, personnel allocation and design for systems and machines. The orientation towards the problem has dominated the development of the techniques and more particularly the underlying taxonomy or classification problem. Nevertheless it is now clear that task/skill analysis is the essential initial step in any personnel sub-system problem from machine design to interface design, job aid design, training, selection, manpower allocation and even education. Although the evidence and progress in developing these techniques has been so context-dependent it would seem reasonable to approach the problem more academically and see if a taxonomy of tasks or skills can be developed without regard to particular problems. One approach to this is to use factor analysis in the hope that clearly identified factors selected from a variety of performance data will form an independent taxonomy of skills or at least of factors determining skills.

FACTORIAL TASK ANALYSIS

Fleishman (1966) has been the central figure in the psychometric approach to task analysis. His early work developed from association with Fitts and Gagne (Gagne and Fleishman, 1959) and during the 1960s he developed his own group of associates concerned with these problems at the American Institute for Research in Washington.

The origin of the work is in the problem of selection of Air Force personnel, particularly pilots. Selection is of course a matter of identifying individual differences and thus it belongs in one of what Cronbach (1957) called the two disciplines of psychology – experimental and differential. These two disciplines are often regarded as totally separate – Jones (1966) characterizes differential psychology as "passive, speculative and leisurely" in contrast to experimentalists who are "active, hard-boiled and harried". From the time of Spearman (1927) differential psychologists have been interested in genetic variations and early experience, while for the experimentalist the past of his subjects is of little concern and variations between their individual performances are a tiresome irrelevance classified as error variance. Although Fleishman's interests and methods stem from differential psychology he would not accept that the division is inevitable or necessary and in much of his work he attempts to manipulate variables, i.e. do experiments, within situations which are analysed by correlation methods, the basic tool of the differential psychologist.

To cope with the selection problem of predicting performance at one task (the real one) on the basis of performance at another task (the test) it is assumed that there is an underlying entity called an ability which is required for both. Broadly the psychometric evidence is consistent with this assumption; there are sets of tasks with high intercorrelations of performance different from other sets of tasks which do not show high intercorrelations, although to complicate the issue almost all such correlations are positive. Hence another assumption of a general ability and the need for elaborate statistical analysis to separate the various underlying factors identified as specific abilities each making a particular contribution to the performance variance. Some abilities may be innate, in which case they are called capacities, but more usually there is a learned component superimposed on the genetic component. Since abilities are subject to learning there is a problem of distinguishing between abilities and skills. Fleishman (1966) considers that abilities are "fairly enduring traits" or "organismic factors which the individual brings with him when he begins to learn a new task". Thus ability is person-oriented, while skill on the other hand is for Fleishman a task-oriented term, referring to level of proficiency on a specific task such as flying an aeroplane or operating a lathe. Skills do, however, have general characteristics such as spatial–temporal patterning, interaction of responses with input and feedback processes and learning.

During learning the relative importance of particular abilities changes. Jones (1966), from the evidence of superdiagonal form in correlation matrices (a given trial consistently correlates most highly with the one immediately preceding it, less highly with the one following it and even less highly with trials other than those immediately following and preceding), considers that the range of factors or abilities involved in a task decreases as learning proceeds. Fleishman considers that some abilities may have a dominant influence early in learning but other abilities become dominant later. For example, in a two-hand co-ordination task Fleishman and Rich (1963) were able to show that within a group of subjects those of high spatial ability performed best early in the learning but this difference disappeared after half an hour of practice, whilst those of high kinaesthetic sensitivity were performing better after this period although the kinaesthetic sensitivity did not discriminate in the earlier trials.

Fleishman (1975) also takes up the problem of defining a task. He points out that the totality of what is considered to be a task can vary from a specific action required (e.g. pressing a button) to a complete situation with a context and an ambient environment; some concepts of a task are based on what is imposed on a subject, others on what the subject perceives. These variables will influence the classification of tasks which he considers can be approached in at least four different ways: categories of what is done, e.g. handling, analysing, negotiating; categories of required behaviour, e.g. scanning, storing, decision making; categories of required abilities, e.g. dexterity, speed, precision and external characteristics of the task, e.g. goals, stimuli, instructions, procedures. Independently of the basis of the classification there are various criteria which it should meet or at least be assessed against, these include reliable nominal scaling, mutual exclusivity, exhaustiveness, behavioural implications, efficiency and utility for communication.

Table 1.4   Fleishman's (1975) ability taxonomy

1. Verbal comprehension	14. Visualization	27. Choice reaction time
2. Verbal expression	15. Speed of closure	28. Reaction time
3. Ideational fluency	16. Flexibility of closure	29. Speed of limb movement
4. Originality	17. Selective attention	30. Wrist–finger speed
5. Memorization	18. Time sharing	31. Gross body co-ordination
6. Problem sensitivity	19. Perceptual speed	32. Multilimb co-ordination
7. Mathematical reasoning	20. Static strength	33. Finger dexterity
8. Number facility	21. Explosive strength	34. Manual dexterity
9. Deductive reasoning	22. Dynamic strength	35. Arm–hand steadiness
10. Inductive reasoning	23. Stamina	36. Rate control
11. Information ordering	24. Extent flexibility	37. Control precision
12. Category flexibility	25. Dynamic flexibility	
13. Spatial orientation	26. Gross body equilibrium	

Fleishman's own preference is for an abilities taxonomy based on factor analysis conducted within many interrelated studies of human performance. The object is to maximize the range of human performance studied and to minimize the range of independent ability factors required to describe this performance. In this way he has arrived at the thirty-seven abilities shown in Table 1.4. Each of these needs to be defined as precisely as possible and preferably in a way which bridges the gap between laboratory tasks and real world tasks. For each ability, scales are developed, located by bench-marks defined by common but reasonably specific tasks, e.g. the scale of verbal comprehension has bench marks at understanding a comic, a newspaper article and a legal contract. Some of his associates (Farina and Wheaton, 1971) have used the external task as the basis for the taxonomy shown in Figure 1.3. The same principle of generating a scale of seven points with appropriate bench marks is used.

It will be noted that this approach is not oriented towards a particular operational problem such as training. Rather the aim is to develop a method of analysis which describes what is happening when a person performs a task. The criterion of utility is success in predicting final performance at a specified task on the basis of a knowledge of individual abilities..

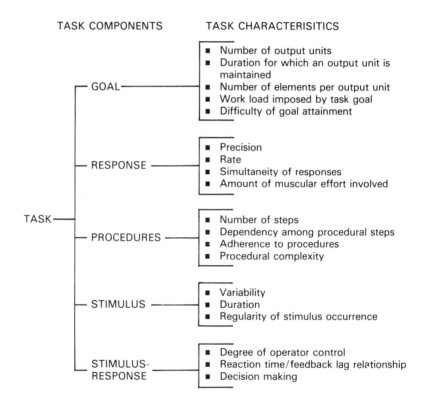

Figure 1.3   Farina and Wheaton (1971) task taxonomy

TASK ANALYSIS FOR TEACHING

R. M. Gagne has for many years been interested in the application of task analysis to education (1965, 1974). There is no clear borderline between studies of task analysis as carried out for example by Miller, where the aim is improved training, and task analysis as carried out for example by Gagne, where the aim is more specifically focussed on teaching–learning in itself. Not in strict isolation of course, since even the purest form of education must take some account of the community context, but nevertheless with a clear emphasis on the learning system as such rather than the training service to some operational system. Even though this emphasis is accepted the criterion problem remains crucial. How does one measure the success of efforts to improve the effectiveness of teaching–learning? Gagne (1975a) emphasises the distinction between construct validity and content validity by analogy with psychometric theory. The former relies on the conceptual background behind whatever is being taught – the course designer feels secure because he understands what he is doing in some theoretical sense – whereas content validity depends on demonstrating that the learning outcomes are relevant to some external context or objective. Gagne considers that construct validity can be based on information processing theories of learning and memory, in particular this enables the different phases of the learning/memory process to be identified and progress assessed for each phase. "One can observe the output of the sensory register and thus test the *selective perception* process of learning. One can observe the output of the short-term memory and thus test the *encoding* process of learning. One can observe the output of the long-term memory as *retrieval* of what has been learned. One can observe the output of the response generator as *response selection and organization*." (Gagne, 1975a; his italics). This proposal can be regarded as the application of a kind of skills analysis to the learner at different learning stages. His own description of Task Analysis is again best provided by quotations from Gagne (1974). "First, each task must be broken down into behaviour capabilities that are not themselves the task but are contributors to the performance of the task. Second, these contributions must be further classified, if possible, into types that serve to identify different optimal conditions for their learning . . . Task Analysis, then, was conceived as a technique which could be brought to bear on the problem of how to get from known human tasks to designed optimal conditions of instructions which would yield competency in these tasks . . . task analysis was proposed as a method of identifying and classifying the behavioural contributors to task competence, for which differential instructional design was possible and desirable." Gagne (1965) considers that there are many different types of learning from simple stimulus–response connections to problem solving with complications from verbalization and rule learning. This variety results in five categories of learning outcome; besides intellectual and motor skills there are attitudes, cognitive strategies and verbalizable information (Gagne, 1974). These latter represent distinct classes of human performance which can be used in the first stage of task analysis. He points out that the bridging operation between the real task and the training design makes necessary a distinction between *job tasks* and *learning tasks*. Job tasks are parts of jobs, learning tasks involve activities which are relevant to jobs but are not carried out as such within jobs. For example learning the meaning of all symbols used in highway signs is a learning task relevant to the job of driving but not practised directly by the driver in the way in which learning competence will be tested. Thus the analyst needs to distinguish between carrying out a job-task analysis and a learning-task analysis. The purpose of task analysis is to identify different classes of learning outcome and identify for each class the most appropriate learning conditions. This is complicated by the hierarchial nature of these classes which might be regarded as skills. A target task will have identifiable pre-requisite skills. These prerequisite skills will be utilized and perhaps modified to suit the current task; for example, Gagne (1962) points out that the operator establishes shunting and filtering conditions which change with learning. *Shunting* involves setting up the required transformations between inputs and outputs which may not require interpreting the full meaning of the inputs – identifying the appropriate output may be carried out on a limited range of the available input characteristics. Correspondingly *filtering* involves selectively responding to only part of the total range of potential inputs. The introduction of the term skill emphasises that we are now discussing internal rather than external aspects of the task performance. The hierarchy is more a characteristic of the performer than of the task itself. Gagne sees the process of task analysis as always working backwards in two different senses, from the response to the stimulus and also from the learning outcome to the appropriate instructional situation.

All this is to do with learning processes; the instructional situation cannot be planned on this basis alone, it is also necessary to consider the phases of learning outside acquisition and retention. Before these aspects there are motivational and attentional aspects and beyond them there are aspects such as generalization and performance–feedback loops leading to reinforcement. Similarly, outcomes of learning go beyond the subject matter to include changing dispositions as well as capabilities. For example, becoming a respiratory physiologist will almost certainly increase the disposition to avoid smoking cigarettes. Thus Gagne (1976) identifies the questions to be answered in relation to teaching–learning as divisible into three classes: processes (learning, retention, transfer), phases (sequences of transformations) and outcomes (capabilities and dispositions). This situation becomes even more complex if one considers the broader context of education as a national effort. The goals which this involves vary from simple instructional objectives to human capabilities, curricula, manpower and social aspects as well as national characteristics (Gagne, 1975b). This may appear to be way beyond the purview of task analysis but there is no obvious borderline which delimits the concerns of the task analyst. In addition it does illustrate that since task analysis usually has a purpose connected with learning the analysis of operational tasks inevitably overlaps with the analysis of learning tasks, which in turn overlaps with the analysis of training or teacher or educationalist tasks.

Returning to more limited issues, the problems of task analysis were highlighted by another learning development in the 1960s, the introduction of programmed instruction usually in the form of teaching machines. Wallis *et al.* (1966) outline the following characteristics of programmed instruction: there is a statement of objectives (often in the form of a specification of terminal performance), the material to be learned has been itemized, the sequence of items is controlled, frequent responses are required and feedback about the correctness or otherwise of each response is given. Decisions are required about whether the sequence of material should be linear, intrinsic branching or adaptive, whether there should be no pacing, group pacing or partial pacing and whether the presentation should be single or multisensory. It will be clear that such a systematic approach to learning requires correspondingly systematic analysis of the task to be learned. Indeed it can be argued that the main dividend from programmed instruction has been the manifestly required discipline of task analysis for both the operational task and the learning situation. Biel (1962) considers that the whole field of training devices can be subdivided into teaching machines, concept trainers, skill trainers, procedure trainers and simulators. Behind this taxonomy is an assumption of three kinds of learning: verbal material or knowledge, concepts such as fault location principles, and skills including setting up procedures and on-line operation. Wallis *et al. (op. cit.)* point out that the early use of programmed instruction concentrated on acquisition of information and intellectual skills; later it was extended to cover procedural, perceptual and control skills with control skills subdivided into craft, operating and coding skills. The full range of training areas finally arrived at is divided into ten categories: physical fitness, procedural and routine skills, perceptual skills, control skills, acquisition of information, intellectual skills, character building, managerial skills, identification with group and system activities (Wallis, 1975).

Thus the main contribution of the teaching-based task analysis approach has been in exploring the range of training and learning outcomes and in attempting to devise comprehensive taxonomies, to encompass this range. Although this problem cannot be regarded as completely solved there has been considerable progress and certainly the complexity of what a learner can acquire and what a practitioner can exhibit in the performance of a task has been more thoroughly explored than hitherto.

ERROR ANALYSIS

Singleton (1971) divided Ergonomics as practised at that time into three categories: *classical ergonomics,* the original study of environmental conditions, work spaces, displays and controls based essentially on the results of laboratory experiments, *systems ergonomics* concerned with allocation of function between man and machine, training and interface design where task analysis is the basic technique for acquisition of evidence, and *error ergonomics* where the objective is to minimize human error and the corresponding source of evidence is error analysis. The study of errors is important not only in the accident context where there is a potentiality for personal injury but also in the wider field of man as the big system monitor, controller and mender (Singleton, 1974). Systems failures can be extremely expensive and inconvenient as well as damaging. Cherns (1967) has connected errors and accidents very closely by defining an accident as "an error with sad consequences". Unfortunately there is no correspondingly elegant definition of what an error is. It is a failure of human performance; the performer is pursuing some objective and either does not achieve it or departs significantly from the acceptable path towards it.

One can approach the description of errors either from the operational stand-point by studies of what happens in practice, or from the theoretical stand-point in terms of what we understand about why humans err. Most approaches attempt some compromise where there is some potentiality for utility and also some conceptual support for the approach adopted. The operational classifications of error are summarized in Singleton (1972b). Statistically one can distinguish between systematic errors (bias) and random errors and between formal errors of logic and substantive errors of inadequate problem definition. Other classifications are based on the established principle that humans are very good at error correction; these include detectable/undetectable, reversible/irreversible and recoverable by man or machine or neither. The commission/omission distinction relates to the decision theory approach where a decision criterion can alter the relative proportions of false positives and negatives. The most commonly utilized theory to aid in classifying errors is information theory. Kidd (1962) traced the path of information through the human operator and identified possible errors and causes/remedies for these errors at the different stages of processing. The stages he identified were failing to detect a signal, incorrectly identifying a signal, incorrect value weighting, error in action selection and error in commission. De Greene (1970) has developed a similar classification with main divisions of inputs, decisions and outputs and three or four subdivisions within each of these. One can attempt to classify directly by remedies such as errors due to design faults, selection and training faults and instructional faults, or less directly by locating the responsibility: incorrect diagnosis, insufficient attention, wrong procedures or wrong instructions. Welford (1973) considers that errors occur either when the human operator reaches a limit of his capacities, that is, he tries to cope with too much information or when he receives inadequate information; this leads to four categories: ignorance, speed, span of apprehension and presence of random activity. Information theory is only one of many theoretical tools; other relevant theories are described in Singleton (1973). These range from the psychoanalytic approach through social theories, field theories, and statistical theories to performance theories. Zeller (1970) proposes a three-fold approach to human limitations: the physical organism with time lags and sensory limits, the biochemical plant subject to fatigue and many stresses including toxicity, and the psychic being with aptitudes, attitudes and emotional needs. The study of error as a failure of skill as distinct from error as a failure of performance brings error analysis close to skill analysis. The skills approach to error analysis emphasises the concept of a skilled man in a situation extended in time and in space (Singleton, 1976a). There is no point in looking for simple cause–effect relationships because a response at a given instant is never merely a function of the stimulus at that time. If an error is regarded as a disorder of skill then its origins will be not only in the immediate stimulus environment but also in the history and training of the person involved as well as in his personality and emotional state. Similarly in considering the action, it is not enough to look at the choice of a particular response at a particular instant; the whole pattern of output leading up to that response is relevant. In their particular taxonomy of errors Meister and Rabideau (1965) included a category of out-of-sequence performance together with failure of performance, incorrect performance and non-required performance. Singleton (1976b) suggested that errors can be regarded as failure of either perceptual skills or motor skills. Evidence of a motor skill failure appears in timing mismatches and sequencing disorders, while perceptual skills fail when the mental picture or model which the operator is using doesn't correspond to reality sufficiently closely, so that the model used is either inadequate or just wrong. This somewhat abstract approach can be given a more utilitarian aspect by linking the skill failure to possible remedies of which there are only three: redesigned equipment, changed procedures or modification of training.

A very different and more direct approach to error analysis is possible if one ignores the aetiology and the possible remedies and just treats the human operator as a device subject to error. The problem then becomes one of estimating the error rate in a given situation by analogy with the procedures which engineers use to estimate the failure rates of mechanisms. This is similar to the predetermined motion time systems used in work measurement. The procedure is to identify the basic elements which can be assumed to have standard error rates and then to sum the error rates for these elements as they occur in the task under analysis (Swain, 1963, 1970).

The operational difficulty is that error rates for simple movements tend to be very small, about 10^{-4}, so that the probabilistic sum of such small quantities tends to vary little with the variety of elements contained in the analysis and with the exact numbers attached as the failure rates for particular elements. The theoretical difficulty is in the assumption that error rates even for small elements are consistent and independent of context. Nevertheless, this is the sort of technique which appeals to reliability engineers because they are familiar with it for other purposes and because it does contain, however insecurely, a possibility of predicting error rates for systems still at the design stage.

Although the problem of error analysis is so important in relation to human safety and to system reliability more generally, progress is slow. This is because the background to every error is so complex and the range of relevant theory is so extensive and diverse. Fundamentally, understanding why people make mistakes is the same problem as understanding human behaviour. Correspondingly, on the operational side human errors react in such complex ways with the external environment, so that what is from the initiator's point of view the same error can have no consequences or can lead to a catastrophe.

Nevertheless the skilled analyst can make a contribution; he has more awareness than others of the complexity of the situation he has to handle and he is acquainted with the many relevant theories and taxonomies of error. It is a question of adapting the analysis to the particular problem and the particular resources available to deal with it by selecting the most relevant theories and techniques.

PROCESS CONTROL ANALYSIS

The process control operator has a very different job from that of the more traditional industrial worker from whom Work Study techniques were developed. His energy output is small, usually confined to strolling around the plant and more particularly the display and control consoles, occasionally pressing buttons, turning knobs, making telephone calls or entries in log books and chatting to other people. He is surrounded by a vast amount of data from chart and dial readings and winking lights to vague smells and noises coming from the operating plant: most of this data is ignored. His skill consists of detecting departures from normality, in the form of changes in particular readings or in the complex overall pattern of presented data, which signal the need for his participation, and of the identification of possible strategies and the choice of a particular strategy leading to a course of action or inaction. Normally everything, including system behaviour and his own actions takes place slowly with no time stress, but occasionally there may be a need for very rapid and decisive action. The slowness itself may be a problem in that the extensive lag between his actions and their consequences makes anticipation essential.

The analysis of this situation was first discussed in detail by Crossman and his associates (Crossman, 1960). They were concerned with the analysis and description of at least three aspects of the situation: the distribution of the operator's attention, the establishment of links between patterns of operator input and output and in particular the ways in which the operator copes with time lags in the system, and finally with more general ways in which the operator interacts with the system. There are four different methods of acquiring evidence; the first two are the traditional field and laboratory ones of observing what happens and talking to those involved and supporting this by carrying out experiments in which the number of variables is reduced so that their separate and interactive influences can be more readily traced. In addition to these there is a theoretical approach based on man as a good controller, where the arguments runs logically that this is what he must be doing to be effective, and finally a cybernetic method similar to Miller's robot in which a physical control or problem solving device is postulated which has certain limitations of capacity and speed similar to those of the human operator, its performance is examined to identify similarities to human performance and their origins. The pioneers of this last technique were Newell and Simon (1963). Crossman *et al.* (1964) analysed the sampling interval in observing a particular structure of displays where only a few values may change in terms of the rate of growth of uncertainty, the penalty attached to error and the cost of sampling. One relevant theory is the Saunders modification of the Shannon–Weiner sampling theorem in which frequency and duration of sampling is a function of the variability and the required accuracy. This seems to fit reasonably well if one calculates the relevant bandwidth using the highest frequency component of random fluctuations having a peak amplitude greater than the assigned tolerance. There are other complications, due for example to forgetting and the lags after control changes. Quite reasonably the operator does not sample after a control change until after the appropriate lag in system response.

In examining input–output linkages for the process controller it is not usually adequate to consider one stimulus such as a dial reading or one response such as a control change. Rather one has to examine the system state where a number of variables have values in a pattern sufficiently consistent to regard this as one state within a multi-dimensional system space. Correspondingly there are categories of action state where the sequence or pattern of control achieved consistently results in a desired change in system direction. These can be explored in the working situation, e.g. Beishon (1969), or in laboratory tasks typifying this situation, e.g. Crossman and Cooke (1962). This kind of system state/action state modelling not only provides insight into the operator's procedures but also suggests where his limitations might be restricting performance, e.g. in short-memory or in dynamic behaviour such as anticipation or other tracking strategies. Assessment of the factors limiting performance can lead in turn to suggestions about how these might be compensated for either by training or by improved information coding and presentation.

Beishon (1967) summarizes the problems and methods of describing the process controller's task. These tasks involve cognitive processes which are not well understood theoretically and they involve complex feedback systems where the dynamic properties are complicated by non-linear human characteristics. Two methods of analysis and description have proved useful: the signal flow graph and the activity chart. The signal-flow graph is a technique taken over from the analysis of electrical networks. Circles indicating various kinds of physical parameters such as temperature and pressure called nodes are connected by lines or paths which are used to indicate the quantitative relationship between the connected values. In addition to providing a valuable map or display of the total system such graphs can be manipulated and simplified by algebraic-type reduction and can also include human participation with particular operator transforms as system elements. An activity analysis involves preparing a multi-line time chart of changes in the system and operator actions from which relationships can be traced.

Such descriptions of the overt behaviour of the system including the operator can only be extended to descriptions of what is going on inside the operator by rather tenuous logic often amounting to no more than guessing. Rather more direct evidence about his internal processes can be obtained by asking him to 'think aloud'; this commentary is recorded and later analysed and related to the overt behaviour. The main exponent of this technique has been L. Bainbridge (Bainbridge *et al.,* 1968; Bainbridge, 1969). The operator is regarded as having a set of aims to fulfil and there are sets of actions or action strategies associated with each aim. These can be traced by action/ information trees or algorithms. The course of thinking reported by the operator can also be structured into an information tree with branches indicating new streams of thought. Insight into the skills can be obtained by, for example, comparing the stream-of-thought trees for skilled operators and for other subjects such as undergraduates attempting to carry out the task without the benefit of long experience. It emerges that the operator carries a 'mental picture' of the process including what has happened and what might happen over perhaps the next hour. He updates this picture continuously but irregularly. The irregularity arises from the scanning flexibility, from the switching between sequences of activity and from interrupts, for example through a digression such as a tea-break.

Such activity makes considerable demands on memory and Bainbridge (1975) has explored this in detail. Working storage involves data items and routines which need to be related for a specific action strategy but which are essentially independent in that the same data may appear in different strategies. Purposes and routines have an analogous flexible connection; the purpose may in fact be specified by a data item. This can be recorded graphically by using 'boxes' to represent data values – a series of boxes is used for a list of values. The boxes represent the constants of the situation (although of course the values of the items in the boxes can be changed by observation or calculation) linked by the routines for changing values either in one operation or by progressive refinement as more dimensions of the situation are considered. Thus the operator is seen as engaged in routines for changing data items in boxes. The routines are not hierarchial but the items are in the sense that there is a set of main items or context with supporting items.

This technique of analysis and box/routine descriptions goes some way towards matching the complexity and flexibility of human performance in process control. However, such a description deals mainly with the control of process variables. Crossman (1963) suggests that this is one of six process task elements, the others being manual operations where the operator is in direct contact with materials, the sequencing of process operations, fault detection and remedy, communication with colleagues and coping with emergencies such as fires.

CONCLUSION

It is clear that the method of analysis including both the techniques and the taxonomy cannot be separated from the purpose of the investigation or from the type or level of task studied. In short, skills analysis techniques are context-dependent.

Advancing technology has changed the predominant characteristics of human work from high energy expenditure and fast manipulative activity to high sensory loads and complex cognitive activity. Similarly the predominant objective of work improvement has changed from high individual output to reliability and safety. These of course are overall generalizations, and it is probably true that the interests of the skills analysts are running ahead of changes in jobs for the community as a whole. There are still plenty of jobs requiring heavy and fast work with production dependent on the effort of the operator and thus there is still scope for the traditional work study techniques of analysis.

Rapid change of jobs and associated required skills particularly in the military field during the 1960s shifted the emphasis to training requirements with the corresponding interest in what is normally called task analysis. In aerospace, transport and industry the increased potential consequences of accidents as the power available in systems increases has resulted in the need for better error analysis and prediction.

On the academic side current interest varies from factor analysis of human performance data, through the design of experiments to support and examine hypotheses formed in field studies, to protocol analysis aimed at the greater understanding of fundamental cognitive processes. The relevant model of the human operator has changed from a stimulus–response organism to a model-maker, picture-builder and navigator within internally generated multi-dimensional system parameter maps.

The central problem requiring improved theory and practice is the increased utilization of man–computer partnerships in on-line control of process systems and more ambitiously in complex decision making, using the computer as the central data bank and communication vehicle within a team of human operators.

(Whitfield, 1976). The degree to which these future system designs can be effectively realized depends on progress in analysing and describing the relevant human cognitive processes. Greater understanding is also needed of the more affective processes involved in motivation and in interactions within teams of human operators collectively involved in the control of large scale systems.

References

Annett, J., Duncan, K. D., Stammers, R. B. and Gray, M. J. (1971), Task Analysis. *Training Information Paper 6, Dept. of Employment*. (London: HMSO)

Bainbridge, L. (1969). Analysis of verbal protocols from a process-control task. Reprinted in Edwards, E. and Lees, F. P. (1974) (eds.). *The Human Operator in Process Control*. (London: Taylor and Francis)

Bainbridge, L. (1975). The representation of working storage and its use in the organisation of behaviour. In Singleton, W. T. and Spurgeon, P. (eds.). *Measurement of Human Resources*. (London: Taylor and Francis)

Bainbridge, L., Beishon, R. J., Hemming, J. H. and Splaine, M. (1968). A study of the real time human decision making using a plant simulator. In Edwards, E. and Lees, F. P. (1974) (eds.). *The Human Operator in Process Control*. (London: Taylor and Francis)

Barnes, R. M. (1949). *Motion and Time Study*. (New York: Wiley)

Beishon, R. J. (1967). Problems of task description in process control. In Singleton, W. T., Easterby, R. and Whitfield, D. (eds.). *The Human Operator in Complex Systems*. (London: Taylor and Francis)

Beishon, R. J. (1969). An analysis and simulation of an operator's behaviour in controlling continuous baking ovens. Reprinted in Edwards, E. and Lees, F. P. (1974) (eds.). *The Human Operator in Process Control*. (London: Taylor and Francis)

Biel, W. C. (1962). Training programs and devices. In Gagne, R. M. (ed.). *Psychological Principles in System Development*. (New York: Holt, Rinehart and Winston)

Cherns, A. B. (1967). Accidents at work. In Welford, A. T. *et al.* (eds.). *Society: Problems and Methods of Study*. (London: Routledge and Kegan Paul)

Cronbach, L. J. (1957). The two disciplines of scientific psychology. *American Psychologist*, **12,** 671

Crossman, E. R. F. W. (1956). Perceptual activity in manual work. *Research*, **9,** 42

Crossman, E. R. F. W. (1960). Automation and skill. DSIR booklet reprinted in Edwards, E. and Lees, F. P. (1974) (eds.). *The Human Operator in Process Control*. (London: Taylor and Francis)

Crossman, E. R. F. W. (1963). Analysis of non-repetitive manual work. *Ergonomics*, **6,** 302 (abstract)

Crossman, E. R. F. W. and Cooke, J. E. (1962). Manual control of slow-response systems. Reprinted in Edwards, E. and Lees, F. P. (1974) (eds.). *The Human Operator in Process Control*. (London: Taylor and Francis)

Crossman, E. R. F. W., Cooke, J. E. and Beishon, R. J. (1964). Visual attention and the sampling of displayed information in process control. Reprinted in Edwards, E. and Lees, F. P. (1974) (eds.). *The Human Operator in Process Control*. (London: Taylor and Francis)

Duncan, K. D. (1975). An analytical technique for industrial training. In Singleton, W. T. and Spurgeon, P. (eds.). *Measurement of Human Resources*. (London: Taylor and Francis)

Edwards, E. and Lees, F. P. (1974). *The Human Operator in Process Control*. (London: Taylor and Francis)

Farina, A. J. Jr. and Wheaton, J. R. (1971). *Development of a Taxonomy of Human Performance*. (Washington: American Institute for Research)

Fleishman, E. A. (1966). Human abilities and the acquisition of skill. In Bilodeau, E. A. (ed.). *Acquisition of Skill* (New York: Academic Press)

Fleishman, E. A. (1975). Taxonomic problems in human performance research. In Singleton, W. T. and Spurgeon, P. (eds.). *Measurements of Human Resources*. (London: Taylor and Francis)

Fleishman, E. A. and Rich, S. (1963). Role of kinaesthetic and spatial–visual abilities in perceptual motor learning. *J. Exp. Psychol.*, **66**, 6

Gagne, R. M. (1962). *Psychological Principles in System Development.* (New York: Holt, Rinehart and Winston)

Gagne, R. M. (1962). Human functions in systems. In Gagne, R. M. (ed.). *Psychological Principles in System Development.* (New York: Holt, Rinehart and Winston)

Gagne, R. M. (1965). *The Conditions of Learning.* (New York: Holt, Rinehart and Winston)

Gagne, R. M. (1974). Task analysis – its relation to content analysis. *Educational Psychologist,* **11**, (1), 11

Gagne, R. M. (1975a). Observing the effects of learning. *Educational Psychologist,* **11**, (3), 144

Gagne, R. M. (1975b). Taxonomic problems of educational systems. In Singleton, W. T. and Spurgeon, P. (eds.). *Measurement of Human Resources.* (London: Taylor and Francis)

Gagne, R. M. (1976). The psychology of teaching methods. In *Seventy-Fifth Yearbook of the National Society for the Study of Education,* Chap. II (Chicago: University Press)

Gagne, R. M. and Fleishman, E. A. (1959). *Psychology and Human Performance.* (New York: Holt-Dryden)

Gershoni, H. (1972). A laboratory approach to work study. *Int. J. Prod. Res.*, **10**, (2), 147

Gilbreth, F. B. (1911). *Motion Study.* (New York: Van Nostrand)

Gilbreth, F. B. (1973). *Applied Motion Study.* (reprint of 1917 edition) (Easton: Hive Publishing Co.)

Gilbreth. F. B. and Gilbreth, L. M. (1916). *Fatigue Study.* (New York: Sturgis and Watkin)

Glaser, R. (ed.). (1965). *Teaching Machines and Programmed Learning.* (Washington: National Education Association)

de Greene, K. B. (1970). Systems analysis techniques. In de Greene, K. B. (ed.). *Systems Psychology.* (New York: McGraw Hill)

de Greene, K. B. (1970). (ed.). *Systems Psychology.* (New York: McGraw Hill)

Gregory, G. (1961). A note on a method of estimating the precision of time study observations. *Int. J. Prod. Res.*, **1** (1), 63

Hollinshead, W. H. (1976). *Functional Anatomy of the Limbs and Back.* (Philadelphia: Saunders)

Jones, M. B. (1966). Individual differences. In Bilodeau, E. A. (ed.). *Acquisition of Skill.* (New York: Academic Press)

Kidd, J. S. (1962). Human tasks and equipment design. In Gagne, R. M. (ed.). *Psychological Principles of System Development.* (New York: Holt, Rinehart and Winston)

Meister, D. and Rabideau, G. F. (1965). *Human Factors Evaluation in System Development.* (New York: Wiley)

Miller, R. B. (1962). Task description and analysis. In Gagne, R. M. (ed.). *Psychological Principles in System Development.* (New York: Holt, Rinehart and Winston)

Miller, R. B. (1967). Task taxonomy: science or technology. In Singleton, W. T., Easterby, R. S. and Whitfield, D. (eds.). *The Human Operator in Complex Systems.* (London: Taylor and Francis)

Miller, R. B. (1975). Taxonomies for training. In Singleton, W. T. and Spurgeon, P. (eds.). *Measurement of Human Resources.* (London: Taylor and Francis)

Moores, B. (1968). Comparison of basic time for six operations as determined by MTM and normal time-study methods. *Int. J. Prod. Res.*, **7**(2), 151

Newell, A. and Simon, H. A. (1963). GPS – a program that simulates human thought. In Feigenbaum, E. and Feldman, J. (eds.). *Computers and Thought.* (New York: McGraw-Hill)

Rogers, W. and Hammersley, J. M. (1954). The consistency of stop-watch time-study practitioners. *Occ. Psych.*, **28**(2), 61

Sanfleber, H. (1966). An investigation into some aspects of the accuracy of predetermined motion time systems. *Int. J. Prod. Res.*, **6**(1), 25

Seymour, W. D. (1954). *Industrial Training for Manual Operations.* (London: Pitman)

Seymour, W. D. (1966). *Industrial Skills.* (London: Pitman)

Seymour, W. D. (1968). *Skills Analysis Training.* (London: Pitman)

Shaw, A. G. (1952). *The Purpose and Practice of Motion Study.* (London: Harlequin Press)

Singer, E. J. and Ramsden, J. (1969). *The Practical Approach to Skills Analysis.* (London: McGraw-Hill)

Singleton, W. T. (1957). An experimental investigation of sewing-machine skill. *Br. J. Psychol.*, **48**(2), 127

Singleton, W. T. (1960). An experimental investigation of speed controls for sewing machines. *Ergonomics*, **3**(4), 365

Singleton, W. T. (1964). A preliminary study of a capstan lathe. *Int. J. Prod. Res.*, **3**(3), 213

Singleton, W. T. (1966). The skills of the driver and the response of the vehicle. *Proc. Inst. Mech. Eng.*, **181**, pt. 3D, 51

Singleton, W. T. (1967). *Ergonomics in Systems Design*, **10** (5), 541

Singleton, W. T. (1971). Psychological aspects of man–machine systems. In Warr, P. B. (ed.). *Psychology at Work*. (Harmondsworth: Penguin)

Singleton, W. T. (1972a). Total activity analysis: a different approach to work study. *Le Travail Humain*, **35**(2), 241

Singleton, W. T. (1972b). Techniques for determining the causes of error. *Appl. Ergonom.*, **3**(3), 126

Singleton, W. T. (1973). Theoretical approaches to human error. *Ergonomics*, **16**(6), 727

Singleton, W. T. (1974). *Man–machine Systems*. (Harmondsworth: Penguin)

Singleton, W. T. (1976a). The model supervisor dilemma. In Sheridan, T. B. and Johannsen, G. (eds.). *Monitoring Behaviour and Supervisory Control*. (New York: Plenum)

Singleton, W. T. (1976b). Skill and accidents. In *Occupational Accident Research*. (Stockholm: Gotab)

Singleton, W. T., Easterby, R. S. and Whitfield, D. (eds.). (1967). *The Human Operator in Complex Systems*. (London: Taylor and Francis)

Singleton, W. T., Whitfield, D. and Stammers, R. B. (1973). Task analysis of the tractor driver. *Paper 2, Proceedings of NIAE Subject Day*, October, 1973

Singleton, W. T. and Spurgeon, P. (1975). *Measurement of Human Resources*. (London: Taylor and Francis)

Smith, R. G. (1964). *The Development of Training Objectives*. (Alexandria Vg: Hum. RRO)

Smith, K. U. and Sussman, H. (1969). Cybernetic motor learning and memory In Bilodeau, E. A. (ed.). *Principles of Skill Acquisition*. (New York: Academic Press)

Spearman, C. E. (1927). *The Abilities of Man*. (London: Macmillan)

Swain, A. D. (1963). A method for performing a human factors reliability analysis. *Monograph SCR-685*. (New Mexico: Sandia Laboratories)

Swain, A. D. (1970). Development of a human error rate data bank. In Jenkins, J. P. (ed.). *Proceedings of US Navy Human Reliability Workshop*. (Washington: Naval Ship Systems Command)

Taylor, F. W. (1911). *The Principles of Scientific Management*. (New York: Harper)

Tippett, L. H. C. (1934). A snap reading method of making time studies of machines and operatives in factory surveys. *Shirley Institute Memoirs*, **13**, 73

Wallis, D. (1975). A concluding commentary on the conference papers. In Singleton, W. T. and Spurgeon, P. (eds.). *Measurement of Human Resources*. (London: Taylor and Francis)

Wallis, D., Duncan, K. D. and Knight, M. A. G. (1966). *Programmed Instruction in the British Armed Forces*. (London: HMSO)

Welford, A. T. (1973). Causes of human error. *Paper to Royal Australian College of Surgeons*.

Wells, K. F. and Luttgens, K. (1976). *Kinesiology*. (Philadelphia: Saunders)

Whitfield, D. (1976). Man–computer symbiosis: A 1975 review. *AP Report 57, Applied Psychology Department, University of Aston in Birmingham, UK*

Zacks, S. (1962). The determination of optimal sample size for some work measurement procedures. *Int. J. Prod. Res.*, **1**(4), 43

Zeller, A. F. (1970). Accidents and safety. In de Greene, K. B. (ed.). *Systems Psychology*. (New York: McGraw-Hill)

2
Occupational Disability

W. T. SINGLETON

INTRODUCTION

There is no simple way of determining the number of people who come within the group described as occupationally disabled persons. One legally recognized category is the registered disabled who make up about 2% of the working population. However, since there are few advantages in claiming to belong to this group except facilities such as privileged car parking and since many individuals object to being classified as disabled there are many who could register but who do not. It has been estimated that only about half of those who could reasonably claim to belong in this category are currently registered. If one inquires of a company how many disabled employees they have, the intelligent response is to ask who is to be included. The smallest group is the registered disabled, the next largest is the pensioned disabled, the next includes all those with some physiological impairment and the largest includes all those with any kind of psychological disability. This last group can be increased or decreased indefinitely according to the definition of psychological disability which is acceptable – for example, whether it is intended to include only those who have been treated for mental illness or all those whose work effectiveness has at one time or another been affected by psychological influences. This last group of course includes everyone. Even if one tightens the definition to imply only those for whom there has been a significant negative effect on performance this still includes widespread industrial problems such as absenteeism and unpunctuality. These are not normally considered to be problems of disability although there might be some value in looking at them from this point of view. The objection which would occur to most people is that absenteeism, for example, is not entirely a characteristic of the individual; it is also a working group phenomenon and there is an interaction effect between the individual or group and the employer. Much depends on the definitions, attitudes and rules which stem from the company or other institution. In fact however, various interaction effects occur for all kinds of disability. Even for a simple anatomical impairment such as a missing finger, whether or not this is a disability obviously depends as much on the occupation as it does on the nature of the defect. From this background there is a current consensus (Wood, 1975) that at least three different labels are needed — impairment, disability and handicap. *Impairment* is intended to describe what is wrong with the individual in clinical terms — Harris (1971) defines it as "lacking part or all of a limb or having a defective limb or having a defective organ or mechanism of the body which stops or limits getting about, working or self-care". *Disability* is the functional description of the consequences, and *handicap* is the effect in terms of occupation and more generally in quality of life. Thus we have residual disability, functional disability and socio-economic disability respectively. Another associated term *invalidity* is currently used to describe the need for state support in the form of money (pensions and allowances) or services such as appliances and help in the home.

Impairment is essentially a clinical and mainly a medical problem and its description is strongly influenced by the need for curative treatment and therapy. Disability is seen in a wider context; there is still a therapy aspect and the assessment remains clinical but the objective is to consider defects in terms of needs and aspirations from self-care to self-fulfilment. Handicap is very much a social and economic matter ranging from facility for personal interaction to the required or desired standard of living. It will be seen that these concepts overlap; each shades into the next one and into other fields not usually thought of as disablement. The term disablement is sometimes used to cover the whole field while disability is restricted to functional aspects.

Thus there are at least two sources of complexity and ambiguity. Firstly there are no boundaries readily identifiable by the presence of discontinuities or step functions in measurable parameters; each definition at best focusses on an arbitrary region within some continuous parameter. Secondly, there are many disciplines involved including medicine, psychology, sociology, law and each brings to the topic its own characteristic set of techniques, procedures, models, theories and even values.

THE SIZE AND NATURE OF THE FIELD

The Harris (1971) survey indicates that, of the working age group of thirty-four million people (about twenty-five million actually wish to work) one and a half million are impaired — about 4%. Details are shown in Table 2.1. On average the impaired left school earlier and are less highly qualified than those of normal health. They tend to retire early and this trend is more marked among women than men. The longer they have been away from work the more

Table 2.1   A comparison of the general population and the impaired in Great Britain

		General population* (thousands)	Impaired in the population† (thousands)	Impaired as a percentage of their age group	
Over 65	Men	2 451	599	24·4	
	Women	3 988	1 184	29·7	
50–64	Men	4 683	401	8·6	Men 3·9
	Women	5 118	433	8·4	
15–49	Men	11 943	247	2·1	Women 3·8
	Women	11 946	209	1·7	
Under 15	Boys	6 241	not given	–	
	Girls	5 932	not given	–	

* Figures derived from 1966 Census
† Figures from Harris (1971)

they drift out of contact with their own doctors and with hospitals. These facts emerge from Martin and Morgan (1975). Of those who work only about 4% are in any kind of sheltered employment, 62% are in private companies and the remainder are evenly distributed between nationalized industries, local authorities, the civil service and self-employment. About half those working consider that their impairment is of no disadvantage, that is, they are not handicapped. For the other half the handicap manifests itself mainly in limiting the opportunity for different kinds of work and to a lesser extent in an inability to work hard. The most common cause of impairment is diseases of the circulatory system; this together with diseases of the respiratory system and the locomotor system account for more than three-quarters of the complaints keeping people off work for more than a year as shown in Table 2.2. It will be noticed that diseases of sense organs account for only about 3% of the total while mental disorders account for 10%. These data are not readily transferable into functional terms but, if one assumes that circulatory and respiratory problems will restrict energy expenditure, about 60% of those off work for a long time have this disability while about 20% have restricted movements. However, it must be borne in mind that few jobs now extend the worker near his limits of energy expenditure while there are many which demand high versatility of hand and body movement. The age trends confirm that bronchitis and rheumatism are much more evident in the last quarter of working life, indeed particularly in the North of England some degree of such impairment is currently regarded as normal for the over fifties. It is to be hoped , as housing and working conditions continue to improve, that these affects will diminish but, for the present, it is difficult to regard chronic minor symptoms of these two diseases as anything other than the apparently inevitable consequences of increasing age. Thus disability, like health, is age-dependent. One definition of disability (Disabled Persons Employment Act, 1944) is "a person who on

Table 2.2   Complaints keeping people off work (OPCS Survey 1972/73)

	Percentage kept off work for	
	1 month	12 months
Infective and parasitic diseases	3	2
Neoplasms	2	3
Endocrine, metabolic, nutritional disorders	1	2
Diseases of blood and blood-forming organs	1	2
Mental disorders	8	10
Diseases of sense organs	2	3
Diseases of nervous system	3	5
Diseases of circulatory system	13	38
Diseases of respiratory system	20	24
Diseases of digestive system	13	6
Diseases of genito-urinary system	5	3
Complications of pregnancy	1	—
Diseases of skin and subcutaneous tissue	3	1
Diseases of bones and organ movement	16	20
Accidents	25	8
Amputations	1	1
Uncodable	—	—

account of injury, disease or congenital infirmity is substantially handicapped in obtaining or keeping employment or in undertaking work on his own account, of a **kind** which apart from that injury, disease or deformity would be suited to his **age,** experience and qualifications".

Behind this definition there is clearly a model of the individual seeking work in a competitive society and subject to two kinds of liability. The first kind are handicaps including injury, disease and infirmity, the second kind includes time-dependent factors such as age, inexperience and absence of qualifications. A substantial liability of this first kind is called disablement but one of the second kind, although it similarly limits the range of feasible jobs, is nothing to do with disability. Behind this again are some deep conventions of society, for example that the business of maintaining the community by work is the responsibility of those in the middle age range, say 16–65 years; those outside this range are entitled to support from society, and there are also some within this range who need support for various reasons of impairment and they are the occupationally disabled. Just how much support these latter need either financially or in terms of sympathy and co-operation depends on the kinds and degree of impairment and on the attitudes, fashions and available resources of a given society at a given time. Broadly the blind are considered to require more than the deaf, for example, and although this seems rational enough in terms of likely handicap it does sometimes seem that the deaf are relatively hard done by in terms of understanding by the rest of us. The situation in relation to intellectual impairment is particularly complex. Mild impairment merely warrants lack of respect and a low standard of living – they are the dull-witted, suitable for the most menial jobs and low financial rewards.

However, at some rather arbitrary intelligence level this shades into the subnormals who need looking after by positive discrimination in the education system and later by sheltered employment.

This is connected with the competitive element mentioned earlier. If an individual is similar to ourselves he is one of our group and competes normally for the jobs and resources we must share between ourselves. If however his impairment is of a degree such that he is manifestly not one of us then our attitude to him changes markedly and we accept that he can be treated more favourably. However, the subtle social penalty associated with these favours is that he is outside our group. There is more to this than merely pointing out the irrationality of group behaviour. There is a fundamental problem here about which many disabled individuals feel very strongly – they naturally wish to be a part of society rather than a separate, if favoured, group. It can also have direct and serious consequences in relation to rehabilitation. For example, one could take a series of routine industrial tasks and by minor redesign of jobs and procedures plus the design of appropriate training schemes it might well be possible to create a highly competitive work-force from intellectually subnormal individuals. They would be less likely to get bored, they would accept discipline and they could produce the manufactured article in a regular fashion. In a narrow sense these persons are now completely rehabilitated. However, what happens to the self-esteem of the original work-force who now see their job being done equally well by the subnormals? They now have to accept that they belong to the same group as these disabled or alternatively, being human, they will find a way of stopping the scheme, perhaps through the Trade Unions, so that they are not subject to this threat. Correspondingly, there would be middle-class people, not themselves in danger of being classed as the same group, who would attack the scheme savagely on the grounds that the subnormal individuals were being exploited.

This is, of course, a hypothetical situation and in practice the variety and complexity of particular projects is such that these simple confrontations do not arise, but it does illustrate some of the potent and not always positive forces at work behind what superficially may seem to be a straightforward, well-intentioned and desirable rehabilitation process. Although occupational disability is ultimately a complex social, economic, legal and political issue it always begins with the individual who has some impairment which results in a handicap.

PERSON-CENTRED ISSUES

At various stages during his life the individual needs occupational guidance. This is true for everyone when full-time education ends and the working life begins and it applies also when changes of career direction occur, for example, after injury leading to handicap.

In principle the guidance process for the disabled is essentially the same as that for other groups in the community. Differences such as age and skill level are at least as important as disability in modifying the procedure. Thus the process for school leavers is somewhat different from that for the redundant worker in his fifties, and the process for professionals and senior executives is different from that for manual workers, but the presence or absence of minor disability makes relatively little difference to what happens. There is one unique factor in the disability context in that sheltered employment or permanent unemployment can be considered as positive options for the seriously disabled. The task of the guidance specialist is to help his client to scan the total occupational field so as to reduce it by criteria such as feasibility, suitability and availability to a perceivable set of alternatives between which a decision can be made by the client (Singleton, 1975). The foundation of the process is the specialist/client interview supported by various tests of and reports about the client (the assessment) and information about occupations. Tests and reports are usually about physical and intellectual capacities although tests of personality and interests are also used. The aim is to clarify the client's realistic view of himself or, in other jargon, to improve his self-concept. This includes aspirations as well as interests and aptitudes. In the case of the disabled and particularly the intellectually impaired there has been and still is a tendency to treat the individual as a patient rather than a client – that is, someone subject to examination by experts who, although they will call it advice, will in fact tell the person what he should do and what is going to happen to him. Although this situation is improving as everyone in society including the expert becomes more sensitive to the importance of the dignity of the individual, disabled or otherwise, one factor acting in the opposite direction is that as costs of guidance and assessment rise so there is more of a tendency to treat the client as a unit to be processed rather than a person. This tendency could be reinforced as assessment procedures become more technologically sophisticated and the whole process is aided by computers. It need not happen – it depends on the designer of the systems being aware of these issues.

The general model is related to that mentioned earlier in which, as the individual proceeds through life, he is expected to work in the middle phase, but in doing so he should be able to satisfy his personal needs as well as community needs. This does not often lead to conflict because the personal needs in the well-adjusted individual are so much conditioned by and interactive with the community as he has learned to understand it, that his expectations match his abilities (Lancashire, 1971). The capacities and abilities of the individual have a stable core but overlying this there is continuous change with maturation and experience. The interests and aspirations also change in time so that although guidance must operationally be an isolated, static and discrete occurrence it should ideally be seen as just one event within a life-long or at least career-long process of adjustment.

Another complication for the disabled is that assessment and occupational guidance get inextricably mixed up with therapy and rehabilitation. There is usually no clear point at which medical rehabilitation gives way to occupational rehabilitation. Some medical specialists argue that rehabilitation begins, for example, in the operating theatre after an accident when the treatment is carried out bearing in mind the future employability of the patient. Others, the vast majority at present, consider that medical treatment should be entirely divorced from anything to do with work. These latter see themselves as doing what can be done to restore the patient to as unimpaired a condition as possible, and then it becomes someone else's problem.

There is an analogous situation in education. In the special schools for the blind, the deaf, the locomotor disorders and so on, how far should the curriculum be oriented towards preparing the child for work as opposed to the traditional broad educational aim of full development of the individual? There is certainly a difficult problem for the disabled at the transition from school to work (Singleton and Debney, 1978).

Returning to rehabilitation, the compromise approach currently used in the Employment Rehabilitation Centres is team assessment; a medical doctor, a psychologist, a social worker, a rehabilitation officer and one or more trades' specialists each get to know the individual, carry out their own form of assessment, and then come together to arrive at a collective decision about the advice which should be given. Formally this is regarded as assessment and guidance but in practice there is a strong, often a dominant, element of therapy. This process takes a long time, several months, and it is very expensive compared, for example, with the straightforward surgical treatment of an injury. There are a few experimental centres such as Banstead Place, Surrey, carrying out a similar assessment process for disabled school-leavers.

JOB-CENTRED ISSUES

The attitude of employers in British manufacturing industry at present is fairly consistent if not entirely rational. When a person is injured at work in a way which leads to handicap some effort will be made to find that person a job, preferably in the same shop where he worked previously, and if this is not possible then in some other part of the company. He will often be guaranteed the payment that he was receiving before his accident for the remainder of his working life. The intensity of the effort put into this rehabilitation process will depend on an unstated but very real assessment of whether or not the individual was a 'good worker' before his disability arose. This asessment includes factors such as length of service, reliability, degree of co-operativeness and general contribution to the company. The rehabilitation effort would be much less, often none at all, if the same person were to have an accident outside work leading to the same handicap. For diseases such as heart attacks the rehabilitation effort will again depend on an assessment, in this case intuitive and of doubtful validity, as to whether or not the disease was caused by effort on the company's behalf. Accepting handicapped people not previously employed by the company is very different. This is approached cautiously; there is some goodwill if the person has not worked previously but, if he has, then the attitude is that his previous company should be looking after him. The most sympathetic approach will be to school-leavers. Older handicapped persons have very little chance of successful consideration. Although one would expect nationalized industries and government employers to be more sympathetic there is in practice little difference. They are not so dominated by the profit motive as private industry but on the other hand they are not so fiercely conscious of the company image and of carrying their own problems. In all instances what is done is based entirely on the individual case with everyone involved making ad hoc decisions about redesign of the work space, access to work, problems of fire and safety regulations and so on. There are few principles and no theory about these activities. The company medical officer, if there is one, will contribute his professional knowledge and skill and so also will the personnel and training officers and the engineers who design special equipment aids. The issue is treated as one of management which is to be solved by common sense from a background of company policy and knowledge about the disabled person concerned, both based on long experience.

Sometimes a technical management problem will emerge. For example, many companies now have very tightly controlled production systems with continuous data generation in the form of man-hours, material costs, production, quality and so on which may be used to monitor performance and as the basis for individual and group bonus schemes. If one handicapped worker, for good reasons, can only generate, say, half the production of an average worker there is a problem. The difficulty is not so much that the company objects to carrying this minor excess cost but rather that it confuses the smooth monitoring of the system and may affect the pay of the group containing the disabled worker. Altering the computer programmes which manipulate the data may be difficult, and even if it is worth doing someone has to decide what proportion of an average worker's output is a fair expectation of this individual. The snags here are that there are few principles about how to make such a judgement other than on experienced clinical-type opinion and many handicaps are not consistent in their effects. Some days the individual may be virtually normal, at other times he may be almost completely disabled, this again can cause problems in management control, which is not usually designed to cope with fluctuations in worker performance.

SKILL-CENTRED ISSUES

Disability is relatively permanent; in this it differs from illness where there is only a temporary problem of restoring the individual to his healthy state. The disabled person cannot be so restored. There is some limitation of his capacities which distinguishes him from the non-disabled. After accepting this he has two strategies: he can modify his aspirations and he can develop new skills which compensate for his specific capacity limitation. The appropriate mix of these two strategies will be different for each individual but there are some broad characteristics of groups which can be identified. Three groups of disabled can be considered: the congenital, the traumatic and the progressive.

The congenitally disabled such as those born with serious visual or spinal problems are faced with subtle difficulties in skill development which often lead to the underestimation of their potential. In the previous volume in this series the way in which skills develop continuously from birth at both the motor level and the perceptual level was described. This development can only proceed normally for those fortunate enough to have intact sensory, central and motor systems. A defect will have repercussions across the whole range of basic skills. Any kind of sensory or motor problem will slow down and reorient the progression from enactive models, through pictorial models to symbolic models. The child will be in danger of being regarded as dull and slow, perhaps as difficult because of the inevitable frustrations arising from trying, as it were, to build these complex structures with imperfect tools and materials. Looked at in this way the extraordinary thing is that disabled children do succeed in conforming so closely to the standard pattern of development. However, they are likely to take longer; this leads to phasing problems both in communicating with others and in fitting in with the standards of various institutions of society. For example, both psychologists and educationists have implicit time- and age-based standards. If a child at the age of ten can only obtain test scores appropriate for an eight-year-old, then he is regarded as that much lower in potential although for a disabled child it may be merely a delay. Most psychologists would in fact be aware of this but tests are often given and interpreted by people who are not psychologists. Similarly educational systems assume that a particular development such as learning to read will take place at a given age and a disabled child who is delayed is in double jeopardy. He has his impairment and he now has to cope also with having 'missed the bus' and got out of phase with the system. At the social level also, because they may not be able to mix so readily with other children and because they have perhaps overprotective parents, disabled children take longer to mature. These difficulties are tiresome enough in schools but they become really serious when the transition to work begins. The consensus seems to be that for a child with any kind of serious disability but who otherwise has average capacities, he can be expected to be at least two years behind his contemporaries in development. This clearly needs to be taken account of in any assessment, prediction and general guidance in relation to choice of career.

The traumatically disabled have a different set of problems in that they probably went through the normal process of skill development and then suddenly one or more of the foundations of the elaborate skill structure disappears. It is interesting to note that it is common practice to assume that, whatever the impairment and occupation, there is some important residue of skill and knowledge. Every attempt is made to keep the individual in the job at which he is experienced. This is probably to do with knowing people, materials and procedures rather than motor skills, although this obviously depends on the specific job and on the nature of the handicap which arises. Nevertheless there does seem to be an assumption based on experience that skills are not dependent on particular bodily functions unless there is complete blockage of an input or output mechanism. For example, a blind person cannot drive a road vehicle and a legless person would not be a very good tennis player, but apart from such extremes skills seem to be resistant to loss of particular physiological support systems.

For the progressive diseases such as multiple sclerosis or rheumatism, the loss of function is not sudden and complete nor is it continuous and regular. There are usually erratic phases of improvement and deterioration and the effect on work is correspondingly difficult to predict and adapt to. Adaptation to losses of receptor and effector functions often takes the form of more elaborate cognitive skills and less reliance on motor skills. Thus the ageing games player will try to win by attacking the morale of his opponents rather than by attempting to defeat them by force and speed. The motor mechanic with an arthritic hip will spend more time thinking out what is wrong and less time climbing under the car or bending under the bonnet to try out hypotheses with minimal planning. The general strategy in colloquial terms is that 'if your body deteriorates you use your head more'. This kind of rational trade-off is at present better carried out by exploration and experiment on the part of the individual concerned rather than by formal training methods or other procedures. This is partly because each case is so different and partly because, if there are potential principles and theories, they have not yet been developed.

For all kinds of disability a more detailed skills analysis in relation to the job concerned, and of the individual before his disability and afterwards as appropriate, would seem to be a reasonable way of making progress. Unfortunately little work of this kind seems to have been done to date.

OPERATIONAL ISSUES

The principles of all personnel processes − guidance, placement, training and job design − are the same for the case of disabled as for other kinds of workers. In either case these are all matching processes where the capacities of the person concerned are related to the demands of the particular job. Every problem has three parameters as indicated in Table 2.3: the personnel processes, the characteristics of the job and the characteristics of the worker either as an individual or as a group such as the paraplegics.

Table 2.3   The total set of operational issues

Personnel processes	Kinds of worker	Kinds of job
Guidance	⎧ skills	Manual
Placement	Special ⎨ knowledge	Manipulative
Training	⎩ personality	Routine procedural
Job design	Special limitations	Dynamic control
		Perceptual
		Intellectual
		Social

Every method of skill analysis described in the previous chapter will generate evidence relevant to the problem. Which one or which combination is most appropriate changes with the particular case. The main variable is the kind of job but the other parameters can also affect the choice. For example if the investigator was concerned with a manipulative industrial task such as assembly he would use a method-study-type analysis, but if he were concerned with a perceptual task such as chemical plant monitoring he would use a process-control-type analysis. These would be appropriate for guidance and placement in both cases, but if the investigator were a training officer he might decide that the assembly task warranted a task analysis, and if he were a disablement resettlement officer dealing with a potential chemical plant controller confined to a wheel chair he might use a method-study analysis to check that the work space design did not generate any special problems.

Work space and job design for the disabled is mainly a matter of carrying out specific adaptations to suit the person concerned (Griew, 1969), for example the designing of special seats for jobs which are normally done from the standing position, such as machine tool operation. Since the seated man's reach area is less than that of the standing man some controls might need to be repositioned or alternatively the seat can be arranged to slide across the work space. Special jigs, measuring instruments and limb supports can be designed for example for those who are blind, who only have one hand or have limited muscular control. Griew (op.cit.) illustrates a particularly ingenious solution from the Netherlands to the problem of designing a job in which mentally retarded workers are required to pack one hundred plastic letters into bags. To avoid counting, a frame with one hundred cells is provided where each cell will only hold one letter, so that the task becomes one of filling each cell and then operating a release mechanism which transfers all the contents to a bag.

For training schemes it is again necessary to match the kind of training to the kind of job and to the kinds of personnel. Wallis et al. (1966) provide a more detailed taxonomy of jobs than that in Table 2.3 and relate it to the various instructional methods which range from self-instructional/student-centred methods through instructor-centred methods to equipment-centred methods such as simulators.

The key to successful training is always knowledge of results which has two separate but complementary effects. It makes learning possible in that there can be no learning without some kind of knowledge of degree of success of previous efforts. In addition the sensitive timing and content of knowledge of results can facilitate and direct the learning process and knowledge of results is a potent additional motivator in those who have some primary drive to learn. These principles are well established by experimental data (Annett, 1969) and by experience of operational training schemes (Seymour, 1968). The International Labour Office has developed the principle of "modules of employable skills" (Dowding, 1973). A module is defined as the smallest volume of skills or group of skills and the necessary related knowledge required to permit remunerative employment. It is also related to a coherent learning process which leads to a distinct package not only by the criterion that it is usable in employment but also that it is an integrated unit for which the progress of performance can be measured as a whole and for sub-modules. The modules are seen as progressive in that a trainee can, at any time, add further modules to his skills and thus increase his employment opportunities. This concept conforms to the principle of adequate knowledge of results and consequent skill development with motivational reinforcement both during training and at work. It is highly feasible and adaptable to general cases and to individuals so that it particularly suits the requirements of the disabled (Cooper, 1977). Cooper stresses the "total care" concept in which training is only one part of the rehabilitation process which must incorporate guidance, placement, job design and also the special problems which arise for the disabled from the design of buildings. At present, because of the orientation of ILO, these ideas are being utilized more in developing countries, although in principle they are equally applicable to advanced countries.

It will be noted that the foundation for decisions about all the personnel processes from selection to job design is an extensive range of data from information about the job or range of jobs to information about the person or range of persons being considered. The study of skills attempts to encompass the range in that it links jobs or tasks and people, but each end of the range is marked by another kind of analysis: job descriptions and personnel assessments respectively. These are not entirely separate; each is a focus which leads into the other one. A useful job description cannot be carried out in the abstract. The way it is done depends on why it is being done; a job description carried out by a production engineer will not be the same as one carried out by a training officer. For the disabled the job descriptions usually concentrate on job demands so that the loci of particular problems for those with particular disabilities will be identified. There are many forms for job assessment in use in various countries, different industries and for different kinds of disability. Typical is the one quoted by Griew (*op. cit.*) and devised by the Danish National Association for Infantile Paralysis; the structure of this analysis is shown in Table 2.4. Since the association is concerned with what is functionally an output limitation there is a strong emphasis on locomotor aspects of the job.

Table 2.4 Work demand analysis form devised by the Danish National Association for Infantile Paralysis

Group	Heading	Content
1.	Locomotion	Walking with obstacles: Slippery floors, ladders etc.
2.	Working positions	Standing, sitting, stooping
3.	Total movements	Kneeling, reading, bending, manipulating
4.	Muscular forces	Pulling, lifting, carrying
5.	Energy output	Pulse rate, calorific expenditure
6.	Working conditions	Heat, cold, noise, dirt
7.	Senses co-ordination	Seeing, hearing, touch
8.	Skill, intelligence, character	
9.	Education or payment	

Personnel assessments can be much more complete but again this depends on whether they are attempted in the abstract or how far the assessment is oriented towards occupations or changes of occupation. For example, an industrial medical officer would probably start from the job his patient did before disablement and consider whether there are now any aspects of functional incapacity which would interfere with his work. If not, and if the objective is simply to get him back to work, then there is no need for more detailed assessment. This is one example of an assessment principle also implicit in Table 2.3, which includes special skills and special problems of disability. The individual need only be described in terms which note his departure from the average, or from some standardized demand such as the requirements of a particular job either positively or negatively. By contrast a youth employment officer dealing with a school-leaver seeking guidance about possible employment will need to go through the whole background of his client including education, interests, family, housing, transport and so on. Table 2.5 shows the structure of the assessment used by the Birmingham Youth Employment Office (Hegginbotham, 1973).

In general the practical problems of occupational disability are so complex and multivariate that there cannot be standard procedures for collecting evidence or making decisions. With so much potential evidence available, that which is worth obtaining and accumulating must be determined by its relevance to the specific problem. This conclusion is a difficult one to accept for those organizational specialists who like to have general rules and procedures and for the systems analysts who prefer standard computer programmes. Nevertheless it does seem to be true that like the general problem of skills analysis introduced in the previous chapter, any operational problem of occupational disability is a unique people-interaction problem involving the disabled and the experts including medical officers, personnel officers, engineers, managers and others. They all use their particular skills to devise a procedure that suits the case.

Table 2.5   Occupational classification by the Birmingham Youth Employment Service

1.	'Level'
H	professional/technical with at least 3 'O' levels
C	craft, clerical and secretarial type training
X	little or no planned training

2.	'Manual to Verbal'
1	Metal ⎫
2	Wood ⎬ designing, making, repairing
3	Other materials ⎭
4	Building, Civil engineering, etc.
5	Agriculture, Horticulture, Forestry
6	Transport and Communication
7	Laboratory and Scientific
8	Medical, Nursing, Pharmacy, etc.
9	Sales
10	Hotel and Catering
11	Entertainment
12	Other service industries
13	Shorthand/typist
14	General Office
15	Office machines

e.g. A plumber's mate is in category 4X
     A computer programmer is in 15H

THEORETICAL ISSUES

The conclusion above is not of course an adequate excuse for leaving the situation to continue indefinitely in a largely pragmatic fashion. The pragmatism is necessary at present because of the multi-dimensionality of the problems but also because the theory and principles are so weak. It is a multi-disciplinary activity where the separate disciplines have very different concepts and objectives which do not readily coalesce. Consider the process in which the disabled person is involved from identification of disease to settlement in work. This is shown in outline in Table 2.6. The first approach to the problem is a medical one, where the theories and taxonomies have developed over centuries with the primary objective of treatment and cure. At some stage when most of this is complete the patient enters a transition phase of rehabilitation which is partly medical and partly occupational. He is then subject to occupational assessment and this may vary from a purely medical appraisal to the purely psychological appraisal of the occupational

Table 2.6 The rehabilitation process

	Procedure	Relevant assessment and classification
Clinic	Diagnosis Treatment Rehabilitation	Medical taxonomies
		Disability taxonomies
Work		
	Assessment Guidance Selection Allocation Training Work design	Person taxonomies Function taxonomies Skill taxonomies Job taxonomies

guidance counsellor. As mentioned already, if assessment is to be comprehensive it must be interdisciplinary in the way developed by the Employment Rehabilitation Centres. The common language here is functions: what the person can and cannot do independently of why not. Beyond this we come to the skills approach which is essentially functional but which emphasises also the dynamic characteristics of functions based on the comprehensive human learning capabilities. Finally these must be related to job taxonomies which vary from person- and skill-oriented descriptions to task- and system-oriented descriptions. The daunting variety of taxonomies currently used within and across these fields has been reviewed by Singleton (1979).

There is some justification for suggesting that the study of skills is central to the field. Skills bridge the gap between person-attributes and jobs and this is the ultimate purpose of occupational disability studies. If we had a complete taxonomy of skills this could form the core to which all other taxonomies could be related and here would be the beginnings of a general theory of occupational disability. Unfortunately this is not yet available but we can make progress with a related aspect by considering the general demands on people at work from an ergonomics point of view. The first requirement for any kind of work is energy, which is generated by the digestive system in co-operation with the respiratory system and the circulatory system, which also does the distribution. Thus any malfunctions in these systems could lead to a limitation of energy expenditure. The energy emerges by the application of forces through muscles and joints and this has consequences for locomotion and for finer manipulations mostly relying on the hands. The triggering, grading and direction of these forces is controlled by the sensory inputs, mainly through vision and hearing with feedback through touch and kinaesthesis. The planning and longer term control requires central functions while the general drive and orientation towards objectives comes partly from the central nervous system and partly from the endocrine system. This taxonomy (Table 2.7) has the advantage of a basis in the human sciences but equally it is

Table 2.7   Structure of occupational disability: job demands and human functions

Resource	Physiological support systems subject to malfunction
Energy	Circulatory, respiratory, digestive
Locomotion	Skeletal, muscular
Manipulation	
Co-ordination	Special senses
Cognitive	Central nervous system
Connative	CNS and endocrine

manifestly relevant to man at work. It is not likely to be superseded by any developments in science or by any changes in work due to developments of technology and society generally. It is depersonalized and treats workers as human operators rather than human beings but the disabled are seeking technical help from the expert rather than sympathy. It is encouragingly similar to the *PULHEEMS* system (*P*hysical capacity, *U*pper limbs, *L*oco-motion, *H*earing, *E*yesight, *M*ental capacity, *S*tability) developed by experience for medical assessment in the British Armed Forces (Fletcher, 1949).

CONCLUSION

Returning to the total issue, an occupationally disabled person is one for whom there is some limitation of function which reduces the possibility of realizing what otherwise would be legitimate employment aspirations. What is legitimate for an individual depends not only on his capacities but also on the opportunities provided by the state of development of the society of which he is a member, the available educational and training systems, the work opportunities, family traditions and privileges and so on. Most of these factors are not readily quantifiable or even describable in detail but they are the setting for the comprehension of the rather arbitrary matters considered to be included under the label disability. We have an individual of working age with a range of capacities which he must match against his aspirations. His capacities are only subject to minor changes through maturation and rehabilitation so that the degrees of freedom open to him are in the adjustment of aspirations and the development of skills.

The category of the occupationally disabled incorporates every individual whose characteristics, in the opinion of that individual, do not fit him to compete without some handicap for jobs which determine his place in society. This place in society determines or is described by his consumption of resources provided by that society and his contribution to it. Normally his opinion will be shared by society generally and more specifically by the individuals and institutions with special responsibility for the disabled. If the opinions do not match then either communication takes place to improve the match or the individual withdraws from general contact with society. If he does withdraw a primary aim of rehabilitation must be to restore communication so that some better matching is possible.

The optimum match is a function of a given society in a given state of political, economic and social development as well as of the individual's physiological and psychological state. These two basic factors, society and the individual's state, are not independent; they influence each other. Thus achievement of an appropriate match is the key to all therapy, education, training and retraining. No form of treatment or training can be successful without some co-operation from the individual recipient and also some communication between society and the recipient. Co-operation varies from docile and passive to dedicated and enthusiastic. So also does the communication from the state. These factors are the basic predictors of the likely degree of success of the process. Co-operation is determined by a complex set of interacting parameters incorporating the individual's appraisal of the value of the process to him personally, and this in turn is determined by the comparison of his situation with that of others who are similarly placed. The concept of those who are similarly placed is culturally determined. In egalitarian countries it can incorporate all other citizens but in other countries with more hierarchical societies an individual's personal comparison group will only include a particular set which might be defined by a mix of class, occupational and economic status.

From this broad conclusion it follows that objectives, equity, improvements, feasibility and in fact every facet of occupational disablement can only be assessed in the context of a particular country at a particular time. However, having perceived the factors making for differences at every level from the individual to the nation, the art of enduring research is to seek out the underlying constants of principle, methodology and technique. For example, implicit in the above discussion is the principle that disablement is primarily a problem of and for the individual. There are grosser problems of putting individuals into categories or devising taxonomies and of preparation of statistics about regional and national situations but these are essentially secondary. The problem is an individual one not only in the sense that interaction and treatment must be specific but also in the sense that the individual must make his own decisions.

However, he needs assistance in making these decisions. Much, probably most, of this help comes and will continue to come from relatives, friends, acquaintances and colleagues at work, but there is a place for experts. These come from established professions for whom occupational disability is a peripheral interest including medicine, psychology, sociology, law, architecture, engineering and management. There are at present no specialists who encompass the whole field except a few individuals with a background in one or more of the above professions, who direct their energies and expertise to these problems but who inevitably start from the biased point of view of their particular professional training. Yet the problem is very large in terms of numbers of clients and costs on a nation-wide scale. There is increasing interest in the field from politicians and the community generally but since this interest tends to be emotionally rather than intellectually based there is a considerable and urgent need for more theoretical development. The study of skills is bound to come into this and although it would be premature to postulate that the role will be the key one it is likely to be an important one.

References

Annett, J. (1969). *Feedback and Human Behaviour.* (Harmondsworth: Penguin)

Cooper N. E. (1977). Vocational reintegration of handicapped workers with assistive devices. *International Labour Review,* **115** (3), 343

Dowding, A. E. (1973). An introduction to vocational training using modules of employable skills. *International Labour Review,* **107** (6), 553

Fletcher, R. T. (1949). Pulheems: a new system of medical classification. *Br. Med. J.* **1,** 83

Griew, S. (1969). *Adaptation of Jobs for the Disabled.* (Geneva: International Labour Office)

Harris, A. I. (1971). Handicapped and impaired in Great Britain. Part I. *Office of Population Censuses and Surveys.* (London: HMSO)

Hegginbotham, H. (1973). Occupational classification in the Birmingham Youth Employment Service. *Occ. Psych.* **47,** 111

Lancashire, R. D. (1971). Occupational choice theory and occupational guidance practice. In Warr, P. B. (ed.). *Psychology at Work.* (Harmondsworth: Penguin)

Martin, J. and Morgan, M. (1975). Prolonged sickness and the return to work. *Office of Population Censuses and Surveys.* (London: HMSO)

Seymour, W. D. (1968). *Skills Analysis Training.* (London: Pitman)

Singleton, W. T. (1975). The role of the computer in vocational guidance. In Singleton, W. T. and Spurgeon, P. (eds.). *Measurement of Human Resources.* (London: Taylor and Francis)

Singleton, W. T. (1979) Chapter 1 – Introduction. In Singleton, W. T. and Debney, L. M. (eds.). *Occupational Disability: the approaches of government, industry and the universities.* (In Press)

Singleton, W. T. and Debney, L. M. (eds.). (1979). *Occupational Disability: the approaches of government, industry and the universities.* (In Press)

Wallis, D., Duncan, K. D. and Knight, M. A. G. (1966). *Programmed Instruction in the British Armed Forces.* (London: HMSO)

Wood, P. H. N. (1975). *Classification of Impairments and Handicaps.* WHO/IL09 RC75.15. (Geneva: World Health Organisation)

3
Skill and Mental Retardation

T. NETTELBECK

INTRODUCTION

This chapter considers the contribution that a skills approach might make to the education and training of mentally retarded persons. Although there has been considerable agreement about the general goals of such education, few specific techniques have been found for achieving these aims. Special education has therefore been less successful than it might otherwise have been, despite the large resources that have been devoted to its development. However, preliminary work suggests that what is already known about the development of skilled performance might profitably be applied to these issues.

Defining mental retardation

Persons whose intellectual and adaptive abilities are observably well below average are described as 'mentally retarded'. The definition formulated by the American Association on Mental Deficiency (AAMD) avoids reference to aetiology, recognizing the difficulties of differentiating between individuals on the basis of cause (Grossman, 1973). In the research literature a distinction is usually made between cases where retardation is the consequence of known organic disorders due to injury, disease, genetic factors or chromosomal anomalies, and retardation that cannot be attributed to any obvious biological deficiency. However, distinctions between brain damage, specific categories of disability like mongolism (Down's syndrome), and cultural–familial retardation provide only a rudimentary classification system; within such categories similarities in behaviour may result from a diversity of biological, psychological and social factors. Thus retarded persons should not be regarded as constituting a homogeneous population (Sanders, 1970).

The degree of retardation is usually described by the individual's score on a standard test of general intelligence (IQ), although motivational and learning factors relevant to social and vocational areas of behaviour may also be considered. Intelligence tests measure the capacity of the individual to cope with complex situations, blurring differences between individuals in the means by which they reach solutions. Such instruments indicate the consequences of particular cognitive deficiencies rather than the causes of those deficiencies. They can identify persons likely to fail within a traditional education system, particularly in areas of achievement like reading and writing, or the use of numbers and money. However, they are not suited to the objective of understanding why some persons fail and what might be done to help such persons cope more effectively.

SPECIAL EDUCATION FOR THE RETARDED

The aims of special education

Children with IQ scores between 50 and 80 are commonly termed educable mentally retarded (EMR). (In Britain, the term 'educationally subnormal' (ESN) has much the same meaning.) In recent times a majority of such children have been educated within special classes and schools. The objectives of this special education system reflect society's belief that despite differences in ability all members of the community have the same basic rights to care, protection, education, training and a decent standard of living. Virtually all programmes have as their aim the development of the individual, taking into account a wide spectrum of physical, intellectual, emotional and social considerations (Rosenweig and Long, 1960). Thus, the broad purpose of special education is the same as that of general education. Differences in specific aims arise only in so far as they reflect the more limited capabilities of retarded children.

Since the early 1970s there has been a marked expansion in the educational services available to a smaller group of Trainable Mentally Retarded (TMR) children – those with IQ scores between 20 and 49. The aims of these services are usually more specific than is the case with education for EMR children, probably because the functional needs of TMR children are more obvious. Many have additional physical and sensory handicaps and require help to attain acceptable standards of self-care and socialization. Although some TMR persons eventually find employment, usually within a sheltered setting, most training programmes for them are concerned more with issues essential to some measure of independence within the community – like travel, following directions, or recognizing signs – than with work preparation (Robinson and Robinson, 1976).

Methods in special education

To date, administrative and curriculum practices in special education have been shaped largely by ideology or by pragmatic considerations about available resources, rather than being derived directly from an established body of knowledge. This has resulted in a great deal of experimentation, change, and controversy about procedures best suited to the needs of mentally retarded persons. While increased commitments by governments have led to widespread improvement in the standard of equipment and buildings available for this purpose, other areas of importance have not necessarily kept pace. Surveys of special schooling have revealed the widespread use of inappropriate teaching methods involving simplified normal elementary school curricula (Guskin and Spicker, 1968). The 1970s have seen an increasing concern with the systematic development of teaching materials and procedures suited to the individual child (Meyen and Horner, 1976). It is fair to say, however, that the impetus for this work has come largely from practical experience rather than from research findings, and it is as yet too early for changes made to have been evaluated.

An evaluation of special education

On the whole, special school arrangements for TMR children do not appear to have improved the social competency of those attending over and above gains found among similar children living at home (Guskin and Spicker, 1968). There is some suggestion, however, that such programmes are of indirect benefit to parents (Robinson and Robinson, 1976).

A recent reaction against self-contained classes and schools has resulted in the widespread acceptance of the desirability of 'normalization' or 'mainstreaming' (Wolfensberger, 1972). According to this policy, integrating retarded children within the main educational system will avoid problems arising from such children being labelled as handicapped. Proponents of 'normalization' point to research findings that isolated special schooling for retarded children is no more effective than regular schooling for similar pupils, and may even result in slower progress (Quay, 1963; Kirk, 1964).

Others have urged caution, insisting that results from research into the relative advantages of different class arrangements are by no means clear. Some retarded children do not achieve levels of development commensurate with mental age in either special or regular classrooms. Thus, as presently constituted, neither setting appears to cope satisfactorily with the requirements of EMR children. As a number of authors have pointed out, the case against separate special educational facilities has not been proved. Poor effectiveness is as likely the result of inadequate curriculum content and poor teacher training as due to the 'isolated' training environment (Cruickshank, 1974).

Problems in special education

Special educators have been faced with two major difficulties. The first has been to define objectives that were specific, unambiguous, and not stated in general, idealized terms not readily translated into reality (Engelmann, 1967). The second has been to develop training procedures that improve the individual's practical self-help skills, communication and interaction with others, and occupational adjustment, even where such aims were fairly specific. Problems arising from a lack of general direction have been if anything more marked where the children involved were more severely retarded (Gunzburg, 1970).

Psychological theories of cognitive development and learning have provided useful guidelines for general special educational practice, but have not led to solutions that can be applied to individual cases with confidence (Engelmann, 1967). Piaget's theories do not attempt to account for individual differences in cognitive development or deal with factors that might underlie such differences. While operant conditioning methods have frequently proved effective for modifying simple behaviour, they have been less so where the behaviour was more complex (Robinson and Robinson, 1976). On the whole, programmed instruction has not proved superior to traditional teaching procedures (Guskin and Spicker, 1968). Yet, lacking knowledge about the fundamental nature of behavioural limitations and dysfunctions, it has not proved possible to establish with any degree of certainty precisely how such inadequacies might be offset.

EMPLOYMENT FOR THE RETARDED

Selection

Only a small proportion of a person's difficulty at work seems attributable to those areas of behaviour measured by IQ and other aptitude tests. Many retarded persons achieve much higher levels of competence than would be expected on the basis of initial test performance (Wolfensberger, 1967; Gunzburg, 1970). On the other hand, batteries of psychomotor tests and work sample tests simulating real industrial tasks have not generally been more successful at predicting satisfactory adjustment of retarded persons in work settings, and have frequently been less so (Wolfensberger, 1967; Gold, 1973, 1975). As Whelan (1973a) has stressed, this is probably because the selection of batteries has been determined by pragmatic considerations, and not the extent to which their contents reflected skills required in the areas of work involved.

Work adjustment

Although many studies during the 1950s suggested that most mentally retarded adults with IQs greater than about 50 achieved a high degree of social and work adjustment, more recent research has been less optimistic. Findings vary widely, most studies reporting that between about 50 and 80% of retarded persons find employment. Much of the variability between studies is attributable to differences in how 'successful adjustment' is defined (Mahoney, 1976a), and many surveys may have overestimated the numbers achieving satisfactory work adjustment (Wilson, 1970).

A wide body of evidence confirms that retarded persons are slower to acquire acceptable levels of the range of self-help and interpersonal skills essential to satisfactory adjustment at work (Gunzburg, 1968). Not surprisingly then, when compared with non-retarded workers, retardates frequently display a higher incidence of behaviours that affect relationships with others adversely, like rudeness, laziness, temperamental instability, unreliability, and inappropriate sexual attitudes (Mahoney, 1976b). Moreover, since employers are on the whole concerned more with appropriate work behaviour than with specific work skills, maladaptive social behaviour is a frequent cause of job failure (Heber and Dever, 1970).

Areas of employment

On average, retarded persons attain only poor levels of general living conditions and security in employment (Mahoney, 1976b). With only occasional exceptions the jobs they obtain are unskilled – predominantly assembly and packaging (Mahoney, 1976c). Many cannot find employment outside of sheltered work settings. In open employment retarded persons are found more frequently in jobs having a high level of turnover among employees, and are more likely to be retrenched than non-retarded workers, particularly when prevailing economic conditions are generally depressed (Goldstein, 1964).

Despite a widely held opinion among managers of sheltered workshops, there is little evidence to suggest that retarded workers prefer to be employed on tasks that are simple and repetitive, with a short operation cycle. This 'dull work for dull minds' dictum appears to derive from early research by Kounin (1941), who found that moderately retarded adolescents tended to persevere longer than children of the same mental age on simple drawing tasks. Clearly, however, conclusions from these experiments should not be generalized to all degrees of retardation. Nor does it seem likely that rigidity in a brief experimental situation of this kind would provide a reliable index of behaviour at work. Retarded workers have sometimes been reported to be more consistent and more stable than non-handicapped employees where repetitive work was involved, but whether this is because of some cognitive deficit is at least open to question. Zigler (1973), for example, attributes such persistence to social deprivation rather than to inherent rigidity. He maintains that retarded persons persevere in relatively boring situations so as to gain the attention of those responsible for their welfare.

The need for training

Reports from those responsible for the education and training of retarded persons typically emphasise that such people are slow to learn new skills. Furthermore, they often seem not to retain such skills over a period of time. Yet poor learning may be the consequence of an assumption by the teacher that the pupil has understood more than he actually has, particularly if he is told *what* to do, rather than *how* to go about it (Salvendy and Seymour, 1973). If teaching depends heavily on incidental learning then poor understanding may result, preventing the acquisition of those skills required to do the task. Because of poor performance, many tasks come to be regarded as too difficult for retarded persons. Yet this conclusion underestimates what such persons can do if assisted by training.

Most jobs in sheltered workshops require minimal levels of skills that are already well within the capabilities of the clients. Gold (1973, 1975) has argued that this policy is shortsighted for reasons which have both economic and personal implications. Such contracts are usually transitional, making it difficult for management to standardize production procedures, and are less remunerative than more complex work requiring higher levels of skill. Repetitive jobs with a very short cycle time also have the additional disadvantage of being tedious. This can exacerbate problems of poor attendance, punctuality, concentration and perseverance while working.

It is now well established that the level at which most retarded workers function can be raised appreciably by appropriate training. The initial performance of such persons on a learning task is a poor predictor of the level eventually achieved, provided that sufficient time is available and appropriate training techniques are applied. Thus, management energies expended on maintaining facilities that are not self-supporting might more profitably be directed towards the effective training of retarded workers for more challenging jobs. Of course, more interesting work is usually also more complicated, so that suitable training procedures would first be required.

A SKILLS APPROACH TO EDUCATION AND TRAINING

The basic model

The basic psychological model underlying this approach regards man as an extremely complex servo-mechanism, actively seeking information and using it in conjunction with previously developed plans to guide actions. Thus, ongoing behaviour is modified as a result of feedback from previous action (Welford, 1968, 1976). Limitations to performance can lie in sense organs, in the size and shape of the person, or the structure of limbs and members, but most importantly, in the brain's mechanisms involved in perception, memory, shaping and ordering movements, and using feedback from actions. The objective of a skills approach to mental retardation is to measure individual limitations to performance, rather than to compare the performance of different persons.

In these terms, widely supported general goals for the education and training of retarded persons, such as 'maximizing their potential', must be redefined as specific objectives related to particular deficiencies or difficulties.

If the approach advocated here were pursued, then ideology and practical considerations would to some extent determine the broader issues towards which education and training were directed – for example, socially desirable objectives like self-help, social adjustment, occupational independence and so on. However, the progress of an individual within any particular area, as defined by the actual level of functioning achieved, would be determined by the success of research: firstly, in delineating the skill requirements for specific activities; secondly in focussing on specific deficits underlying related learning problems; and thirdly, in matching limitations and requirements. The demands of any situation would need to be defined in terms of the various processes limiting performance – that is, in terms of the contribution to decision making of processes like attention, perception, memory or the use of feedback. The different capacities of a particular individual would be defined by the extent to which he coped with the various situational demands confronting him. Such capacities could be 'maximized', either by special training designed to structure the learning situation appropriately, or by redesigning the activity itself so as to compensate for particular deficits. Within such a scheme, the 'best interests' of the individual would be determined by the extent to which training reflected current knowledge, and the degree to which developed skills matched the demands of the situatioñ within which the individual functioned.

Skills analysis

The task of developing the taxonomic system proposed here is formidable. Far from requiring less assessment then has been undertaken hitherto, it needs more – but of a different kind to the mental tests relied upon to date. New means of assessment are required to uncover the nature of specific deficits, rather than the consequences of those deficits.

Some instruments already available may prove useful in this regard. Matthews (1974) discusses the possible application of a battery of tests developed by Reitan to detect the presence of localized brain damage, by sampling a wide variety of sensory, motor, problem solving, attention, memory and other abilities. This battery would be most useful if it proved sensitive to previously undetected dysfunctions responsible for specific disability.

A wide variety of checklists and rating scales are available for evaluating retardates' social adaptability and work behaviour (Wolfensberger, 1967; Robinson and Robinson, 1976). The Adaptive Behaviour Scales designed to measure independent functioning and personal and social responsibility (Nihira et al., 1969) and the WARF scale of personal work adjustment (Bitter and Bolanovich, 1970) appear promising, in so far as they sample a number of behavioural domains. However, only preliminary work has yet been done to establish their reliability and validity. As yet none of the many scales available has been linked directly to resources that would provide detailed guidelines for teaching required skills.

Whelan (1973a, 1973b) advocates applying a predetermined motion time system derived from the content of real work to identify individual work training needs. He anticipates that areas of poor performance can then be improved, either by using operant techniques or by intensive practice in perceptual—motor exercises. At first sight this approach seems promising, since a time and motion system provides a standardized taxonomy for highlighting operations that are difficult to learn. However, the units of analysis within such a system are a number of basic movements, rather than the psychological processes controlling these. The success of this approach will therefore depend ultimately upon the extent to which exercises can be devised that focus on deficits underlying basic motions.

Breaking down a job into its component operations and arranging these sequentially by work study methods can help to identify overall objectives more precisely. However, as Salvendy and Seymour (1973) have emphasised, ascertaining how component operations are to be done requires more than an analysis of the sequence and the pattern of movement involved in the job. An account of the sensory, perceptual, and decision activities governing those movements is also necessary. When breaking a job down it is common to proceed only to the degree of detail required in order to make a proposal about how to train (Annett et al., 1971). These authors have outlined how both the cost of failure and the probability of failure assist in arriving at a decision as to whether further analysis is required. The second factor is clearly of particular relevance where mental retardation is involved, and can only be ascertained in the light of what is known about the precise nature of the deficit limiting performance.

Skills analysis is readily applicable in a number of areas essential to independent functioning (e.g. dressing, toileting, eating behaviour). Similarly, it could be used to improve methods for teaching basic reading and number skills. Although one may question the relevance of academic skills to the education of retardates, some reading and arithmetic is necessary for direction finding, telling the time, and handling money. Nettelbeck and Kirby (1975,

1976a) have used skills analysis when training mildly retarded persons to use tools and machinery. Procedures developed to aid the acquisition of various social and interpersonal skills might also be adapted without difficulty to the needs of retarded persons.

LIMITATIONS TO LEARNING

Human performance

When retarded persons are compared with non-retarded, their psychomotor functioning and development is almost always less proficient. Baumeister and Kellas (1968) have proposed that inconsistent behaviour rather than an intrinsic general slowness may be responsible for the poorer performance of retardates in sensory–motor tasks. The cause of this inconsistency is not yet known, but evidence is accumulating that attentional processes are important contributors.

Zeaman (1973) has proposed that the retarded child has limited attentional processes, particularly in the breadth of attention, and is therefore less able to use redundant aspects of the stimulus when learning which dimension to attend to. Once this initial discrimination has been accomplished, however, learning to select the correct cues proceeds at much the same rate as is found among non-retarded children (Zeaman and House, 1963). Others have suggested that the retarded person is more readily distracted by irrelevant stimuli, perhaps because of an impaired ability to focus attention on relevant sources. However, experimental evidence concerning this is equivocal. Zeaman (1973) suggests that retardates may have a more marked preference for old rather than new information, and there is some evidence that they have weaker orienting reflexes towards novel stimulation (Karrer, 1966). Thus, rather than being more distractable, it may be that retardates are deficient in their ability to distribute attention appropriately. Attention may not only be less actively directed, but also less influenced by feedback. This suggestion is supported by Folkard's (1974) finding that mildly retarded children distribute their attention among more stimulus sources than do normals of the same mental age.

Evidence from a variety of sources suggests that although retardates develop expectancies about when predictable events will occur, they are less efficient than normals in this regard. They are less accurate at anticipating when a stimulus will occur, even when the duration of the preparatory interval is always the same (Baumeister and Kellas, 1968). Taken together, a wide body of research suggests that poor performance reflects a failure to identify and select essential cues in the task situation, rather than inadequacies associated with the registration of information.

Gold (1972) has shown that moderately and severely retarded young adults can learn to do complex assembly work if the situation is engineered to overcome attentional deficiencies. Workers in sheltered employment settings learned to assemble a 15-piece bicycle brake much more quickly and efficiently when the surface of each part facing the worker if positioned correctly for assembly was painted. This made both form and colour dimensions relevant and redundant. Subsequently workers trained in this way transferred successfully to assembling a 24-piece brake without the aid of colour coding. A study 12 months later involving about 80% of the original participants found a high level of retention, although none of them did work of this kind during the interim.

Gold and Barclay (1973) have demonstrated the effectiveness of an easy-to-hard training sequence in which the relevant dimension is initially made very prominent. Moderately and mildly retarded workers learned to sort bolts of different lengths by beginning with bolts of very different length, and progressing subsequently to more difficult discriminations. Nettelbeck and Kirby (1975) used a similar procedure to train mildly retarded girls who previously were unable to identify the correct side of twill material and position it on a sewing machine. Initial training used pieces of corduroy with pattern configurations the same as for twill, but enlarged so that critical features were readily discernible. Progress to finer degrees of discrimination was dependent upon success. This procedure was very effective, virtually eradicating error for most trainees. A similar technique was used to design an appropriate training procedure for mildly retarded employees of a work training centre who were learning to sand furniture veneered with timber. These young men were previously sanding beyond the level of finish required, ruining the veneer. However, this problem disappeared once attention was directed towards critical aspects of the task, like the degree of pressure to apply and the appearance and feel of the properly sanded surface.

Direct evidence linking slower perceptual speed with retardation is provided by recent investigations of the rate at which a person can accumulate information from a visual display (Lally and Nettelbeck, 1977). Nettelbeck and Brewer (1976) have investigated differences between RTs for different fingers in an 8-choice RT situation, comparing mildly retarded with non-retarded subjects. Results suggest that retardates are not only slow when accumulating information, but also make more observations than non-retarded subjects except where prominent cues are available. When retarded subjects were prevented from seeing their hands while responding, RT decreased appreciably, particularly for the ring and middle fingers. However, errors increased from about 6% when the hands were visible to about 10% when they were not. Among normals error rate was about 5% in both conditions and RT remained unchanged. Thus, part of the longer RTs registered by retardates when response selection is difficult can be attributed to their visually checking a response before it is made (Brewer and Nettlebeck, 1979).

Both a slower perceptual speed and a tendency to make additional checks would disadvantage a retarded person when learning unless materials were presented at an appropriate rate. This suggestion seems particularly pertinent to the training of retarded persons in areas of work frequently held to be beyond their capabilities. If machines were modified during training, enabling operators to take in new information and feedback from actions at a slower rate, then the smooth co-ordinated actions of skilled performance might be achieved more readily. Operating speed could then be increased in accordance with progress.

Belmont and Butterfield (1969) conclude from a review of short-term memory studies with retarded children that poorer performance is related to differences in acquisition and retrieval, rather than to structural defects limiting retention. O'Connor and Hermelin (1971) reach similar conclusions with regard to long-term storage. From evidence available it is reasonable to infer that retarded persons process information in memory in essentially the same manner as do non-retarded persons. However, most retardates are deficient at organizing material to be remembered and require help in acquiring appropriate strategies for acquisition and retrieval. They remember more effectively when information is presented in small amounts, but require more time at all stages of processing.

Frith and Frith (1974) have summarized observations from a number of sources that Down's syndrome children are slower to develop ambulating skills, generally clumsy throughout childhood and adolescence, and poor at motor tasks requiring feedback control, like arm movements, finger-tapping, and rotary pursuit tracking. Structural differences in the brain may underlie these motor deficits.

Cultural–familial retardates have been found consistently to be deficient in physical development, gross motor abilities like maintaining balance either when stationary or moving, and fine motor acts requiring complex co-ordinations or manual and finger dexterity. However, as Bruininks (1974) has emphasised, it is often difficult to determine the extent to which poor performance is the consequence of reduced opportunities to participate in motor activities. On the whole, researchers have not attempted to take account of possible motivational influences, or of confounding perceptual, memory and other conceptual requirements of the motor tasks employed.

Motivation and feedback

Retarded children are often found to show less curiosity, confidence, and lower motivation to succeed than non-retarded children (MacMillan, 1971). Zigler (1973) has argued that this is the consequence of poorer socialization. Reduced cognitive abilities result in frequent failure, so that the child comes to expect failure. Withdrawing from problems and challenging situations helps to avoid failure and associated anxiety. Difficulties in coping are assumed to play some part in the development of 'character disorders', although why this occurs is only poorly understood. On the other hand, when ways are found to ensure success then confidence is enhanced and general personal adjustment improved. Zigler's motivational theories emphasise the importance of experiential factors and their influence on the development of personality. Whereas deficient cognitive functions cannot be restored, motivational and personality factors relevant to competent social adjustment are modifiable.

Numerous studies have established that, as a general rule, retardates respond to incentives in much the same way that non-retarded persons do. Most work has used extrinsic, tangible rewards, like food, money, tokens and sensory stimulation, but intrinsic incentives like praise, reprimand, competition, co-operation and information about performance have also been applied. Research has focussed mainly on the effects of these various motivating factors on psychomotor performance (Baumeister and Kellas, 1968; Bruininks, 1974), and on work related behaviours (Gold, 1973). As would be expected from learning research, incentives are most effective when reinforcement is contingent upon behavioural change, and delivered immediately. The success of financial reward therefore often depends on whether the person paid associates this directly with performance (Campbell, 1971). This relationship may not be understood properly if wages are not received until the end of the week, or if payment is made directly to parents or into a bank account.

Praise can improve performance (Zigler, 1973). An interesting study by Waters (1978) demonstrates that the working behaviour of mildly retarded adolescent girls can be improved appreciably by supervisory approval. Waters' procedure required very little additional effort on the part of the supervisor.

Although behaviour modification procedures derived from conditioning principles provide powerful means of controlling behaviour, there are some circumstances in which they are difficult to apply – for example, where behaviour cannot readily be observed. Furthermore, individual differences in response to reinforcement can be difficult to account for and overcome. Welford (1968, 1975) outlines a general framework for investigating individual differences in how motives operate. Following Woodworth (1958), he assumes that man's fundamental motive is to "attempt to secure results from action". Behaviour is corrected and directed in accordance with knowledge of the results of previous actions. Thus, motivation is considered in terms of a feedback mechanism, and achieving results depends upon the development of specific skills.

On the basis of evidence from diverse sources, Welford suggests four extensions to a simple servo model, each of importance to an understanding of individual differences:

(1)   The incentive effect of action depends in part upon the effort required to achieve it. Although considerable effort may subsequently enhance the value of an achieved outcome, action is more readily undertaken where the ratio of result to cost is favourable.

(2)   A situation with feedback from sub-goals on the way to the main objective will be preferred to one where many actions are required before any result is achieved.

(3)   Any situation can be represented as a series of sub-tasks, each with its own immediate objective, but also as co-ordinated within a larger hierarchical organization of tasks and goals. A long-term objective can therefore lend purpose to shorter tasks, resulting in different actions on different occasions. Conversely, several motives can contribute to a single outcome.

(4)   An organism attempts to achieve an optimum state of arousal or stability, avoiding extremes of stimulation, but seeking moderate change.

Although Welford's conception of motivation is as yet largely untested in any rigorous sense, his proposals are of considerable heuristic value. In these terms, mentally retarded persons are clearly disadvantaged. They frequently expend disproportionately large degrees of effort in order to achieve relatively modest outcomes, their daily lives often lack variety, and their long-term goals sometimes seem to be poorly formulated or understood. There is a need then for educators and trainers to find ways in which these problems can be overcome.

CONCLUSIONS

Acquiring skill

In the light of the limitations to learning discussed above, several well established training principles assume particular importance when teaching retarded individuals.

(1)   *Understanding what is required* – The poor performance of retardates can be due to a failure to identify and select key perceptual cues in the task situation, rather than to memory deficiences. It is essential to maintain their interest when teaching new skills, and to direct their attention to features critical for the initiation and termination of action. Effective strategies for manipulating and organizing material to be learned must be taught beforehand.

(2)   *Active participation* – Training that relies heavily on instruction and demonstration is poorly suited to the needs of retarded persons. Passive observation is less stimulating than active participation and its effectiveness often depends on incidental learning by the trainee. Instead, the trainee should wherever possible be guided to do what is required.

(3)   *Knowledge of results* – Accurate knowledge, which immediately follows the outcome of action, is essential. Welford (1975) makes the additional suggestion that records should emphasise an overall trend, so that variability in performance should not be given undue weight. Where it is necessary to

eradicate behaviour feedback is equally important, since awareness of an inappropriate response facilitates its modification.

(4) *Part training* – The task to be taught should be split up into a number of independent operations, each sufficiently small so that objectives are clearly defined and information processing requirements able to be dealt with without undue difficulty. Welford's suggestion that a satisfactory balance between result and cost be achieved can be applied usefully here, especially where different tasks must be graded for relative difficulty.

Nettelbeck and Kirby (1976b) have confirmed the advantage of part-training procedures when teaching mildly retarded workers to thread an industrial sewing machine. A progressive part-training procedure in which the various operations were gradually combined and synthesised after initial isolated practice was only slightly more effective than pure-part training. However, despite the greater preparation required to train by this method, a progression procedure might yield more substantial training gains where the synthesis of skill elements was more complicated.

(5) *Distributed practice* – There must be adequate opportunity for material to be learned thoroughly, and relearned on subsequent occasions where necessary. Criteria defining satisfactory achievement must be established beforehand, so that progress can be evaluated. During early training the time spent learning should be divided into short periods for practice in a variety of relevant tasks. However, periods of practice should subsequently be combined and extended in a controlled manner, so that stamina on particular tasks is developed.

(6) *Separate training* – The disadvantages of isolated and therefore artificial social environments notwithstanding, educational and training programmes for retarded persons are best carried out in areas separate from the mainstream. However, as far as possible these areas should be located near to, or even within, similar services for the non-retarded. This arrangement has the advantage of protecting trainees from distracting events around them and the discouragement of competing with normals, while enabling the provision of the specialized help that retarded persons require. At the same time the worst aspects of isolation are avoided.

(7) *Counselling* – Any educational or training programme should include a counselling service to help the individual cope with residual day-to-day problems that can disrupt learning but that cannot be dealt with readily in other ways. Although such problems may arise within the learning situation, many will be related to life at home or in the community at large. Frequently, an opportunity to discuss these problems with some interested and sympathetic person seems to provide the first step towards a satisfactory solution. Even where the problem is less easily solved, regular contact with the counsellor can reduce its distracting influence in the educational or training setting.

The transition from school to adult life

At the present time, for most retarded adolescents the change from school to a work setting is abrupt. Although most schools would aim to help the pupil to adjust gradually to the responsibilities of adult life, an important event like starting a job is accomplished in perhaps a single day. Yet a natural progression governed by capabilities and needs is as important here as in any other aspect of training.

Significant improvements in habilitation, together with substantial reductions in the stresses and costs of real work training, should follow if the various services and agencies responsible for the education and vocational development of mildly retarded persons could co-operate in developing an integrated system of training for work. This suggestion faces a major difficulty, in that these two areas are usually administered separately, and communication between personnel is therefore limited. A possible solution is for special education to develop its own vocational guidance and preparation services. In the meantime, persons already familiar with vocational rehabilitation and industrial requirements should be included in special teacher training programmes wherever possible. This would serve to establish contacts between the educational and employment spheres that might enhance placement opportunities. It should also help to correct imbalance in school curricula caused by any over-emphasis on the development of language, literacy, and computational skills. Thirdly, it should help schools to develop work preparation programmes having the relevance to real employment opportunities that has often been lacking.

Training and associated evaluation procedures that focus on requirements for functioning in adult society should be incorporated within the educational programme for a number of years before the school leaver is required to seek employment. Such procedures should aim to simulate the demands of real working conditions as closely as possible.

Such schemes would need to be sufficiently flexible at all stages to allow for individual differences in training requirements and in the rate of progress. Whereas some persons might be placed in sheltered or open employment with little difficulty, others might require additional preparation in certain areas of behaviour, or in order to acquire specific job skills. Work training within the school would not always be specific to certain jobs. A policy of exclusively specific training would restrict both training and placement opportunities. In any case, skills learned at school may become obsolete in time. On the other hand, some specific training would be essential for the purposes of realism. Actual work experience might be accomplished by placing the individual in real settings on a part-time basis. Such experience could then be extended progressively as the time approached for the person to leave school. This procedure would serve the additional purpose of enabling a prospective employer to appraise the school leaver's potential on the job.

Even after the person has left school, close support from school personnel should be available if required. Such a follow-up system should provide assistance with difficulties associated with either employment or living outside of working hours. The service could be withdrawn gradually, records of progress being used to ensure that independence was not accompanied by any decline in performance.

Putting theory into practice

Most of the training considerations outlined in this chapter have been known for some time. One may ask, therefore, why they are not in use on a wide scale? One reason is that our knowledge about the nature of retardation is still insufficient to permit reliable assessment of the individual and precise formulations about how to help him. The skills approach advocated here does not provide a single, 'cure-all' prescription for solving all practical problems confronting those responsible for the education and training of retarded persons. Rather, it provides a conceptual framework that might be used to develop a comprehensive, systematic programme for work preparation (Singleton, 1972). Thus, it might help define objectives consistent with the reality of what the person may or may not do, formulate the steps by which these might be attempted, and permit evaluation of progress (Budde and Menolascino, 1971). Within such a system, no single 'right way' for overcoming a particular problem exists. Skills analysis may help to define the direction in which a solution is to be sought, but ingenuity and insight on the part of the teacher as to what is required remain essential ingredients for success.

A second reason may be that establishing and maintaining a new training programme requires effort additional to that already being made by staff responsible for training and supervision. At the same time, possible gains are often far from obvious, and associated with long-term habilitation objectives. Staff within schools and employment settings are already extremely busy coping with the existing demands of their jobs. One can understand their scepticism when an outside 'expert' to whom they have turned for help confronts them with a set of requirements that actually demands more of them. It may be then that progress charts, graphs, and the like are as salient to supervisory staff as to the trainees for whom they are intended. Clearly also it is essential that procedures developed for teaching and training be evaluated by research, and modified or discontinued as findings suggest.

A third reason is that even where appropriate training procedures are introduced, they all too often erode with the passage of time. This is particularly a danger where those responsible for carryin out training planned by others are not already thoroughly familiar with the methods involved.

References

Annett, J., Duncan, K. D., Stammers, R. B. and Gray, M. J. (1971). *Task Analysis.* Department of Employment Training Information Paper 6. (London: HMSO)

Baumeister, A. A. and Kellas, G. (1968). Reaction time and mental retardation. In N. R. Ellis (ed.). *International Review of Research in Mental Retardation.* (New York: Academic Press)

Belmont, J. M. and Butterfield, E. C. (1969). The relations of short-term memory to development and intelligence. In L. P. Lipsitt and H. W. Reese (eds.). *Advances in Child Development and Behaviour.* (New York: Academic Press)

Bitter, J. A. and Bolanovich, D. J. (1970). WARF: a scale for measuring job-readiness behaviours. *Am. J. Men. Defic.,* **74,** 616

Brewer, N. and Nettelbeck, T. (1979). Speed and accuracy in the choice reaction time of mildly retarded adults. *Am. J. Men. Defic.* (in press)

Bruininks, R. H. (1974). Physical and motor development of retarded persons. In N. R. Ellis (ed.). *International Review of Research in Mental Retardation.* (New York: Academic Press)

Budde, J. F. and Menolascino, F. J. (1971). Systems technology and retardation: Application to vocational habilitation. *Ment. Retard.,* 9 (1), 11

Campbell, N. (1971). Techniques of behaviour modification. *J. Rehabil.,* **37**(4), 28

Cruickshank, W. M. (1974). The false hope of integration. *The Slow Learning Child,* **21**(2), 67

Engelmann, S. (1967). Relationship between psychological theories and the act of teaching. *J. Sch. Psychol.,* **5,** 93

Folkard, S. (1974). Expectancy in educable subnormal children and their normal mental age controls. *Quar. J. Exp. Psychol.,* **26,** 495

Frith, U. and Frith, C. D. (1974). Specific motor disabilities in Down's syndrome. *J. Child Psychol. and Psychiatr.,* **15,** 293

Gold, M. W. (1972). Stimulus factors in skill training of the retarded on a complex assembly task: acquisition, transfer and retention. *Am. J. Men. Defic.,* **76,** 517

Gold, M. W. (1973). Research on the vocational habilitation of the retarded: the present, the future. In N. R. Ellis (ed.). *International Review of Research in Mental Retardation.* (New York: Academic Press)

Gold, M. W. (1975). Vocational training. In J. Wortis (ed.). *Mental Retardation and Developmental Disabilities: an annual review.* (New York: Brunner/Mazel)

Gold, M. W. and Barclay, C. R. (1973). The learning of difficult visual discriminations by the moderately and severely retarded. *Ment. Retard.,* **11**(2), 9

Goldstein, H. (1964). Social and occupational adjustment. In H. A. Stevens and R. Heber (eds.). *Mental Retardation: A Review of Research.* (Chicago: University of Chicago Press)

Grossman, H. (ed.). (1973). *Manual on Terminology and Classification in Mental Retardation.* (Baltimore: Garamond/Pridemark Press)

Gunzburg, H. C. (1968). *Social Competence and Mental Handicap.* (London: Tindall and Cassell)

Gunzburg, H. C. (1970). Pedagogy. In J. Wortis (ed.). *Mental Retardation and Development Disabilities: An Annual Review.* (New York: Grune and Stratton)

Guskin, S. L. and Spicker, H. H. (1968). Educational research in mental retardation. In N. R. Ellis (ed.). *International Review of Research in Mental Retardation.* (New York: Academic Press)

Heber, F. R. and Dever, R. B. (1970). Research on education and habilitation of the mentally retarded. In H. C. Haywood (ed.). *Socio-cultural Aspects of Mental Retardation.* (New York: Appleton-Century-Crofts)

Karrer, R. (1966). Autonomic nervous system functions and behaviour: a review of experimental studies with mental defectives. In N. R. Ellis (ed.). *International Review of Research in Mental Retardation.* (New York: Academic Press)

Kirk, S. A. (1964). Research in education. In H. A. Stevens and R. Heber (eds.). *Mental Retardation: A Review of Research.* (Chicago: University of Chicago Press)

Kounin, J. S. (1941). Experimental studies of rigidity: I. The measurement of rigidity in normal and feeble-minded persons. *Character and Personality,* **9,** 251. II. The explanatory power of the concept of rigidity as applied to feeble-mindedness. *ibid,* **9,** 273

Lally, M. and Nettelbeck, T. (1977). Intelligence, reaction time, and inspection time. *Am. J. Ment. Defic.*, **82**, 273

MacMillan, D. L. (1971). The problem of motivation in the education of the mentally retarded. *Except. Child.*, **37**, 579

Mahoney, D. J. (1976a). The success of the mentally retarded in employment. *Austr. J. Ment. Retard.*, **4**, 19

Mahoney, D. J. (1976b). Factors affecting the success of the mentally retarded in employment. *Austr. J. Ment. Retard.*, **4**, 38

Mahoney, D. J. (1976c). A review of jobs undertaken by the mentally retarded. *Austr. J. Ment. Retard.*, **4**, 24

Matthews, C. G. (1974). Applications of neuropsychological test methods in mentally retarded subjects. In R. M. Reitan and L. A. Davison (eds.). *Clinical Neuropsychology: Current Status and Applications*. (New York: Wiley)

Meyen, E. L. and Horner, R. D. (1976). Curriculum development. In J. Wortis (ed.). *Mental Retardation and Development Disabilities: An Annual Review*. (New York: Brunner/ Mazel)

Nettelbeck, T. and Brewer, N. (1976). Effects of stimulus–response variables on the choice reaction time of mildly retarded adults. *Am. J. Ment. Defic.*, **81**, 85

Nettelbeck, T. and Kirby, N. H. (1975). Training the mildly mentally handicapped worker. *Ergonomics*, **18**, 517

Nettlebeck, T. and Kirby, N. H. (1976a). Training the mentally handicapped to sew. *Educ. Train. Ment. Ret.*, **11**, 31

Nettelbeck, T. and Kirby, N. H. (1976b). A comparison of part and whole training methods with mildly mentally retarded workers. *J. Occ. Psychol.*, **49**, 115

Nihira, K., Foster, R., Shellhaas, M. and Leland, H. (1969). *Adaptive Behaviour Scales: Manual*. (Washington DC: American Association on Mental Deficiency)

O'Connor, N. and Hermelin, B. (1971). Cognitive deficits in children. *Br. Med. Bull.*, **27**, 227

Quay, I. C. (1963). Academic skills. In N. R. Ellis (ed.). *Handbook of Mental Deficiency*. (New York: McGraw-Hill)

Robinson, N. M. and Robinson, H. B. (1976). *The Mentally Retarded Child: A Psychological Approach*. (New York: McGraw-Hill)

Rosenweig, L. E. and Long, J. (1960). *Understanding and Teaching the Dependent Retarded Child*. (Darian, Connecticut: The Educational Publishing Corporation)

Salvendy, G. and Seymour, W. D. (1973). *Prediction and Development of Industrial Work Performance*. (New York: Wiley)

Sanders, C. (1970). Terminology and classification. In J. Wortis (ed.). *Mental Retardation: An Annual Review*. (New York: Grune and Stratton)

Singleton, W. T. (1972). Total activity analysis: a different approach to work study. *Le Travail Humain*, **35**, 241

Waters, L. K. (1978). Social reinforcement of the working behaviour of retardates in a rehabilitation centre. *Austr. J. Psychol.*, (In Press)

Welford, A. T. (1968). *Fundamentals of Skill*. (London: Methuen)

Welford, A. T. (1975). Motivation and handicap: a second look. In S. K. Steel and F. R. G. Hodgetts (eds.). *A Conference for sheltered workshop personnel and rehabilitation workers in related fields*. (Canberra: Australian Council for Rehabilitation of Disabled)

Welford, A. T. (1976). *Skilled Performance: Perceptual and Motor Skills*. (Glenview, Illinois: Scott, Foresman and Co.)

Whelan, E. (1973a). Developing work skills: a systematic approach. In P. Mittler (ed.). *Assessment for Learning in the Mentally Handicapped*. (Edinburgh and London: Churchill Livingstone)

Whelan, E. (1973b). The 'scientific approach' in the practical workshop situation. In H. C. Gunzburg (ed.). *Experiments in the Rehabilitation of the Mentally Handicapped*. (London: Butterworth)

Wilson, W. (1970). Social psychology and mental retardation. In N. R. Ellis (ed.). *International Review of Research in Mental Retardation*. (New York: Academic Press)

Wolfensberger, W. (1967). Vocational preparation and occupation. In A. A. Baumeister (ed.). *Mental Retardation: Appraisal Education and Rehabilitation*. (Chicago: Aldine)

Wolfensberger, W. (1972). *Normalisation*. (Toronto: National Institute on Mental Retardation)

Woodworth, R. S. (1958). *Dynamics of Behaviour*. (London: Methuen)

Zeaman, D. (1973). One programmatic approach to retardation. In D. K. Routh (ed.). *The Experimental Psychology of Mental Retardation*. (London: Crosby Lockwood Staples)

Zeaman, D. and House, B. J. (1963). The role of attention in retardate discrimination learning. In N. R. Ellis (ed.). *Handbook of Mental Deficiency*. (New York: McGraw Hill)

Zigler, E. (1973). The retarded child as a whole person. In D. K. Routh (ed.). *The Experimental Psychology of Mental Retardation*. (London: Crosby Lockwood Staples)

4

Hearing-impaired Children

J. G. KYLE

INTRODUCTION

There are many problems which arise out of a relatively simple handicap of not being able to hear properly. Hearing loss can affect social behaviour when it cuts off friends and colleagues. It affects employment prospects when written exams are involved. It changes speech because of the lack of feedback from one's own voice. It affects school placement when it occurs early in a child's development. Finally, if it occurs at or before birth and is severe, it can effectively remove the communication capability in respect of hearing people.

Two factors important in estimating such a handicap are the degree of the hearing loss and the age of onset. Other factors such as cause of deafness, type of schooling and family history are largely overridden by a third variable of measured intelligence. The hearing loss effect can be expressed in a number of ways but a simple grouping on the decibel scale from a notional zero of the threshold of hearing people for pure tones is useful: hearing loss up to 65 to 70 dB is labelled *partial hearing;* beyond this and up to 85 or 90 dB is usually termed *severe hearing loss* and beyond 90 dB is the area of *profound deafness.* The first group are the hard-of-hearing whom most people have encountered at one time or another. In the absence of other handicaps, their problems need only be minor, as benefit may be obtained from the use of a hearing aid. One could expect people in this group to cope on the whole, in a hearing world. The second group obtain rather less benefit from a hearing aid and if the loss has existed from birth are likely to be backward in language development and have some speech difficulties. The third group constitutes the most serious problem and occupy about half of the places in schools for the deaf. At this level, it is unlikely that the sound of one's own voice can be heard unaided and only very minimal help will be available from a normal hearing aid.

These are the problems in outline and they are so determined in their nature by the various factors of hearing loss, onset age and intelligence and their interaction with the environment that it is meaningless to talk about 'the deaf child' as a single entity, though it is frequently used to designate those for whom special educational provision has been made. There are also a number of notions about the deaf which are as well rejected at the outset. Firstly, there is a commonly held belief that the other senses somehow compensate for lack of hearing. Schiff and Thayer (1974) and others have shown this to be inaccurate. Secondly, there is an idea that lip-reading almost automatically takes the place of hearing. Lip-reading is a very difficult and complex skill. Even in ideal conditions of lighting and position, the lip-reading performance can be sustained for only a short period of time except when the conversation is very basic. Also, natural limitation of lip-reading (the fact that certain sounds are virtually invisible on the lips) and the inevitable physical movement of the speaker combine to reduce this performance even further. A final belief is that congenitally deaf people, partly due to their lack of language development, cannot manipulate abstract concepts. This is not the case as has been consistently shown (Furth, 1971, gives a review). The deaf are able to 'think' and what this consists of will occupy a later part of this chapter.

From the above it will be realized that a large proportion of deaf children will have difficulties with even the basic skills in education. The tradition in the UK has been to design the educational programme around low aspirations based on perceived goals for society's acceptance of the hearing-impaired. Broadly speaking, this has meant instructions in three primary skills: speech, the understanding of speech and reading. These will be examined in turn.

First, however, a brief word is necessary on the educational ethos for deaf children. This discussion now centres on children deafened at an early age. The approach which has dominated for the last hundred years, the oral method, involves the teaching of a child to speak and to lip-read and generally discourages the use of the hands in communication since this would only isolate the deaf community further. Part of this approach utilizes the residual hearing of a child. The child is taught how to use this hearing, effectively taught 'how to listen' in order to be able in the end to discriminate speech sounds with the help of his hearing aid. At present, there is a move away from this approach both in Britain and in USA in favour of a more flexible approach to communication.

The educational provision for children varies slightly from area to area but generally allows three levels of support. First, children with serious difficulties will be placed in a school for the deaf, whether day or residential depending on location. Children with lesser problems might be in a similar school setting with other partially-hearing children. Second, children might be placed in a Unit attached to a hearing school if it is thought that the child may be able to cope in a hearing class for at least part of the school day. Support in other subjects will be given by the Unit teacher, a teacher of the deaf, as well as training in speech and lip-reading. Third, the child may be placed in a hearing class all of the time with perhaps a weekly short visit from a peripatetic teacher of the deaf.

In the UK there are no easily available, accurate, figures of the number of children in special education for their hearing impairment. Estimates for the total population of adults with a hearing impairment range from 1 million to $2\frac{1}{2}$ million. However, figures provided for Northern Ireland by the Secretary of State, when adjusted for the UK, suggest a population with a very severe impairment of approximately 62 000 of whom over 20 000 will have been deaf since before the age of 3 years. DES statistics (1975) show approximately 1 in 1100 children in special education because of their hearing impairment.

Turning to the basic skills, these can be examined in terms of the goal of producing a fully communicating deaf person and in terms of methods of assessing them.

SPEECH

The approach to speech in deaf education has been modelled largely on the poor articulator or person with a speech defect. The basic assumption is that speech is still the best mode of communication even in profound deafness and the discrimination and production of speech sounds represent a case of retardation in the deaf. A child is taught to copy facial movements of an adult in close proximity and, by shaping, moves closer and closer towards the expected sound pattern. Modern methods include the development of 'visual speech' machines which allow representation, on a visual monitor, of characteristics of the words spoken by the teacher and the child, usually in the form of a curve. It should allow a visual matching by the child who can practise until his match is close to the short sample presented on the visual display.

Where there is useful residual hearing one is led to expect the development of speech which is intelligible (Ewing and Ewing, 1964). Where powerful amplifying devices are provided as speech trainers a child will obtain greater auditory feedback and therefore speech should improve. Since this system is often used with seriously hearing-impaired children from the age of 3 years onwards and certainly will be used with partially hearing children from age 5, one might imagine that speech clarity would develop. The results, however, are disappointing. Brannon (1964) found only 20–25% of deaf children's word utterances intelligible to listeners. Markides (1970) with a younger group noted only 19% of speech was intelligible to listeners. Conrad (1975) showed, as part of a large study, that less than 10% of the speech of profoundly deaf children was intelligible, after approximately 10 years of education. While the different options available of using tape-recorded spontaneous speech or read sentences, played back to listeners, may be questioned, the overall picture of the poor quality of speech must be upheld. Kyle (1977) has shown the closeness of the relation between speech and hearing loss and it may be supposed that the relation is a causal one. The varying levels of hearing loss reflect the 'success' of the method with partially-hearing children (up to 85% of their speech may be clear to listeners), but the inappropriateness of the method for the profoundly deaf where intelligibility drops almost to zero. The question to be posed is whether the level of aspiration is appropriate for such children when the means to attain the goals through acoustic feedback is inadequate.

LIP-READING

Myklebust (1964) treats lip-reading as a receptive language process involving the association of meaning with lip-movements. He points to the difficulties involved in such an activity which hearing people with a great wealth of word knowledge may not realize. In lip-reading, the speakers must always be facing the reader thus precluding any simultaneous activity on the part of the speaker. The speaker must also be prepared to adjust to the needs of proximity and lighting, therefore making lectures rather difficult. According to Gustason (1975) between 40 and 60% of speech sounds are invisible on the lips. Perhaps in the light of all this it is surprising that the hearing-impaired can lip-read at all.

The type of training a deaf child receives in lip-reading begins usually in the home when the mother is attempting to convey instructions and consists of talking clearly and distinctly face to face with the child, with minimal gesture. The child will learn to read facial expression as a contributory factor but the emphasis is on the association of the meaning with the lip-movements. Children who are partially-hearing often do not use lip-reading as they can hear sufficient to understand the message. Though one cannot establish a fixed cut-off, children with hearing losses up to 75 and 80 dB may have enough information through their hearing aids to make lip-reading only supportive, while beyond 90 dB the lip-reading ability is probably the primary method of gaining information.

Very few studies have actually tried to evaluate lip-reading performance against an absolute criterion. This is understandable because performance is so context- and speaker-dependent and because items used may not be representative of the same level of ability for all children. The DES (1972) reports subjective assessments indicating poor standards of performance but other studies (Montgomery, 1968; White and Stevenson, 1975) examine the relationships of lip-reading with other abilities or with other means of communicating information (signs, reading). Conrad (1977a) compared profoundly deaf and hearing children 'deafened' by white noise on a speech comprehension measure. While deaf children could identify up to 70% of the very simple items used, hearing children performed at the same level without the benefit of extensive training that the deaf children had had. While there is a confounded language variable in this comparison it does cast doubt on lip-reading as a viable, teachable skill. Kyle *et al.* (1978) illustrate the variations in speech comprehension performance for children with different hearing losses. The Donaldson lip-reading test was used. In this case all children wore hearing aids so strictly speaking lip-reading may not have been necessary for at least the group with small hearing losses. For partially-hearing children, the performance is 95% correct but it drops to 65% for the profoundly deaf. These figures are slightly ambiguous since they represent close to maximum performance in almost ideal conditions of lighting and proximity, when the material is very simple. It may not reflect peformance in everyday life which deaf people claim is very difficult.

READING

If one acknowledges the severe communication problems of the hearing-impaired, the other traditional means of expanding the experience of language is through the written word. It is of critical importance to a hearing-impaired person as it maintains an indirect link to other people's experiences and views. It allows development of further skills by the dissemination of knowledge and when mastered can be a major source of growth. Clearly, people who become deaf after the acquisition of reading ability are at an enormous advantage over those who are deafened before, and children in the former position will often continue to function satisfactorily in a normal educational setting because of the support available through written notes.

Nearly all children who are in the second category of being deaf before reading manifest some backwardness in reading. Myklebust (1964) refers to a 7–8 year retardation at the age of 15 years, but dependent on degree of hearing loss. The teaching of reading is a process of association of words and pictures as with hearing children, but also of association of lip-read shapes and sensory feedback from articulation. The overall strategy seems to be one of teaching as if the child were simply a slow learner such that the instruction progresses very slowly as the semantic associations to the written word are built up. There are variations on this method using greater or smaller parts of words, phrases, and sentences. According to Gibson and Levin (1975) the approach has not been particularly successful and has been very slow to change. Practices are altering in the light of different beliefs in the usefulness of a sign system for the deaf in the teaching of reading. Garretson (1976) and Stuckless (1976) have discussed the incidence and efficacy of the other communication forms in the practice of reading.

Despite concern about the level of reading and the difficulties of its acquisition, few empirical studies have presented clear pictures of reading standards.

Murphy (1957) in a comprehensive study of 12-year-olds showed that word recognition related to comprehension but did not present an assessment of comprehension in the deaf. Numerous other small scale studies give limited information about the effect of hearing impairment on reading (Owrid, 1970; Hine, 1970; Vernon, 1976) but generally find retardation. A major study in the USA examining educational attainments of 17 000 hearing-impaired schoolchildren has been published by Di Francesca (1972). It indicates a mean reading age of just over 9 years for deaf children aged 15 and 16 years. Conrad (1977b) reports a large-scale study of reading level in the UK. Testing the total population of 15- and 16-year-olds in special education for the deaf, an overall reading age of 9 years was found. However, there are clear differences according to hearing loss. Children designated partially-hearing read at a median level of 10 years 8 months, while those in the most severe hearing-impaired group read at a level seven years below their chronological age. Further to this, a study by Hammermeister (1971) followed up deaf children up to 13 years after leaving school and found no significant improvement in reading. Obviously, there ought to be concern at these figures no matter whether one accepts a lower reading level as adequate for daily purposes. Again the educational aspirations of teachers and of the pupils differ significantly from the reality of what is achieved. If these difficulties are present when a child is at school it must have implications for his employment and adjustment beyond the school.

ENACTIVE SKILLS

However, it is always possible that though development has not occurred in the skills traditionally required by education, abilities may manifest themselves in other ways. Though the educational system attacks the cognitive skills, with special regard to the above instances, the question of physical skills described as body image or enactive skills is not really raised. It is easily seen in schools that there is a great deal of encouragement in sporting and outdoor enterprises and capabilities for any activity involving hand—eye co-ordination seem unimpaired. The notion of the deaf excelling in such things *because* of their deafness, however, seems to be unfounded. Myklebust (1964) equates the deaf and hearing in terms of this type of skill but always in the context of the deaf being no poorer than hearing groups. Also, while there are examples of individuals who became deaf and still excelled (Beethoven might be an interesting example), the silence introduced by adventitious deafness is irrelevant if one has never experienced hearing. Woods (1970), in a passionate book called *The Forgotten People,* highlights a number of deaf successes. Edison, who apparently had progressive deafness from the age of 12 onwards, and Gregg, the inventor of shorthand, are examples. Marr, an architect, one of the few who were pre-lingually deaf, attended a school for the deaf. Schein and Delk (1974) found a large proportion of the deaf in poorer than expected jobs and, though there was also a large group of craftsmen, there is still traditional pressure on certain occupations like shoemaking. One can only conclude that there is no evidence to suggest the deaf are poorer in enactive skills, but equally it cannot be maintained that deafness itself acts as an aid in such skills by reducing interference. In relation to the cognitive skills upon which doubt was cast by the performance tests, it is reasonable to open the question of whether this is due to a lack of the processing capability or simply to an inappropriate application of such a capability.

SPATIAL/PICTORIAL SKILLS

Although one might expect this to be the basis of communication among pre-lingually deafened individuals, there is little research specifically on this topic. Hermelin and O'Connor (1973) examined a task where digits were presented in a way which could be encoded in temporal sequential order or spatial order, and found that deaf groups produced a far greater degree of spatial ordering. O'Connor and Hermelin (1973) discovered that deaf children remembered the order of presented faces better than the order of syllables (the opposite of a hearing group). This was proposed as evidence of a post-iconic visual store. O'Connor and Hermelin (1976) supported this when they found that the deaf performed better in backward recall than did the hearing. More evidence is clearly necessary but this work does indicate capabilities of using a spatial system as a basis for some pictorial processing.

SYMBOLIC SKILLS

A great deal more work has been done in this area. Furth (1966, 1973) is one of the most prominent of those claiming that the deaf do have inherent capabilities for thinking and problem solving, despite their linguistic deficit which he seems to translate into an experiential deficit. He says that failure in a task is often due to lack of experience with the materials and deaf children, once they have been exposed to the methodology for a period of time, can complete tasks in the same way as hearing children. His approach is very much a Piagetian one using tasks to indicate levels of development. Therefore, if after repeated exposure to a task, a deaf child succeeds where a hearing child has in the first trial, then the deaf child is said to have performed at the same level as the hearing. One can have sympathy with this approach but it runs counter to many methods of achievement testing. Furth (1971) lists a great deal of this type of work where solution of a problem involves the under-standing of a particular principle. Youniss (1967) showed a considerable lag of spontaneous logical behaviour in the deaf but, with added task information and demonstration, the performance reached approximately the level of hearing children. Piaget (1966) reports retardation in the development of conservation, though it followed the normal pattern. He suggests that these differences are due more to the methods of communicating the task. This lack of understanding consistently appears in reports of this type of work. Ross (1969) found that in a test of memory span of up to nine binary symbols (+, −), deaf and hearing children were no different in errors. It may well be the case that when there is no obvious language representation in the task as in principles of conservation or in memory for symbols, the deaf need not be disadvantaged.

The role of language representation is taken up by Conrad (1970) when he reports differences between 'articulators' (children who made confusion errors according to the articulation of the word) and non-articulators in the recall of homophone and non-homophone lists. Whereas the articulators had more difficulty with the words which sounded alike, the other group manifested no difference in recall of the different material to be remembered. Conrad (1973) showed that profoundly deaf children predominantly did not use a speech encoding to memorize words and had more problems with words which were visually similar. When this 'internal speech' was used, it greatly enhanced overall performance. The nature of the encoding used by the majority of deaf children is not clear but one is tempted to suggest some form of visual representation in the light of the above studies. These findings have been confirmed in a larger scale study of all 15- and 16-year-old deaf children in England and Wales (Kyle et al., 1978). In this case it was shown that reading performance was greatly enhanced by the presence of a speech coding, independent of hearing and intelligence. Similar results appeared for lip-reading and memory, indicating the need for the use of a representation system which could be used in the language task.

This idea of speech coding is elaborated by other studies in illustrating this representational difference and can show the deaf as more competent than the hearing. Chen (1976) in a task involving cancellation of the letter 'e' in a piece of prose found that the deaf were much better than the hearing in cancelling 'e's which were silent (or would not be pronounced if the prose were read aloud) and also cancelled more accurately in general. The deaf were less dependent on the context of word sounds than the hearing. One would predict this result from the model of processing that the work by Conrad proposes. The question still remains nevertheless as to what type of coding allows the deaf to perform in this way and whether it can be used in a constructive framework. Bellugi et al. (1974) studied memory for words presented in sign language and found that errors were made which were quite clearly visual in nature. In comparing deaf in the signed condition with hearing subjects in the auditory condition, they found no overlap in the intrusion errors produced. Despite the fact that the deaf knew the words in written form − they wrote down their recall − they appeared to be using a representational system based on sign. This sign system, according to Bellugi *et al.*, is not just "English on the hands" but rather a completely different language with different lexical rules. Bellugi and Klima (1975) give more information on this. The sign language, or in their case American Sign Language (ASL), is not just a loose connection of gestures. but rather a native language for up to 20% of deaf people, and there is a total of around 500 000 users in USA. Signs are not analysable as linear sequences as words are but do have major characteristics of a human language. Wilbur (1976) claims sign language exhibits *creativity,* the capacity of reconstruction of new sentences, *features of language use,* the arbitrary matching of words to objects, *displacement,* the capability of reference to objects not physically present and it can also be used to *learn other languages.* It also manifests useful syntax and can carry abstract concepts. It differs from English in that it does not have indefinite articles but neither does Russian, Czech or Japanese. It does not have a passive but neither does Thai. Effectively it can be seen as a language system rather different from English but capable of carrying the meaning required for all communication purposes.

The question of whether it can be as effective as a representational system as English is the important one. Huttenlocher (1975) raises some doubts as to whether ASL permits categorization in the way required in English and also queries the difficulties in decoding messages in ASL which require spatial construction, such as imagery problems studied by Brooks (1968). The point is supported by O'Connor and Hermelin (1973) as the encoding is often spatial; thus, though it is easier to represent spatial problems in ASL it may also be more difficult to use the code without confusion. However, this is a problem faced by any language code. Another question which is perhaps more easily tackled, arises from a suggestion by Mattingly (1975) that the load on the receiver is much lower in speech than in other types of communication such as sign. Hoemann (1972) studied a task where a sender and receiver communicated either by sign or by speech the contents of one of a set of pictures. The pictures often differed only in perspective and thus fine discrimination on the basis of the sender's communication was critical for the receiver. The results showed speech as a more efficient communication channel than sign but the issue was clouded in the study by problems of estimation of the adequacy of the message sent.

Bellugi *et al.* (1974) found, in their short term memory task for signs (deaf subjects) and written words (hearing subjects), that the deaf have a memory span of 4.9 while the hearing have a span of 5.9. However, since response was by writing the recalled words, the task might favour the hearing group. White and Stevenson (1975) attempted to assess the amount of information assimilated through different methods of communication. In order to convey information they used oral, manual or written instructions or total communication methods. While rather strangely the written or read version was easiest for deaf children, the manual methods were much better than the oral. None of these studies are without difficulties, mainly because of the attempt to evaluate a 'foreign' language in terms of tasks in English, and one must be careful of applying it directly to communication between experienced signers. Jordan (1975) examined a similar task situation to Hoemann's (1972) but found very clear evidence that deaf signers communicated the information content of pictures as well in sign as hearing people did in speech.

A number of other studies have examined the nature of the representation rather than just the capacities of the system. Odom et al. (1970) found deaf subjects performed significantly better in memory on words for which there was an exact sign than on those where there was not, but they also found in contrast to Bellugi et al. (1974) a difference in recall between deaf and hearing, in favour of the deaf. Locke and Locke (1971) give evidence of a similar outcome for paired consonant letters. Moulton and Beasley (1975) showed that paired associates with common sign and semantic relation are very much better recalled than pairs without these links. The conditions in the experiment make conclusions a little difficult but a clear implication is that sign representations are related to semantic storage. Moulton and Beasley try to link this to current models in information processing where meanings (in a cognitive or long-term storage system) are accessed through the representation in working memory. This appears to open up a complete new area of investigation of representational or organizational structure in the deaf. Green and Shepherd (1975) partly examine this possibility in studying the semantic structure of the deaf, using the semantic differential. They used rather difficult concepts like 'freedom' and 'war' but claimed that the children understood them at some level. Their results gave Evaluation and Potency factors as is usual, but not Activity, which suggests the deaf use a scale of sensory representations. In effect, it presents the deaf as having a different language 'space' which might be congruent with Myklebust's (1964) notion of organismic shift because of experience. This notion arises from a simple discovery that the deaf group studied/performed better on a Knox cube test which measured the ability to observe, organize, retain and reproduce patterns of movement. He suggested that early sensory deprivation ensures that the organism must modify its means of maintaining adequate environmental contact. The shift in perceptual organization may induce different features of semantic organization. He takes the idea no further but one would expect an organismic shift of some magnitude. Kyle (1978) examines this on the basis of the physiological data but the data are incomplete. Meadow (1976) indicates that deaf people need to have specific examples in explanation rather than vague references and exhibit social characteristics which suggest a different perceptual organization. It is an interesting problem which cannot be resolved here.

If one is allowed a brief summary at this stage, it must present a picture of unattained goals for a deaf child. It can be demonstrated that the child is capable of processing in similar ways to hearing children but the nature of the representation is different. Since the method of instruction does not really come to terms with this, it is not too surprising that he fails to perform well in the standard achievement tests. Inevitably this has affects on further employment beyond school and it is worth examining the provision made for children when they enter the adult world.

EMPLOYMENT AND SUPPORT SERVICES

The major implications of the lack of the three traditional skills is, immediately, reduced job opportunities. Recently schools in general have begun to offer more applied programmes to give a background to employment beyond school. For a deaf child this becomes particularly important and the basis of work skills can be explored further in the further education schemes which appear to be on the increase. These types of schemes often attempt to bridge the gap between the protective school environment with its low level goals and the job where different demands are made. Day release classes from school help and a major aim, as with hearing children, is to take the student through certificate courses which are of value in his chosen career. However, a particularly acute problem is the lack of instructors who can communicate with a deaf person in such a situation. Though colleges now attempt to provide a counsellor who has experience with the deaf and can therefore help with general difficulties, there is often no support in specialized subjects.

This has been seen as important in the USA where the National Technical Institute for the Deaf has been set up, and it is purpose-built for the further education of deaf students. Communication in lectures and seminars is tailored to the needs of the deaf individuals who attend. Courses are offered and qualifications given in a range of specialized technical subjects. Their follow-up programmes suggest that their students are successful in finding and keeping jobs. The major differences between this education provision and other schemes are in the designing of a setting suitable for the non-hearing person (plenty of light, visual aids, small group settings) and the establishment of a sufficiently flexible communication method to encompass all hearing-impaired students. Unfortunately it can only cater for a small proportion of the deaf student population. A very large population still have to make the adjustments themselves. Bolton (1976) describes this personal adjustment as the most critical factor in rehabilitation. Whether the individual has just become deaf or has gone through an educational programme for the deaf, he must still make the necessary relation of his ideas to attainable goals. Deaf individuals are continually under-employed, despite Montgomery and Miller's (1977) optimistic statement that they do make surprisingly good adjustments in employment and in social life. They tend to be pushed into areas of unskilled work.

Lerman (1976) summarizes the findings of a number of studies of vocational status. Less than 10% of deaf males are to be found in professional or managerial roles but over 60% are in skilled or semi-skilled posts. Deaf women appear in semi-skilled or commercial jobs to the extent of 55% but there are less than 10% with professional status. Over 20% of the deaf are in unskilled jobs. These findings are generally supported by studies in the UK. Storer (1977) found males and females predominantly in semi-skilled or unskilled jobs even when hearing loss was relatively slight. Montgomery and Miller (1977) found no significant difference in the pattern for profoundly deaf and partially-hearing. They have found strong links between the home and later vocational adjustments. Montgomery and Miller put this adjustment in terms of establishment of self-identity. Rodda (1970) discovered lower levels of aspiration in more severely hearing-impaired groups. He points out that the higher levels of aspiration in the partially-hearing may cause problems of frustration. Unfortunately, the group studied were not followed up far enough beyond school to test these points.

As far as higher education is concerned, there is very little provision for the deaf. In the USA, Gallaudet college gives a liberal arts education with appropriate communication arrangements, while in the UK the Open University courses are compatible with deaf students' requirements. Durham University is in the process of setting up support services for the deaf student.

The general picture emerging is of the availability of further educational training but of the under-achieving deaf moving out into under-employment partly because of their lack of the basic skills which would allow easier inter-action and instruction. The lessons of further education lie in the interaction part since the availability of a medium of communication is extremely im-portant and in many circumstances this is designed to suit the capabilities of the deaf rather than to fit in with the normal system of instruction. When the communication is attained, realistic goals may be attempted. If the perfor-mance skills required of the deaf group can be as poor as suggested above, some other skills must be substituted.

DISCUSSION

It can be seen that in traditional skills of speech and reading the deaf perform rather poorly. In any task which can have a language component their responses are not as good as the hearing. At the same time, they do appear to follow the same cognitive development though at a slower rate. Their communication is greatly improved by the use of sign language, rather than lip-reading, though it is not clear just how powerful the system is. The value of this communication is that it leads to a representation internally which allows control of information in memory. Whether one adopts a low-level claim as Conrad (1970) of a non-articulation group of deaf children or a higher one such as Bellugi *et al.* (1974) of a sign language code, its presence is of importance. Recent work (Kyle *et al.,* 1978) has shown that the presence of an internal speech code gives an advantage of over 2 years of reading to a child, and is a fundamental factor in language-based skills. The significance of this is that theoretically a method of representation which is not spoken language may be used as a code in much the same way. One might disagree with Furth that thinking can be done "without language", and replace it with the phrase, "thinking in a different language."

The extent to which different language principles can be invoked as systems of control for the mechanisms of search, retrieval and storage in current psychological models remains to be explored. What the previous research has done is to state the lack of progress, under present approaches, in the development of relevant ability in deaf people. Whether it is measured through low-level achievement measures of reading and speech, or whether through job distribution, the deaf group are underperforming. A critical difference between school and counsellors in employment is that the latter propose to fit the communication system to the capacities of the deaf individual. Denmark (1973) is one of the leading advocates of the use of communication methods which are relevant to the needs of the deaf child. He argues that a deaf person will in any case learn sign language very quickly after leaving school.

The main point presented is that currently, or at least until very recently, the deaf have been presented with unattainable goals. Conrad (1977b) suggests the need for the organization of goals which will lead to meaningful progress rather than frustration. Furth (1973) makes virtually the same plea and adds that current educational practice is a denial of deafness and presents the deaf child with a crisis of non-attainment when he leaves school. To a certain extent this is true; the deaf child is treated mainly as a slow learner rather than as someone requiring different communication facilities. Nevertheless, the problem of setting up a deaf community, who can interact with one another but not with the outside world, is the outcome to be countered. The main argument is quite simply that under the present system of instruction this is what happens anyway (Denmark, 1973) and therefore there are strong grounds for using the processes which the deaf have available for teaching any system of language. The argument for and against different systems of education has traditionally been a passionate one, dominated by individual casework and personal feelings. Psychologically, the greater part of it is misplaced, since it can be shown that some children succeed in one system and some succeed in the other. The key point is that success does not mean *only* in one system but given one language acquisition will allow the development of the other. One tends not to argue that the use of Japanese in childhood precludes reading in English at a later stage. The acquisition of a representation system based on a formal language must aid cognitive and conceptual manipulation. In altering his capacities for language development, the handicap of deafness produces a critical gap between society's aspirations for its members and the interactional capabilities of the individual. The educational system, in narrowing this gap mainly by lowering aspirations, does not explore the full capabilities of a deaf child, unless there is a considerable amount of residual hearing. In exactly the same way, the deaf find jobs through lowered aspirations in isolated trades, even when possibilities exist in higher level jobs for reducing the communication load or improving the environmental acoustics. It is essential that job analysis be carried out in relation to capabilities and not in relation to supposed deficits. The change in approach seems to be in progress and, with a more fundamental understanding of the basis of the learning of skills, the extent of the crisis of non-attainment should decrease.

In bringing this back into the context of the creation of skills in the individual, one can appreciate the inherent 'unfriendliness' of the deaf person's environment. The skills model (e.g. Welford, 1976) however, insufficiently characterizes the abilities of deaf individuals in dealing almost completely with capacities. To a considerable extent the deaf are similar to the hearing in the presence of the processes in the information flow model (the cognitive/symbolic skills section has presented evidence of this). They can remember, they can turn perception into action, they have control over effectors; the difference is hidden by the 'arrows' which designate information flow. The nature of the information is different, the way it is represented leads to different performance outcomes.

The picture of the deaf individual dominated by environmental factors is realistic in one sense but the dominance is not incapacitating. Unlike groups with other permanent handicaps (mental handicaps, physical disability), where compliance is constant and inevitable, the pre-lingually deaf, in interaction with other deaf persons, manifest all levels of skill and the dominating communication deficit disappears. Paradoxically, the adventitiously deaf may suffer the most serious adjustment problems, and the loss of control over one facet of environmental interaction may prove incapacitating to what were previously normal relations. This dual picture is rather important in evaluating the skills framework for those affected by lack of hearing. Performance skills are affected very seriously when the language medium is central but, by altering the communication environment, the processes underlying performance can be shown to contribute very markedly to other aspects of the abilities and skills of the individual.

References

Bellugi, U. and Klima, E. S. (1975). Aspects of sign language and its structure. In J. F. Kavanagh and J. E. Cutting, (eds.) *The Role of Speech in Language,* (Cambridge, Mass: MIT Press)

Bellugi, U., Klima, E. S. and Siple, P. (1974). Remembering in signs. *Cognition,* **3,** 93

Bolton, B. (1976). *The Psychology of Deafness for Rehabilitation Counsellors.* (Baltimore: Univ. Park Press)

Brannon, J. (1964). *Visual feedback of glossal motions and its influence upon the speech of deaf children.* Unpublished Ph.D. dissertation, Northwestern Univ.

Brooks, L. R. (1968). Spatial and verbal components of messages in the act of recall, *Canad. J. Psychol.*, **22**, 349

Chen, K. (1976). Acoustic image in visual detection for deaf and hearing college students. *J. Gen. Psychol.*, **94**, 243

Conrad, R. (1970). Short term memory processes in the deaf, *Br. J. Psychol.*, **61**, 179

Conrad, R. (1973). Some correlates of speech coding in short term memory of the deaf, *J. Speech Hear. Res.*, **16**, 375

Conrad, R. (1975). Speech quality of deaf children. In S. D. G. Stephens (Ed.)., *Disorders of Auditory Functions – 2*, (London: Academic Press)

Conrad, R. (1977a). Lip-reading by deaf and hearing children, *Br. J. Educ. Psychol.*, **47**, 60

Conrad, R. (1977b). The reading ability of deaf school leavers, *Br. J. Educ. Psychol.*, **47**, 138

Denmark, J. (1973). The education of deaf children. *Hearing*, **28**, 284

Department of Education and Science (1972). *The Health of the School Child, 1969–70*, (London: HMSO)

Department of Education and Science (1975). *Statistics of Education*, (London: HMSO)

Di Francesca, S. (1972). *Academic Achievement Test Results of a National Testing Programme for Hearing-Impaired Students*, U.S.: Spring, 1971, (Report No. 9, series D), Gallaudet College, Office of Demographic Studies, Washington, D.C.

Ewing, A. W. G. and Ewing, E. C. (1964). *Teaching Deaf Children to Talk*, (Manchester: Manchester Univ. Press)

Furth, H. G. (1966). *Thinking Without Language.* (London: Collier–Macmillan)

Furth, H. G. (1971). Linguistic deficiency and thinking: research with deaf subjects 1964–1969. *Psychol. Bull.*, **76**, 58

Furth, H. G. (1973). *Deafness and Learning.* (Belmont, Calif: Wadsworth)

Garretson, M. D. (1976). Total communication. In R. Frisina (ed.). *A Bicentennial Monograph on Hearing Impairment–Trends in the U.S.A.* (Alex G. Bell Association for the Deaf)

Gibson, E. J. and Levin, H. (1975). *The Psychology of Reading*, (Cambridge, Mass: MIT Press)

Green, W. B. and Shepherd, D. C. (1975). The semantic structure in deaf children, *J. Commun. Disord.*, **8**, 357

Gustason, G. (1975). Signing exact english, *Gallaudet Today*, **5**, 11

Hammermeister, F. K. (1971). Reading achievement in deaf adults, *Am. Ann. Deaf*, **116**, 25

Hermelin, B. and O'Connor, N. (1973). Ordering in recognition memory, *Canad. J. Psychol.*, **27**, 191

Hine, W. D. (1970). The attainments of children with partial-hearing. *Teacher of the Deaf*, **68**, 129

Hoemann, H. W. (1972). The development of communication skills in deaf and hearing children. *Child Devel.*, **43**, 990

Huttenlocher, J. (1975). Encoding information in sign language. In J. F. Kavanagh and J. E. Cutting (eds.). *The Role of Speech in Language*, (Cambridge, Mass: MIT Press)

Jordan, I. K. (1975). A referential communication study of signers and speakers using realistic referents. *Sign Lang. Stud.*, **6**, 65

Kyle, J. G. (1977). Audiometric analysis as a predictor of speech intelligibility, *Br. J. Audiol.*, **11**, 51

Kyle, J. G. (1978). The study of auditory deprivation from birth. *Br. J. Audiol.*, (in press)

Kyle, J. G., Conrad, R., McKenzie, M. G., Morris, A. J. M. and Weiskrantz, B. C. (1978). Language abilities in deaf school leavers, *Teacher of the Deaf*, **2**, 38

Lerman, A. (1976). Vocational development. In B. Bolton (ed.). *The Psychology of Deafness for Rehabilitation Counsellors*, (Baltimore: Univ. Park Press)

Locke, J. and Locke, V. (1971). Deaf children's phonetic, visual and dactylic coding in a grapheme recall task. *J. Exp. Psychol.*, **89**, 142

Markides, A. (1970). The speech of deaf and partially hearing children with special reference to factors affecting intelligibility. *Br. J. Commun. Disord.*, **5**, 126

Mattingly, I. G. (1975). The human aspect of language. In J. F. Kavanagh and J. E. Cutting (eds.). *The Role of Speech in Language*, (Cambridge, Mass: MIT Press)

Meadow, K. P. (1976). Personality and social development of deaf persons. In B. Bolton (ed.). *Psychology of Deafness for Rehabilitation Counsellors*. (Baltimore: Univ. Park Press)

Montgomery, G. W. G. (1968). A factorial study of communication and ability in deaf school leavers. *Br. J. Educ. Psychol.*, **38**, 27

Montgomery, G. W. G. and Miller, J. (1977). Assessment and preparation of deaf adolescents for employment. *Teacher of the Deaf*, **1**, 167

Moulton, R. D. and Beasley, D. S. (1975). Verbal coding strategies used by hearing impaired individuals. *J. Speech Hear. Res.*, **18**, 559

Murphy, K. P. (1957). Tests of abilities and attainments. In A. W. G. Ewing (ed.). *Educational Guidance and the Deaf Child*. (Manchester: Manchester Univ. Press)

Myklebust, H. R. (1964). *The Psychology of Deafness*. (New York: Grune and Stratton)

O'Connor, N. and Hermelin, B. (1973). Short term memory for the order of pictures and syllables by deaf and hearing children. *Neuropsychologia*, **11**, 437

O'Connor, N. and Hermelin, B. (1976). Backward and forward recall by deaf and hearing children. *Quart. J. Exp. Psychol.*, **28**, 83

Odom, P., Blanton, R. and McIntyre, C. (1970). Coding medium and word recall by deaf and hearing subjects. *J. Speech Hear. Res.*, **13**, 54

Owrid, H. L. (1970). Hearing impairment and verbal attainments in primary school children. *Educ. Res.*, **12**, 209

Piaget, J. (1966). Surdi-mutite et conservations operatoires. In *Etudes d'epistemologie genetique* (No. 20) (Paris: Presses Universitaires de France)

Rodda, M. (1970). *The Hearing Impaired School Leaver*. (London: Univ. of London Press)

Ross, B. M. (1969). Sequential visual memory and the limited magic of the number seven. *J. Exp. Psychol.*, **80**, 339

Schein, J. D. and Delk, M. T. (1974). *The Deaf Population of the U.S.* (Maryland: National Assoc. for the Deaf)

Schiff, W. and Thayer, S. (1974). An eye for an ear? Social perception, non-verbal communication and deafness. *Rehabil. Psychol.*, **21**, 50

Storer, R. D. K. (1977). The vocational boundaries of deaf and partially hearing adolescents and young adults in the West Midlands. *Teacher of the Deaf*, **1**, 134

Stuckless, E. R. (1976). Manual and graphic communication. In R. Frisina (ed.). *A Bicentennial Monograph on Hearing Impairment-trends in the U.S.A.* (Alex G. Bell Assoc. for the Deaf)

Vernon, M. (1976). Communication and the education of deaf and hard of hearing children. In *Methods of Communication Currently Used in the Education of Deaf Children*, (London: RNID)

Welford, A. T. (1976). *Skilled Performance: Perceptual and Motor Skills*. (Glenview: Scott-Foresman)

White, A. J. and Stevenson, V. M. (1975). The effects of total communication, oral communication, and reading on the learning of factual information in residential school deaf children. *Am. Ann. Deaf*, **120**, 48

Wilbur, R. B. (1976). The linguistics of manual language and manual systems. In L. L. Lloyd (ed.). *Communication, Assessment and Intervention Strategies*. (Baltimore: Univ. Park Press)

Woods, W. H. (1970). *The Forgotten People*, (Florida: Dixie Press)

Youniss, J. (1967). Psychological evaluation of the deaf child: observations of a researcher. *Eye, Ear, Nose and Throat Monthly*, **46**, 458

Illustrations The aging process is no respecter of persons. This unusual collection of pictures of Sir Winston Churchill demonstrate the changes seen during the course of a full life-span *(Reproduced by kind permission of Birmingham Post and Mail (upper left and middle centre), The Mansell Collection (upper centre and right), Camera Press Ltd. (middle left and lower left) and London News Services (middle right))*

5
Skill in Aging

A. T. WELFORD

INTRODUCTION

Human performance results from the interaction of three sets of factors. First are *demands* made by, or resulting from, the environment and the individual's attitudes, aims, ambitions, hopes and fears. These demands thus include the requirement to secure certain necessities such as food, water and shelter in order to survive, the need to guard against natural hazards and dangerous animals, social pressures exerted by other people, responsibilities at work and in the family, and also desires for self-realization in the material and social world. Second are *capacities*, both physical and mental, for receiving information, making decisions and executing action, and for memory, learning and thinking. Third are techniques and methods or, as they have come to be called, *strategies*, by which capacities are deployed in order to meet demands.

All these sets of factors differ between individuals and for any one individual at different times. Demands vary with circumstances, and the average level is higher for some individuals than for others. People differ in the patterns of capacities they possess and, for any one individual, capacities change with states of fatigue. illness, lack of sleep and other temporary conditions. Especially is there variation between individuals in the strategies they employ. This is understandable because strategies are formed in the course of experience and thus reflect the subtle variations of situation and circumstance that have occurred during an individual's life. Indeed it is essentially in the development of strategies that training and learning from experience have their effects.

Attempts to improve performance fall broadly into three classes according to the type of factor they seek to influence. The ergonomic approach of 'fitting the job to the man' tries to reduce demands and so bring a wider range of tasks within the capacities of any given individual. Regimens of exercise designed to produce fitness increase capacity for physical work, although it can be argued that they only bring out a potentiality already there and do not affect fundamental capacity. Whether mental exercises can truly develop mental capacity is doubtful, but they can and do develop and refine strategies, making them more effective and efficient. It is the use of such refined strategies that seems to be implied by the term *skill* (Welford, 1978).

Both demands and capacities change with age. It follows that strategies also must change if they are to remain effective and efficient. This does not seem always to be fully attained, but many of the changes in the method and manner of performance as people grow older can be construed as attempts, sometimes conscious, sometimes not, in this direction. The main changes of demand come from two obvious sources: first the transition from dependence to independence when adulthood is reached, followed by marriage and the upbringing of a family which eventually moves away; and second the transition from school and student days to work, followed by the gradual assumption of increasing responsibilities and the shedding of them again at retirement.

The main changes of capacity with age are again two: first the various bodily mechanisms of sense organs, muscles, joints and the nervous system including the brain, rise to a peak of capacity during the early twenties and thereafter decline slowly to the age of about 70, then more rapidly (see Birren and Schaie, 1977). Second, as against these declines, experience and knowledge increase continuously, and, at least up to the age of 60 or so, usually more than offset any forgetting that may occur (Foulds and Raven, 1948; Botwinick, 1977).

As regards strategies, if as the result of increased demand or reduced capacity an individual becomes overloaded, there appear to be four broad ways in which he can attempt to restore a balance between the two. First, he can try to ensure that the small-scale strategies and techniques he uses are as efficient as possible; second, he can increase effort; third, he can shed part of the load by restricting interests, aims and activities; and fourth, he can shift load by recruiting help from others.

The changes of performance that occur at different periods of life are the result of interactions between various features of demand and capacity and the broad strategies used. How far the appropriate strategies are chosen and modified as demands and capacities change depends upon the extent to which an individual maintains flexibility in his approach to the tasks of work, home and everyday life − in other words, how far he is *able* to modify his strategies and how far is he *willing* to do so. These inevitably involve fundamental questions of *learning* and *motivation* in relation to age, which will be considered in turn.

ABILITY TO CHANGE − PROBLEMS OF LEARNING

It is commonly assumed that, as one grows older, learning becomes extremely difficult, but this is by no means universally or necessarily so. Although some skills, especially those such as car-driving which involve complex sensory–motor co-ordination, appear often to be difficult to acquire fully after the twenties, many other skills can be developed at almost any age during adult life. Moreover, research has shown that at least some skills normally considered to be impossible to learn after the teens can be acquired in middle age if suitable training methods are used (e.g. Belbin, 1958). Skills once mastered seem usually to be well maintained with age in the sense that basic principles and techniques are not forgotten, and often, although not always, in the sense that strategies are gradually modified to optimize performance in the face of changing capacities and demands. At the level of managerial skill, a fascinating account of how a number of high-level executives gained insight into their methods and modified them as they grew older has been provided by Birren (1969), who portrays the men he interviewed as becoming increasingly aware of both their competence and their weaknesses, of recognizing the need for help from others and mastering ways of obtaining it, of enabling others to bear responsibilities delegated to them, of maintaining authority and efficiency together with easy social relationships, and especially of dealing with problems in the broader terms – larger 'chunks' – that increased understanding had made possible.

Considerable success in training people in middle and early old age for certain kinds of shop-floor work has been achieved by the use of the so-called 'discovery' method. With this, a minimum of direct instruction and demonstration is given. Instead, the trainee is given the time and opportunity to discover for himself the nature of the task and the way in which it should be done. In the early stages care is taken to ensure that correct actions are indicated or are easily inferred from the way the task is arranged, so that errors are prevented, or if they are made are quickly corrected. The result is a training in which the trainee is not a passive receiver of information, but has actively to think about the task and so gains insight into it and commitment to it (Belbin and Shimmin, 1964; Belbin and Downs, 1966; Belbin, 1965, 1969).

The factors important in discovery learning seem to apply also to the acquisition and maintenance of skills in general at work and in everyday life, whether or not formal training is provided, and to the preservation of flexibility in middle and old age. They can be divided broadly into three types:

(a) *Acquisition and retrieval of information.*
Learning and memory imply a series of stages. First, the material to be learnt has to be comprehended. Second, it has to be held for a few seconds by some kind of ephemeral, dynamic process to give time for a third stage of more permanent memory traces to build up in the form of enduring biochemical or microstructural changes in the brain. Fourth, the traces have to endure until recall is required and a fifth stage of recovering the material by reactivating the appropriate traces begins. In the 1950s it seemed plausible to suppose that

difficulties for older people sometimes lay in the first of these stages when the task was complex (e.g. Belbin, 1958), but that the main difficulties occurred in the second and fifth stages (Welford, 1956). The view had some introspective support; many older people complain that they forget immediately what they have been told and that they cannot recall names or other items when they

Recent evidence indicates, however, that the main source of difficulty lies rather in the third stage. Older people fail to retain material in memory, not because they forget more rapidly, but because they do not register it as thoroughly in the first place. The complementary result is that, because the traces are weak, they are less easy to recover when recall is required. Failures of both learning and recall among older people seem therefore to be due to poorer initial registration of material in long-term memory (Welford, 1979).

The implication is that older people need to take special care to ensure adequate registration. General studies of learning suggest that powerful aids to registration are close attention to the material, the spending of a little extra time, and immediate attempts to rehearse. They are epitomized in the custom when being introduced to a stranger: "This is Mr. Bongleton", of immediately replying: "How do you do, Mr. Bongleton". The intention to repeat the name ensures close attention to it when it is heard and guarantees that it is retained for at least a few seconds, and the actual repetition acts as a rehearsal.

(b) *Feedback and correction of error*
One consequence of difficulty in learning is a tendency to rely on already acquired facts, techniques and ideas and to apply these to new situations even though they are not fully appropriate. Older people seem to be especially likely to do this. In such cases initial performance of a new task is likely to contain some errors, and subsequent learning is mainly concerned with getting rid of these (Kay, 1951). Eliminating errors is more difficult than initial learning because the erroneous response competes with the correct one which has, in consequence, to be learnt more thoroughly than it would otherwise be in order to be distinguished clearly from the error. It is probably for this reason that learning is faster if conditions are arranged to prevent errors being made in the early stages (von Wright, 1957).

In the laboratory, correction of errors and the mastery of new tasks depends on knowledge being available to the subject of the results of previous attempts which is relevant, clear and given in a way that enables it to be related easily to the performance concerned. These principles also have obvious applications to work and many aspects of everyday life. Most interestingly, perhaps, they offer an explanation of an observation made by an eminent management consultant that, in his experience, those in trade and commerce tended to remain more flexible in middle and old age than did their opposite numbers in industry. Why, he did not know, but it seems reasonable to suggest, on the basis of what is known about feedback, that the effects of actions and decisions which are readily recognizable will tend to weigh to a greater extent in shaping future actions and decisions than will more remote effects, even if these are recognized eventually. A young man usually obtains knowledge of the effectiveness of his work relatively quickly – and often vigorously – from those above him. A man who moves to a responsible position in business, say in the retail trade, still obtains fairly clear and immediate feedback from his customers and is thus kept alive to changes of demand and to the satisfactoriness or otherwise of the goods he is selling. In many kinds of manufacturing industry, however, a man obtains less and less immediate knowledge of the results of his actions and decisions as he attains more senior positions. Contact with customers, if it exists at all, is indirect through a sales organization. Such feedback as he does get comes mainly from colleagues and from those under him in his factory. Relations with these will tend to be pleasant and trouble avoided if changes are kept to a minimum. Changes often also mean a temporary rise in the cost of manufacture which may be difficult to justify. The senior man in industry can thus easily, on a short view, find inflexibility rewarding.

There may well be parallels to this in other walks of life. Does, for example, the academic who is exposed to the searching questions of students and who risks the criticism of colleagues by speaking at conferences retain adaptability better than one who sits firmly in the proverbial 'ivory tower'? Is the medico in a large hospital, where others will know whether or not his actions are sound, more flexible in outlook than an isolated practitioner who can judge the efficacy of his actions only by the dubious criterion of whether or not the patient returns? It seems fair to suggest that those who in any way put themselves beyond the reach of criticism expose themselves to the risk of inflexibility, and that the opportunity to do this increases with age. The older man or woman, especially in a senior position, has therefore a special need to develop self-criticism, seek opinions of others and look for new knowledge, however troublesome these tasks may sometimes appear.

(c) Opportunity to learn

Industrial managers, university teachers, medical practitioners, politicians and many others often find this last problem compounded by the fact that increasing responsibilities in middle and early old age leave them little or no time to learn anything new, even within the immediate area of their work. The same is often true of the shop-floor worker whose slowing performance means that he has to work more continuously in order to keep up with his younger colleagues and cannot, therefore, stand back and think about how to improve his methods. There is need for a deliberate effort to ensure time to learn. The need is probably best recognized in universities, where the substantial periods of vacation and sabbatical leave are not the holidays they are often popularly supposed to be, but give time for study – provided they are not eroded by administration and committee meetings. Some moves have been made to allow periods of leisure for learning in other walks of life, but so far these have been relatively few. It seems fair to argue that, since failure to exploit new techniques and to understand needs for change can have disastrous effects for industries and businesses, substantial efforts should be made to ensure that those concerned in such organizations, especially those in senior positions, take time to read, discuss and listen in order to keep abreast of developments. In the short term, this time may seem ill afforded from the hectic daily round, but in the long term such discipline would undoubtedly be rewarding, not only for the individuals concerned but even more for the organization as a whole.

MOTIVATION

It used to be thought that lower performances by older people at many laboratory tasks and mental tests were due to poorer motivation. Older people were thought to regard the tasks as trivial and not worth serious effort, and it was assumed that if only they could be stimulated to do their best, they would do as well as those younger. More recent evidence has shown this view to be false. To take only one trivial example, average reaction times become shorter if electric shocks are administered as a 'punishment' for slow reactions, but the shortening is no greater for older than for younger subjects (see Welford 1977).

However, on a broader scale, we should expect the changes of demand and capacity that occur during the course of a lifetime to be reflected in changing motivation. Willingness to take action depends upon a balance or ratio between the costs of the action in terms of effort, difficulty or unpleasantness and the benefit, either material or in terms of satisfaction or other desirable result, likely to be obtained. Both costs and benefits are likely to change with age. Any loss of capacity will mean that the cost in terms of effort to be expended in order to attain a given result will rise. At the same time, the achievement in middle age of a well-structured and ordered way of living will mean that the benefits to be gained from many activities will tend to diminish. The overall result will be an increase of cost–benefit ratio leading to a reduced tendency to take action.

The change provides a theoretical basis for the tendency already noted for older people to fall back on established routines rather than learn new ones. It is almost always more difficult – 'costly' – to work out and learn a new procedure than to apply one already known. Thus, for example, any change of working conditions, whether in factories or offices or elsewhere, will tend to produce a temporary rise in cost–benefit ratio unless the change produces a very great improvement in the cost–benefit ratio inherent in the job. Even then, the need to learn new procedures will mean that the full benefits of the change will not be realized immediately.

More generally, changing cost–benefit ratio can account for many shifts of interest in later life as a person moves away from activities such as vigorous games and sports where reduced capacities have raised costs, or from pursuits where altered needs have reduced benefits, and moves towards other concerns such as for security, where benefits are likely to rise with age. Looking at changing interests and activities in this way is not to be construed as a criticism of older people. It is in line with the sound biological principle that the organism designs its activities to make the best use it can of its capacities and opportunities. If so, much of the behaviour of older people which seems to an outsider to be crabbed, unadventurous, inward-looking or otherwise unsatis-factory needs to be judged with caution. What the old people concerned get out of life may not be what others would choose, but it may be the best they can achieve.

Four further points about motivation in relation to age deserve mention. First, while a high cost–benefit ratio tends to deter action, it appears also to enhance the value subsequently placed on achievement. Why this is so is not clear, but it seems to be a further influence affecting willingness to learn and change; we tend to value not only possessions, but also skills and pursuits that have been attained with difficulty, and to be unwilling to relinquish them even though their cost–benefit ratios have become unfavourable.

Second, knowledge of results of action – feedback – in addition to being important for learning and the attainment of accuracy, has been shown often to act as a powerful incentive and stimulant to performance. This is under-standable on the seemingly improbable but in fact very plausible view that the one fundamental human motive is to secure results from one's actions (Wood-worth, 1958; Welford, 1972). Some studies have shown, however, that feedback can have a *dis*incentive effect. The conflict seems capable of recon-ciliation on the commonsense view that so long as the feedback indicates a favourable cost–benefit ratio for action taken, it will be an incentive, but if it indicates an unfavourable one it will have the reverse effect. In so far as the cost–benefit ratio of any particular activity changes with age, the effects of feedback from the activity are therefore likely to change also.

Third, emotional stability as measured by several personality tests seem to vary little with age, although small trends towards increased stability have been observed at least until middle age (Heron and Chown, 1967). However, emotional stability in another sense seems likely to increase more substantially. By late middle age most people seem to have taken the measure of life and come to terms with their ambitions, some of which have been achieved and others quietly forgotten. Obviously their stability in this sense is due in large measure to better organization and structuring of experience, but we can fairly wonder whether changes in the thalamus and limbic system, paralleling those in the cortex, reduce the intensity of emotions as age advances and in doing so make it easier to deal with personal, and thus with social, situations objectively. If so, it is an interesting example of the complexity of relationship that can arise: a *fall* of emotional capacity precipitates a change of strategy which leads to a reduction of self-imposed demand and *improved* social performance.

Lastly must be mentioned one point about the way people view their achievements which, unless recognized and allowed for, is likely to condemn old people to chronic frustration. Satisfaction with achievement seems not to be gained from reaching a standard one regards as 'good', but rather in doing better than one's previous best. Since the standard of this previous best will tend to rise progressively with age, the chances of such satisfaction would diminish even if all one's capacities remained unchanged. The eventual way out of this unsatisfying situation for most *men* is retirement, which involves moving into a situation where no attempt is made to maintain or improve on previous achievement, at least as regards work. Until that time, considerable maturity and poise may be needed to maintain effort without continually striving for the impossible. For *women* whose life work has been at home, the need for such maturity and poise continues because they do not retire. Perhaps for both them and their menfolk one of the most skilful achievements of old age is to acknowledge that failure to better one's previous best may not so much reflect present shortcomings, as be a cause for satisfaction at high achievement in the past.

FROM YOUNG ADULTHOOD TO OLD AGE

Various changes of demand and capacity and changes of strategy to meet them tend to become important at characteristic ages – some early, some much later. Let us now look at age changes as they seem typically to appear in the successive decades from the twenties onwards. In doing so it must be emphasised that we are concerned only with broad average trends; the demands made upon individuals at any given age vary widely, and individuals differ greatly in the rates at which their various capacities change; a man or woman of, say, forty may be typical of his or her age in some respects but resemble the average of those many years younger or older in others. It is, therefore, not appropriate to argue policies for older people on the basis of a few individuals who may be exceptional, nor is it fair to lay down conditions which preclude all applicants over a set age from obtaining particular jobs, driving licences or travel facilities. It may be desirable to require applicants over a set age to pass defined standards of competence or fitness, but exclusion on grounds of age alone will bear harshly on some individuals and, unless the age bar is placed very low, allow in others who should be excluded.

The twenties

This is the decade during which sensory capacities, bodily strength and power to perform 'mental gymnastics' in manipulating data in the abstract are all at their peak. Understandably, therefore, those in their twenties tend to enjoy energetic pursuits, are quick mentally if they are ever going to be, and tend to be sentimental and to become emotionally involved with a wide variety of other people. Their limitation lies in lack of the experience and practice necessary to develop the strategies to use these powers efficiently. Productivity at work is thus relatively low (e.g. Wackwitz, 1946; King 1956), enthusiasm is patchy and behaviour often seemingly irresponsible. On the roads, rates of accidents and offences among men (although not among women) are relatively high, due mainly to rashness (McFarland *et al.*, 1972; Road Traffic Board of South Australia, 1972).

There are thus often several changes of job, leisure activities, friends and actual or potential sexual partners in the search for what are felt to be suitable long-term choices. The instability of such a period means that although life is full of excitement and hope, there is often a great deal of emotional turmoil and uncertainty which can be intensely distressing. Also, the break from the parental home and the beginning of married life, usually with limited financial resources, mean that many insistent demands of living have to be faced for the first time. Viewed by other people, those in their twenties usually seem likeable and well-intentioned, but their lack of social skill, and their greater consciousness of new powers and freedoms than of the limitations of inexperience, make them often appear thoughtless, selfish and arrogant.

The thirties

By the early thirties the main changes of capacity that will be continuous to old age have already begun. Eyes and ears will have lost a little sensitivity. An athlete will no longer be the sprinter he or she once was, but will still be able to perform well in competitions demanding endurance. Many sensory–motor performances will be a little slower or, alternatively, a little more liable to error. However, all these declines are likely to be more than compensated by increased knowledge and experience. Skills learnt during the 'teens and twenties thus come to maturity. At the same time, most people have by the end of the thirties found their niche in life, and have settled into it as the responsibilities of a growing family bring realization of the need for a steady income and stable living conditions.

As a result of these tendencies, the thirties are commonly the age of peak performance at shop-floor industrial work and other activities in which knowledge is important but not *all*-important, and they are the beginning years of safe and law-abiding driving on the roads. In terms of the compensatory strategies mentioned at the beginning of the chapter, the thirties are a time during which the detailed tactics of performance are developed and become fully efficient.

The forties

During this decade many feel that they reach a watershed or 'point of no return' when they realize they have lived more than half their likely span of life. Physical powers are still adequate for activities involving considerable endurance where very severe instantaneous effort is not required; for instance, many long-distance runners are in their forties. Sensory changes have, however, become appreciable and many who before did without spectacles now take to them for reading. In industry people begin to move away from the most strenuous physical jobs to lighter work (Powell, 1973). In semi-skilled work performance tends to slow, but this is still commonly compensated by improved strategies and skill in deploying them, and these lead also to greater reliability. Widening experience enables problems to be dealt with in broader terms, and it is usually only by this age that people attain the stature required for bearing really large responsibilities.

At home, the situation may be less happy. Increased responsibilities at work may lead a husband to neglect his wife and family. The fact that the children are nearly grown up and are becoming restive to throw off parental constraints and leave home can be distressing, especially for their mother. Consciousness of age changes may lead to unwise attempts to demonstrate that youthful prowess has not departed, by trying desperately to compete with those younger at such activities as squash and skiing. Waning of sexual powers and desires, especially if it occurs earlier in one partner, can lead the other to seek stimulation from someone younger and thus break up a hitherto stable marriage. Especially may this occur if over the years one partner has also developed to a greater intellectual or social extent than the other.

Both at work and at home, the forties are a time for taking stock, reconciling oneself to moving definitely into middle age and realizing that, skilfully lived, the middle years have potentialities more important than those of youth.

The fifties

By the early fifties some age changes of both demand and capacity have reached a point at which more definite adjustments are needed to the manner of life and work. On the domestic side, the last children probably leave home and mother must make a difficult adaptation to a life with substantially reduced home responsibilities. The transition is often eased by the arrival of grandchildren – commonly a source of pleasure and vicarious pride. Fathers usually cope more successfully than mothers with the family changes. Mothers traditionally tend to resent their daughters-in-law and to interfere with the upbringing of grandchildren, while fathers take more benign and tolerant attitudes. Why there should be this difference between the two parents is not known for certain, but part of the reason is probably that daughters normally learn their domestic skills from their mothers. Because of this, a daughter-in-law introduces techniques and methods of running a home and looking after her mother-in-law's son which are strange and resented as a threat to the mother-in-law's expertise. Fathers are not affected because the skills on which their self-respect rests lie outside the home. Perhaps, however, one can see tensions analogous to those between mother and daughter-in-law when a man finds younger people at work developing new ideas and taking responsibilities in areas where formerly his skill and knowledge were unchallenged.

On the work side, the trend away from very strenuous jobs accelerates, and in lighter industries most shop-floor workers move from jobs on conveyor lines or those which otherwise lay stress on speed, to those in which the pace is more flexible and under their own control (Belbin, 1953; Welford, 1966). Analogous moves are probably made on the management side although, so far as the writer is aware, they have not been systematically studied. Many people make these adjustments easily and without fully realizing they have done so: for example an appreciable number of people are promoted out of jobs they would have been unable to sustain for long had they stayed in them. For some people, however, adjustment is not so easy: they gradually find it more and more difficult to keep up performance, and so they become less and less effective. In an effort to compensate, they sacrifice accuracy for speed, but the errors they make, the confusion these lead to and the time it takes to correct them serve only to increase their feeling of harassment. Often they blame their inefficiency on others or on circumstances and become obstinate or disagreeable, and these attitudes at work may spill over to relationships at home. For such people a change of job, when it comes, is often not acknowledged as due to age. Instead it is made following a short illness which in itself is too trivial to account for the change, but provides a rationalization of it which is not damaging to self-esteem (Richardson, 1953). The strategy of coping employed by such people is that of trying to maintain achievement by expending extra effort, and it tends to result in signs of stress. In gross cases these take the form of cardiac incidents, hypertension or ulcers in one or other part of the alimentary tract.

As regards more specifically intellectual functions, some difficulties seem to begin, although they are largely unconscious, in following statements by others, especially complex arguments, and this often leads to a tendency to talk more and listen less. The change is understandable in that listening is a task paced by the other person, whereas the pace of talking is under the speaker's control. The danger is that failure to listen may not only make one a bore but effectively close the mind to an important source of new ideas. It is in the fifties also that complaints of difficulty in learning and remembering become frequent, and it becomes important to apply the countermeasures designed to increase efficiency of learning that were outlined earlier. Not only must one give oneself time to learn but must recognize that many long-cherished ideas may thereby be put into disarray, and may have to remain so until they can be thought through again to an acceptable conclusion.

The fifties are the age at which most men have reached as far as they are going to, and at which those who have reached high usually have to bear the full weight of their responsibilities. Probably it is also now that the balance of intellectual agility and maturity of experience fits them best to do so, at any rate under conditions of reasonable stability.

Whether or not a man at this age consolidates his hold on his position and perhaps starts to advance still further depends very much upon two factors: first an understanding of how to conserve his energies, shedding unnecessary interests – but not too many so that he becomes narrow – and establishing labour-saving, and especially worry-saving, routines. The second factor is his attitude to what he has already attained. If he is content with it he is likely, as Parkinson (1958) recognized in his remarkably shrewd book *Parkinson's Law,* to do better than if he is disgruntled. The reason is probably not merely that a contented man is a pleasanter colleague and a more humane leader, but that the human brain has a limited capacity for work, so that any effort expended on watching others to see one is not outstripped or worrying about one's own position detracts from the effort available for one's main job.

The sixties

This decade brings two major changes. First, the shift from mental agility to experience as a basis for work performance and daily living becomes much more substantial. Often it means that to be successful a person must adopt the role of a sympathetic and constructive user of younger people's ideas and agile brains, acting as the conductor of an orchestra, the individual instruments of which he could not possibly play himself. Scientific knowledge of how to achieve this position is lacking, but we may perhaps surmise that if a person has taken the right turnings during the preceding years and kept up to date, he will have taken the measure of life and attained a degree of social skill and understanding which enable him to bring out the best in younger people under his charge and lead them to make more of themselves than they ever could without him. Doing so will demand effort, and will require self-discipline to avoid jealousy, but can yield a profound satisfaction.

Second, it is usually in the sixties that retirement from work takes place. Of the many changes of demand and circumstance that this brings, two seem especially important in the present context. First, for many *men* it brings a moment of truth: they have climbed their tree during working life, and now have to step down from it. Many are content to do so, glad to relinquish responsibilities and tasks which have been becoming increasingly onerous over the years. Some, however, bitterly resent the reduction of income usually involved and, even more, what they feel as a loss of status. Either attitude is likely to have effects beyond the individual himself: our attitude to ourselves tends to be reflected in our attitudes to others — we are never so generous-minded to others when we are pleased with ourselves, or so critical of them as when we know we have failed.

Contentment in retirement seems to depend less on economic or other circumstances than upon certain personality characteristics (Reichard *et al.*, 1962). Those who are kindly, patient, tolerant and unpretentious are happy. Those who are over-competitive or who look back with anger or regret live in states of chronic discontent. These personality characteristics seem not to be the product of retirement itself but have, in the main, been present in the individuals concerned during most of their lives. Earlier, however, they have not had free play because of the exigencies of work and of bringing up a family. It has been suggested that it is the freeing of older people from these exigencies that produces a tendency in many cultures for old men to become, on average, more passive as they abandon their active work roles of early and middle life, while women become, on average, more aggressive and domineering once the need for nurturing children has passed (Gutmann, 1977). One must wonder, however, whether the very universality of these sex differences does not imply that more fundamental biological factors also play a part.

The other important change that retirement brings is increased leisure. This, of course, gives opportunities to pursue hobbies and other interests which had to be set aside during working years, and allows more time for husband and wife to enjoy each other's company. Here, however, often lies a problem: the company of relatives and friends, and for many even of their spouses, is enjoyed only in small doses. We all have at least a few irritating habits which can be tolerated when they occur only in the early mornings, evenings and week-ends, but become unreasonably annoying when they are experienced all day and every day. The problem is especially acute for the houseproud wife: men tend on average to be less tidy than women, so that when a husband is around the house continually, the burden of having at frequent intervals to tidy the newspaper and straighten the cushions may quickly become intolerable.

Probably the main reason for this kind of difficulty is that human beings need variety. During the working years a man gets this in the continual alternation between work and home, and a woman gets it in bringing up her children. After retirement, every day and every hour of the day tend to be much more alike. In such conditions, horizons contract and attention comes to be focussed down onto small details that would otherwise be neglected. The lack of variety may be made worse by lack of money which would enable the monotony to be broken by excursions, shows, meals out and other changes of routine. Further, it tends to be cumulative in its effect so that, in time, listlessness and apathy can render people unwilling to take opportunities for variety when they occur. Lack of variety may be exacerbated by physical disabilities that make getting about difficult. Except in severe cases, however, the effects of these are usually less serious than those of sensory or mental disabilities: people seem able to compensate for and overcome physical handicaps to a remarkable extent, so long as their intellectual capacities remain.

Coping with problems of retirement seems to require a skilful mixture of load-shedding and load-retention. It is important to shed unnecessary loads such as a large house, excessive furniture and a big car. These are not only costly at a time when money may be short, but often impose burdens of responsibility and worry which are only fully recognized after they have been removed. Some tasks and interests need to be retained however, in order to preserve variety in life even if they are moderately demanding. Many retired people, if they can be humble enough, find satisfaction in part-time work either paid or voluntary. Others enjoy hobbies such as gardening with its variation between seasons of the year, or keeping pets or animals. These may indeed be profitable – for example fattening pigs for market. All these activities impose some discipline: things have to be done at set times. Many people recoil from this, yet man is constituted in such a way that, without effort, there is no real satisfaction. Retirement as a pleasurable time to do nothing or to follow one's whims is a myth: the ordinary minimal demands of living seldom allow it, and even if they did we should not enjoy it for long. However, the deep-seated belief that idleness is preferable to work, and the sagging of interest that seems to result from monotony, mean that people need to be strict with themselves, or have others be strict with them, if they are to achieve contentment. It may be noted that if they do push themselves to take an active part, they seem not only to be happier but also healthier than they would otherwise be (Kleemeier, 1951).

Many people think of the sixties as the decade in which responsibilities are shed, but it is clear that the task of achieving this successfully is as challenging and demanding of skill as any tackled earlier in life.

The seventies and beyond

For most people, the seventies and after are a period in which the problems of the sixties have given place to a settled pattern of living in retirement. For some, however, and an increasing number as the years pass, two further problems arise – dependency and loneliness. Understanding of both can be helped by applying to social situations the principles of motivation outlined earlier in this chapter. Consider two people in social contact. Each person observes the other's reactions and, in turn, reacts to them, in a continuous series of exchanges. If these exchanges yield a favourable cost–benefit ratio, we have the conditions for friendship: each will lower his cutoff point so that the tendency to act in response to the other will be increased and mutual exchanges will grow. If, on the other hand, the cost–benefit ratio is unfavourable, tendency to act will decrease, mutual contacts will be reduced and, if one party presses them, the other may make active efforts to prevent them: in short, hostility may develop (Welford, 1971, 1976).

Dependency arises when physical, medical or in some cases mental changes have taken place to an extent that a person is no longer able to cope with the normal demands of life without help from others. In other words, he is forced to adopt the strategy of supplementing his own efforts with those of others. The need for skill in handling this situation arises from the twofold result that dependency improves the cost–benefit ratio for the person concerned, but impairs it for those on whom he depends. The first of these results means that dependency can be highly satisfying, and many people seem to become addicted to it, enjoying the attention and feeling of power over others it brings. For instance, the improved geriatric care that became available in the late 1940s, which put many elderly, bedridden patients on their feet again, was often bitterly resented by them.

Ways of keeping the cost–benefit ratio as favourable as possible for those providing care and help are suggested by two factors important in preserving good human relationships. First, a dependent person seems usually to remain on good terms with those caring for him so long as he is reasonable in his demands, grateful for what is done and, perhaps most important, more interested in the donor, other people and matters of general concern than in himself, so that he is a better listener than talker and what he says is likely to be interesting. In these ways he will provide the lowest possible costs for the donor. Second, relationships tend to be better when a dependent person is cared for in appropriate special accommodation than in their own home by a relative or in a relative's home. The reason appears to be in part that at home the attention demanded of relatives, often involving both day and night care, imposes a cost they cannot bear for long without severe strain, whereas the staff of an institution are on duty for limited periods only and have the added benefit of wages or salary for what they do. In part also, natural feelings often make it easy to obtain care from relatives so that, in accordance with what was said earlier about the relationship between cost and value, it is not fully appreciated. For example, if an elderly widow has two children and lives with one of them, it is often the other for whom she has the greater regard: the child with whom she lives does too much for her too easily, and is therefore valued less than the other child whose cost–benefit ratio is less favourable.

Loneliness seems to occur when the feedback loop between a person and those around is broken, and is thus a state in which there is neither friendship nor hostility from others. Some loneliness is obviously likely to arise following the deaths of close friends and especially of a spouse, but the wounds caused by these losses are commonly assuaged with time even if they are never completely healed. The most serious problems of loneliness seem to occur when bereavement is coupled with a particular type of personality. The people in which they are typically found are not physically isolated from others, but are surrounded by relatives, neighbours, welfare workers and acquaintances. Their loneliness seems to arise because either the communications from these people are ignored, 'or because communications to others are not accepted. In either case, the circular relationship with people around is broken. The reason seems usually to be that the lonely individual is self-centered. He or she is thus not interested in most of the communications that come from others – the cost of listening to them is regarded as outweighing the benefit of doing so. At the same time, communications to others, couched, say, in terms of how clever the lonely person and his or her children are compared with others, has an adverse cost–benefit ratio for listeners. In short, such people are bores. They tend to become persistent seekers for attention, and may prefer even hostility from others to being ignored.

It is clear that seeking to help them by providing visitors, clubs and similar means of contact with others will have only a limited effect and not touch the hard core of the problem. What is needed is to overcome self-centredness and conceit. These, as we have noted, are often deep-seated, and the task is therefore difficult. The fundamental cure would seem to be, first, to ensure that their present behaviour is unrewarding and, second, by a mixture of training and psychiatric advice, to convince them of the causes of their loneliness and the benefits of improving their social skills. Such a cure is unlikely to be welcomed and may at first sight seem cruel, yet it appears to be the only way to relieve a condition that is undoubtedly distressing both for the individual concerned and for those around.

RECIPE FOR CONTENTMENT

What has been said in this chapter will have seemed depressing reading to many, yet a moment's reflection will reveal that it should not be so. It seems to be a fundamental biological characteristic, which has important survival value, that our main attention is given to what is painful, unpleasant and troublesome. An organism that dwelt exclusively, or even mainly, on what was comfortable or pleasant would not advance. The first essential for contentment at any age is, therefore, to recognize its problems and seek to cope with them, or even better to anticipate them and take appropriate preparatory action: as Maurice Chevalier once remarked, "Growing old is inevitable for all of us. The clever thing is to accept it and always plan your next move well in advance."

What can be done to give effect to this advice? As regards basic changes of capacity with age, the answer must be 'very little' because the extent to which various capacities change with age, and the rate at which they do so, is largely determined genetically. However, two lines of action are possible and worthwhile. First, many people's capacities are not fully developed so that, for example, regimens of exercise designed to maximize physical fitness have often been found to increase effective physical capacity. Second, some losses of capacity at later ages are not the result of true ageing processes but of disease or misuse earlier in life; for instance, hearing losses with age are greater than normal among orchestral players and those who work in very noisy factories, and are somewhat greater among town than among country dwellers.

Much more can be done to modify demands and strategies. As regards external, environmental demands, many of the problems of middle and early old age in industry could be greatly eased by the application of ergonomic principles (e.g. Griew, 1964) and appropriate methods of training. The same is true of the design of accommodation for old people and of equipment for the frail and handicapped. The largest scope undoubtedly lies, however, for ageing individuals to adopt strategies which reduce internally generated demands such as unrealistic aims and unnecessarily burdensome styles of living, and which maximize efficiency in dealing with the demands that remain, concentrating on pursuits within the range of existing capacities and exploiting the fruits of experience, being willing to make extra efforts on occasion, and ready to accept gratefully the help of others when necessary. Again it is important not only to deal with the present situation but to prepare for the future. Especially does it seem desirable to make some provision in earlier years to ensure adequate variety during retirement. For example, many people look forward to travelling when they retire, only to find when the time comes that the problems of passports, planes, luggage and lodging fill them with anxiety and make their tour a burden instead of a pleasure. They would have fared much better if they had learnt the techniques of dealing with these things earlier in life.

On the whole, it is probably fair to say that most people grow into a contented old age, coping with their problems more skilfully than either those concerned with the welfare of the aged or they themselves realize. If asked whether, if they could have their lives over again, they would have wished them to be different, many people might answer "Yes". If, however, they were asked whether they would like to go back to their earlier years *in all respects,* the honest answer would almost always be "No". Despite any difficulties and drawbacks that come with the years, there are important ways in which most people find each decade better than the one before. Those who yearn for lost youth are looking for an impossible best of both worlds, epitomised in the words of the song "I wish I were a little bit younger and know what I know now".

References

Belbin, E. (1958). Methods of training older workers. *Ergonomics,* **1,** 207
Belbin, E. and Downs, S. (1966). Teaching paired associates: the problem of age. *Occup. Psychol.,* **40,** 67

Belbin, E. and Shimmin, S. (1964). Training the middle aged for inspection work. *Occup. Psychol.*, **38,** 49

Belbin, R. M. (1953). Difficulties of older people in industry. *Occup. Psychol.*, **27,** 177

Belbin, R. M. (1965). *Training Methods for Older Workers.* (Paris: OECD)

Belbin, R. M. (1969). *The Discovery Method: an International Experiment in Retraining.* (Paris: OECD)

Birren, J. E. (1969). Age and decision strategies. In A. T. Welford and J. E. Birren. (Ed.). *Decision Making and Age.* pp. 23–36. (Basel: Karger)

Birren, J. E. and Schaie, K. W. (Eds.). (1977). *Handbook of the Psychology of Aging.* (New York: van Nostrand Reinhold)

Botwinick, J. (1977). Intellectual abilities. In J. E. Birren and K. W. Schaie. (Eds.). *Handbook of the Psychology of Aging.* pp. 580–605. (New York: van Nostrand Reinhold)

Foulds, G. A. and Raven, J. C. (1948). Normal changes in the mental abilities of adults as age advances. *J. Ment. Sci.* **94,** 133

Griew, S. (1964). *Job Redesign: the Applications of Biological Data on Aging to the Design of Equipment and the Organisation of Work* (Paris: OECD)

Gutmann, D. (1977). The cross-cultural perspective: notes toward a comparative psychology of aging. In J. E. Birren and K. W. Schaie. (Eds.). *Handbook of the Psychology of Aging.* pp. 302–326. (New York: van Nostrand Reinhold)

Heron, A. and Chown, S. (1967). *Age and Function.* (London: J. and A. Churchill)

Kay, H. (1951). Learning of a serial task by different age groups. *Quart. J. Exp. Psychol.*, **3,** 166

King, H. F. (1956). An attempt to use production data in the study of age and performance. *J. Gerontol.*, **11,** 410

Kleemeier, R. W. (1951). The effect of a work program on adjustment attitudes in an aged population. *J. Gerontol.*, **6,** 372

McFarland, R. A., Tune, G. S. and Welford, A. T. (1964). On the driving of automobiles by older people. *J. Gerontol.*, **19,** 190

Parkinson, C. N. (1958). *Parkinson's Law.* (London: John Murray)

Powell, M. (1973). Age and occupational change among coal-miners. *Occup. Psychol.*, **47,** 37

Reichard, S., Livson, F. and Petersen, P. G. (1962). *Aging and Personality.* (New York: John Wiley and Sons)

Richardson, I. M. (1953). Age and work: a study of 489 men in heavy industry. *Br. J. Indust. Med.*, **10,** 269

Road Traffic Board of South Australia. (1972). *The Points Demerit Scheme as an Indication of Declining Skill with Age*

Wackwitz, J. D. (1946). *Het Verband Tusschen Arbeidsprestatie en Leeftijd.* (Delft: Waltman)

Welford, A. T. (1956). Age and learning: theory and needed research. *Experientia,* Suppl. IV, 136

Welford, A. T. (1966). Industrial work suitable for older people: some British studies. *Gerontologist,* **6,** 4

Welford, A. T. (1971). *Christianity – A Psychologist's Translation.* (London: Hodder and Stoughton)

Welford, A. T. (1972). The future motivation of man. *Search,* **3,** 113

Welford, A. T. (1976). *Skilled Performance: Perceptual and Motor Skills.* (Glenview, Illinois: Scott Foresman)

Welford, A. T. (1977). Motor performance. In J. E. Birren and K. W. Schaie. (Eds.). *Handbook of the Psychology of Aging.* pp. 450–496. (New York: van Nostrand Reinhold)

Welford, A. T. (1978). Mental work load as a function of demand, capacity, strategy and skill. *Ergonomics,* **21,** 151

Welford, A. T. (1979). Perception, memory and motor performance in relation to age. Proceedings of *World Conference of Institut de la Vie, Vichy, 1977* (Oxford: Pergamon) (to be published)

Woodworth, R. S. (1958). *Dynamics of Behavior.* (New York: Henry Holt and Co.; London: Methuen)

von Wright, J. M. (1957). A note on the role of 'guidance' in learning. *Br. J. Psychol.* **48,** 133

6
Institutionalization: Hospitals and Prisons

P. SPURGEON and M. THOMSON

INTRODUCTION

The very use of the term 'institution' has almost come to represent a negative value or at least an expression of regret that the building and collection of individuals being referred to have come to exist in their present form. Since the initial work of Goffman (1961a) in which the damaging and demoralizing impact of long-term stay in mental hospitals was graphically described, many subsequent studies have followed and endorsed this negative orientation. This perspective has tended to influence research, especially action-oriented programmes; the emphasis is very much upon effects on the inmate/patient. It is interesting to consider the individual in more detail and to assess his strategies and abilities to cope with the pressures in many different ways and to varying degrees.

OBVIOUS GOALS

Prisons

One can look at the goals of the prison from three points of view – society, the inmates and the prison staff. Although the prison rules contain words to the effect that the object of imprisonment is to enable the inmate "to lead a good and useful life", it is not clear how this is to be done. Society may view the aims of the prison in terms of isolation from society, to stop current crime, punishment or revenge, deterrence or prevention of further crime, and rehabilitation or 'treatment', and individual members or groups of society may often have different goals in mind.

For the inmate the prison has no obvious goals which are consciously presented, and each individual's perceived goals will vary depending on his view of his 'criminality', varying from a need to be punished, efforts at rehabilitation with a need for help, or to avoid being touched at all by the institution and leave the prison unchanged.

The situation is rather more complex for the prison staff. They will, as individuals, reflect society's own views, but the aims of the prison are set out in the Prison Rules. However, the report on the regime for long-term prisoners (HMSO, 1968) acknowledged, for the first time in widely published print, that the aim of a long-term prison establishment is "humane containment". This is a tacit goal of many prisons incorporating the ideas that no-one escapes, the prison is run quietly, and inmates are kept as comfortable as possible within the accepted standards of current society. There is of course considerable attention paid to 'treatment', and many of the staff are highly committed to this as a goal, yet it is a secondary one to security and confinement in the final analysis. This is different from the situation found in hospitals, where 'treatment' is the goal for inmates and staff. In common with all institutions, prisons have less definable goals relating to employee satisfaction and working conditions; for example most staff are provided with free accommodation, or special allowances for 'prison conditions' and there are opportunities for training and specialization. As no prison could run without the tacit co-operation of the inmates, a basic level of support and 'inmate satisfaction' is also required. In summary, the main goals would appear to be:

Humane containment and isolation from society

Treatment and rehabilitation of inmates

Employee satisfaction

Maintenance or development of day-to-day acceptance of prison routine.

Hospitals

Institutions like hospitals exist to meet particular goals defined by society as appropriate and necessary. Even during periods of relative economic success there are limitations upon the resources available to any single institution. There would probably be little dispute with the argument that a hospital must mobilize its resources in pursuit of what might be termed its instrumental goals (treating patients, maintaining employee commitment). However, it is perhaps the over-zealous pursuit of these laudable objectives that results in a failure to meet satisfactorily other more diffuse goals such as the demands and needs represented by individual patients within the hospital. The patient's need for emotional support and psychological gratifications are the areas in which institutions have found most difficulty in meeting demand. The absence of such support represents not only a social loss, it is becoming increasingly recognized that there may be negative implications for the therapeutic and rehabilitation work of hospitals. The point is well made by Rudd (1974) in describing some of the difficulties institutional life may create. "The violent changes of living pattern which people undergo on entering hospital, even on a short-term basis, is seldom appreciated. The normal routine, which is at least under partial control of the individual is suddenly interrupted. The character and quality of his food is no longer subject to choice; the daily timetable is at another's disposal and even the choice of diversion, such as radio and television is dictated by others. From being an active agent, the patient suddenly becomes a passive one, operated upon instead of operating. He is often denied communication and subject for long hours of the day to the whims of others. In short-term situations acute boredom results while in circumstances where a prolonged stay is necessary, mental stagnation develops." The lack of choice, of privacy and of the challenge in deciding one's personal affairs are other important consequences noted by Rudd. This view is echoed by comments of patients, for, as Phillips (1975) seems to be saying, the collective call of patients to the medical staff is that "you know and understand all the rules and regulations, we don't, please give us time and help us to adjust".

In summary then the goals of the hospital system may be simply identified as the most effective, economic treatment of patients. There is, however, the less readily recognizable goal of providing emotional support for the patient. It is a requirement receiving increased attention as it is appreciated that ignoring this demand may impair the fulfilment of the primary goal.

SIZE OF THE FIELD

Prisons

The White Paper, *People in Prisons* (HMSO, 1969), gives a figure of approximately 35 000 individuals in prison. Of that number about 1 in 20 were serving sentences of 10 years or over, and approximately 7500 individuals were serving sentences of 3 years or over. Following the Criminal Justice Act of 1967 there was an increase in the number of life sentences, and also in fixed sentences of 14 years and over. Long sentences increased also as a result of the abolition of capital punishment. In 1968 there were some 15 000 staff within the prison system and projections for the future indicate an increase in both inmate and staff numbers. Within the framework of an increase in the number of establishments dealing with long-term prisoners is the need to look at the implications of imprisonment for human skills in the widest sense. Cohen and Taylor (1972) draw attention to the very real fear amongst inmates themselves of the personality, physical and cognitive deterioration as a result of their long prison terms.

Hospitals

The hospital population is enormous and extremely varied. In 1976 there were almost 600 acute hospitals and these were involved with approximately two and a half million patients. However, the average length of stay was comparatively short, 9.56 days. In contrast the psychiatric–mental handicap hospitals were concerned with approximately 150 000 patients with the average length of stay varying from 209.60 days in hospitals treating mental illness (including children) to 961.53 days in hospitals dealing with severe adult handicap.

It is clear that quite different situations exist within the range of hospital types and the effects upon the patient should not be generalized across hospitals without regard to these differences.

THE INSTITUTION IMPOSING ITS DEMANDS

Prisons

The prison may be viewed as a system in two ways, firstly simply as a series of routines or actions which are performed on the inmate, and secondly as a more complex social or institutional system.

A good example of the former is the induction procedure for inmates. In prisons this takes the form of a reduction in individual identity; inmates are allocated numbers, and subsequently are formally addressed by these rather than by name. Prison clothes are issued, and most personal belongings are removed, and various depersonalizing processes take place. Cohen and Taylor (1972) graphically describe the 'dehumanizing' routine.

Goffman (1961b) has introduced the concept of a total institution which he describes as follows: "First, all aspects of life are conducted in the same place and under the same single authority. Second, each phase of the members' daily activity is carried on in the immediate company of a large number of others, all of whom are treated alike and required to do the same thing together. Third, all phases of the day's activities are tightly scheduled, with one activity leading at a pre-arranged time to the next, and the whole sequence of activities being imposed from above through a system of explicit formal rulings and by a body of officials. Finally the contents of the various enforced activities are brought together as part of a single overall rational plan purposely designed to fulfil the official aims of the institutions."

This description fits the prison situation closely, where there is an authoritarian structure based on specific rules, and little communication with the outside world. Another approach is the consideration of the prison as an organization. Katz and Kahn (1966) describe organizations as examples of open systems which as such have an output (product or outcome) not necessarily identical with the individual purposes of group members. Of the system functions, some are intrinsic (immediate and direct outcomes), and some extrinsic (outcomes affecting other systems). Intrinsic functions of a prison appear to be humane containment of offenders, i.e. security, keeping people in gaol. Extrinsic functions would be rehabilitation and labour. Under a typology of organizations Katz and Kahn describe prison as a political organization, although having a socialization or normative function. From Etzioni's (1961) typology of organizations (coercive, rational, legal and normative), the prison system is obviously a coercive authority, with the implication that the involvement of its members is alienative, i.e. the individual is not psychologically involved, but coerced to remain a member – although as will be seen from the adaptations of inmates, some do become psychologically involved.

In general coercive types of organization tend to reduce performance in industrial terms to the minimum. Although it is dangerous to generalize too readily from industrial organizations to prisons one can draw parallels if one defines 'productivity' in terms of accepting the prison goals for (a) humane containment ('doing one's bird quietly') and (b) rehabilitative attempts. Table 6.1 presents Katz and Kahn's model for the activation of legal compliance, with additional comments relating to prisons in brackets.

Table 6.1 Conditions affecting the activation of legal compliance

Objective conditions	Mediated by psychological variables	Outcome
1. Use of appropriate symbols of authority (prison staff)	Recognition and acceptance of symbols	Produces minimally acceptable quantity of work (viz. situational withdrawal, intransigence of prison goals)
2. Clarity of legal norms and requirements (clear-cut rules and regulations)	Lack of subjective ambiguity permitting wishful interpretations	Can reduce absenteeism (not applicable directly, perhaps dependence).
3. Use of specific penalties (e.g. loss of of remissions, further sentence)	Individual expectations of being caught	May increase turnover (inmates unable to leave, may lead to development of alternative system – inmate sub-culture)
4. Expulsions of non-conformers (solitary confinement)	Desire to stay within system: dependence on system as way of life	Affects innovative and other behaviour beyond call of duty (viz. colonization and conversion)

Hospitals

Nearly all patients when interviewed say that they are very grateful for the treatment received and appreciate the efforts of the nursing and medical staff. Nonetheless the negative viewpoint is consistently present although perhaps seen as something the patient must endure.

The first major impact of the system in re-structuring the patient's life style is the admission procedure. If the patient is able, form filling represents the first initiation ceremony and although perhaps friendly it will also be impersonal. Once in the ward, at least for the ordinary patient, his bed, surroundings and room-mates are chosen for him. His possessions and clothes are taken, ostensibly for safe keeping, but they also inform that patient that he has now left his previous lifestyle behind and faces something new, if temporarily. Finally, once fully installed, the trappings used to establish his identity outside have disappeared and part of his individual character is lost. Although not a stated aim of the procedure, this aspect of the system would appear to be creating a psychological dependency. As Miller and Gwynne (1972) point out, many institutions are organized such that the various sub-processes operating within create a continual and increasing dependence by removing the patient's capacity or confidence to perform tasks on his own. They felt there were few, if any, organizational activities geared to promoting independence behaviour. Similarly, Derdiarian and Clough (1976) found dependence behaviour to increase during the hospitalization period. They again suggest that a valuable modification in organizational activities would be to develop procedures that positively encouraged more independent behaviour. They argue that such a change would be of value in rehabilitating patients to life outside.

The transition from a free agent to a hospital patient is continued and reinforced by a process that might be seen as a condensed socialization into a new environment. The routines and procedures play a large part in structuring the new environment. The success of this process in producing patients compatible with the hospital's image will vary from patients who are fully socialized and acquire both the values and behaviours seen by the staff as appropriate to hospital life, through patients who retain their own values but behave in an acceptable way, to patients who acquire neither and are often classified as 'difficult'. Much of the conflict between staff and patients can be viewed in terms of differential socialization. The staff have undergone a long and fairly directed socialization into the practice of medical and nursing knowledge and skills. A failure to recognize that patients do not have this perspective on hospital routine may account for friction between staff and patients, especially when patients are seen as demanding.

The term socialization is an important one in terms of the view of the patient suggested here. Socialization implies that a learning process is operating and that the patient is learning about his new temporary world and the appropriate behaviours in this new environment. When one considers the severity of the change imposed on the patient by the hospital system it is not surprising that he needs to adjust and adapt to his new setting. During a period of considerable stress in his life he finds that the people and objects familiar to him have disappeared and the markings of his individuality have been removed. Previous behaviours are no longer appropriate and he must acquire the skills that will enable him to cope with his new situation.

ADAPTATION OF INMATES

Prisons

One of the early concepts of 'social' reactions is that of 'prisonization' (Clemmer, 1958). This may be defined as 'a continuous and systematic destruction of psyche in consequence of the experience of imprisonment and the adoption of new attitudes and ways of behaving which are not only unsuited to life in the outside world, but which frequently make it impossible for the individual to act successfully in any normal social role'.

This is seen as a cumulative process of deterioration, the autonomy, identity, and responsibility of the individual being affected. It is all the more pronounced and serious in individuals who may already be inadequate or pathological. The degree of prisonization is affected by the number of times a person has been in prison, by how much contact he maintains with the outside world, by how far he accepts the codes and dogmas of the prison sub-culture and by the prisoners' relationships within the prison. In relation to this a typology of reaction to prison has been suggested. While there is bound to be some over-generalization and overlap, it may be useful to go through the categories.

(1) *Conformity* – the inmate accepts, initially, the objective or goals of the institution, and recognizes that he has done wrong and must be punished for his own good, and society's. He thus recognizes the legitimacy of the regime and conforms to its demands. It is suggested that few people adapt like this, as it might involve abandoning their own self-concept. Conformity is therefore only superficial, and co-operation may only be to preserve order and stability, rather than sharing the values of the system.

(2) *Innovation* – the inmate may accept the official objectives but rejects the institutional means to attain them. He may produce ideas about how the prison should be changed.

(3) *Ritualism* – in this case although the inmate has rejected socially approved goals, he behaves in a strictly conforming manner, changing to the safe routines and norms of the institution and goes with the system. This may be divided into ritualism of dependence, where initiative is lost, and the

individual may become dependent on the system, feeling secure only in prison, and secondly, ritualism of identification, consisting of ambivalent attitudes, for example a person may take a responsible job and look down on other inmates.

(4) *Retreatism* – the inmate rejects both goals and the means to attain them, 'in' society, but not 'of' it. It is suggested that this is fairly rare, but may occur in extreme institutionalization, or mental illness. The individual may refuse work, and becomes withdrawn or passive; long termers may be especially prone to this. The lack of privacy in prison may prevent some people completely withdrawing, but for others, it may be the last straw for breakdown or suicide.

(5) *Rebellion* – here the individual seeks to overturn the existing structure of goals and means, and substitute an alternative. In these cases there is generally no social cohesiveness or purpose, as authority reasserts itself, and you have an individual against the system. Thus an irrational contest may exist between the individual and authority. More severe punishment may only serve to increase his status, and he may often be a scapegoat.

(6) *Manipulation* – here the behaviour is more rational than the rebels, the individual attempting to outwit rather than conflict with the institution. The means by which he does this are not necessarily illicit and the goals set up are not necessarily totally unacceptable to the system. This individual is often knowledgeable about prison matters and may have power from his status inside or outside the prison or from money.

Apart from these reactions to prison, other types of adjustment may take place as a person tries to retain his individuality, such as the solution of escape, although this may be due to outside pressures. Failure to adjust and retain one's individuality may lead to prisonized participation – a deepening of criminality, trafficking, fiddling etc. – or prisonized withdrawal where people remain in their cells and become isolates.

A further concept is Barton's (1966) idea of institutional neurosis. This is characterized by lack of interest in events which are not immediately personal, by a lack of initiative, submissiveness, lack of interest and inability to plan for the future, deterioration of personal habits, and a general resignation.

The factors producing this kind of response are in the general environment and may be summarized as:

(1) *Loss of contact with the outside world* – this includes such things as locked doors, retention in custody, few letters and few visits.

(2) *Enforced idleness* – this may be the result of life being ordered and structured for the inmate, signs of activity and/or initiative often being construed as aggressive or suspicious, and a lack of worthwhile things to do. He cannot make his own decisions.

(3) *'Bossiness' of staff* – produced by an authoritarian regime (not only

individuals) with the presence of rules and regulations governing almost anything. He is ordered about.

(4) *Loss of friends, possessions and personal events* – visits tail off, the inmate is excluded from things like family birthdays, weddings etc. There are restrictions on personal possessions, he can't decide his own entertainments and may feel generally cut off from his own life.

(5) *Drugs* – too many and continuous sedatives and tranquilisers.

(6) *'Ward' atmosphere* – this applies to the general environment which may be rather drab and uninteresting, dirty or smelly.

(7) *Loss of prospects outside the institution* – this includes such things as finding a place to live, and getting a job. The longer one is inside, the more difficult it becomes finding a job and also adjusting to outside conditions generally. The loss of friends and a fear of future loneliness is also allied to this.

Goffman (1961b) describes what he calls secondary adjustments to a total institution, enabling the inmate to keep some control over his own life by obtaining forbidden satisfactions or permitted ones by forbidden means. A general adaption is the development of an institutional sub-culture or mores, where a fraternalization process gives rise to mutual support, slang and social stratification based on illicit commodities and action. More specific adaptions are as follows:

(1) *Situational withdrawal.* Here the inmate withdraws attention from all events except those immediately surrounding him. This 'prison psychosis' results in isolation, and may build up an illusory system of private persecution, yet omnipotent power within his own cell which he will try not to leave (McCleery, 1961).

(2) *Intransigence.* The inmate may refuse to co-operate with staff, involving a deep personal commitment and his morale. This often implies paradoxical attention by the organization, and may result inattempts to 'break' the individual by the institution (Schein, 1956). This is often a temporary stand or phase of reaction however.

(3) *Colonization.* A stable existence based on the procurement of the maximum satisfaction provided by the institution is built up. This involves comparisons of the outside world in a negative way – the institution being a haven from troubles and anxieties – a sort of 'home from home'. Continual recidivism has been related to similar constructs used by inmates. The 'old lag' often deliberately commits an institutional offence to prevent discharge, and also incidentally sustains the counter-moves of the solidarity amongst inmates.

(4) *Conversion.* The individual may try to act out the the institutions view of a perfect inmate. This may take the form of becoming a 'trustee' and even adopting the style and mannerisms of the staff.

These are obviously broad categories, and will involve some overlap; the effect on the inmate by the institution seems to be a generalized type of adaption or behaviour.

It has been pointed out by Garrity (1961) that these general adaptive behaviours will depend on individuals' previous personality, and using Schrag's typology of inmate social norms he demonstrated different levels of prisonization. Schrag described five social types which comprised the basic distinctions inmates made among themselves: the 'right guy', 'outlaw', 'politician', 'square John', and 'ding'. The 'right guy' is an anti-social offender, stable and oriented to crime, criminals and inmates. The 'outlaw' is an asocial offender, undisciplined, bound by no outside constraints. The 'politician' is the confidence man, a sophisticated pseudosocial type of offender, the 'square John' is prosocial, oriented to society and the prison administration, and without a criminal self-conception. The 'ding' category includes socially shunned offenders, the neurotic, psychotic, mentally retarded and the 'rapo' (a non-violent sex offender). Garrity summarizes: "Since social control is greater within the 'right guy' category, prisonization also should be most rapid there. The antisocial attitudes and values, criminal commitments, etc. which are characteristic of a 'right guy' further contribute to the ease with which a 'right guy' can conform to the inmate code. Although the 'politician' might be expected to become prisonized relatively rapidly, his ambivalent position between inmate and administrative social structures prevents him from doing so. The position of the 'square John' in the inmate social order is such that prisonization can only occur very slowly, and never beyond the limits of simple necessity. Similarly, the 'outlaw' is an isolate and for that reason he should be only slightly prisonized, despite the fact that his parole violation rates are high."

Hospitals

It is not surprising in view of the function of hospitals that patients should be subject to varying degrees of stress. Those events seen as stress-inducing by patients have been studied and documented by Volicer (1973, 1974). It is interesting to note that apart from the expected apprehensions about physical pain there are a number of less tangible expressions of patient anxiety such as inadequate explanation of treatment, change in amount of independent behaviour and change in awareness of world or local events. Kornfield (1972) has pointed to the continuing sophistication of technical equipment now available in the treatment of patients as an additional force dividing the medical staff from the patient. Although the medical staff may well have adjusted and indeed become immune to working in a highly technological environment, it may well be very stressful to the patient. Also as he (the patient) is less likely to understand the process at work the possibility of effective communication between hospital staff and patient is further diminished. Kleeman *et al.* (1976) demonstrated how important the physical aspects of the environment can be in terms of patient behaviour. As a result of various architectural and structural changes they were able to report a significant increase in the amount of interaction taking place in a ward of long-term mental hospital patients.

This is a relatively new conception of the patient's position and one which has been subject to very little empirical enquiry. However, it is a construction that is gaining ground. Levitt (1974, 1975) provides a good example of how this approach may be utilized in understanding patient behaviour. The patient must initially perceive his illness as being sufficiently serious to warrant seeking professional medical help and agreeing to become an in-patient. In accepting his illness and right to treatment he must also accept a new set of obligations. The patient must conform to the routines and systems operating within the hospital, and co-operate in treatments and procedures. It is unlikely that he will refuse as patient strikes are unknown. Nonetheless compared with his previous life it is a considerable undertaking. He has surrendered control of his body and related functions, lost autonomy and effective decision making about himself. He is consequently likely to feel increasingly anxious and thus the first aim of his coping behaviour will be to cope with this anxiety. An initial mechanism available to the patient is to become ego-centric and constricted in interest. He co-operates readily with the treatments and procedures in order to reduce the conflict that may be experienced in potentially unpleasant or frightening situations. Levitt argues that it should not be seen as a simple distortion of events but "an altered perception of experience that permits tolerable and positive emotions to be felt in situations that might otherwise be quite demoralizing". The preservation of self-esteem may be seen as an outcome of an efficient and smooth transition from person to patient and this in turn may well be a significant factor in the patient's recovery. It is unlikely however that these aspects of human relationships will appear as objectives of the National Health system. There are perhaps two approaches to tackling the problem. The first is to increase the sytem's awareness of the issue and provide directed training for the staff involved. The second is to consider the patient as acquiring strategies for optimally maintaining his own effectiveness within the system.

PSYCHOLOGICAL REACTIONS

Prisons

Cohen and Taylor (1972) draw attention to the very real fear amongst inmates that they are deteriorating psychologically and physiologically during their sentence. They also argue that long-term inmates are sensorily deprived and might be expected to produce similar effects to sensory deprivation. There have been, however, few studies on specific skills and other variables during long-term imprisonment. Studies in concentration camps during World War II (e.g. Krol *et al.*, 1967) and on long-term hospitalization (e.g. Bernstein *et al.*, 1968) show significantly lower performances on intelligence tests, e.g. WAIS, as well as impairment of social judgements. This, coupled with Hebb's (1958) demonstration of deprivation 'raising susceptibility to propaganda, provides a psychological rationale for the social conformity and withdrawal.

Bannister *et al.* (1973) administered a wide range of cognitive tests, and also undertook a follow-up study of released men and 'detainees', to control for the effects of imprisonment versus a possible individual difference resulting from the overall characteristics of offenders. The sample was based on men serving sentences of 10 years or more, and controlled for the total number of previous sentence lengths. There was no general intellectual deterioration based on the WAIS scores, but there was a reduction in performance tests and on tests of perceptual motor speed. There was, however, no clear-cut relationship between length of time served, and the above deterioration. In general they conclude that there are some similarities, particularly the retention of 'verbal' skills and the reduction of 'performance' skills, between the effects of long-term imprisonment and the correlates of the aging process. This perceptual-motor deficit was shown to be the result of imprisonment, although no theoretical rationale was postulated.

The previous sections on institutionalization and social reactions suggest that one might expect personality variables to be affected (viz. apathy, anxiety). There has been considerable work on the personality characteristics of prisoners, notably Trasler (1962), Eysenck (1964), Eysenck and Eysenck (1971), suggesting that they show lower scores on introversion and higher on extroversion, which have been related to social learning and conditioning. There is also evidence (Caine *et al.*, 1967) for higher scores on hostility measures. With this background in mind Heskins *et al.* (1973) attempted to examine the effects of long-term imprisonment on personality variables. They found that there was an increase in hostility, particularly directed towards the self, and also a trend of declining extroversion (increasing introversion), but no clear-cut differences on the other measures which could be defined as resulting from the effects of imprisonment. For example the 'releases' scored higher on the Sixteen Personality Factor Questionnaire C (16 PF – emotional maturity) than the 'detainees', suggesting a possible factor in differential parole decisions.

The increase in intropunitive hostility (guilt, self-criticism), as opposed to paranoid hostility and criticism of others, suggest the inmate is introjecting his social rejection into self-rejection during long-term imprisonment. The extroversion results are more difficult to interpret, possibly suggesting a similar 'inward-looking' trend, or an increase in 'conditionability'. However, the results showed no evidence of initially higher extroversion or impulsivity scores for this group compared to the normal population. There is little empirical evidence on attitudes. Watt and Maher (1958) found no firm evidence for anti-authority attitudes, and Hulin and Maher (1959) reported that increasing lengths of imprisonment resulted in increased hostile reactions towards authority. Heskins *et al.* (1973, 1974) found a decline, as well as low evaluation, scores for 'myself' showing a marked decline, as well as low opinions for the concept 'prisoners'. This supports some of the sociological effects, and was also interpreted as an increasing identification with fellow inmates during imprisonment. There was also a consistent decrease for the concept 'work' suggesting a deterioration of attitudes towards work within the institutions. A further decrease in scores for the concept 'father'. One possible interpretation could be the lack of contact between inmates and their families, and the deterioration of external relationships. However, there was no deterioration of attitude towards prison officers, law, police etc. (although these were initially low), suggesting that the prison 'culture' was having little effect on these variables.

A longitudinal study was also carried out on the same sample of men who were still in prison after an average of 19.07 months (Bolton *et al.*, 1976), and compared them with a similar group of non-prisoners. Here the results were in contrast to the above, with no decrease in intellectual functions, and a *reduction* in hostility. To quote the authors: "In summary, the results of the longitudinal analysis offer little support for the idea that long-term imprisonment is associated with psychological deterioration, as assessed by a large battery of psychometric tests. Intelligence remains intact and hostility declines over the test–retest period. These results may be due to changes in prison atmosphere between first and second testing, but the fact that it is those men who show an increase in emotional maturity over the test–retest period who also show a reduction in hostility suggests that im- prisonment itself may sometimes be associated with beneficial effects which are rarely, if ever, discussed. The most consistent trend observed in the second cross-sectional analysis was a decline in emotional maturity with increasing mean lengths of total imprisonment. This result is interpreted as arising in large part from the selection for parole of the emotially mature prisoner."

Hospitals

Hospitals are increasingly sensitive to the attitudes of their patients and as the review by Ley (1972) indicates patient complaints are well researched and documented. Despite this the complaints tend to be fairly consistent and related to specific areas. Furthermore, patients grateful for the treatment received tend to structure their comments in terms of how the hospital stay might have been improved. It is Levitt's (1975) contention that this underlying good humour and tolerance is in fact a sophisticated cognitive structure to avoid such uncomfortable feelings as anxiety, fear or depression. One or two examples from her survey data may serve to make the point. One patient had been told little about his condition or treatment but by overhearing medical staff discussing his case he was able to get a picture of his situation. As a response to a question about adequate information it might seem more reasonable to suggest that proper information had not been given and that he had acquired details in a haphazard and piece-meal fashion. The fact that he did not say this suggested that he had settled into his passive and compliant patient role. It is unlikely that he would have found it satisfactory to acquire information about a railway timetable in the same incidental manner. Patients who are unable to restructure their view of things in such a way are much more likely to find their hospital story a stressful and upsetting experience. Similarly the signing of the consent form provoked far less reaction from the patients seen by Levitt than the significance of the document warrants. It is in fact one of the few, perhaps only, times at which the patient finally acknowledges that he has handed over control of crucial decisions about himself to others. Very few patients actually read the form as this might have been interpreted as questioning the medical staff's competence or right and may have been an awkward confrontation. The almost total compliance involved in this behaviour is further evidence of adaption to a passive coping strategy.

Perhaps it is worth considering at this point if a rather more general psychological model can encompass this form of behaviour. As part of a general debate around Festinger's (1957) model of Cognitive Dissonance, a paper by Bem (1967) attempted to supply the motivational aspect apparently lacking in Festinger's original proposition. The basic notion in Bem's model is that subjects in experiments are concerned to present to the experimenter and other subjects a consistent and stable view of themselves. In dissonance situations where the subject is confronted with his own behaviour appearing inconsistent with his expressed views he is able to preserve his self-image as a sensible and stable individual by altering his views such that they are consonant with his behaviour. Now the hospital patient is confronted with situations which may well be undignified, embarrassing and threatening to his self-esteem. On the other hand he has agreed to be treated and thus to be difficult and troublesome would be inconsistent with his stated view that he wishes to receive the correct treatment and be cured. Thus he can adopt a passive and compliant strategy, accepting the more onerous features of his treatment and presenting to the world an image of an individual who is sensible and ready to adjust to difficult circumstances.

The communication pattern between staff and patients poses a critical feature of the adjustment process. It is perhaps the most consistent criticism voiced by patients that they are not given sufficient information to understand the details of their condition and treatment. There are a number of pressures that lead to this situation. Staff may be reluctant and unwilling to provide too much detail as it is perceived as slightly threatening to their position of control and proxy decision making. As Skipper and Leonard

(1965) argue it is a form of self-defence on the part of the staff and protects them from potential criticisms of their actions. This non-communicative role is further strengthened by the implicit collusion between staff and patients that questioning and seeking information is at the initiative of the patient alone. Thus, at a time in his life when an individual is most exposed and vulnerable, he can hardly be expected to assert himself in the face of a new and high status work group; it is not surprising that patients opt for the compliant role and accept the cloak of mystery. In very few other areas of life would such acceptance be seen as appropriate. Perhaps for just this reason individuals who come from relatively authoritative positions find the transition to the patient role most difficult.

The hospital system itself is not the only agent involved in instructing the patient about his new environment. Rosengren and Leftomn (1969) point out that a hospital like any other group develops its own sub-culture and the informal leadership provided by other patients is a powerful force in changing the patients' behaviour. There is a difference here between long-term and short-term hospital situations. In the former the pattern of group life will be very clear and detailed, affecting virtually all aspects of the patient's life, while the latter is inducted into an acceptable role but one which will have relatively limited affects. The power of group pressures are very great in such circumstances as the patient is in need of support and comradeship. It is likely that the cultural values of the group will be compatible with those of the medical staff, once more pressure is upon the patient to conform and not to disturb the status quo of hospital life.

THE UNSUCCESSFUL/SUCCESSFUL INMATE

Prisons

The various adaptions/reactions to institutionalization as outlined above may be broadly fitted into those which are maladaptive and those which are adaptive. However, these will depend very much on the 'successfulness' in terms of the institution or the inmate. The institution may define the successful inmate as one who 'causes no trouble', conforms quietly and doesn't upset the system or escape, and who is 'rehabilitated' in the sense that he is less criminally inclined and less likely to commit a further offence. The situation is more complex for the inmate, he may be 'successful' if he retains his individuality and does not deteriorate physically or psychologically. This often will not imply conformity, and a further complication is that some inmates may wish to 'retain their criminality', whereas others may wish to be 'changed for the better'. With these points in mind a summary table (Table 6.2) is presented incorporating the various adaptations. Some of these are new skills which are learnt during the sentence, others involve a loss of previously held skills. These are presented in the inmates' and the institutions' terms. Those seen as 'successful' or 'unsuccessful' by both are in both columns.

Table 6.2 Adaptations of 'successful' and 'unsuccessful' prison inmates

	Successful	Unsuccessful
Institution (assuming humane containment goal)	Colonization Conversion Conformity Ritualism No deterioration in attitudes towards authority	Situational withdrawal Intransigence Innovation Retreatism Rebellion Manipulation
Institution (assuming rehabilitative goal)	No deterioration of intelligence Reduction of hostility and gains in emotional maturity for some individuals	Colonization. Perceptual–motor deficits. Increase in self-directed hostility Increase in negative reactions to work Decline in emotional maturity in some men Increase in negative attitudes to family 'Aging' effects of long-term imprisonment
Inmate (assuming retention of individuality and self)	Intransigence Innovation Rebellion Manipulations No deterioration of intelligence	Situational withdrawal Colonization Conformity Ritualism Retreatism Perceptual–motor deficits Increase in self-directed hostility Decline in emotional maturity 'Aging' effects
Inmate (assuming desire to be 'rehabilitated')	No deterioration of intelligence Increase in emotional maturity Reduction of overall hostility	Colonization Intransigence Innovation Rebellion Manipulation Negative attitudes to world and family 'Aging' effects

Bearing in mind some of the more equivocal results of the studies on psychological variables not in the above, there are broad agreements when both inmate and institution have rehabilitative goals. Here the successful inmate is one who avoids deterioration of psychological functioning, develops an increased emotional maturity and whose attitude towards authority does not interfere with his long-term aims in rejoining a society with rules and laws. A certain level of co-operation and conformity within the prison setting is required, in the sense that a rejection of the institutional goals would be counter-productive, as would complete subjugation of personality. A balance is required, and the successful inmate is one who neither overdoes his personal individualism, in the sense that he does not fit into the day-to day regime, nor develops increasingly negative attitudes to authority, work and family, nor loses his individuality by conforming totally and perhaps deteriorating in self-esteem and cognitive skills, becoming inadequate in terms of returning to the outside world.

However, it is where the institutional goals are geared to containment that serious conflicts arise. Here 'success' and 'failure' are almost diametrically opposed. For the institution the successful inmate is the one who 'knuckles under' and conforms, even to the level of becoming depersonalized and inadequate, whereas to the inmate success is a retention of his previous self, by conflict with authority and even an increase in hostility or 'deepening' of criminality. In summary overall success and failure in the inmate's terms is the difficult balance between self preservation, retention of previously learnt skills and avoiding conflict in the prison on the one hand and acceptance of rehabilitative goals with consequent modification of attitudes towards un-acceptable behaviour (in society's terms) on the other.

Hospitals

Some parallels may be drawn here with the work of Cohen and Taylor (1972) on the effects of time in prison. A view frequently expressed by hospital patients is that there is not enough to occupy their thoughts, not enough activities to provide the link between the infrequent medical procedures. In essence they suggest that time passes very slowly, and it is surprising how fundamental and critical the passage of time can become when we are not occupied. In normal life the conglomeration of people, events and activities lead us to take the concept of time passing for granted. For the long-term patient, especially, the relatively infrequent events provide little structure for this time concept. The proliferation of time checks available (radio, television and the millions of phone calls made simply to establish the correct time) are evidence of the importance attached to the concept in society. The hospital patient needs to adapt his ordering of the world to his new routine. Time is relative and the patient who fails to establish an alternative time perspective is more liable to experience boredom and depression.

A related concept is that of motivation. Psychologists have struggled with the exact nature of motives, the distinction between primary and secondary desires being rather hazy. However, there is some consensus that motives may be seen as hypothetical constructs that help us to organize and structure our daily lives. For the hospital patient – and again the problem is exaggerated for the long-term patient – he may have difficulty in setting intermediate goals that provide some structure to his life. The overriding goal and desire to recover may not be enough to give pattern to day-to-day activities. If it exists as the sole aim it may lead to a neurotic and obsessive concern with treatments and details of the illness. The patient able to adopt strategies that provide realistic and meaningful goals may well find the rehabilitation process easier. This is perhaps part of what Berger *et al.* (1974) describe as an individual's lifeplan which represents a total construction of time, motives and events. Most of us have sets of events, people or activities that provide a context for our life development. This may be at a limited level of consciousness and may only be considered intermittently in the whirl of daily life. The hospital patient may have a lot of time to consider but relatively little daily activity that can fit into any life plan. The long-term patient is likely to experience this loss and feeling of alienation more than short-stay patients.

Finally, it is relevant to consider whether the concept of the 'good' or 'bad' patient is a meaningful one. We have seen that there are various pressures within the system that lead the patient to behave in certain ways. It is not surprising that the view of patients is very firmly that the 'good' patient from the staff's viewpoint is passive and compliant. It has also been shown that the strategies adopted by patients in response to system pressure tend to reinforce this view of patients. However, especially in the work of Rudd and of Levitt we have seen that this staff–patient relationship may not be entirely satisfactory. The patient certainly has strategies to cope with life in hospital but a patient who is questioning may be viewed as demanding and therefore described as having not fully adjusted to the system. Perhaps the adjustment must be seen in two distinct aspects. The first is directly the responsibility of the patient and is in terms of how he cognitively structures his new environment in order to preserve as many as possible of his facilities for decision-making or self-esteem. The second is more of a compromise between system and patient where the two move toward a rather more active patient (both in terms of physical activities and seeking information about themselves) and a more responsive system actively seeking to meet the human relationship needs of its patients.

DISCUSSION

It may be seen from the previous discussion that the two institutions examined have a number of parallel processes at work within their day-to-day activities. As they exist for very different reasons one can only surmise that the overlap and commonality stems from the operation of a large institution rather than the similar purposes of the institutions.

Thus a prerequisite for any organization in the light of the influences identified is that it must be clear not only about the goals being pursued but also and perhaps even more critically the means to achieve these ends. The majority of the less favourable influences stem from sub-system activities and it is extremely hard to recognize the repercussions when these are only related to overall goals. Although there is a gradual increase in awareness of the influence of various processes it is easy to appreciate why the staff involved do not readily recognize what is happening. In situations of staff shortage and pressure it is very difficult to step outside one's daily task and assess the longer term impact of the system or one's own behaviour upon a patient or inmate.

The development of more directed and purposeful activities would be a reasonable recommendation but more fundamentally there is the need for staff to recognize and understand the situation. Coupled with this is the need for a willingness to assess the source of present influences and to adopt policies and routines appropriately.

References

Bannister, P. A., Smith, F. V., Heskins, K. J. and Bolton, N. (1973). Psychological correlates of long-term imprisonment; 1. Cognitive variables. *Br. J. Criminol.*, **13,** 312

Barton, R. L. (1966). *Institutional Neurosis.* (Bristol: J. Wright)

Berger, P. L., Berger, B. and Kellmer, H. (1974). *The Homeless Mind.* (Harmondsworth: Penguin)

Bernstein, A. S., Klein, E. B., Berger, L. and Cohen, J. (1968). Relationship between instituitionalisation, of the demographic variable and the structure of intelligence in chronic schizophrenics. *J. Consult. Psychol.*, **29,** 320

Bem, D. J. (1967). Self-perception: An alternative interpretation of cognitive dissonance phenomena. *Psych. Rev.*, **74,** 183

Bolton, N., Smith, F. V., Heskins, K. J. and Bannister, P. A. (1976). Psychological correlates of long-term imprisonment IV. A longitudinal analysis. *Br. J. Criminol.*, **161,** 38

Caine, T. M., Foulds, G. A. and Hope, K. (1967). *Manual of the Hostility and Detection of Hostility Questionnaire.* (London: Univ. of London Press)

Clemmer, D. (1958). *The Prison Community.* New edition. (New York: Rinehart)

Cohen, S. and Taylor, L. (1972). *Psychological Survival: The Experience of Long-term Imprisonment.* (Pelican Books, Penguin)

Derdiarian, A. and Clough, D. (1976). Patients' dependence and independence levels on the pre-hospitalization – post-discharge continuum. *Nursing Res.*, **25,**(1), 27

Etzioni, A. (1961). *A Comparative Analysis of Complex Organization.* (New York: Free Press)

Eysenck, H. J. (1964). *Crime and Personality.* (London: Routledge and Kegan Paul)

Eysenck, S. B. G. and Eysenck, H. J. (1971). Crime and personality: item analysis of questionnaire responses. *Br. J. Criminol.*, **11,** 49

Festinger, L. (1957). *A Theory of Cognitive Dissonance.* (Evanston Ill: Row, Peterson)

Garrity, D. L. (1961). The prison as a rehabilitation agency. In Cressey, D. (ed.). *The Prison Studies in Institutional Organization and Change.* (Holt Rinehart)

Goffman, E. (1961a). *Asylums: Essays on the Social Situation of Mental Patients and Other Inmates.* (New York: Doubleday Anchor Books)

Goffman, E. (1961b). On the characteristics of total institutions: The inmate world. In Cressey, D. (ed.). *The Prison: Studies in Institutional Organization and Change.* (Holt Rinehart)

Hebb, D. O. (1958). The motivating effects of exteroreceptive stimulation. *Am. Psychol.*, **13,** 109

Heskins, K. J., Smith, F. V., Bannister, P. A. and Bolton, N. (1973). Psychological correlates of long-term imprisonment: II Personality variables. *Br. J. Criminol.*, **14,** 150

Heskins, K. J., Bolton, N., Smith, F. V. and Bannister, P. A. (1974). Psychological correlates of long-term imprisonment: III. Additional variables. *Br. J. Criminol.*

HMSO (1968). *The Regime for Long-term Prisoners in Conditions of Maximum Security: Report of the Advisory Council on the Penal System.* (London: HMSO)

HMSO (1969). *People in Prison.* (London: HMSO)

Hulin, C. L. and Maher, B. A. (1959). Changes in attitudes toward law concomitant with imprisonment. *J. Crim. Law Criminol. Police Sci.*, **50,** 245

Kahn, M. W. (1968). Superior performance IQ of murders as a function of overt act or diagnosis. *J. Soc. Psychol.*, **76,** 113

Katz, D. and Kahn, R. L. (1966). *The Social Psychology of Organizations.* (New York: Wiley)

Kleeman, W. Jr., Hartford, B. D. and Reeves, R. E. (1976). Interaction on Ward 8: Physical settings and behavioural change. *Proceedings of 6th Congress Int. Eng. Assoc.* Univ. of Maryland

Kornfield, D. S. (1972). The hospital environment: Its impact on the patient. *Adv. Psychosom. Med.*, **8,** 252

Krol, V. A., Pazder, L. H. and Wigdor, B. T. (1967). Long-term effects of a prolonged stress experience. *Canad. Psychiat. Assoc. J.* **12,** 175

Levitt, R. (1974). Becoming a patient. *Community Health*, **6,** 138

Levitt, R. (1975). Attitudes of hospital patients. *Nursing Times*, **March,** 497

Ley, P. (1972). Complaints made by hospital staff and patients: A review of the literature. *Bull. Br. Psych. Soc.*, **25,** 115

McCleery, R. (1961). Authoritarianism and the belief systems of incorrigibles. In Cressey, D. (ed.). *The Prison: Studies in Institutional Organization and Change.* (Holt Rinehart)

Miller, E. J. and Gwynne, G. V. (1972). *A Life Apart.* (Tavistock Publication)

Phillips, D. (1975). The patient is a person. *Nursing Mirror*, **141,** (4), 64

Rosengren, W. R. and Leftomn, M. (1969). *Hospitals and Patients.* (New York: Atherton Press)

Rudd, T. N. (1974). Quality of living. *H. Soc. Serv. J.*, **June,** 1224

Schein, E. H. (1956). The Chinese indoctrination program for prisoners of war. *Psychiatry*, **19,** 160

Skipper, J. K. Jr. and Leonard, R. C. (1965). *Social Integration and Patient Care.* (Philadelphia: Lippincott Co.)

Trasler, G. (1962). *The Explanations of Criminality.* (London: Routledge and Kegan Paul)

Volicer, B. J. (1973). Perceived stress levels of events associated with the experience of hospitalization. *Nursing Res.*, 22(3), 235

Volicer, B. J. (1974). Patients' perceptions of stressful events associated with hospitalization. *Nursing Res.*, 23(3), 235

Watt, M. and Maher, B. A. (1958). Prisoners' attitudes toward home and the judicial system. *J. Crim. Law Criminol. Police Sci.*, **49,** 327

7
Safety and Risk

W. T. SINGLETON

INTRODUCTION

Safety, like health, can only be defined in terms of an objective which we aspire towards but never completely attain. If we think of it as a state or situation of an individual we are clearer about its absence rather than its presence. Something happens only in the absence of safety, namely an accident or a casualty from some cumulative effect such as radiation. Thus we can describe the danger of a situation rather than the safety because we have evidence about danger in the form of accident and morbidity statistics. Such data for given situations over given time periods can be used to describe danger in the form of risk or probability of damage. No one number is sufficient because there are bound to be kinds and levels of damage. Ratios of fatal accidents to severe accidents to minor accidents vary enormously between different situations such as different industries and different kinds of event (Table 7.1) so that there can be no unique quantification of risks. Nevertheless we can reasonably try to minimize risk however defined. It cannot be eliminated because reducing any measure of probability of damage to zero is impossible.

To take an extreme example, risk for the individual cannot be minimized by ensuring effective food supplies and toilet facilities and then putting him to bed in a well heated and ventilated room. It won't do physiologically because most of the systems — respiratory, circulatory, locomotor and so on — deteriorate rapidly if they are underused and it won't do psychologically because the individual in such a situation soon becomes bored and eventually perhaps less interested in survival. Life is optimally sustained in narrow bands of external parameters. It can be too hot or too cold, too noisy or too quiet, too much oxygen or too little oxygen, too much food or too little food and so on. Moreover, although we can describe these bands in numerical terms we cannot

Table 7.1 UK accidents in factory processes, 1975 (HSE data)

	Fatal accidents	Total reported accidents (thousands)
Machinery	63 (27%)	32 (16%)
Transport	48 (21%)	15 (7%)
Falls of persons	39 (17%)	32 (16%)
Struck by falling objects	13 (8%)	12 (6%)
Other contact with goods, objects, persons	6 (2%)	76 (38%)
Others	57 (25%)	37 (18%)
Total	231	204

optimize a particular environment for an individual and keep it constant. Such an environment is de-arousing unless some of the parameters change and it is unnatural because the person involved would not be able to pursue any of his goals without disturbing the parameters.

If we accept that the human being is a purposive or goal-seeking organism then he must take risks. For example, pursuing any objective usually involves, at some stage, moving about and in doing so he is exposed to some of the main risk categories such as falling and things falling on him (Table 7.1). If he claims technological support for his movements by getting into some kind of vehicle than he is further at risk because he is close to some source of energy which may go astray. McFarland and Moore (1971) have pointed out that one useful way of looking at an accident is that there has been an accumulation of energy in the wrong place at the wrong time.

Thus the individual exercises his skills in pursuing some objective and within these skills safety appears as one variable in a complex cost–benefit equation. The degree of danger appears as one of the costs of a particular strategy. Take a simple case of a journey; there must be a set of benefits which make the journey worthwhile in spite of the costs. It might be possible, in principle, to make the journey by walking, cycling, car or train. For walking the cost in time and energy could be too high, for cycling (manual or motor) the cost in terms of danger could be too high, and thus the choice between car and train will be made in terms of cost such as money, time and perhaps the relatively lower risk of going by train. This assessment is made and the decision arrived at without any exact quantification of the relevant factors. Intuitive estimation of factors such as risks is part of the skill and skills also are involved in minimizing the risks while the journey is in progress. Some of these latter skills will be associated with the traveller, e.g. expressed in the way he drives his car, but other relevant skills have been involved in the design of the transport system, e.g. the engineering of the car, the curves and junctions of the road, the signalling system of the railway and the skills of the train driver. In general there seem to be three main categories: the safe situation, the safe operator and the safe climate. The safe situation is a matter of design skills, the safe operator involves setting-up, operating and maintenance skills and the safe climate involves management skills. Table 7.2 shows the main variables associated with these three categories (Singleton, 1976).

Table 7.2   Main variables in safety strategies

---

1. Safe operator: Minimize probability of human error, by selection, training, providing adequate information, avoiding time pressure but maintaining arousal level.
Maximize probability of error corrections, by increasing detectability and potentiality for reversibility, by separating decisions and implementations and by requiring monitoring only of exceptions in machine performance.
2. Safe system: Safety is a by-product of efficient system design where the emphasis is on optimal allocation of function between man and machine, good communication between man and machine through well designed displays and controls, and systematic consideration of personnel sub-system functions such as selection, training, procedure design and contingency planning.
3. Safe climate: The appropriate organizational climate of opinion is created and maintained by leadership, formal and informal, by training of immediate supervisors in sensitivity to safety and by discrete use of propaganda: e.g. by occasional films and posters and by routine dissemination of news about accidents and safety.

In summary, safety is not a static, positive objective but rather the inverse of danger which is measurable over a period in terms of accidents and morbidity. Sustaining the optimally safe state is a dynamic process involving a variety of skills. Some of these skills are practised by the person at risk, others by those responsible for his situation. The situation is created by designers including those responsible for training as well as those responsible for hardware. The situation is maintained by managers who are responsible for devising appropriate procedures partly on the basis of national legislation and company procedures and partly on the basis of their specialized knowledge of the particular situation.

DESIGNING FOR SAFETY

Discussion with designers (Singleton, 1972) invariably generates at some stage the statement that design is always carried out 'with safety in mind'. It is difficult to be exact about what this phrase is meant to describe because it covers such a vast range from the safety factor in the breaking strength of the bolts used to awareness of regulations about machines being capable of 'safe operation given reasonable care'. In addition it is often seen as an inextricable part of the total design effort, as one designer put it "safety is built into the structure and architecture of the machine". This total conception is important also because it is readily possible to have a set of separately safe components which when put together form an unsafe system. Although the designer is aware that safety is one of his objectives, his consideration of it is intuitive and erratic rather than systematic. There are many reasons for this. For small machines or systems such as a guillotine or a welding machine he cannot be too rigorous because he does not have a full picture of what the machine might be used to do, nor does he know very precisely the range of skills of those who will operate it. In these circumstances he might well give himself the rather vague objective of making the machine 'fool-proof'. Even here, however, he is operating in a cost–benefit mode in that the more he assumes diminished responsibility on the part of the operator the greater the cost of the hardware and the more he has to limit the versatility of the system. For big systems such as power stations and airliners the objectives are more exact and the expected skills of operation can be specified, but there are other unknowns in that these systems are near the limit of the technological state of the art and it is correspondingly difficult to carry out detailed contingency planning.

For all these reasons designs and designers tend to be conservative. There is heavy reliance on past experience and on making the next design a progressive development of the previous one so that most of the lessons learned from operating the previous one remain relevant. Radical departures from previous practice always generate unforeseen problems. For example, even in such a well developed technology as motor-car design and manufacture, new models always have teething troubles which can take several years to get under control.

Thus the skills of the designer develop through a long experiential process which may extend for decades. Safety is usually a totally integrated facet of the overall design decision making. This is the background to the objection to so-called safety engineers. Except for the bigger systems, identifying an individual or a team responsible for safety is regarded as a false separation advocated only by those who have never practised as designers.

Experience is regarded as the key feature in skill development because there seems to be no other way of acquiring the range of relevant knowledge. This covers the history of the industry concerned, the ordinary level of skill and cautiousness of machine-operators, the normal quality of supervision and level of discipline, the particular assets and liabilities of all similar machines in the past coupled with a grasp of key incidents such as dramatic machine failures or serious accidents. A particular design decision is made in the context of all this extensive but ill-assorted knowledge. The designer would propose that the essence of his skill is in somehow bringing this whole set of data, incidents and even folk-lore into focus on the specific design issue. He doesn't, of course, know how the process works. It is not a conscious selection of relevant items nor is it an orderly process of scanning possibilities. Rather it seems to be a kind of matching and mis-matching process where cues emerge because they fit the issue. He will be able to debate and describe his decision after it has been made but this is an elaborate post-hoc rationalization. The answer emerges while supporting reasoning proceeds almost independently. This process is by no means infallible. An answer may not emerge or if it does there may be a nagging feeling that it is the wrong one for reasons which are not quite identifiable. Mistakes are made by failing to take account of some aspect which with the benefit of hindsight was relevant and important. Support and correction for this imperfect process is usually provided by repetition and iteration. Each decision is gone over either by the same person, someone else or a committee. Trials are carried out when it seems economic and expedient to do so. Assessing when to devise and insert these checks is another aspect of the skill. The skilled man always seems to have secondary activities going on which monitor his primary activities. This applies to groups as well as to individuals.

The attempt to analyse and formalize the design process has been going on for a long time (e.g. Jones, 1970) and is now making some contribution to the training of designers, but it seems to have been less successful, so far, in raising the effectiveness of practical design decision making. On the specific issue of safety there have been attempts to devise checklists which formalize the objectives the designer should pursue. The categories of questions in relation to these objectives cover such factors as the appropriateness of the work space dimensions, what the operator actually does, whether he receives adequate information to decide what to do including warning lights and design of guards.

SAFE OPERATING

There are clearly differences in risk levels between individuals engaged in a particular task. For example, McFarland (1970) has calculated that the accidental death rate per 100 000 flying hours is 0·12 for scheduled airline pilots, 1·4 for business pilots and 10·0 for private pilots. The risk of accident to car drivers of different ages is shown in Figure 7.1. The teenage driver is the most dangerous and risk falls with age up to the sixties (Munden, 1966). Although it is true that younger drivers do more of their driving in the dark this accounts for only a small proportion of the age trend (Johnson, 1972). The differences are not necessarily due to differences of skill. In the case of pilots one would guess that formality of procedure is more important and in the case of driving on the road the individually acceptable level of risk probably changes with age.

It is desirable to clarify as far as possible safety factors which can be related to skill and those which are more appropriately related to other aspects

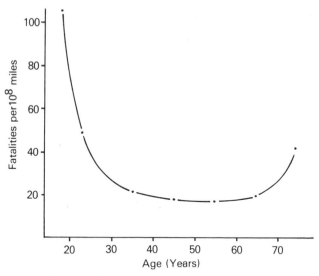

Figure 7.1   Risk of road accident and age of driver. Drivers fatally and seriously injured per 10^8 miles driven, plotted against age (Munden, 1966)

of human performance. The issue is confused in that skill aspects cannot easily be separated from other models of human performance or from other variables affecting performance. For example, the 'information processing model' overlaps with the 'skill model' even though there are fundamental differences of approach (Singleton, 1975). The model of the human operator as an information processing device is behaviouristic in origin and basically treats the individual as a stimulus–response device. This is hardly appropriate for the study of safety since it is well established that accidents rarely have a single identifiable cause in terms of the action of a human operator. To describe comprehensively any accident it invariably seems to be necessary to look at the whole series of events which led up to it and very often to the parallel pattern of coincidental events taking place at the time. This is not to suggest that there is nothing to be learned from information models about the human errors which lead to accidents. Concepts such as limited channel capacity and single channel operation clearly have some relevance to understanding behaviour in conditions of overload. The possibility of a short 'refractory phrase' following on action where no new signals can be received because of the check on the previous action (Welford, 1968) could in principle generate a dangerous situation if an operator in an emergency missed a key signal for this reason. For example, a process control operator whose plant is subject to some fault may need to take rapid action in response to a variety of warning signals and missing one of these signals could lead to a wrong diagnosis of the under-lying fault. This theory not only explains why the operator might make a mistake but also suggests ways of minimizing this possibility. The task should be designed so that stimuli are tied together into integral packages and the required responses are simple and generate rapid feedback about the effectiveness of the action, the training should be such that standard responses are overlearned to the point where no internal check of action is needed, thus economizing on attention time, and the procedure should be designed so that the operator is discouraged from premature action so that he awaits an adequate series or array of signals before making any response. Finally converging situations where increasingly rapid responses are needed to increasingly rapid sequences of stimuli should be designed out of the system. If they can be foreseen they are best dealt with automatically rather than by relying on the human operator. Bartlett (1943) pointed out that as fatigue increases the range and variety of signals attended to by the operator is likely to decrease and the threshold level below which he considers it inappropriate to make any response at all is likely to increase. If follows that working periods, methods and even tasks should be arranged so as to minimize the possibility of fatigue and to take account of it. This is no more than commonsense but some of the potential remedies suggested by the theory are not so obvious. For example, the criterion for warning signals or other key sources of information is not merely that they should be perceptible by the operator when he is fresh and alert but that they must be capable of gaining his attention towards the end of a shift when fatigue effects might be present. This can be done for visual signals by keeping them towards the centre rather than the periphery of his field of view and for auditory signals by designing them so that they are most distinctly different from the ambient noise in either loudness, pitch or continuity.

Russell Davis (1958) discusses three mechanisms relevant to the origins of human errors in transport accidents, illustrating their effects from various accident investigation reports of rail and air crashes. These are "the false hypothesis", "preoccupation" and "emergency mechanisms". He points out that the meaning attached to any signal is influenced by what the operator is expecting; if this expectation is wrong then the signal may be either ignored or totally misinterpreted. To quote Russell Davis, "People may fail to see what stares them in the face if their looking is guided by a false hypothesis." By definition an emergency is an unusual or unexpected happening and thus the conditions are intrinsically favourable for its misinterpretation. A train driver may miss a clearly visible red signal simply because in all the times he has travelled on that route it was always green. Again the significant contribution is not so much in the explanation of why these things happen but rather into what the particular remedies are. Russell Davis suggests that proneness to false hypotheses increases with anxiety level (either endogenous or task-induced) and with associated defence mechanisms, such that the individual finds it personally satisfactory to pursue the hypothesis he starts with however strongly the external evidence contradicts it. Related to this is the persistence of reliance on cues which have already pre-empted the situation and a refusal to give due weight to cues which were unjustifiably assigned less importance.

This takes us into Russell Davis' second category of "preoccupation", which also is reinforced by anxiety. Anxiety has similar effects to Bartlett's skill fatigue in that increased anxiety can cause the components of a task to become disarticulated. Attention is focussed more and more on particular components of the task at the expense of others which may be equally important but are not recognized as such. This tendency is particularly strong for individuals of obsessional personality who are normally conscientious and efficient. The third category – "emergency mechanisms" – is best explained by reference to adaptive behaviour for more primitive man who, when faced with danger, reacted more forcibly and with less evidence as he felt increasingly threatened. Such behaviour is normally not adaptive for the human operator in high-powered technologically based systems but it may emerge when in fact the situation calls for restrained and accurate rather than sudden and energetic responses. Hasty, ill-considered action almost inevitably makes the situation worse, which leads to a vicious circle of even less adaptive reactions and finally to disaster. This panic reaction has its equivalent on the perceptual side where, if the individual cannot make sense of what is happening, he may try a whole series of increasingly bizarre hypotheses about what has gone wrong. This has been graphically described as "kaleidoscopic perception"; it can lead to hallucinations or it may cause the central mechanisms to get so involved in trying to resolve the situation that they become cut off from the external world leading to a 'freeze' either on inputs or outputs or both. Paradoxically the extensive over-reaction or under-reaction which appear to be the remote extremes may well be very similar in aetiology.

Branton (1970) found that peak periods of reported accidents in a light engineering factory coincided with increased variability of performance and that this variability could be detected in what he called "unsuccessful hand movements". These represent a relatively small proportion of total hand movements but they cause a disproportionate disturbance of the whole performance because an unsuccessful movement needs to be checked and corrected by further involvement of perceptual mechanisms. They are symptomatic of a breakdown of semi-automatic activity and a requirement for an increased rate of decision making. Kay (1971) describes this phenomenon in terms of the distinction between the "environmentally controlled mode" in which stimulus–response pairing is detectable, and the "pre-programmed mode" in which performance is serially organized and one response triggers the initiation of the next one. The latter is much more efficient than the former in the sense that it can be much faster, although it is less versatile and demands a higher level of skill. There are correspondingly greater differences in individual ability, accidents can happen because of delays in switching between different programmes or in switching from an extensively programmed response to a simple stimulus–response sequence.

Although these authors use different terminologies the picture which emerges of the skilled operator in distress is a consistent one. He functions normally in a mode where inputs and outputs proceed as complex patterns in space and time almost independently and with central organizing processes and monitoring facilities not restricted to operation in a narrow band of real time. The immediate past is very much with him through memory processes and so also is the immediate future through anticipatory processes. This wide-band window moving in phase with real time but not confined by it can be disturbed. These disturbances may be predominantly external in origin when an unexpected event or a mistake in interpretation occurs. Each of these encourages the other. Alternatively they may be predominantly internal in origin because of fatigue, anxiety or inadequate learning. In either case the process which follows is the same. The operator needs to slow down because the mis-matches create more work for the central processes. However, an inappropriate action is likely to demand faster rather than slower further actions so cumulative disruption becomes more likely. There then follows the familiar ineffective functioning in the form of hasty inadequate responses following correspondingly inappropriate interpretations and decisions. Later analysis of what happened does not make sense because the context is missing. What the operator did or didn't think and do cannot be understood outside the total process as it occurred at the time. Hence the difficulty of justifying specific actions either by the operator himself recalling events or by others trying to find out what happened.

MANAGING FOR SAFETY

The manager is responsible for the physical, organizational and social environments within which the operator functions. Safety is a specific problem in its manifestations through accidents but in the control of the origins of these accidents there is considerable overlap with other management objectives such as productivity and quality of work. Fortunately the optimal conditions for the meeting of these different objectives usually coincide.

It is possible to think of cases where superficially there might appear to be a conflict. For example, in feeding metal components into a press the machine is often arranged so that the operator must insert the component, close a guard which ensures that his hands are isolated from the work-point and then operate the press. If there were no guard and he could operate the press as soon as the component was correctly positioned, the job would be faster but less safe. Such situations often turn out to be instances of bad design; for example, in the above case the operator is involved because he can check the quality of the components and because of his manual dexterity in inserting them. He can still perform these functions if he inserts the components in a jig which is then moved automatically and safely under the press: moreover he can insert one while the previous one is being pressed. This change will speed the process even further and yet still improve the level of safety. There may be exceptions but it is a useful discipline to believe that if a procedure designed for safety interferes with efficiency then it is a badly designed procedure and there ought to be a better way of doing it. If this can be achieved then the operator is not tempted to increase his risk in order to increase production.

In the specification of environmental conditions the characteristic positive relationship of safety, productivity and quality emerges. An optimal environment of heat, cold, lighting, noise and vibration will simultaneously minimize risks and encourage production and quality. This is because safety and quality are linked by the intervening variable of human error and safety and production are linked by the intervening variable of optimal arousal level. Thus the management problem is to be aware of the appropriate levels of these parameters and arrange matters so that they are achieved. The range of human adaptability is such that one does not normally need elaborate data and measurements to get these things right; the skill of the manager from this point of view is in being sensitive to what seems about right for the job. Conversely, the unskilled manager is the one who is in contact every day with a job where the operator obviously cannot see properly or is too cold and yet it does not occur to the manager to take any action.

The situation is not so straightforward in relation to organizational matters and particularly procedures. The fundamental difficulty here is that, in matters of safety, the human operator is not a self-correcting and stabilizing mechanism. The operator learns or develops skills by knowledge of results from his actions on every time scale from kinaesthetic and touch feedback for separate hand movements to success in achieving objectives on a scale of months or even years. The skill of minimizing risk cannot be developed by individual experience because accidents are too rare in relation to the working life span. Obviously no-one learns from the individual experience of a fatal accident and serious accidents, even in situations recognized as dangerous, have a long average period between events. For example, using the data from Figure 7.1, if every driver stayed the same age indefinitely and drove 20 000 miles per year regardless of being killed and injured at intervals, he would have a fatal/serious accident about every fifty years if he was young and about every two hundred years if he was a safe middle-aged driver. Clearly his theoretical learning curve from personal experiences would need to be plotted over many centuries. This problem is dealt with in primitive societies with unchanging tasks by the development of myth and folk-lore which summarizes the collective experience and encourages safe behaviour. This process cannot function in technological societies because the tasks and their associated risks change too rapidly. For example, the young farmer will be reasonably safe in his handling of dangerous bulls because the techniques for doing this have developed over many generations. However, he may well be doing himself serious damage from vibration in high-speed ploughing for eight hours a day; he does not have the warning of his grandfather sitting in the corner with a damaged back because, at his age, his grandfather was doing the job at a tenth of the speed by walking behind two horses. Preservation of safety and health for the present-day tractor driver cannot emerge from experience; it has to come from theory and experiment on the long-term effects of given vibration levels, from the design of tractor seats, from data collected over many countries and finally from the specification of safe procedures. This is the management responsibility. It may appear to have elements of paternalism but it is necessary for the reasons described above and because, as one consequence of the rarity of accidents, individuals develop irrational attitudes: for example the common belief in personal immortality and impregnability. This is reinforced by the fact that a serious accident has not happened yet and perceptual anticipation indicates, as a first approximation, that the future will be a repeat of the past.

Thus, particularly in work based on high technology, an elaborate management system for designing and implementing safe procedures is required. This begins with the theory of potential damage, e.g. in the setting of radiation level exposure standards, but since the theory is never sufficiently comprehensive it needs to be reinforced by checks of what happens on the basis of experience. This in turn takes two forms: routine accumulation of data about incidents which may or may not have actually resulted in accidents and routines for investigating specific serious accidents or other casualties in detail leading to identification of causes and recommendations for revised procedures or designs. Accident investigation procedures are well developed and extensively used in the transport industries. Historically this no doubt began with railways as one of the first high power systems and for ships where accidents have always been dramatic and expensive. There is also a feeling, with some justification, that innocent unskilled persons such as passengers are entitled to special protection. These trends have been followed in road transport and in aviation. The investigation is quasi-legal in character because there may be consequences in the form of proceedings in law courts and because the legal method of requiring those involved and experts to state their evidence verbally and to be subject to questioning, some supportive, some hostile and some neutral is well developed as a procedure for revealing what happened in a complex situation. These procedures are currently much more sophisticated in the physical and medical sciences than in the social sciences. There is, for example, a tendency to think that the investigation is complete when a cause such as 'human error' has been located without sufficient further inquiry into the origins of that human error. Such investigations, e.g. of an aircraft crash, can be extraordinarily expensive both in terms of the investigation itself and the consequences in the form of financial compensation for victims and their relatives. Such costs, including insurance, are a significant proportion of the total costs of systems such as airlines.

The complementary activity of accumulating data about incidents relevant to safety including accidents and health of personnel tends to be shared between national bodies such as the Health and Safety Executive, Government

Ministries, trade and professional associations and so on. These bodies can operate with larger and more appropriate sample sizes than the independent organizations and companies, although these latter are ultimately the data source and the data can never be better than the original records. The skills in interpretating these data depend not only on statistical expertise but also on the ability to trace global data back to its origins and to consider the likely validity from this view-point.

The design of procedures, which is one of the main objectives of these investigations, requires considerable skill because there are many trade-offs involved. For example, at a fundamental level there are decisions about when to rely on the versatility of the operator and when to provide him with a drill which is to be followed. The advantages of versatility are that not everything can be foreseen and so there must be an ultimate reliance on the initiative of the man on the spot – he is the one familiar with what is happening in its unique context and when he also knows that he must exercise initiative then he can be more involved in the job. Providing drills for everything can be self-defeating in that they have to be learned or manuals have to be provided together with methods of scanning the manuals.These can become very elaborate as, for example, on the flight deck of a civil aircraft where there is a small library of procedures. On the other hand there are great advantages in providing procedures; they increase uniformity, reduce anxiety and stress and, in most cases, make for faster and more appropriate responses.

Ensuring the implementation of procedures is a management responsibility at all levels from the operational team leader to the senior management and including management services such as training and safety. More broadly, the maintenance of a safe climate starts with the interest and concern of senior management in safety and works its way down to the team leaders and senior operatives in the examples they set, both in leadership itself and in matters such as discipline and what is usually called good housekeeping. These terms are not easily defined in detail partly because they have not been fashionable research topics.

SAFETY RESEARCH

The research worker seeking data in this field is always tempted to begin by looking at accident statistics. The analysis of such data in meaningful ways is much more difficult than it might seem at first sight. Consider for example Table 7.1; there are more than two hundred thousand accidents which seems like a reasonably sized chunk of evidence. However, if one pauses to think where it comes from, the source is hundreds of people: safety officers, doctors, nurses, first-aid personnel and so on in factories across the country who have filled in various kinds of report forms. The origin in most cases was that someone needed medical help but this varied from full-scale surgery to treatment of a minor abrasion – whether, when such help is provided, it is reported at all, depends on the policy of the company, the attitude of the person who gave the help and even on whether or not he or she happened to be busy at the time. Beyond this is the question of why the worker asked for first-aid; if he is busy and his morale is high the wound would have to be quite serious before he takes any action. On the other hand if he is bored and feels like a walk away from the work space followed by a chat with the nurse any excuse will do to obtain treatment following a minor accident. Thus, reported accidents are a sample of accidents, not necessarily a random one and containing probably less than half of the accidents that could have been reported. Then there is the taxonomic question of how to divide the reported accidents into categories, what are the criteria for selecting categories? Traditionally a set of data is divided into 7 ± 2 categories with approximately equal numbers in each category and with definitions of categories as unambiguous and discrete as possible. Unfortunately this last criterion is impossible to meet; categories always overlap and someone has to make a fairly arbitrary decision about each accident to select the most appropriate category. Suppose, for example, that in 1975 I was walking through a factory and to avoid a fork-lift truck I suddenly stepped sideways, bumped into a machine operator, slipped and fell with part of the machine falling onto me. Where would this incident appear on Table 7.1? It could be in any of the categories.

One can avoid some of these difficulties by concentrating only on fatal accidents. Here at least there is little ambiguity about the consequence of the accident and there will be few, if any, unreported. There is in fact a slight ambiguity in that there has to be an arbitrary decision about the length of the period after the accident beyond which the death of the victim cannot be attributed to the accident. Because this period differs in different countries fatal accidents between countries are not always strictly comparable. This period in the U.K. is 366 days. We now also have a sample size problem in that there are 231 cases in a year across the whole of British industry. There is also the difficulty of the chance nature of the injury associated with a particular accident. Returning to my walk through the factory a negligible difference in the way I fall might result in a fatal bang on the head or, alternatively, a minor bruise. From the point of view of accident prevention the incident is the same but the consequences can be so very different. In general, accident statistics give some indications of the pattern of relevant events and trends in time or across industries or factories but useful detailed analysis requires a specific hypothesis which can have its origin in practical experience or in a theory.

Reliance on formal accident investigations also has its difficulties. The problem here is that the procedure and objectives are dominated by legal and other requirements which may or may not coincide with a scientific point of view. There is a certain arbitrariness in reaching conclusions about causation; this usually takes the form of one or a very few main causes with others regarded as contributing factors.

In general the whole business of safety and accidents is so diffuse and pervasive that nothing is likely to be achieved by a broad approach of the 'let us find out about' kind. One needs an orientation from a real problem or a theory or preferably both. Theories about accidents are not easy to construct because of their heterogeneous nature. It seems reasonable to begin with people as the common factor. Accidents happen to people and they are caused by people making mistakes. Thus the theory of human errors seems to be one valid starting point (Singleton, 1973). The study of skill would also seem an appropriate conceptual background.

We know that there is always a complex pattern of events preceding an accident, that people expose themselves to danger because they consider that the objective is worth the risk and that many mistakes can be traced to misinterpretations of the situation. All this can be readily translated into skill terminology. Consideration of the total stream of activity is the distinguishing feature of skill psychology compared with stimulus–response psychology. Skilled performance has meaning because it is integrated by and linked to the pursuit of an objective, and the concept of dynamic internal models into which the human operator fits all new data is fundamental to the approach.

We can note also that the accident research worker is a skilled operator and he has the problem of categorizing, which is another fundamental aspect of the skills approach. In fact the categorizing phenomenon links the actor or victim in an accident with the observer or research worker. Devising categories into which the likely array of events can be divided is a basic, although not always conscious, process within the development of skill. In the interests of economy and efficiency, categories into which events are equally likely to fall are ideal but difficult to achieve because multi-parameter situations tend towards normally distributed outputs rather than outputs across rectangular distributions. Thus to keep the categories more or less equally loaded with events the ranges within a category have to be larger at the periphery than in the centre of attention. This is difficult and what he may do instead is to accept that an event rarely needs to be fitted into a peripheral category; when such an event actually does occur it will be unexpected and will be placed in the wrong category – this amounts to not believing what has happened and distorting it towards what one expected would happen. For example, commuters driving in rush-hour traffic have well-developed models and rules and categories about what is going to happen at particular junctions and regions where there are necessary lane changes; the traffic flows quickly and safely because all the drivers are experienced at this particular game and have a consistent set of categories of likely routes.However, when the holiday season starts and tourists get mixed up in this traffic they change the expected pattern of events and behave in unexpected ways. Accidents are now much more likely. Or consider a game of tennis at the international level, the two players have played against each other very frequently so that nice tidy routines of rallies can develop with responses at a speed quite beyond not only the average player but also any other international level player who has not been in the circuit recently and has not got a matching range of event–sequence categories. However, should one of the players by a fluke or by some extraordinary effort deliver at some instant a response which does not fit into the categories of his opponent then the opponent will be completely baffled. He will either stop and make no response or he will make a wildly inappropriate response.

Similar, if less dramatic, dangers confront the research worker trying to make sense of some accident data. He will develop a set of categories and will feel satisfied when the accidents come out neatly, preferably with about the same frequency, in each of the categories he has devised. If there are events that do not fit nicely into his categories he has two choices – he can either make them fit by distorting or ignoring some evidence or he can revise his categories. Being human he is always reluctant to do the latter because like a train-driver passing a signal at danger he would have to make an extra effort to accept that this anticipations have been incorrect and that his categories do not fit. One lesson from this is that the research worker, more than most people, needs to keep his categories flexible and he must be prepared to modify them if the evidence does not fit or if the problem being investigated changes.

Consider, for example, the problem of accidents to tractor drivers. A task analysis (Singleton *et al.*, 1973) reveals that actually driving the tractor is only one part of the job. Even when it is being used as a transport vehicle (for which task incidentally it is badly designed) the driver spends much of his time getting on and off the machine to open gates and so on and in these phases new risks develop; he may stumble when getting on or off and he may attempt to drive the machine through a gate whilst walking beside it. There are other risks while attaching implements and in driving with them attached where the stability of the system, particularly on sloping fields, may be a matter of concern. The tractor driver also does a great deal of maintenance. In all these tasks there are sequences of events from which he should not depart for safety reasons; this is a considerable memory load, particularly when one notes that tasks are seasonal and it is often about a year since he last did a similar task, e.g. there is at least one fatality each year following an action such as removing the flexible hydraulic hose without first reducing the pressure and making the machine position independent of this pressure. The probability of a tractor being in an accident in a given year has been stable at about 3×10^{-3} for the last twenty years or so, although the number of tractors has increased. The probability of a fatal accident involving a particular tractor in a year is about 10^{-4} and has tended to increase over the past twenty years possibly levelling off in the last few years. There are about seventy fatalities per year. The unusually high ratio of fatal to non-fatal accidents is, of course, a matter of reporting; an accident has to be quite serious before anyone takes the trouble to report it but fatalities are very carefully dealt with. Each has to be reported to the police who inspect the scene, often accompanied by a specialist agricultural safety inspector. There is an inquest which the inspector attends and from which he sends a detailed report back to the Ministry. These reports are collated and later each is summarized into an account of about fifty words explaining what happened to whom and in what context. Note that there is no attempt to classify these events except along the sequence of time, each one is treated as a unique incident and this is an invaluable source of uncontaminated raw data which can be analysed in the way which best suits a particular purpose. For example, if the data are analysed into failures of inputs, decisions and outputs, it emerges that even for this superficially manual task it is inputs (40%) and decisions (36%) rather than outputs (18%) where most of the fatal errors probably occurred (Singleton et al., 1973). One has to accept that such analyses into categories are neither comprehensive nor exclusive and there would inevitably be differences between two observers who attempted to classify the data by the same criteria; the important question is whether or not such differences would alter the interpretations, the conclusions and the consequent recommendations. There are always a few accidents where nothing can be done to avoid similar occurences in the future – e.g. an implement triggers an unexploded bomb which has been dormant for thirty years or an aircraft crashes onto men ploughing in the middle of a field. Such accidents or 'Acts of God' are best removed before further analysis. So also are the totally irrational incidents such as driving into a clearly visible obstacle. These may be examined in detail to try to discover any reasons for the total failure of attention but there are always a few per year which defy explanation so that they cannot be classified by any other criterion. The criteria for analysis might be theoretical, aimed at a better broad understanding of the skills such as the separation of failures of cognitive modelling from wrong sequencing, or they may be operational, starting from what can be done in principle to remedy the situation – this includes machine design, training and procedure design. Alternatively, they may be intermediate between theory and practice, such as the separation of failures of perceptual skills and failures of motor skills, which is theoretically interesting and also has implications for the design of training schemes. Examples of all these methods are given in Singleton (1975). Yet another approach is to use a risk-type taxonomy where accidents in which someone took a reasonable risk (low probability events do happen sometimes) are separated from those where the risk is unreasonable. This provides a target for the final success of safety procedures since there is always a residual core of accidents which were unavoidable even by a skilled and reasonable operator (Singleton, 1977). This highly flexible approach is not to everyone's taste and there are inevitably problems in that numerical data cannot be isolated from a context defined in great detail, and consequently there is little scope for the use of sampling statistics of significance which makes some research workers feel insecure. However this diffuseness can be regarded as an inevitable concomitant and acknowledgement of the variability and complexity of human skilled activity.

CONCLUSION

Accidents which have happened are investigated principally to reduce the probability of further similar accidents. There are other objectives such as establishing who should provide compensation for victims, but even when the search is for culpability this is not an end in itself but a step towards improved training or changed attitudes or perhaps punishment, and all of these are again justified in terms of reduced likelihood of accidents in the future. This is, of course, routine skilled behaviour. One studies the past and the present in order best to predict and control the future. Excepting very short time scales this prediction is done by generating a model which has some characteristics in common with the real situation. The model can be manipulated to provide some prediction. For any complex situation the model is bound to involve categorizing. For a particular purpose, such as making a response or assessing risks, categories are developed for which the outcome is operationally the same. The devising of categories is a fundamental characteristic of skilled behaviour required of individuals involved in risk situations. Useful insights into these processes of categorization progress the theory of what is happening, and through the development of theory we can improve safety or reduce danger by better machine design, procedures design and training design.

References

Bartlett, F. C. (1943). Fatigue following highly skilled work. *Proc. Roy. Soc. B.*, **131**, 248
Branton, P. (1970). A study of repetitive manual work in relation to accidents at the work place. *Int. J. Prod. Res.*, **8** (2), 93
Johnson, H. D. (1972). Ages of car driver casualties in 1970. *Road Research Laboratory Report* L.R. 431. (Crowthorne, U.K.)
Jones, J. C. (1970). *Design Methods*. (London: Wiley)
Kay, H. (1971). Accidents: some facts and theories. In Warr, P.B. (ed.). *Psychology at Work*. (Harmondsworth: Penguin)
McFarland, R. A. (1970). Human factors during the next decade 1970–1980. *Presidential Address to the Human Factors Society, 1970.*
McFarland, R. A. and Moore, R. C. (1971). Safety engineering. *(Encyclopaedia Britannica)*
Munden, J. M. (1966). The accident rates of car drivers by age. *Int. Rd. Saf. Traff. Rev.*, **14** (1), 28
Russell Davis, D. (1958). Human errors and transportation accidents. *Ergonomics*, **2**, 24
Singleton, W. T. (1972). The ergonomics of safety and design. Evidence submitted to the Robens Committee on Safety and Health at Work. A. P. Report No.
Singleton, W. T. (1973). Theoretical approaches to human error. *Ergonomics*, **16**, (6), 727

Singleton, W. T. (1975) Skill and accidents. In *Occupational Accident Research*. (Stockholm: Swedish Work Environment Fund)

Singleton, W. T. (1976). *Human Aspects of Safety*. (London: Keith Shipton Developments, Special Study No. 8)

Singleton, W. T. (1977). Accidents in agriculture. *British Association Symposium on Human Error*. University of Aston A. P. Note 62

Singleton, W. T., Whitfield, D. and Stammers, R. B. (1973). Tasks analysis of the tractor driver. Paper No. 2. Proceedings of National Institute of Agricultural Engineering, subject day on Tractor Ergonomics. (U.K.: Silsoe)

Welford, A. T. (1968). *Fundamentals of Skills*. (London: Methuen)

(Reproduced by kind permission of Submex Ltd.)

8
The Commercial Diver

D. GODDEN and A. BADDELEY

THE UNDERWATER ENVIRONMENT

Physical characteristics

Conditions underwater are spectacularly different from those of a normal working environment. Low temperatures and the high thermal conductivity of the water mean that the diver must often wear cumbersome protective clothing in the form of wet-suits, dry suits and thick woollen undergarments, or suits that can be heated either electrically or by a constant flow of hot water. The old 'hard hat' with a heavy brass headpiece screwing on to a leather suit is rarely if ever used these days, although some form of head protection may be worn. Both this protective clothing and the viscosity of the water itself impede movement. Thus even the use of simple tools such as a hammer becomes difficult. Unless he is heavily weighted, which in many cases would be impractical, the diver will often be neutrally buoyant, making it difficult for him to gain purchase on a surface or to exert a torque; in some cases he may have to tether himself to the work surface. Furthermore, although suitably buoyed heavy objects may be easily moved underwater, they can become hazardous in moderate currents, since, although weightless, they retain their inertia. Vision is restricted by the size and design of the diver's face plate, and is distorted by the water/glass/air interface. Finally, water conditions may reduce visibility, sometimes almost to zero, further adding to the physical difficulties facing the working diver.

Physiological complications

As the diver descends, the pressure increases by 1 bar for each 10 m of depth.

To avoid being crushed, the cavities in a diver's body – lungs, sinus, middle ear – must contain gas at local ambient pressure. Thus, breathing gas is supplied to the diver at this ambient pressure through a pressure-regulating device. This, however, produces a number of physiological complications.

Gases in the breathing mixture dissolve in the diver's body tissues. The rate at which this happens depends on the pressure of the gas (and therefore the depth) and the rate at which the diver is compressed. When the diver surfaces after the dive, the pressure is reduced, and the gas which has dissolved under pressure has to escape. If it is allowed to diffuse out too quickly, it will form bubbles in the tissues which cause extreme pain, can cause permanent damage and sometimes result in death. The condition is known as 'the bends', as the bubbles tend to concentrate in and near joints. To avoid it, the diver must decompress slowly, according to an established schedule depending on his depth–time profile for the dive. For surface-oriented dives which are relatively shallow and usually of short duration, decompression may take place in the water, with the diver stopping at certain depths for set periods of time to enable gas diffusion to proceed at the correct rate. For deep or prolonged medium depth dives he may complete decompression in a surface chamber, and for bell dives he will always do so. During such decompression, oxygen may be administered as it helps to flush out the dissolved inert gas absorbed from whatever breathing mixture was being used. Other forms of decompression sickness can occur; bubbles of nitrogen can appear in the blood, for example, causing what used to be known in the trade vernacular as 'the chokes' or 'the staggers'.

If the surface-oriented diver has to ascend rapidly for some reason, he can suffer pulmonary barotrauma; the pressure of the air within the lungs rises compared with the surrounding pressure and they distend to the limit of their elasticity: after this point they will burst and allow air to spill out. Thus, during a fast emergency ascent, the diver must resist the temptation to breathe normally, and instead must breathe out continuously to allow the expanding gas to escape. A full account of decompression sickness will be found in Schilling *et al.* (1976).

The depth at which the air diver can operate is limited by two factors. The nitrogen in the air becomes narcotic at increased pressure: the onset of this effect, known as nitrogen narcosis, is generally expected to appear below about 30 m. Furthermore, as the partial pressure of oxygen approaches 2 atmospheres, it too can become toxic, producing oxygen convulsions. For these reasons, carefully controlled gas mixtures for breathing have to be supplied. Helium, which is much less narcotic than nitrogen, is used to replace it, and the proportion of oxygen in the mixture is reduced to avoid oxygen convulsions. A common mixture is 94% helium, 6% oxygen; helium and oxygen mixtures are generally referred to as 'heliox'.

The replacement of nitrogen by helium causes some further problems. The high thermal conductivity of heliox means that the diver's core temperature would drop rapidly if the gas mixture was not heated; heating systems are thus necessary, but are just one more piece of hardware that can go wrong. Furthermore, heliox changes the resonant frequencies of the vocal tract; due to the increased velocity of sound, they are moved upwards. Intelligibility decreases with pressure and with the proportion of helium in the mixture, and speech becomes almost completely unintelligible at depths where 90% helium is needed in the mix. This is known as the 'Donald Duck' effect producing high squeaky voices that sound too fast. Divers can adapt to this, though only partially; helium unscramblers have also been developed that partially alleviate the problem.

Finally, there is the 'high pressure nervous syndrome' or HPNS. When high pressures for particularly deep saturation diving are required, a condition of motor dysfunction can appear, characterized by tremor and jerking muscles, and accompanied by somnolence, visual disturbances, dizziness and nausea. Changes in the EEG are detectable. This is not the same as inert gas narcosis and can in some ways act against it. The onset and severity of HPNS depends on both the compression rate and the pressure. It can be minimized by slow compression with stops. Divers tend to adapt with time at depth and recover from the symptoms, although some impairment in mental performance continues to be present at depths exceeding 300 m.

Psychological factors

An attempt has been made here to group the material, first in terms of the stress involved, and then to relate the effects of each stress on two components of performance: memory and other cognitive tasks, and psychomotor performance. Work on social and personality characteristics, and response to extended periods of social isolation, is then reviewed in relation to saturation diving.

Thermal stress – In practice, more and more deep dives are being made using heated suits, the most common medium being pumped hot water. However, cold stress will continue to be a problem; heating systems can fail, and there is always the difficulty of heating the extremities. Furthermore, exploration and exploitation are expected soon to extend north into the Norwegian Sea, and the Arctic regions off Canada, Alaska and Greenland.

Exposure to low temperatures obviously causes numb fingers and impairs manual dexterity. If hands are maintained at about 18 °C (65 °F), performance level remains relatively high, while if their temperature is lowered, performance will deteriorate (Gaydos and Dusek, 1958; Gaydos, 1958). Springbett (1951), using various tests of manual dexterity and motor performance, found that subjects with cold hands showed significant impairment whether their bodies were warm or cold, and conversely, subjects with warm hands showed no impairment, whether or not their bodies were warm or cold. While these studies are not based on divers, there is ample evidence for impaired manual dexterity as a result of diving in cold water, with or without gloves (e.g. Bowen, 1968; Stang and Wiener, 1970).

The effect of cold on cognitive efficiency is more complex. While a drop in body temperature appears to impair memory performance (Baddeley et al., 1975; Bowen, 1968; Davis et al., 1975) and time estimation (Baddeley, 1966a), Teichner (1954) found reaction time to be unaffected by cold. A similar result was obtained by Baddeley et al. (1975), who also found no impairment in speed or accuracy of verbal reasoning, or in vigilance, despite a marked drop in body temperature during a dive in water at 4 °C. Davis et al. (1975) did observe a cognitive decrement in cold water, but the decrement was just as great at the beginning of the dive, when body temperature was normal, as it was at the end when rectal temperature had dropped. This suggests that the impairment was due to distraction by the sensation of cold rather than to an effect of cold on the efficiency of the central nervous system.

The effects of breathing hyperbaric gas – The depth of effective air diving is limited due to the onset of nitrogen narcosis. This results from breathing nitrogen at increased partial pressures and can induce subjective feelings that resemble drunkenness, and which may be accompanied by a range of symptoms such as tunnel vision, nausea and aggression. Sight, sound and smell perception may also be affected. It is normally expected at depths below 30 m (Kiessling and Maag, 1962), has been demonstrated as shallow as 10–20 m (Poulton et al., 1964), and the onset, experience and degrees of susceptibility are subject to a large amount of individual variation. However, few divers can work effectively on air below 60 m and only very exceptional or well-adapted divers can do anything useful below 90 m. (Schilling et al., 1976). Most experimental work has studied performance in a dry chamber at pressures equivalent to the relevant depth. There is, however, evidence that performance in the open sea may show a much more dramatic impairment (Baddeley, 1966b). This appears to be particularly characteristic of psychomotor performance, and to be dependent on the anxiety level of the diver (Baddeley, 1966 and 1967; Davis et al., 1972).

Substituting heliox for air reduces the narcosis problem, and a number of studies have found no impairment in performance at depths ranging up to 450 m (Bennett et al., 1967; Bennett and Towse, 1971; Biersner and Cameron, 1970; Bühlman et al., 1970; Parker, 1969). However all these studies were carried out in dry pressure chamber conditions, typically using very small numbers of subjects and beset with problems of inadequate experimental design. In an open sea study Baddeley and Flemming (1967) observed a decrement in manual dexterity at a depth of only 65 m. It seems likely however that anxiety played a major role in this effect. Such an interpretation seems less plausible in the case of the cognitive decrements which are now beginning to be reported in dry chamber dives at depths exceeding 300 m (Baddeley, 1977; Carter, 1977). It now seems clear that heliox will alleviate the narcosis problem but will not cure it.

Weightlessness and environmental distortion – Movement underwater is restricted by viscosity; the diver (if free swimming) is often neutrally buoyant and will have to use restraining aids if he needs to exert any degree of force on a work face. Consider an impact wrench, for example: if a neutrally buoyant diver tries to apply it to a bolt without some way of controlling the reactive force, he is more likely to rotate than is the bolt. Viscosity also affects force production, and Streimer *et al.* (1971) found that output from a continuous rotary movement underwater was down as much as 36% over surface performance. Further ergonomics details of working underwater (forces, oxygen consumption, load carrying etc.) can be found in Schilling *et al.* (1976).

The direction of the gravitational vertical is given by visual, vestibular and tactile–kinaesthetic cues. Underwater, tactile–kinaesthetic and visual cues are reduced and under some circumstances the diver may find himself not knowing which way is up. Laboratory experiments (Nelson, 1967) and open water trials (Ross *et al.*, 1969) have shown that the size of error is about 7%, and with the head down, about 30%. Furthermore, misperceptions of the angles of tilt of other objects increase underwater (Ross, 1974). There is a report (personal communication) that during a training task involving the erection of a right-angled scaffolding frame, a team of divers took 15 minutes to completion on the surface, and 5 hours underwater. This was because each pair down found that the previous pair's attempts to bolt their piece at the correct angle was woefully out of line.

Distance and directional abilities underwater have also received some attention. Ross *et al.* (1970) had divers swimming blindfold, assisted by ropes, round two sides of a triangle. They then tried to complete the third side unguided. There was a marked tendency to veer from the straight line somewhat erratically. Sound, too, is distorted underwater. It travels approximately $4\frac{1}{2}$ times faster in water, frequencies are higher and phase differences at the ears are difficult to detect, making sound localization difficult. Sensitivity to sound is reduced by roughly 60 dB, and with heliox or under greater pressure, by even more.

Anxiety – That anxiety impairs performance, and that it can be present to some extent in diving, is obvious. It is often said that it is a poor diver who doesn't have a healthy respect for fear, and a much used homily is that "there are old divers, and there are bold divers, but there are no old bold divers". Just how anxiety will affect performance, however, is dependent on a number of things, environmental conditions and experience being more or less quantifiable, but individual reactions to similar stress levels being more elusive. Weltman *et al.* (1974) review the literature and conclude that psychomotor tasks in general show a greater decrement if subjects believe themselves to be in a stressful environment than if there is no knowledge of the stress cf. Baddeley, 1966). There is also evidence that anxiety may result in 'perceptual narrowing' when attention becomes 'narrowed' on to a central task and peripheral cues become harder to detect. Weltman *et al.* (1966) asked novice divers to monitor a peripheral light either alone or while performing a central addition task while dial watching. When diving, sub-groups of the dual task subjects significantly increased response times to peripheral stimuli while maintaining constant performance on the central task. Weltman *et al.* (1971) used non-divers in a simulated pressure chamber (the deception perpetrated by moving dials and hissing air). The subjects detected 40% less visual peripheral signals when performing a central, self-paced task than did controls. Anxiety was inferred as the cause since the 'chamber' subjects showed significantly higher heart-rates and anxiety test rating scores than controls. Baddeley (1969) proposed a speculative model for 'perceptual narrowing'. He suggested that a dangerous situation will tend to increase the subject's level of arousal, which in turn will focus his attention more narrowly on those aspects of the situation he considers to be most important. If the task he is performing is regarded by him as most important then performance will improve; if, on the other hand, it is regarded as peripheral to some other activity such as survival, it will deteriorate.

All commercial diving can be in some senses regarded as dual task performance, the two tasks being to do the job at the same time as staying alive. Perceptual narrowing, if it exists in the experienced commercial diver (once again, both studies reported here involved novices or non-divers), could have serious implications for safety. If the diver is narrowed on to the job, peripheral cues indicating that something is going wrong (slight pulls indicating fouling lines, faint noises suggesting impending equipment failure, emergency instructions coming faintly over a noisy communication channel, changes in current etc.) may go undetected. Similarly there are implications relevant to efficiency; if the diver is narrowed on to his own safety, the job may be poorly done.

Social stresses – In addition to all the other stresses that a commercial diver will have to endure while actually working, there are a number of social stresses that go with the job. The offshore commercial diver will spend a number of weeks offshore followed by a rest period ashore; the actual amounts of time involved will depend on the job and the company for whom he works. If the company is large enough, his offshore location each time will vary and may be anywhere in the world. Thus there are no constraints on where he lives and comparatively less opportunities to form social relationships with workmates when away from the job. The diving population is a small, elite group and experienced divers are consequently in great demand. As recently as 1973, Jugel (1975) estimated that there were only 2300 commercial divers in the whole United States, and of these 770 were free-lance or part-time. Unsubstantiated estimates of the numbers now working in the North Sea vary from 1500 to 2000. With these comparatively small numbers, a diver, even during his rest period, will often be on call, and may have to drop everything to be 'choppered' out to a rig somewhere where an expensive emergency is happening at 3.15 in the morning. On the rig, barge or diving boat, he lives in cramped, noisy conditions in an all-male society, although conditions on the rigs are usually made as comfortable as possible under the circumstances, with good food, TV and films. On the spot firing for sometimes trivial reasons is fairly commonplace. This is perhaps not as unfair as it sounds as, purely for safety reasons, the supervisor must get rid of anyone who he considers to be a potential troublemaker within the team, or to be inadequate for the job. There is no room for anyone who won't or can't pull his weight.

It is not surprising, then, that the commercial diver has a reputation for being a latter-day cowboy who tends to go berserk on arrival back in the rig's base port. This is not necessarily true, but many divers like to keep up the illusion. The lack of constraint on where he lives means that the younger, unmarried diver may well be comparatively rootless. Although no reliable data are available, personal experience indicates that the divorce rate among married divers, especially those who were married before taking up diving for a career, is high, which again is not surprising.

One might thus imagine that it takes a fairly exceptional personality to withstand the stresses of this particularly demanding life-style. Various studies have attempted to isolate the personality characteristics of the diver, but with mixed results. Radloff and Helmreich (1968) found that more successful divers tended to be older, more experienced and shared motivational interests with other divers, but this seems to be largely a truism. Nichols (1969) propounded that divers were more intelligent, affected by feelings, surgent, tough-minded, hard to fool, and forthright, but not as self-sufficient or bloody-minded as for example climbers. Biersner (1973) reported that navy divers (before joining) were different from fleet controls in running away from home, playing truant, receiving traffic tickets and being arrested for non-traffic violations. He concluded that they rebelled earlier against the restrictions of social institutions and were successful in directing this activity and aggression towards an occupation in which these characteristics may not only be useful, but necessary.

There is certainly a case for a rigorous and intensive study of the working, successful commercial diver, since most studies have concentrated on either navy divers or sport divers. However, it is unlikely that any single trait or cluster will emerge as dominant. Personal observation of commercial diving teams gives the impression that a good team is rarely if ever made up entirely of highly dominant extrovert leaders; such a team would probably be disastrous. One should avoid a situation where there are too many chiefs and not enough indians, and, living at close quarters on the rig, and especially in saturation, it may be a positive advantage to be able to withdraw from the foibles of others. Many saturation divers occupy their time off shift by taking correspondence courses, often in languages. Saxophonists are not encouraged.

Commercial divers are these days required to go into saturation for increasingly longer periods of time, where confinement is closer than under normal circumstances. Studies of such confinement and social isolation have been made, both under normal atmospheric and under hyperbaric conditions. Because of the constraints imposed by the high cost and low living volume of such operations, the number of subjects in any given study must be small, which unfortunately makes it difficult to generalize from the results.

During August–October, 1965, 3 teams of 10 US navy divers spent 15 days in the SEALAB habitat at 6.2 m (SEALAB II) under saturation, in an experimental test of the feasibility of scientific working in habitats having independence from surface support. From sampling of activities, analysis of communications of the teams with each other and the outside world, it was found that successful accommodation to conditions of isolation and confinement were accounted for by three clusters of attributes: task orientation, emotional stability and social compatibility. Gregariousness and dedication to work were the main characteristics of the best members of the teams. It seems, then, that the successful saturation diver must be a bit of a contradiction. He must be not only 'hard-headed' and 'tough-minded' in order to do his job, but gregarious *and* tolerant, and at the same time must be able to withdraw from irritations.

THE JOB: CLASSIFICATIONS AND CATEGORIZATIONS

Diving techniques

The most useful distinction on the grounds of environment, social and working conditions, jobs mostly performed and diving techniques can perhaps be made between shallow inshore compressed-air diving and offshore oilfield work. The former can be defined as being limited to construction, repair and maintenance in harbours and dockyards and is usually referred to as civil engineering diving. The latter will be operationally based on platform, barge or diving boat, and will involve offshore shifts mostly varying from 2 weeks to a month with variable shore periods depending on the contractor. It embraces the whole range of diving techniques, from shallow compressed-air diving to deep saturation and habitat working dives.

We will concentrate first on the *harbour and dockyard diver,* whose job is easily defined, and for whom the existing records are well standardized. The working and social conditions of this kind of professional diver are probably much closer to those of his counterparts in shore-based industries than those of any other professional diver. He has a steady, guaranteed job, a home base, and he will rarely be called upon to work outside normal industrial hours or away from home. Most of his work will be carried out in comparatively shallow water. This has the advantage that he can work for extended periods of time without needing decompression. The major drawback, and possibly a major point of interest from the psychological and human factors point of view, is that, in addition to all the other potential diving hazards, the state of the water in the average harbour is such as to reduce visibility to almost zero.

Within offshore and oilfield diving one can isolate sub-categories.

Surface-oriented shallow compressed-air diving — This overlaps with the civil engineering classification in that the equipment and diving techniques will be substantially the same but the jobs performed are rather different since they involve more 'scientific' measurement using devices such as welding crack detectors, and more cleaning, preparing, constructing and maintaining metal structures, usually in at least moderate visibility. Divers typically use surface demand, rarely SCUBA, and often operate from a cage lowered from a derrick on the barge or platform, from which they can be conveyed to a dry decompression chamber immediately on surfacing, should the schedule demand it. This kind of diving will be much more affected by adverse weather conditions than harbour and dockyard work, especially when working from a boat where swell can render a job impossible.

Bell-oriented 'no lock out' diving — involves inspection, measurement or estimated measurement, or the searching and location of objects from the inside of the diving bell. Since the diver does not have to leave the bell, the bell is not 'blown down' to ambient pressure and no decompression will normally be involved.

Bell-oriented 'lock out' diving — involves the diver leaving the bell. His life support is provided via umbilical hoses from the bell, will normally involve mixed gas (usually heliox) for breathing, such dives tend to be comparatively deep, and will often involve the circulation of warm water to heat the diver's suit. A variable period of decompression depending on the depth–time profile of the dive will normally be required.

Saturation diving — is required where the depth of the job, or the depth–time profile, is such that the divers' tissues become saturated with absorbed gas, thus requiring a maximally long decompression schedule for the relevant depth. Once saturated, the diver can be kept at the working (or storage) pressure for as many days as may be required to complete the operation, then brought back to the surface according to a special kind of slow decompression procedure. While under the storage pressure, he will live in a chamber on the barge or rig which varies in size, providing accommodation for up to six men in a rather cramped environment. To get to the work site, which may be up to 200 m deep (this depth will certainly increase as exploration gets progressively deeper), the divers in saturation, usually 2 at a time, will enter a bell which can be locked on to and off from their living chamber. This will have been blown down to the working ambient pressure, will be lowered to the working site, and the divers will work from the bell as in 'bell-oriented lock out diving' above. Psychologically, this kind of diving is characterized both by long periods of confinement in a small space and the prospect of high remuneration for the job, as well as the as yet largely unknown effects of continual exposure to high pressure. Confinements for periods of up to 20 days are now not uncommon.

Submersibles, single atmosphere suits and lock-out submarines — can either be a way of conveying a diver to work at ambient pressure, or closed, single atmosphere and highly specialized vehicles for deep recovery operations. Single atmosphere reinforced and jointed suits, such as JIM and SAM, keep the individual diver in a normal atmosphere, allow him to work with his hands using various kinds of prosthetics, and enable a diver to perform manual tasks at great depths without elaborate or lengthy decompression schedules. Lock-out submarines are the equivalent of diving bells, but mobile. There is little data yet available on the operation of these systems.

Task categorization

The jobs a professional diver is required to perform require adaptability, insight, inventiveness and a multitude of skills, the possession of almost any single one of which would on its own provide a man with a steady surface industrial job. A tentative categorization of activities at the task level has been arrived at via an analysis of a series of structured interviews conducted with a variety of diving supervisors and divers from a number of different sources.

Diving activities can be divided into three broad areas. The first is construction and maintenance, the second is inspection, and the third consists of practice, equipment testing, rehearsal and 'catch-all'. The third cannot usefully be sub-categorized. The first two, on the other hand, can be subdivided into tasks as shown in Table 8.1. This preliminary classification system could be improved; for example, riding a jet-sled could be classed both under "Excavation" or "Guiding surface". Nonetheless, the system has been developed through consultation with those most in touch with underwater working, and may serve as a basic framework.

The civil engineering diver operates at shallow depths but for long periods. While the effort exerted was mostly recorded by the divers as 'medium', it is probably true to say that a major requirement of this form of diving is considerable stamina. The general range of skills and tools required is quite considerable. Operations are biassed towards manual labour but the emphasis would seem to be on adaptability. Personal observation leads to the conclusion that the successful civil engineering diver tends to be inventive; he will often, for example, design and make for himself personalized all-purpose tools for particular kinds of job. The fact that most of the jobs are manual, involving hand tools, coupled with the comparatively long duration of each dive and the fact that most dives take place in conditions of poor to zero visibility indicate that certain personal qualities must be of prime importance. The diver certainly must possess a high degree of manual dexterity and should be able to work largely from a highly developed sense of touch that can be maintained underwater for two to three hours. He should also be persistent and not subject to giving up easily.

For offshore and oilfield commercial diving we move into the realm of the deep and hostile open ocean. This kind of diving is the prerogative of what

TABLE 8.1   Construction and maintenance

Action	
Emplacement	Placing a sizeable object in a well-defined position
Heavy assembling/dismantling	Using power tools
Light assembling/dismantling	Using hands, hand tools
Rigging/unrigging	Fork-lifting, emplacement etc.
Demolition	Explosives
Excavation	Trenching, digging, jetting etc.
Building	Cementing, grouting, mortar etc.
Protection	Lagging, epoxy coating etc.
Welding	Self-evident
Cutting	Hand saw, power saw
Burning	Oxyarc, thermic lance cutting etc.
Drilling	Hand or power tools
Cleaning	Remove marine growth, debris etc.
Inspection	
Investigation	Routine checking, check repairs etc.
Measuring	Simple measurement of objects using tape, rule
Surveying	Detailed plan of area for construction or repairs
Searching	Look for lost objects, damage etc.
Sampling	Mud samples, core samples, grouting samples etc.
Photography	Still camera, video
Guiding surface	Positioning crane, barge etc.
Scientific measurement	X-ray welds etc.
Estimation	Estimating dimensions with no direct measurement

is popularly known as 'the deep sea diver', where hard and sometimes dangerous work is performed under conditions which can be truly harsh. Some insight into the demands of this job can be obtained from critical incident studies. Strictly speaking, a critical incident should be defined as a set of circumstances that could have led to an accident or to a botched job, but didn't. Such circumstances, however, are not generally recorded, at least on dive summary records. Bends and accidents are usually recorded, as are equipment failures. As mentioned previously, it is certainly possible that minor accidents and difficulties do not get recorded as divers in general tend to avoid anything that might in any way make them appear incompetent. Childs (1976) conducted a study of 114 incidents in the North Sea where the diver actually lost consciousness or showed other similar symptoms of distress. He reports problems occurring immediately before the incidents concerned which break down roughly as follows: thermal (heat, cold) 8%; unsteadiness or weakness (dizziness, faintness, confusion, disorientation) 18%; neurological problems (visual disturbance, convulsions, tremor) 12%; effect on consciousness (impending unconsciousness, memory loss, erratic behaviour) 13%; respiration problems (breathing difficulty, hyperventilation) 25%; general distress 4%; Psychological problems (undue unease or apprehension, diver failure) 15%; dysbaric problems (compression or decompression) 12%; equipment problems, 13%.

In 1976 we carried out a survey of operations carried out by several offshore diving contractors. About 1800 dives were involved from a variety of vessels and structures. The accidents that were recorded in our sample involved 147 separate incidents, comprising 8.2% of the total dives in the sample. Of these, about half were due to equipment failure involving varying degrees of risk to the diver. Limitations caused by adverse weather conditions accounted for a third of these incidents, while there are only 7 recordings of incidents that can be reasonably attributed to human error. Only two recorded injuries, one from a water jet exhaust, and the other a badly cut finger, required the divers concerned to be sent for hospital treatment. Of 7 recorded incidents involving bends, all were successfully treated by modifying decompression schedules accordingly.

A survey of experienced commercial diving supervisors was conducted to discover which tools and tasks and individual divers' personal characteristics were generally considered to be most important. Rigging tools (shackles, rope, lifting strops etc.) emerged as the most important, while spanner, hammer, and wrench followed closely; some tools mentioned here were specific to offshore work. Pneumatic or hydraulic tools such as the impact wrench and the use of still photography and video systems were mentioned fairly often. The most surprising rating was the low score given to the welding gun, but this may be due to bias in the sample. Various scientific instruments (welding crack detectors, magnetic particle detectors, and so on) were also mentioned; they have a comparatively low rating as they are largely regarded as 'specialist', although they are used extensively on certain kinds of contracts for non-destructive testing (NDT).

The survey also asked the recipients to rate, on a scale of 0 to 100 in terms of importance, two lists of personal characteristics relevant to the good diver and to the poor diver. These lists were derived from earlier semi-structured interviews with experienced commercial divers, on the basis of the number of times each characteristic was mentioned. The divers' own opinions about both what makes a good diver and a bad diver were somewhat at variance with the popular image of the 'latter day cowboy'. Reliability, common sense and honesty rate highly as desirable personality characteristics, as do staying power, level-headedness and knowledge. Strangely enough, sociability was not rated at all highly, nor the ability to ignore others' faults. To the professional, these are probably seen to be irrelevant to whether or not a man can do a good job but they must at least be important in saturation. A man who asks if he doesn't know something, rather than trying to cover his ignorance, is rated highly. The bar 'super-hero' rates highly on the bad diver scale, as does the man who gives in easily. Respect for fear occupies the middle ranges. Attitudes to drink, part of the popular image, are not rated highly on either scale, although this may be because the diver is forced to be dry at work, and it is considered that what he does ashore is up to him. While experience is seen as a fairly important characteristic of the good diver, inexperience is not viewed as an important characteristic of the bad diver; that is, a diver is not discriminated against if he is inexperienced as long as he is willing both to learn and to pull his weight. Finally, the low ratings given on both scales to attitudes towards high financial reward reflect a possible general feeling that most divers are in the job for the money rather than for the love of the job. As one supervisor put it: "I think that all divers are in the job for the money, mainly because it is purely a short-term career, say 10–15 years of active diving." Few divers are fortunate enough to 'graduate' to even the lower range of management.

Civil engineering work is generally harder and less comfortable than shallow off-shore work. Dive durations for the former peak at between 3 and $3\frac{1}{2}$ hours, whereas the offshore sample summary peaks at less than half an hour, the more arduous work being done in saturation. In terms of tools and equipment usage (at the work face itself) both kinds of diver spend a high proportion of their time using simple hand tools such as hammers and spanners. Certain pieces of equipment, such as the airlift, are less prominent in offshore work than in civil engineering, and the opposite goes for metal-oriented tools such as the oxyarc cutter. Equipment that reflects the wider range of offshore activities, such as video, still camera, scientific measuring devices and so on, is not used in civil engineering. Offshore diving requires a much more even distribution of skills than civil engineering, across the whole range of tasks. Demolition, heavy assembly, photography (still or video), guiding the surface, scientific measurement and estimation are not mentioned at all in the civil engineering survey, and burning, welding, and sampling were negligible; all these tasks, however, are carried out to varying extents offshore. The majority of civil engineering constructions and maintenance jobs fell into the light assembly/dismantling category, demanding skill with hand tools, with building and excavation figuring fairly prominently as well. Tasks most often done offshore were rigging, emplacement, heavy and light assembly, cleaning and burning. Building and demolition (explosives) occupied the smallest estimated percentage of man hours. Rigging, of course, was dominant in the offshore survey; it is possible that this task may be under-represented in the civil engineering data due to its being so commonplace that it may get ignored on records and in questionnaires. A much more even and wider spread of inspection tasks was required offshore, with general investigation taking priority, whereas surveying and searching were prominent in civil engineering.

The good diver emerges as something of a paragon of virtue, but the preferred characteristics are not surprising, considering the hazardous nature of the job, the interdependence of a diving team and the fact that it may sometimes be difficult to check on a diver's work and thus reliance is placed on the honesty of his surface debriefing.

The general range of tools and equipment used was quite considerable for both forms of diving, especially offshore work. In the latter, there is a trend towards the use of more complicated equipment, such as non-destructive testing devices and, with technological advances, diving systems themselves also become more complex. To learn to 'drive' such systems, divers need at least a minimum level of intelligence. It is also perhaps worth pointing out that, due to the international nature of offshore diving operations, instructions for the use of, and the units of calibration of, diving systems can be displayed in different languages – the major alternative to English is French.

Operations are biassed towards manual labour, but the emphasis would seem to be on adaptability. A diver must be quick to learn in new situations, and adaptable to unfamiliar tools and diving systems. He should possess a high degree of manual dexterity and in many cases should be able to work from a highly developed sense of touch that can be maintained underwater; this implies a good visual/spatial memory. He should be persistent and not subject to giving up easily. His intelligence often manifests itself in making personalized all-purpose tools for particular kinds of job.

ADAPTATION, OR WHY THINGS AREN'T QUITE AS BAD AS THEY SOUND

One could be forgiven for wondering, if impairments and stresses underwater are indeed as bad as they appear, and if the requirements of the job are as demanding and varied as they have been shown here, how anything at all ever manages to get done efficiently. The answer, of course, lies in the basic human ability to adapt to almost anything given enough exposure and training. Realization of this basic piece of common sense runs throughout the industry. Having passed a commercial diver training course, even with flying colours, the diving 'graduate' is unlikely to get a job as a diver straight away. He is much more likely to serve an apprenticeship of sorts, as a linesman and tender to a more experienced diver, before he is allowed to operate as a diver himself, even in shallow water.

Adaptation to social stress was demonstrated by Miller et al. (1967) during the SEALAB II human behaviour programme. They found that all three teams spent more time in the water during the second halves of their missions; both the frequency and the duration of dives increased significantly. Furthermore, group cohesiveness improved during the missions. Comparison between pre- and post-mission administrations of sociometric choice questionnaires showed, for all teams, significant shifts towards selection of team-mates.

Experience of working in the underwater environment is obviously a major factor in the individual's ability to come to terms with it. As early as 1937, Schilling and Willgrube found that cognitive tasks such as solving arithmetical problems were consistently less affected by pressure at each level between 1 and 10 ATA for experienced divers than for those with less experience. Weltman et al. (1971) showed that, compared to novice divers, experienced divers displayed virtually no decrement in a complex pipe assembly task between tank and 6 m ocean, or between tank and 15 m cold ocean in poor visibility. Andersen (1968) and Vaughan (1972) found that navigational ability improved with training, while Ferris (1971) found that distance judgement accuracy improved with training and feedback. Standard pipeline lengths may provide feedback for this kind of learning. Incidentally, Godden (unpublished) found that training on the surface for a task involving visual imagery, memory and manual dexterity under conditions of zero visibility was positively harmful to subsequent performance underwater. After surface training, one group's performance when switching to the underwater environment became significantly worse than that of another on their first underwater trial with no prior training at all. Presumably land training taught reliance on cues that were distorted or not available under water.

Many of the performance impairments mentioned here can to a large extent be put down to an interaction between environmental stresses and anxiety. However, experienced divers can adapt to the deleterious effects of anxiety as well, perhaps by invoking some kind of defence mechanism during the activity itself. Knapp *et al.* (1976), in studies involving a 5 day habitat dive and a 305 m 10 day saturation simulation, showed that, although there was an increase in the level of anxiety 30 minutes after completion of these dives, there was a lowering of anxiety immediately before and during the dives themselves, suggesting that subjects developed appropriate defences to prevent the debilitating effects of anxiety at the important stages of the experiment. Finally, Skreslet and Aarefjord (1968) found that divers adapted physiologically to cold stress after six weeks of diving, but the adaptation disappeared when exposure trials were discontinued. It therefore appears that, with experience and persistence, the determined and motivated commercial diver can adapt to offset many of the deleterious effects of his chosen working environment.

SUMMARY AND A LOOK TOWARDS THE FUTURE

Some practical implications

The physiological problems described earlier are comparatively well understood. Considerable research, both naval and commercial, has served to reduce many of them to within acceptable limits; the development of successful compression and decompression schedules to enable simulated dives of over 600 m to be achieved on the one hand, and the successful and continuing commercial development of thermal suits and heated gas systems on the other, serve as examples. Such research will continue as the limits of diving are steadily pushed back.

To draw practical implications from the psychologically oriented work described here is not quite so easy. Applied psychological, social, and human engineering disciplines do not yet have much of a foothold in the industry, which can probably lay claim to being both the newest industry of its kind and at the same time the most conservative. This is due to many factors, not the least being the (often justifiable) suspicions of the contractors who tend to label any investigator in this area as just another 'shrink', and to the lack of immediate relevance of many studies to the commercial world. There are of course other problems. It is safe to say that commercial divers will be subject to cognitive and psychomotor impairments in performance that will be broadly similar to those described here, but to what extent we cannot yet say. This has obvious implications for safety. Perhaps some attempt should be made to acquaint trainee divers with aspects of the available psychological literature during their training, relevant both to the performance decrements and to the possible social consequences. This should, however, be done with the Weltman *et al.* (1974) results in mind (awareness of potential danger interacts to increase impairments) since one does not want, in the industrial vernacular, to 'overspook' them. One important point here is probably to promote awareness of the mechanisms of adaptation. If it is the case, as has been suggested, that many divers leave the profession only to return some months or years later, their latent adaptation will disappear unless they keep up some constant exposure to their previous working environment, and they may return much less capable than they believe themselves to be.

Problems also arise in attempting to draw implications for industrial efficiency. Obviously, efficiency and safety will increase if jobs are planned in such a way as to reduce potential psychological impairments. This might involve developing operational procedures to check periodically on possible impairment, planning briefing and debriefing environments and methods to take account of potential context-dependent memory effects, structuring information in the most easily assimilated forms given cognitive impairments, and so on. As far as implications for the selection of commercial diver trainees is concerned, one can only suggest that they be tested for mechanical ability, memory (especially visual) and a useful standard of numeracy. Research into selection on the grounds of personality has not been too successful in the past and is unlikely to prove so in the future. However, it is strongly suggested that potential trainees should be screened for a reasonable expectation of what they are in for, together with screening for past history of mental disorder or instability. It is also generally agreed that stable domestic circumstances are important to the working diver, and that on no account should a diver be committed to a saturation dive if there is trouble at home. The main implications for training are that, in a rapidly changing technological industry, training organizations must be kept abreast of what is happening, both in terms of equipment and in terms of jobs done. To this end, a continuing job study based on more standardized and detailed records than are currently available should be set up.

Finally, the most immediately relevant and visibly useful research is likely to come from the human engineering approach, and in the development of operational procedures designed to overcome specific and well-recognized problems in the industry. One such is to be found in diver-to-surface communications. The best systems in the world at the moment cannot overcome occasional serious noise in the communications channel, which cannot be avoided on a diving boat or rig, where generators and assorted stray electrical activity are endemic. Helium unscramblers work up to a point, but are not fully efficient and can interact to make the problem worse. This can result in misunderstandings and concomitant safety risk, and a diver may have to be recalled into the bell where he can make himself more intelligible without restrictions of the mask. Furthermore, with any given set of communications gear, there is a wide amount of variation in individuals' intelligibility. Work soon to be started will attempt to establish an overall diving vocabulary, identify intelligibility levels of each word over standard and noisy communications systems, and find either highly intelligible words to substitute for low intelligibility common terms, or alternative operational procedures to reduce the expensive occurrences of bell recall.

Human engineering of equipment design will also be of immediate and visible application. As mentioned previously, most equipment for use underwater is merely the surface item modified solely for corrosive protection, if modified at all. Considerable increase in practical efficiency can be achieved by designing tools to fit the environment, rather than hoping that the man can adapt to the tool. Another common complaint is with the design and layout of control and display systems for various pieces of equipment from communications gear to operating systems for large saturation complexes. In the former, although the facility for multiway communications exists electronically, the controls are often such that, as one diver put it, "to work that lot properly, you'd have to learn to play the harmonium". In the latter case, although the systems are usually superb pieces of engineering, dials that should be continuously watched are often placed where they cannot be comfortably monitored, and sometimes cannot be monitored at all if simultaneous observation is needed. Instructions can be misleading and are sometimes in languages foreign to the operators. In one case an operator, in order to record dial readings, had to sit with his back to the dials. Emergency controls can be in positions where only a dwarf with six foot arms could reach them in a hurry. There is therefore considerable scope for ergonomic consultancy at the early design stages of these systems. As the same diver put it, "when you're down there, narked out of your tiny mind, and something nasty happens, it's nice to know that you're likely to hit the right button, or at least, that the monkey upstairs will".

What we know, and what we ought to know

What we know about diving is rather patchy and disorganized. Unfortunately, most of the data largely concerns the behaviour of navy divers and amateurs. Commercial divers have been involved in very few studies. In view of the findings that navy divers and amateurs can adapt to cold, to anxiety, and to perceptual distortions, one might predict that the successful commercial diver has become highly adapted, and that many of the reported impairments of cognitive function, manual dexterity and so on, may have become greatly reduced through such adaptation. There is therefore a strong case for taking a closer look at the commercial diver from the behavioural point of view and using representative samples of commercial divers as subjects to repeat a number of the studies reported here that might be relevant to the commercial world.

One area of study which has received plentiful attention in the surface and industrial contexts, but no attention whatsoever in the underwater world, is decision making. Now, accurate decision making is obviously an extremely important aspect of a diver's day-to-day existence. Decisions taken before-hand in planning a job, decisions made while working (Is this the right pipeline? Is this corrosion acceptable or not? Should I abort this job now or carry on to finish it? and so on) will have a marked effect on overall efficiency. On the surface, people tend to be rather bad at decision making, especially if it is probabilistic rather then deterministic, and has to be made on the basis of incomplete information (Edwards, 1968). One cannot yet even hazard a guess at what might happen underwater.

One hears of fatal accidents in the North Sea, and access to the relevant circumstances can be obtained, but one rarely if ever hears reports about or can obtain data on non-lethal accidents, and critical incidents where injury or job completion failure might have resulted but didn't. Research into critical incidents on a broad scale might help pinpoint certain common qualities in terms of the situations and circumstances surrounding them, and therefore indicate situations which should be avoided. Anxiety and perceptual narrowing in the experienced and presumably highly adapted commercial diver warrant further study, as do the mechanisms of, and circumstances surrounding, the onset of panic. For both practical and ethical reasons, panic cannot be induced under controlled conditions, but verbal reports and structured interviews might produce a useful data-base.

If we are to find out anything useful about what makes the commercial diver function and how he copes with his working environment and life-style, it is the commercial diver himself who must be studied, and not the amateur sport diver or the navy diver. This of course presents problems, not the least being the availability of subjects and their willingness to volunteer for experimental studies or to participate in surveys, questionnaires or interviews. These difficulties, together with the obvious interest of the naval authorities, have led to the major research effort being directed towards navy diving. Nonetheless, navy diving and the surrounding social and work conditions are vastly different from the general experience of the commercial diver. Furthermore, the majority of experimental study has been oriented towards the categorization and quantification of performance impairments. A shift of emphasis towards a more positive relevance to the commercial diving industry is needed; that is, we should concentrate now more on what the diver *can* do and how he does it, and on ways of improving efficiency and safety in the real working environment.

The changing nature of commercial diving and the direction of future research

Several factors will interact to affect the nature of commercial diving in the coming years, especially in the North Sea, and any future research effort should take them into consideration. The most obvious will be a shift in balance between exploration and production. As more and more platforms go into production, the distribution of required tasks will alter, with maintenance (rather than construction) and routine inspection becoming dominant.

This, however, will be offset by the continually developing technology surrounding underwater operations, and by the push for exploration in progressively deeper and more hostile oceans. The Norwegian Sea and Arctic areas off Greenland and Alaska are now opening up for exploration and the lessons learned in the North Sea can be adapted and extended there. Furthermore, it is not only oil to which the future will look for exploration. Tin exists in some quantities off the Cornish coast, and it is even feasible that mining of manganese modules from the deep Pacific ocean floor might one day become a commercial possibility. New and revolutionary techniques will need development if resources such as these are to be tapped.

The diver has not yet been designed out of the system, and it is unlikely that he ever will be. Pesch *et al.* (1970), evaluating the capabilities of the human operator to perform applied undersea tasks as a diver, in comparison to operating a remote controlled, manipulator-equipped, small submersible, found that divers were faster than manipulators by a factor of 4, although this factor was highly task-specific. Shallow underwater mining will probably involve an interaction between straightforward diving and the use of submersibles in one form or another. At profound depths, however, the diver will probably be operating from single atmosphere subsersibles or bottom crawlers, and will not be able to exit into the underwater environment.

References

Andersen, B. G. (1968). Diver performance measurement: underwater navigation depth maintenance and weight carrying capabilities. *Groton, Conn.: Gen. Dynam. Corp. Elect. Boat. Div.*, Report u-417-68-030

Baddeley, A. D. (1966a). Time estimation at reduced body-temperature. *Am. J. Psychol.*, **79**, 475

Baddeley, A. D. (1966b). Influence of depth on manual dexterity of free divers: a comparison between open sea and pressure chamber testing. *J. Appl. Psychol.*, **50**, 81

Baddeley, A. D. (1967). Diver performance and the interaction of stresses. In Lythgoe, J. N. and Woods, J. D. (eds.). *Underwater Association Report 1966–1967*. (Carshalton, England: T.G.W. Industrial and Research Promotions)

Baddeley, A. D. (1969). Performance in dangerous environments. Presented at NATO Advanced Study Institute in Human Factors/Ergonomics, Mondello, Sicily, Sept. 1969

Baddeley, A. D. (1977). Paper presented to the Undersea Medical Society second workshop in Development of Standardised Assessment of Underwater Performance, Bethesda, Maryland, March 1977

Baddeley, A. D., Cuccaro, W. J., Egstrom, G. H., Weltman, G. and Willis, M. A. (1975). Cognitive efficiency of divers working in cold water. *Hum. Factors*, **17** (5), 446

Baddeley, A. D. and Flemming, N. C. (1967). The efficiency of divers breathing oxygen–helium. *Ergonomics*, **10**, 311

Bennett, P. B., Poulton, E. C., Carpenter, A. and Catton, M. J. (1967). Efficiency at sorting cards in air and a 20 percent oxygen–helium mixture at depths down to 100 feet and in enriched air. *Ergonomics*, **10**, 53

Bennett, P. B. and Towse, E. J. (1971). Performance efficiency of men breathing oxy–helium at depths between 100 feet and 1500 feet. *Aerospace Med.*, **42**, 1147

Biersner, R. J. (1973). Social development of Navy divers. *Aerospace Med.*, July 1973, 761

Biersner, R. J. and Cameron, B. J. (1970). Cognitive performance during a 1000-foot helium dive. *Aerospace Med.*, **41**, 918

Bowen, H. M. (1968). Diver performance and the effects of cold. *Hum. Factors*, **10**, 445

Bühlmann, A. A., Matthys, M., Overrath, G., Bennett, P. B., Elliott, D. H. and Gray, S. P. (1970). Saturation exposures at 31 ata in an oxygen–helium atmosphere with excursions to 36 ata. *Aerospace Med.*, **41**, 394

Carter, R. (1977). Paper presented to the Undersea Medical Society second workshop on Development of Standardised Assessment of Performance, Bethesda, Maryland, March 1977

Childs, C. M. (1976). Investigation into loss of consciousness in divers. Offshore Health Service, Department of Surgery, University of Aberdeen. Copies of the report held by Dr Cocking at Harwell

Davis, F. M., Baddeley, A. D. and Hancock, T. R. (1975). Diver performance: the effect of cold. *Undersea Biomed. Res.*, **2**, 195

Davis, F. M., Osborne, J. P., Baddeley, A. D. and Graham, I. M. F. (1972). Diver performance: nitrogen narcosis and anxiety. *Aerospace Med.*, **43** (10), 1079

Egstrom, G. H. and Weltman, G. (1974). Underwater work performance and work tolerance: final report. *Report N00014-69-A-00200-4034, ONR*

Ferris, S. H. (1971). Absolute distance perception underwater and improvement through training. *U.S. Nav. Submar. Med. Cent.*, Report SMRL 670

Gaydos, H. F. (1958). Effect on complex manual performance of cooling the body while maintaining the hands at normal temperatures. *J. Appl. Physiol.*, **12**, 373

Gaydos, H. F. and Dusek, E. R. (1958). Effects of localised hand cooling versus total body cooling on manual performance. *J. Appl. Physiol.*, **12**, 377

Jugel, K. (1975). An analysis of the civil diving population of the United States. *Manned Undersea Science and Technology Report*

Kiessling, R. J. and Maag, C. H. (1962). Performance impairment as a function of nitrogen narcosis. *J. Appl. Psychol.*, **46**, 91

Knapp, R. J., Capel, W. C. and Youngblood, D. A. (1976). Stress in the deep: a study of undersea divers in controlled dangerous situations. *J. Appl. Psychol.*, **61** (4), 507

Miller, J. W., Radloff, R., Bowen, H. M. and Helmreich, R. L. (1967). The SEALAB II human behaviour program. In Pauli, D. C. and Clopper, G. P. (eds.). *Project Sealab Report, an Experimental 45-day Undersea Saturation Dive at 205 feet*. ONR Report ACR-124

Nelson, J. G. (1967). The effect of water immersion and body position upon perception of the gravitational vertical. *US Nav. Air. Devel. Cent.*, Report NADC-MR-6709

Nichols, A. K. (1969). The personality of divers (and other sportsmen). *Underwater Association Report*, pp. 62–66

Parker, J. W. (1969). Performance effects of increased ambient pressure, II. Helium–oxygen saturation and excursion dive to a simulated depth of 110 feet. *US Nav. Med. Cent. Rep.* SMRL 596

Poulton, E. C., Catton, M. J. and Carpenter, A. (1964). Efficiency at sorting cards in compressed air. *B.J. Indust. Med.*, **21**, 242

Radloff, R. and Helmreich, R. (1968). *Groups under Stress: Psychological Research in SEALAB II*. (New York: Appleton–Century–Crofts)

Ross, H. E. (1974). *Behaviour and Perception in Strange Environments*. Advances in Psychology: 5 (George, Allen and Unwin Ltd.)

Ross, H. E., Crickmar, S. D., Sills, N. U. and Owen, E. P. (1969). Orientation to the vertical in free divers. *Aerospace Med.*, **40**, 728

Ross, H. E., Dickenson, D. J. and Jupp, B. J. (1970). Geographical orientation underwater. *Hum. Factors*, **12**, 13

Schilling, C. W. and Willgrube, W. W. (1937). Quantitative study of mental and neuromuscular reactions as affected by increased air pressure. *US Nav. Med. Bull.*, **35**, 373

Schilling, C. W., Werts, M. F. and Schandelmeier, N. R. (1976). *The Underwater Handbook. A Guide to Physiology and Performance for the Engineer*. (New York and London: Plenum Press)

Skreslet, S. and Aarefjord, F. (1968). Acclimatisation to cold in man induced by frequent scuba diving in cold water. *J. Appl. Physiol.*, **24**, 117

Springbett, B. M. (1951). The effects of exposure to cold on motor performance. *Canadian Defense Research Board, Physiology 3*, 1951

Stang, P. R. and Wiener, E. L. (1970). Diver performance in cold water. *Hum. Factors*, **12**, 391

Streimer, I., Turner, D. P. W., Jolkmer, K. and Pryor, P. (1971). Experimental study of diver performance in manual and mental tasks at 66 feet. *Engineering Psychology Programs*, ONR Contract N00014-70-C-0189

Teichner, W. H. (1954). Recent studies on simple reaction time. *Psychol. Bull.*, **51**, 128

Vaughan, W. S. Jr. (1972). *Diver Performance Capabilities and Endurance in a Wet Submersible*. (Whittenburg, Vaughan Associates, Inc., for ONR)

Weltman, G., Christianson, R. A. and Egstrom, G. H. (1970). Effects of environment and experience on underwater work performance. *Hum. Factors*, **12** (6), 587

Weltman, G., Egstrom, G. H. and Christianson, R. A. (1966). Perceptual narrowing in divers: a preliminary study. *University of California, Los Angeles Report* 66–67

Weltman, G., Smith, J. E. and Egstrom, G. H. (1971). Perceptual narrowing during simulated pressure-chamber exposure. *Hum. Factors*, **13**, 99

(Reproduced by kind permission of R. F. Allen)

9
The Rock Climber

H. DRASDO

INTRODUCTION

Rock climbing, sometimes considered as one branch of expertise subserving mountaineering, more often nowadays as an art or sport in its own right, has a recognizable history of about a hundred years. From its beginnings climbers have praised or criticized the ways in which particular ascents have been achieved, but it is only within the past ten years that systematic descriptions of the previously unwritten codes shaping all forms of mountaineering have been attempted. These codes are often flouted; excuses are offered or the sovereignty of the proposed rules is flatly rejected and argument on matters of principle and detail rages furiously at the time of writing. But the skills of the climber make no sense without mention of the constraints which allow him to display these skills and most climbers would agree broadly with the following summary.

All forms of climbing from greater mountaineering to the ascent of boulders are governed, or ought to be governed, by two codes of behaviour both of which may be infringed at the same time. Despite some protest, the term 'ethics' has come into use to refer to these two codes which may be described as *environment ethics* and *competition ethics*. Environment ethics, matters of temporary or permanent damage or disturbance to the mountain scene, are outside the scope of this essay. Competition ethics, variously called *climbing ethics* or *climbing rules,* matters of the use of assistance or advantage in the ascent of particular climbs, have to be understood in order to follow this discussion.

Mountaineering, Tejada-Flores (1967) proposed, consists of a hierarchy of distinguishable sub-sports or climbing-games. And the purpose of the restrictions set for each sub-sport by competition ethics is "to maintain a degree of uncertainty as to the eventual outcome". Therefore, assistance considered permissible on Everest – say, the use of a ladder to cross a crevasse – would be absurd and unfair on a British outcrop. The less the objective danger and the less the duration of the effort required, the more restrictive the rules become. The factors upon which the whole system seems to rest may be reduced to the need to exert oneself, the need to scare oneself, the need to excel, and the example set by the way in which the classic climbs in each area were first ascended. In British rock climbing the forms of advantage most often debated are the use of *aid* (chock slings, pitons and bolts to allow the climber to rest or make progress where he could not or dare not without this assistance) and the use of *protection* (the same equipment used only to secure the rope in order to mitigate so far as possible the effects of a fall). The rehearsal or inspection of difficult climbs or moves with a top rope or by abseil is often criticized. At the present moment the use of chalk on the hands is the subject of vehement argument. Competition ethics, moreover, respond continuously to change. Sometimes they are eased by common consent when population pressures force climbers to seek new ground on cliffs presenting novel problems or when there is no other way in which a new generation can achieve more than its predecessors. Sometimes they become more restrictive, taking account of a general rise in the level of skill, of new techniques and better equipment, or the results of increases in wealth and leisure.

It will be seen that from this viewpoint rock climbing is clearly a complex *game* (OED: "contest according to rules and decided by skill, strength or luck") continuously modified for the satisfaction of the skilled climber taking particular account of his stress-seeking propensity. It is an ideal model for Bernard's (1968) concept of human energy considered as an article of consumption. However, it should also be noted that competition in rock climbing is of two types (Drasdo, 1974). There is the *collateral competition* between climbers, broadly as described above, with recognition as an important reward. But climbing offers many other rewards distinguishable from this aspect of the activity: the savouring of astounding situations, the beauty of the rock architecture in itself, the tactile satisfactions, the interest inherent in using the gear and in imposing one's rope patterns against the rock structures, the controlled ecstasy of movement as widely varied as dance – its aesthetic and kinaesthetic pleasures in short. And a climber may in fact see himself as involved primarily in *vertical competition,* a contest between himself and the climb to which the transactions of other climbers and their group-agreed standards are to some extent irrelevant. From this viewpoint he may choose to employ as much aid or protection as he feels he needs, though his actions may provoke scorn, even hostility, if they are carried out on popular cliffs and are clearly at variance with local practice.

Every climb has its individual presence and reputation. It is named by the first party to ascend it and it is recorded in a club journal or log book or in a climbers' magazine before eventually finding its way into the guidebook for the area. In this it is credited to the first party, described in sufficient detail to allow all later climbers to find and follow the route exactly, and graded in difficulty by one of a number of reasonably precise systems. The most common classification divides climbs into six or seven main categories, usually taken in Britain as running from Moderate to Extremely Severe. Great prestige accrues to those who succeed on the most desperate enterprises and a tight communications network through magazines and informal channels keeps the national or international elite aware of the latest developments. Rock climbing (it has been said) "pre-supposes a certain language-game . . . its names, its grades, are important to us".

A number of distinguishable sub-sports may be recognized even within Britain and for convenience these may be reduced to *boulder problems, unroped solo, free climbing* and *aid climbing*. Such apparently dissimilar activities as climbing on sea-cliffs or on man-made walls relate essentially in skills and techniques to these four forms. British rock climbing has also been influenced over the past few years by *big wall climbing* overseas.

ASSESSMENT OF SKILL

When a climber is said to be skilful the basis of the judgement may range from a single observation of his performance to a considered evaluation of his achievements. In the former case the bystander would pay attention to two obvious characteristics. Firstly, he would notice the apparent ease of movement, the relaxed and stylish nature of progression; and also, perhaps, the amount of protection the leader of a roped party found it prudent to allow himself. (In passing, 'good style', 'poor style' and so on, often have a special and confusing meaning in climbing today; they indicate that compared with other parties less or more aid or protection, respectively, was used. In this discussion the word is used in its normal sense.) Secondly, he would take some account of the length of time spent in solving the problem. For, although a climber almost never considers speed on a short route as an end in itself, it does give some index of his competence. Two climbers may make an on sight lead of Cenotaph Corner in similar conditions and to the outward eye each may appear perfectly in control throughout; but this 120-foot pitch detains one for only fifteen minutes and the other for an hour and a half. One's assumption has to be that the former is more skilful.

It might be thought that there must be little difficulty in identifying the most skilful climbers by comparing their achievements. The avenues through which recognition and prestige may be gained are clear enough. We notice the ascent of a series of new routes, whether on well-known cliffs or in unexplored areas; the first ascent of a 'last great problem', especially one which has defeated a number of strong parties, and its early repetitions; the soloing of a high standard climb; the 'on sight' solo of any hard climb – its ascent without the soloist having climbed it earlier as a member of a roped party; the 'freeing' of a climb or move on which all earlier parties had used aid. In a loose sense we have usually taken it that anyone who leads top-standard climbs is an expert and, in using such long-lived or briefly fashionable expressions as tiger, hard man, star, the elite, the cream team and so forth, succeeding generations have generally felt that these persons or groups identified themselves easily enough. Yet, when rock-climbing standards are higher now than ever and activity far more intensive, it is not easy to define this upper class with perfect consistency.

The problem stems from how much importance should be accorded to survival as a criterion of skill and from the uncertain significance of chance in survival. If a climber is killed after a meteoric career of three years on the very hardest routes one is tempted to wonder whether he may have been climbing closer to his limits or less finely attuned to them than his surviving contemporaries. It cannot be denied that nearly all experts have fallen at some time or other and that survival in many of these falls could only be attributed to good luck; but it is equally the case that some few experts have never had a potentially serious fall and that some of the greatest who have survived sensational falls – for example, Joe Brown – have in the main won their reputations in periods following these early misadventures. In the end, the question of whether the expert is free to demand a share of good luck is unanswerable; but it seems reasonable to suggest that a fair number of years of successes are required to prove beyond doubt the expert's resources.

BASIC MOVEMENT

In talking about the essential or useful aspects of their art climbers have developed a specialized vocabulary and such terms as technical ability, delicacy, strength, control, confidence and drive have been in use for many years. There has always been a degree of overlap about these expressions and in all discussion of climbing skill, but by adopting the convention of the climbing-game hierarchy as described above it now seems possible to separate the main factors more precisely, even though in action these factors are usually present in combination.

Rock climbing, irrespective of the rock type on which it is practised, has a recognizable basic movement on comparatively easy ground. It copies walking movement; that is, the climber stands and moves in balance on his feet and uses his hands and arms mainly to preserve that balance. For most beginners this is an entirely natural and not a learned movement. Even those persons who have extreme difficulty in adopting it are rarely suffering from some congenital handicap. Rather, the free movement is inhibited either because the beginner cannot believe that the friction coefficient of the rock is sufficient to allow him to maintain this posture or because a generalized fear of falling blinds a rational view of its possibility. In either case he leans forward to reach for and clutch better handholds. At once, he reduces dangerously the angle at which his weight is applied to the footholds, he tires his arms unnecessarily by tensing them, and he hides with his body the footholds he will shortly need.

BOULDER PROBLEMS: MOVEMENT SKILLS

Boulders are rock formations small enough to allow the unroped climber to fall off or jump off in complete or comparative safety. The discussion of advanced climbing skills begins with boulder problems since on these the pure movement characteristics may be observed undistorted by other influences. On boulders the climber is able to discover very quickly the absolute physical limits of his performance and with practice he will extend these limits. He will also learn the frictional values of particular rock types and the techniques favoured or demanded by each type. "Even the most casual appraisal of bouldering cannot fail to recognize that it is the quintessence of the physical act of climbing." (Gill, 1978). A boulder problem, like the key passage of a bigger climb, may often be categorized as belonging to one of various general types. It may be strenuous, delicate, technical, awkward and so forth. The attributes demanded by these types of difficulty merit some description. Strength is easily wasted and is rapidly or ultimately expendable, even for the most powerful climber. A rock-climbing problem, especially in wide and holdless cracks or in flared chimneys whenever the angle approaches the vertical, may demand a huge generalized energy output from the limbs and trunk muscles (in climbing jargon, 'a thrutch'); or, at the other extreme on steep open walls or overhangs it may simply be 'fingery', calling for pull-ups on the finger-tips with little or no support for the body-weight from footholds. In climbing it should be remembered that strength is only significant expressed as a power–weight ratio so that a fit, slightly built girl may effectively be stronger than a muscle-bound weight-lifter. Strength has become steadily more important as climbers tackle progressively bigger overhangs and longer impending walls without aid.

Delicacy is usually understood as an aptitude for making controlled balance movements on steep rock with poor footholds and little or no handhold. It is also expressed as a general stability or relaxed quality in the body when at rest on tiny holds. It may be that it is in part a sign of comparative strength in the leg and trunk muscles which tire much less quickly than the arms; on the other hand it may simply indicate fine bodily co-ordination. Certainly we think of delicacy as a characteristic which is not appreciably reduced by exercise whereas strength is always depleted by exercise. Delicacy is related to control and to the indispensible ability to regain strength in difficult positions by consciously relaxing all those muscles not in use. Some climbers seem to be born with the capacity to move delicately; others acquire it slowly as the refined expression of the basic climbing movement; and, inexplicably, some few display it suddenly after years of performance at a lower standard.

Technical ability refers to the repertoire of methods by which climbers deal with specific problems – an infinite range of variations in jamming, bridging, chimneying, laybacking and mantleshelfing movements. Few of these come naturally to the beginner; they have to be learned by observation and experiment. And whilst these movements often call on strength or delicacy one meets many situations in which a cunning technique evades the need to utilize much of either.

Strength, delicacy and technical ability are easily distinguished. Rock climbing, however, sometimes sets problems – 'awkward' or 'gymnastic', for instance – which cannot be described so categorically. Extreme bodily mobility, as in the ability to raise a foot exceptionally high or to flex the ankle beyond the normal range, is occasionally very useful. Physical characteristics like these depend mainly upon body type and such problems come up rather infrequently. Arduous exercise and long experience usually teach the climber to overcome them by the application of refined techniques rather than by improving his capacities in these unusual and unpreferred directions. Though it is true that on boulder problems of exceptional difficulty acrobatic and even aerobatic moves may sometimes be seen.

It is now possible to generalize on the movement skills in rock climbing and on the learning process. The climber discovers what constitute tenable resting positions and for roughly how long he will be able to hold particular positions before losing strength; and within and around a quickly acquired range of linking movements to transfer from one resting position to another he gradually learns more and more of an infinite number of variations. As his experience is built up he becomes able to assess fairly accurately whether the next position will allow him to rest freely, whether it may tax his strength or his balance, or whether it may be nearly or quite impossible to hold. In this assessment he relies mainly upon sight; but, occasionally, purely on touch, as when a handhold is hidden by an overhang or around a rib and must be searched for. The expert must often make cautious exploratory half-moves, first to see what possibilities are available and then to test the feasibility of alternative ways of utilizing them. The information he draws from his finger-tips, eyes and muscles is continuously monitored and his movements are so smoothly integrated that the fore-going remarks may seem over-analytical. He simply finds the best way, perhaps peculiar to himself, of making the move. But in the long run he is always making compromises, calling whenever possible upon technical ability, delicacy and gymnastic flair to conserve his most easily expendable resource, strength. "This fluid process of movement–balance–perception–movement–balance . . . forms the internal dynamic of climbing." (Csikszentmihalyi and Macaloon, 1975).

Above all, although the most desperate routes often appear to be led at snail's pace, the importance of the time-allowance is critical. Sometimes it is only possible to spare a hand, in order to test subsequent holds, for two or three seconds; often the move itself can only be made in a rapid and decisive manner; occasionally the resting position can only be held for a short space of time. However, it may be possible to rest stressed muscles by moving up and down through a series of hard moves and trying positions whilst attempting to work out the crucial move. A climber may therefore sometimes spend an hour ascending and descending such a series, working from a good resting place, even though at no point could he halt for more than a few seconds.

On the very hardest climbs the right decisions may have to be made very swiftly. As a particular example, one of the more difficult routes on Yorkshire gritstone is the Wall of Horrors at Almscliffe. This climb was named and top-roped many years before it was first led in 1961. The route begins with twenty-five feet of very strenuous, dynamic moves on which it is barely possible to halt before a resting place is gained immediately beneath the key move. The successful leader first attempted the route a number of times with the protection of a top-rope and found that he was unable to hold the resting position for more than fifteen seconds or so. During this period an on sight soloist would have to learn how to overcome the next and crucial move. Since 1961 the route has been led with increasing frequency and sometimes with apparent ease, but an on sight, unprotected lead in the purest sense has yet to be made and its seriousness can be imagined. Perhaps, in any case, it may be impossible today in that the notoriety of the route is almost bound to carry with it information on the best method of solving the problem.

At this point a topic so far undiscussed in climbing literature might be raised. Instructional books usually suggest that the crucial sections of rock climbs should be weighed up and the sequences of moves planned before embarking on them. It is implied that the rational intellect carries out this task and instructs the body to execute the plan as coolly as possible; we do this, in picking out obvious resting places and good holds, in deciding which way to face in corner-cracks and chimneys, and so on. But there is a sense in which expert climbers do not always 'think out' difficult moves, even when they use that very expression to describe what they are doing and to explain any delay. It is more the case that they feel out these moves with the input through sight, touch and muscles transformed into action without the mediation of the conscious mind. Significantly, they say 'work out' more often than 'think out'.

An analogy with driving might be helpful. One may drive at normal speeds, even on unknown roads, with the mind occupied with other matters and with no subsequent memory of landscape, road or traffic patterns. Or one may drive at one's limits with the whole attention concentrated on technique. Or one may respond to a skid or evade a sudden road predicament intuitively. It is clear that climbing moves can be purely automatic or entirely conscious actions. But a more puzzling and complex phenomenon has sometimes been experienced. The climber has attempted a baffling move innumerable times without success in spite of calling on all his resources; and then, to his surprise and momentary consternation, he finds himself climbing it with no memory of a conscious decision to make a final effort. Two observations may be made here. It appears that exceptionally difficult moves can sometimes be made "on the autopilot", as one climber expressed it – adding the purely speculative opinion that it is possible for the expert to climb at least as skilfully in this manner as when carrying out a conscious plan. It also appears that, on impulse or through frustration perhaps, a climber may occasionally make his move before his conscious mind has quite gathered itself to set off; and he may solve the difficulty, sometimes, by a technique not envisaged during the earlier, rationally directed attempts. In this context it may be worth adding that of all the mishaps and disasters to which the human body is vulnerable, slipping or falling are amongst the very fastest to which useful responses are available. The muscles, eyes and labyrinth are geared to initiate reflex corrective actions and hence it might be said that at a primitive level the body is programmed to climb.

UNROPED SOLO: JUDGEMENT SKILLS

All the movement skills involved in boulder problems pertain to all other climbing-games. It is most useful to consider unroped solo next because, although it is in some ways the most serious form of climbing and one of the most hazardous pastimes man has ever devised, another group of skills is easily identified and these will again be partly masked in subsequent forms of climbing. The soloist's essential skills include judgement and three factors are involved: appraisal of difficulty in relation to physical resources, appraisal of control, and awareness of personality characteristics.

Some climbers see the appraisal of difficulty as a purely external task. Misled by the very nature of thought and language and the victims of their refined systems of classification they find themselves objectifying difficulty as a property inherent in the climb itself. Indeed, it is often impossible not to feel that a particular route *is* desperate and another *is* easy, even though semantics tells us that this view is naive and observation shows one climber making the desperate route look easy and another finding the easy route impossible. In essence, we have divided the collective historical experience of climbing into arbitrary grades of difficulty; we have tampered with these grades from time to time and we have matched each new climb against our system; we have classified and reclassified our own performances against the abstract grades. But the collective experience is never a perfect frame for individual performance. A climber of a given standard may have strengths in excess of that standard and weaknesses far short of it; and his performance will vary according to his form of the day and his prior exertions within that day. Therefore the wise climber, even though he may have used a guidebook or a reported grade to select a suitable climb, will shut all classifications out of his mind once he sets foot on the rock.

The soloist, then, has two initial tasks. First, drawing on his awareness of his optimum movement skills, he must see the best means of solving each successive problem. Second, he must judge correctly or learn by tentative experiment whether at that moment in time he has the physical resources to apply his solution successfully. The boulder problemist may be said to be learning about the same two tasks, but it is not absolutely required of him that he get the answers right; usually he can attempt any unlikely move and fall off to his heart's content. The soloist cannot, since if he falls off he will die, and his reading of the rock must therefore be matched by his reading of himself. When he sets off on a long and difficult pitch he must assess correctly not only that he can climb to the next resting place safely but also, in the actual process of making each move, whether he can reverse it if necessary. Descending is usually more difficult than ascending and it may even be necessary to rehearse particular moves in descent in order to fix them correctly in the memory. If the soloist keeps climbing through a series of barely reversible moves his first hope must be that nothing more difficult awaits him. He appraises the pitch, then, in short sections from one resting place to the next. If he has already made a roped ascent of the climb he will know how his effort must be programmed. But in making an on sight solo he must be continuously aware of any depletion of his resources since a miscalculation high on the pitch or climb may reduce his reserves to such a degree that his retreat, however well rehearsed, is no longer possible. Then he starts to wonder why he is there.

It will be seen that an extreme degree of physical and nervous control is of paramount importance to the soloist. From some viewpoints it is no doubt misleading to separate body and mind. But in the rock climber's experience they are sometimes as distinct as horse and rider in that a loss of control may appear to originate with one or the other. Sometimes the horse gets jittery but the rider can force it to do what he wants; sometimes the rider panics before the horse has learned the bad news – but something within the rider may yet be able to reassert control and hold the team together. Perhaps the soloist is in a reasonably secure but rather strained position when his leg develops a muscular tremor; so he shifts his position slightly to rest it and he collects himself. Or perhaps the soloist has misjudged the weather and quite unexpectedly, whilst he is utterly committed to the climb, a few spots of rain fall. If the cliff gets wet he is doomed. A flash of alarm invades him and if his muscles learn about it the end may be near; but his will or directing intelligence or whatever may be powerful and fast enough to recompose himself and apply everything to the best course of action.

In an early essay touching on this subject, Birtwistle (1950) remarked that in attempting to lead a hard roped pitch he always tried to hold one-third of his physical energy and a half of his nervous energy, reckoning from the last protection or resting point, in reserve. He did not explain how he was able to quantify these reserves so neatly; but some such subconscious estimate must never be far from the soloist's mind.

Considering the achievements of some solo climbers over the past few years the outsider or moderate climber might be forgiven for assuming that something in their makeup spares them these anxieties. This is not so; they have all had their moments. Royal Robbins (1973) has expressed the problem of the soloist perfectly: "The terrible thing about free soloing difficult routes that are within one's capacity is the chance that, faced with ultimate danger and the need for ultimate self-control, one's nerve could fail and cause an error. That's the irony of it — that fear could short-circuit skill, that one would die as a direct result of being afraid to die."

The soloist's final necessary sense of judgement is in relation to his own personality; he must be able to recognize and overcome any traits in his character that may threaten his life. This might seem a surprising assertion but examples may illustrate its truth. A solo climber becomes cragfast with no-one within hearing but confined to a comfortable ledge. He knows that he may fall if he continues or attempts to descend. On the other hand he knows that if he were to sit down for an hour or two, or perhaps overnight, he could eventually attract attention and be guaranteed a safe return. But he will not do this because he is too proud of his reputation to be willing to submit to the indignity of rescue. Or, the other face of the same example, a soloist is climbing at his limit on a cliff thick with roped parties and under the eyes of numerous spectators. The crucial moves stop him. If he were roped he could easily abandon the lead, shouting down any one of a number of plausible and unverifiable excuses ostensibly as an exchange between himself and his second but nevertheless informing the unknown listeners of a reasonable justification for his retreat. But the soloist can hardly start shouting excuses to persons he has never met and who have no partnership with him. The more he struggles, the more attention is directed on to him. He registers a quite perceptible pressure and he would feel a fool if he had to climb lamely down in the end; though that might very well be the best course of action. It seems highly likely that a number of soloists have allowed themselves to be ritually sacrificed by spectators. An unnamed interviewee listed as one of the *rewards* or aims of climbing "the one-pointedness of mind". And in the same study Csikszentmihalyi and Macaloon (1975) rightly observe: "Any lapse of concentration, any opening of the postern gate to the concerns of ordinary life, is always potentially disastrous . . ."

FREE CLIMBING: PROTECTION SKILLS AND TEAM SKILLS

When we discuss rock climbing in Britain we usually mean free climbing; roped climbing, that is, without the use of aid but with whatever protection is felt necessary. If a move or two is made with aid this has to be admitted, often being considered a flaw in the ascent. If several points of aid are used, depending on the area and size of the cliff, the route may be given an aid grading as well as a grading for its most difficult free moves. The roped climber can rarely utilize his physical resources quite so utterly as the boulder problemist and his degree of commitment is rarely so high, in principle, as that of the soloist. He operates in the wide region between these two extremes, his use of the rope allowing him to extend himself towards a matching of his physical and psychological limits as in no other form of climbing. Whenever he reaches a crucial move he tries to fix protection immediately and if he finds perfect protection he thereby reduces the move to the status of a boulder problem. He may be prepared to press the move to the point of falling off and he may be prepared to make irreversible moves if they give onto ledges or resting places from which an abseil or a protected descent may be made if further progress is impossible. If he cannot find satisfactory protection he moves nearer to the condition of the soloist, though even on suicidally unprotected runouts some slight current of support is often imagined as running up the rope.

Free climbing introduces two further aspects of expertise. First, the techniques of belaying and of applying protection must be second nature, these techniques having to be learned from others or, by cautious experiment, working from books. It is often the case, incidentally, that the mere placing of protection in the form of running belays, however dubious in the event of a fall, will give sufficient confidence for the hard moves to be made. And the act of fixing it is a sort of displacement gesture, taking the climber's attention off the problem for a few minutes and allowing him to regroup his energies. On the other hand, on some very strenuous routes the fixing of protection can be very tiring in itself. It is occasionally the case that a climber exhausts himself in attempting to protect a pitch he had the strength and skill, but not the confidence, to lead.

Protection techniques involve the appraisal of risk in the form of the assessment of the consequences of a fall. It might be assumed that risk-appraisal relates to the soloist too. However, on any serious climb of any length the soloist knows that if he falls he will almost certainly die. The free climber is continuously considering a changing situation and making decisions as to how closely he dare approach his limits. (Other aspects of risk-appraisal, such as stonefall danger from parties higher up the cliff, relate to all forms of rock-climbing other than boulder problems; but the level of skill, experience or imagination required is not particularly high.)

Free climbing also involves team skills, which are related to protection skills though neither may be said to incorporate the other; it is possible to protect oneself without a companion by the complicated manoeuvres of *roped solo* and some aspects of team skills fall outside matters of protection. Team skills are of uncertain importance in British rock climbing. All roped climbs require competence in rope management, but mainly on the part of the leader who can quickly instruct a less experienced second on what has to be done. And even on the very hardest climbs it is not always necessary that the second should climb at the leader's standard since various rope stratagems allow some assistance to the second. Many of the greatest routes have been achieved entirely on the leader's power, sometimes, indeed, with a second on the brink of total nervous collapse. A fair proportion of notably successful and long-standing teams have consisted of a skilful and audacious leader backed by a cool and resourceful second. Equally, a number of brilliant partnerships of climbers of perfectly matched ability have dissolved in tears. Many experts only gain satisfaction from leading and are not prepared to spend half their time as second, sharing the credit for their successes. On the other hand, two climbers of equal ability can often spur each other on and by alternate attempts at a difficult pitch overcome a problem neither could have solved without such competition and relief. Or a team may comprise a climber who excels on strenuous cracks and another who is best on delicate slabs. On a number of famous occasions, too, arch-rivals have gone into partnership to attempt some unusually intimidating possibility.

The main effect seen when equally powerful climbers with a strong rapport team up is perhaps in the speed of the ascent. Obviously, this shows most strikingly on the big classic climbs overseas. As, for instance, in such 'vertical explosions' as the ascent by Habeler and Messner of the North Face of the Eiger in 1974 in ten hours, or the fifteen-hour ascent by Bridwell, Long and Westbay of the Nose of El Capitan in 1975.

AID CLIMBING: AID SKILLS

Aid climbing is not much practised in Britain today, except, somewhat apologetically, as training for mountaineering or big wall climbing abroad. The whole impetus of British climbing over the past few years has been towards the freeing, whenever possible, of aid climbs. In this free climbers have been phenomenally successful and the acreage of rock to which formerly only the aid climber had access has been drastically diminished. The aid climber draws on all the skills already mentioned but is often able to ascend spectacular routes without approaching the extremes of performance in any of those skills. However, he develops a fine awareness of the properties and structural characteristics of the rock types he works on. Sometimes, for instance, he may have to make a sequence of moves on small pitons penetrating a bare half-inch into the cracks and if the one to which he is attached pulls he may unzip the whole series; but since he is usually operating on otherwise unclimbable overhangs such falls, no matter how dramatic, often involve less risk than falls on easy-angled climbs where an impact with the rock is much more likely.

The aid climber's other need is for method. Aside from being conversant with the complicated systems of aid climbing, including jumaring and sack hauling, he must work in a rigorously organized manner. It is easy to waste hours in sorting out baulked ropes or to drop vital pieces of gear. Speed on the big walls on which his ambitions are set will be essential so that even in Britain he will make certain compromises between safety and security. The harder he drives a peg, the longer his second will spend in extracting it. The perfect aid piton, Chouinard and Frost (1970) have said, is placed with the fingers and a single blow, and is extracted with one blow; an ideal few climbers can ever have attained.

CHARACTERISTICS OF ELITE CLIMBERS

Most rock climbers would go along with this separation of general sets of component skills – movements, judgement, protection, team and aid – within British climbing. They might also agree that these divisions account for real differences in the performances of the experts. Some of the greatest are outclassed on boulder problems; some of the star soloists have never put out an exceptional climb; some of the legendary heroes have never soloed anything worth talking about – the thought of repeating Alan McHardy's solos of a few years ago would strike terror into the hearts of most of the present elite; certainly some of the most impressive aid climbs were made by men who did not otherwise distinguish themselves.

However, although these separate aspects reveal essential specific skills, collectively they are not sufficient to account for the successes of the elite. Note that although free climbing is the central form of the sport and the principal activity of nearly all British climbers nothing more vital than protection skills and team skills have been listed above as its distinctive requirements in expertise. These are far more quickly and easily acquired than any of the other skills so that, in theory, the best performers on boulders ought shortly to become the best performers on reasonably well-protected free climbs; and those cool soloists who are also brilliant on boulders ought to sweep the field. Yet this doesn't consistently happen. So there must be something beyond these qualities on which the great climbers are able to draw.

It seems to me that they have two further qualities, both outside any narrow definition of skill but without which it is impossible to exploit the specific skills to their uttermost limits. These characteristics might loosely be called imagination and determination. And for a peculiar reason, as things stand at present, they are most spectacularly displayed in Britain in free climbing. Boulder problems only boast a modest notoriety; no-one would travel far to attempt a boulder, however celebrated, and the boulder expert usually remains simply a local expert. Sensational aid climbs can be accomplished by persons with quite low levels of the advanced climbing skills and the aid climber is usually on the defensive now, always threatened by the free climber. The solo-ist, in turn, would like to threaten the free climber but he labours under disadvantages. It is always easier to climb a route roped rather than solo and British crags have been under pressure for so long that the soloist can never find unbroken ground. However justifiably he may assert that soloing separates the men from the boys he is always condemned to follow in the roped climber's tracks. His chances of promoting solo as the true form of the sport seem to be negligible. The overwhelming majority of climbers want the security of the rope and everything it lays open, rather than the extreme and lonely world of solo.

In British rock climbing, imagination is chiefly shown in what we speak of as 'an eye for a line'. It might equally be described as the exploratory urge except that it demands a discrimination not seen in all explorers. It is displayed by those who put out new routes. The greatest climber of the nineteen-thirties was probably Colin Kirkus; of the nineteen-fifties, probably Joe Brown. It is a striking feature of their campaigns that, judged on aesthetic grounds, hardly a single route is found lacking. Many of these lines, it is true, are self-determined by obvious natural features: but before they were set up as ambitions a leap of the imagination, striking outside current standards, was required. A number, on the other hand, stand out as masterpieces of route-finding ability, bold implausible creations that force us to describe them as if they were works of art.

Determination is the final and outstanding attribute of the great climbers. It is a personality characteristic easily recognized in action and from the records but not so easily fixed by a single word. Such more or less interchangeable expressions as persistence, tenacity, commitment, drive and push are often used. In a wider sense determination is related to ambition and in execution it may often appear to depend upon audacity, nerve or 'neck'. It represents the overt evidence of motivation. But the nucleus of these meanings can be expressed as well by determination as by any other word.

It seems significant that within the climbing community determination is regarded as perhaps the most fascinating aspect of performance, a subject around which myths accrete; and that, by contrast, a collapse of determination on a particular route is often seen as more crushing and more final than a defeat through simple technical inability. An incisive method of identifying the central demands of such activities as rock climbing is by examining the jargon and catch-phrases their practitioners find it useful to invent or import. Over a period of time this language also reveals a good deal about how these demands change. For instance, in the early fifties the expression 'to gumshoe', meaning to move up a delicate slab by pure friction, had a certain vogue; in the seventies it is no longer heard and a more representative phrase, 'to power it', has appeared, testifying to the steeper nature of modern routes and to the premium put on strength. The development of modern climbing might almost be deduced simply by comparing the very numerous and colourful terms for falling off. In this context an americanism and a gallicism adopted by British climbers are worth notice. The expression 'to psych out' (to psychologize out) has gained currency in a number of sports and seems to be colonizing various other fields of behaviour. At first thought its most apt use seems to be to the surfer, hang-glider pilot or novice parachutist who cannot launch out when his moment comes. But the verb and its derivatives have been used by Californian rock climbers for a number of years and nowhere does it fill a gap better than on the big wall climbs of the Yosemite Valley and on routes elsewhere that imitate and in some cases anticipated these climbs. On these vertiginous, three-thousand-foot, multi-day routes, pitches and rope manoeuvres which would be difficult, tiring, hazardous or terrifying to reverse succeed one another. As the party moves up, bivouacking on tiny ledges or in hammocks pegged to the wall, the accumulation of problems in retreat and the uncertainty about the difficulties of exit above sometimes combine to reach a disabling level. (At the time of writing the maximum period spent on a big wall climb is twenty-eight days without descent, the first ascent of Dawn Wall in Yosemite.) Perfect weather, excellent equipment, reasonable supplies of food, the fitness of the party, are occasionally of no avail. Climbers sometimes drop out of a team at the last moment before starting, on one pretext or other. At an early stage in the ascent one may invent an excuse to leave a larger party and may abseil off alone while this is still psychologically feasible. At a later stage the whole team may come to a halt, occasionally effecting a descent more trying from an objective viewpoint than the actual completion of the route. And these situations arouse more sympathy or more glee than almost any other circumstance. They characterize the anguish of the game. Further, the entire tendency of the sport is towards setting up these tests. The drag exerted by competition ethics is steadily making 'siege tactics' – the abandoning of fixed ropes up key pitches to allow easy escape and a subsequent rapid re-ascent to the high point if desired – more and more unacceptable; so that at a quite early stage on many big wall climbs the difficulties of retreat as well as the uncertainties of progress become a gnawing source of anxiety.

On the great alpine routes determination has often been shown in epic retreats in desperate storms. But it is best exemplified in completed ascents made in the face of bad weather. On innumerable occasions parties have been surprised by catastrophic changes of weather and it has become impossible to follow their progress, a cause of grave disquiet to friends in the safety of the valley. In such circumstances French mountaineers have been observed to shrug their shoulders with the philosophical remark, "a leader will emerge", a phrase which passed briefly, in a mainly humorous sense, into British climbing at the beginning of this decade.

On one extraordinary occasion a number of parties found themselves trapped by a storm high on the North Face of the Grandes Jorasses. In the event a monstrous single rope comprising fourteen persons and five nationalities coalesced and fought its way to the summit. The leader was an English rock climber, Dave Yates, taking for his first climb in the Alps the Eperon Walker, a route which has been a lifetime's ambition for many of the world's best mountaineers. Many members of this party were doubtless technically capable of leading their own teams out and all were far more experienced alpinists than the actual leader. But the fact that all of them were prepared to settle for this solution shows how circumstances may emphasise qualities other than pure skill.

In Britain, determination may be seen in the boulder problemist who attempts the same possibility time after time until his fingers give out, and it was shown quite impressively in the heyday of British aid climbing; the soloist also needs determination but not in excess of his skills or his career will be brief. But chiefly it has been displayed in the campaigns mentioned above and equally in the efforts of those who made it their first ambition to catch up on these advances. For example, when the routes of Brown and Whillans began to appear in the early fifties it was immediately clear that a new standard had been attained. The very small group of others actually capable of repeating at least some of these routes failed to do so for a variety of personal reasons and a hiatus of some years elapsed during which a psychological barrier quite as daunting as the technical obstacle interposed itself. It fell to Hugh Banner to break through this barrier and to open up these routes to merely mortal climbers. Operating, at that time, at a lower level of performance than those he was pursuing, but strong on judgement and determination, Banner's effort in working into these climbs must have required at least as much drive as the original exploration demanded of its makers.

CONCLUSION

In summary, it should be pointed out that the use of the climbing-game concept to isolate the several aspects of climbing skills has been purely a device of convenience. It ought not to be assumed that the beginner should logically develop his skills by following a programme based on this description. On first thought many climbers would say that the skills are usually built up in parallel rather than in series and would point out that many, perhaps most climbers, indulge only in free climbing and contrive to develop everything except aid techniques entirely through that avenue. This analysis, they might say, gives a spurious sense of hierarchy. Yet, when one considers the matter more closely, a correspondence, both individual and historical, between the skills in the sequence presented here and the learning process itself may be discerned.

Virtually without exception, the first self-declared rock climbers in the late Victorian era came to the activity after a long apprenticeship as mountain walkers. On their excursions they progressed gradually on to more and more adventurous ridge and gully scrambles. Here they encountered obstacles which may well be described as boulder problems and on the most exposed ridges these amount to a primitive form of unroped solo. Indeed, the rope techniques used until after the turn of the century, and the types of rope available to the pioneers, place the first free climbing in an ambiguous category with a strong sense of the penalties of solo attached to it. Many climbers still follow a similar course of introduction today.

If we turn to the general factual history of British climbing, the claim the poet Coleridge be regarded as the original boulder problemist might be considered. In making the first known passage of Broad Stand on Scafell in 1802 he was obliged to descend a series of short and awkward rock walls – and his extraordinary journal entry relating this excursion represents a penetrating description of the climbing experience. The first really serious rock climb in Britain was the solo ascent of the Napes Needle by W. P. Haskett-Smith in 1886. The use of ropes came in at about the same time and more difficult routes than the Needle began to be achieved in large numbers during the following decade. Finally, the first sophisticated use of aid techniques occurred in 1914 with the ascent by Herford and Sansom of the imposing Central Buttress of Scafell.

When we consider two characteristic forms of introduction to the sport today we see that something on the same lines may still be observed. A beginner with little experience except of mountain walking is taught to climb by friends and he reaches the status of expert purely through the medium of free climbing. However, his earliest climbs are made as second on the rope, fully protected by the leader: which is to say that the penalties are removed so that his movement skills are developed, in effect, under the same terms as those of the boulder problemist. As the difficulty of his routes increases and as the situations become more unnervingly exposed, the protection often comes to seem less reassuring so that the judgement skills are slowly brought into focus whilst the protection techniques are being learned. Soon he moves onto easier climbs but in the capacity of leader and for the first time his skills are tested realistically.

Increasing numbers of climbers, on the other hand, are now entering the activity through the artificial environment of man-made climbing walls. These walls force the movement skills rapidly. (Though many existing walls offering only vertical problems must develop strength at the expense of delicacy and awareness of friction characteristics.) These climbers usually progress first onto the more accessible outcrops rather than the more distant high mountain crags. And on these outcrops the fine line between safe bouldering and hazardous soloing will immediately engage their attention.

Essentially, the expert uses and balances two sets of attributes. First, his steadily acquired skills: in a word, his experience. Second, such qualities of personality as imagination and determination which have always been a part of him quite independently of the activity but which have seized onto and express themselves through his aspirations as climber. Without these last to a high degree he can never harness the skills, however great his natural aptitudes, to any real purpose or achievement. Yet it is also the task of the judgement skills reflexively to consider these personality factors, if not in relation to one's commitment to rock climbing, at least in particular relation to the lunatic courses of action they sometimes drive us to embark upon. Birtwistle (1950) concluded his speculations of thirty years ago by presenting a slightly adapted stanza from Spenser and this will serve well enough here:

> And as he looked about, he did behold,
> How over that same door was likewise writ,
> *Be bold, Be bold,* and everywhere *Be bold,*
> That much he mused, yet could not construe it
> By any riddling skill, or common wit.
> At last he spied at that room's upper end
> Another iron door, on which was writ,
> *Be not too bold* . . .

References

Bernard, J. (1968). The Eudaemonists: human energy as an article of consumption. In Klausner S. Z. (ed.). *Why Man Takes Chances: Studies in Stress-seeking.* (New York: Doubleday)

Birtwistle, A. (1950). Thoughts on leading up difficult rock. *Rucksack Club J., Vol. XI, No. 3, Issue 43,* 192 (Manchester: Cloister Press)

Csikszentmihalyi, M. and Macaloon, J. (1975). Deep play and the flow experience in rock climbing. In Csikszentmihalyi, M., *Beyond Boredom and Anxiety.* Ch. 6, pp. 74–101 (San Francisco, Washington, London: Jossey-Bass Publishers)

Chouinard, Y. and Frost, T. (*c.* 1970). *On the Use of Chouinard Equipment.* (Edinburgh: Alma Press n.d.)

Drasdo, H. (1974). In praise of cheating. *Mountain, 39,* 35

Gill, J. (1979). Bouldering: a mystical art-form. In Tobias, M. C. and Drasdo, H. (eds.). *The Mountain Spirit.* (New York: Overlook Press and Viking Press)

Robbins, R. (1973). *Advanced Rockcraft.* (Glendale, Ca: La Siesta Press)

Tejada-Flores, L. (1967). Games climbers play. *Ascent, 1.* (San Francisco: Sierra Club). (In Britain in *Mountain, 2,* 9; *Alpine Journal, 73,* 46 and in Wilson, K. (ed.). (1979). *The Games Climbers Play.* (London: Diadem Books))

Illustrations Jack Nicklaus, the world's best golfer. This sequence illustrates the co-axial cylinder model of the golf swing described in the text. After the wind-up to the top of the back-swing, the downswing sequence (picture 5 onwards) begins with the lower part of the body pulling round the upper part, including arm and club. Each succeeding upper part – torso, shoulders, arms, club – begins to move independently only when the part below it has expended its useful effort. The last part to be released is the club itself. *(Reproduced by kind permission of Chuck Brenkus)*

10
The Golfer

A. J. COCHRAN

INTRODUCTION

The basic idea of the game of golf is very simple. You have to hit a small ball (1·62″ in diameter) into a hole in the ground ($4\frac{1}{4}$″ in diameter) situated anything between about 100 yards and 600 yards from the starting point, in as few strokes as possible. The ball is stationary when you hit it. Important elements in the game are hitting the ball as far as possible, and hitting it in the intended direction. At some point in the play of each hole, 'hitting the ball as far as possible' must be replaced by hitting it the correct distance. For shots of a range down to about half the maximum – say to 100 yards – reduction in distance is usually achieved by using a less powerful (i.e. more lofted) club and swinging at more or less full power, rather than by swinging less powerfully. At a range of less than 100 yards or so it is no longer practicable to do this, and distance is determined by strength of hit. Within 20 yards or so of the hole ('on the green'), the ground is specially prepared to enable accurate shots to be played with a putter, a club with virtually no loft, which sets the ball rolling along the surface, rather than flying through the air as in nearly all other shots.

The above paragraph is a condensed description of a game that has perhaps had more written about it than any other, and whose Book of Rules runs to 87 pages and over 20 000 words; but it serves to indicate that golf is a collection of four or five sub-skills which can be described separately, and to some extent measured and even developed separately. Before considering these sub-skills, however, it is worth noting one of the virtues of discussing skill in relation to a game like golf: data on the level of skill achieved is plentiful and easy to obtain. A golfer's score for his 18-hole round gives quite a precise measure of his skill at the overall activity of playing golf – modified a little by luck, and subject to day-to-day fluctuation. Because of this, the handicaps allotted to all club (amateur) golfers, based on their typical scores, provide a very convenient index of each individual golfer's skill. It is also quite easy in principle, though it requires some organizing in practice, to obtain measures of performance at some of the sub-skills; for example, percentage of putts holed from various distances, accuracy of approach shots, length of drives.

Some of the relationships obtained for groups of golfers turn out to be remarkably simple. For example, in one professional tournament (Cochran and Stobbs, 1968) the average accuracy of approach shots could be expressed as

$$M = 0 \cdot 078 \ R,$$

where R is the range from which the shot was played, and M is the median finishing distance from the hole. For example, half the shots played from 100 yards range would finish within 7·8 yards of the hole. The same study showed that the average number of strokes (N) needed to hole out fitted quite well the relation

$$N = 0 \cdot 0044 \ R + 2 \cdot 35 \qquad (R \text{ in yards})$$

Both of these relationships were valid for $R > 30$ yards though they fluctuated somewhat, depending on local conditions: figures for one hole differed a little from that for another. Similar relationships have been established by other studies.

SKILLS ANALYSIS

Let us now list and examine some of the sub-skills required by the golfer:

Ability to hit the ball a long distance consistently
Ability to hit the ball in the desired direction consistently
Ability to judge distances and translate this into:
(a) Correct club
(b) Correct swing strength
Ability to make complicated judgements of direction and distance on the often sloping or undulating putting green, and translate these into the required movement of the putter
Certain tactical or strategic abilities.

The first two sub-skills in the list are the ones which determine the quality of any golfer's basic 'swing', the swing he uses for all drives and for most of his long approaches (since, as we have already noted, for approach shots of over 100 yards he tends to select a club which will require a full power swing).

With his most powerful club, his driver, a highly skilled golfer will typically hit the ball 220 to 240 yards through the air, with a further 10 to 50 yards roll of the ball depending on ground conditions. Most good professional golfers also have another 20 yards or so 'in reserve', for occasional use at selected holes, but which they cannot, or at least feel they cannot, use all the time for fear of losing control, or the rhythm of their swings. Regarding accuracy, about 70% of these 250 to 260 yard drives finish within $\pm$ 15 yards of the intended direction *in tournament play*. When practising, accuracy is much higher than this – with a deviation perhaps half of the above figure.

Quite a lot is known about the aerodynamics of golf-ball flight, and about the mechanics of impact between ball and club: enough to specify the precise conditions which the expert golfer must achieve with his clubhead to achieve the length, accuracy and consistency just described. At impact, the clubface is in contact with the ball for less than 0·5 milliseconds, during which time the clubhead behaves as a 'freely moving body'; that is, the presence of the shaft and the golfer's hands on it do not affect the impact. In order to hit a 250 yard drive in the intended direction the clubhead must, at impact, be:

(i) Travelling at around 150–160 ft per sec.

(ii) Travelling horizontally along the intended direction of flight

(iii) Oriented such that the face of the club is facing along the intended direction

(iv) Positioned such that contact with the ball is made at a point opposite the centre of mass of the clubhead.*

Of greatest interest, in the context of highly skilled performance, is the extent to which small errors in these affect the shot. The two requirements which are most critical are (ii) and (iii). Failure to combine these two requirements produces shots which exhibit the greatest inaccuracies, at least for reasonably skilled golfers†. For example, a 1° difference between the horizontal direction of travel of the clubhead, and the horizontal direction along which the face is pointing, typically imparts enough sidespin to the ball to make it swerve in flight ('slice' or 'hook') by a total of about 12 yards before it hits the ground – enough, often, to make the difference between an acceptable and unacceptable result to the shot. This effect increases rapidly with clubhead speed. In order to achieve the same accuracy of shot, in terms of yards left or right of the intended direction, the long-hitting golfer who drives 270 yards has to be roughly twice as accurate in his striking as the golfer who drives 180 yards. And to be a high class performer you have to hit the ball both farther and straighter in absolute terms than the ordinary golfer. Failure to

---

*Strictly speaking in a drive, where the ball may be 'teed' an inch or so off the ground, the optimum conditions exist when the clubhead is travelling very slightly upward (2° or 3° to horizontal) and when contact is made about $\frac{1}{4}''$ above the centre of mass.

†For very unskilled golfers, gross failure to meet condition (iv) produces the most obviously bad results: topping, skying, heeling etc. If the error is bad enough a complete miss can result.

satisfy the requirement (iv) relating to the point of contact on the clubface can also produce relatively large errors – mainly loss of distance rather than direction. A half-inch error to left or right in the point of contact causes 10 to 15 yards loss of distance; and of course, a $1''$ vertical error could result in a topped shot, or even a complete miss.

MODELLING THE GOLF SWING

How does the human golfer achieve the levels of power, accuracy and consistency described above? Does he achieve one at the expense of the other? Does the production of maximum clubhead speed militate against accuracy; or does some principle of maximum efficiency tend to produce both great speed and accuracy? Crude calculations based on simple measurements of speed, time and mass indicate that, in the downswing of a skilled golfer, which lasts only 0·2 to 0·25 seconds, the average power developed is about 3 hp. This poses an interesting problem. The rate at which muscle can provide energy is around $\frac{1}{8}$ hp per pound, when working at optimum efficiency, that is moving the right load at the right speed. Under these conditions then, 3 hp would seem to require 24 lbs of muscle; but in any human movement, roughly as much muscle is required to stabilize joints as is used in creating the actual motion. We may say, then, that about 48 lbs of muscle is needed to produce a maximum power golf drive. The total weight of muscle in a reasonably fit male is about 70 lbs, about 40 lbs being muscles that act in or on the legs, and only 20 lbs being muscles acting in and on the arms. It is clear from this that, although the overall impression may be of swinging the club with the arms, the muscles of the arms alone would be quite inadequate to provide the power needed; and that the large muscles of the legs must be involved as a major source of power. Even so, it is still difficult to account for the great power production, since it is unlikely that the loading of the muscles will be optimal throughout; and we shall have to look for some kind of storage of energy developed in the backswing for use in the downswing.

It is in channelling the power from the legs up through the trunk, shoulders, arms and hands, and finally to the clubhead in sufficient quantity, and with sufficient accuracy and consistency, that a large part of the skill of golf lies. It is what is loosely known as 'timing'. In trying to understand this, it is helpful to think of the golf swing in terms of simplified models. Models of any complicated system are, of course, always open to the danger of misinterpretation; of being applied too literally, or outside their proper range of circumstances. Nowhere is this more true than in modelling the golf swing. The models discussed here are primarily to aid understanding of the golf swing; they do not teach directly how to be a skilled golfer, except perhaps in the very grossest features. More specifically, although it is useful in increasing understanding to identify parts of the models with parts of the human golfer, these can only be very rough correspondences.

The two models described can be justified on a number of grounds. First of all, simple mechanical arguments: if we were constructing a mechanical golfer with similar dimensions and power sources to a man's, how would we design it? Secondly, visual evidence, both with the naked eye and by high-speed photography. And thirdly, established teaching practice which represents the thoughts and feelings of expert performers and experienced teachers.

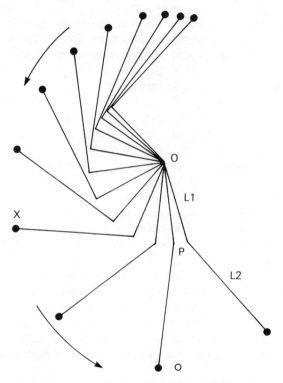

Figure 10.1 The two-lever system shown in a sequence of positions. A model like this can swing efficiently in a manner very similar to a good golfer. The fixed pivot O corresponds to a point between the golfer's shoulders; the upper lever L_1 corresponding to the arms and shoulders, swings around on the fixed pivot. The lower lever L_2 (club) swings around the hinge P (wrists)

The simplest useful model is the 'two-lever model' (Figure 10.1). The lever, L_1, rotates in a plane about a fixed pivot, O, while L_2 rotates in the same plane about a pivot, P, at the end of L_1. The upper lever L_1, corresponds to the golfer's arms and shoulders rotating about some fixed pivot between the shoulders; and the lower lever corresponds to the club, with moving pivot, P, a very simplified representation of the hands on the club. If such a two-lever system is 'wound back' to a top of the backswing position, with a stop preventing complete jack-knifing, and then driven forward by a torque acting at O, the general character of the motion both satisfies the basic mechanical requirements of a golf swing already discussed, and also exhibits some of the features observed in downswings of skilled performers. As the system speeds up, centrifugal force throws the lever L_2 outwards and the angular momentum of the system becomes concentrated in it, with a consequent slowing of the lever L_1. The precise pattern depends on the form and timing of the torques at O and P. Experimentation with this simple model, either mathematically or by building one mechanically, shows that a large fraction of the work done by the driving torques can appear as clubhead energy by the time the clubhead has reached the impact position, provided that the pattern and timing of the torques at the two pivots, and the relative inertias of the two levers, are right. Or, to put it negatively, bad timing of the two torques can reduce the clubhead speed at impact compared with the optimum: specifically, any abruptness in either torque, or too early or too late a release of the hinge. Even this simple model, therefore, illustrates something of the skill of the class golfer in achieving great clubhead speed. It also has relevance to his accuracy and consistency in time after time striking the ball off the same point on the clubface, with the clubhead both facing and travelling along the direction of the shot. Such consistency, one can plausibly argue, is easier to attain the less complicated the swing is in mechanical terms, the fewer degrees of freedom the system has. Thus, the two-lever model described commends itself from basic principles. Contrast, for example, a more complicated system with the arms bending at the elbows to form a third lever; or with the pivot, O, moving laterally.

Photographic evidence confirms the existence of a centre of rotation which remains more or less fixed in the swing of a good player; as indeed do many of the best known golfing adages, such as "keep your head still" and "don't sway". "Straight left arm" fixes the radius of the hand swing. "Point the club towards the target at the top of the backswing" and avoiding "too much inside, or too much outside" are ways of aligning the plane of the swing correctly.

Useful though this simple method is in illustrating some of the key principles of skilled golf, it is too simple in one or two respects – specifically, in helping to understand what happens at the two pivots. We return later to the details of the lower pivot, P: that is, the part the hands play in the system. The other pivot point, O, we have so far imagined to be fixed and we have assumed that somehow a torque is generated there acting on the upper lever. To understand how that torque results from the various turning and lateral forces originating lower in the body we need a more complicated model.

This model (Figure 10.2) consists of a stack of cylinders each turning on a common axis. The cylinders are driven by springs connecting each other, and the lowest one to the ground. The springs decrease in stiffness from the ground upwards. On top of the stack, and fixed rigidly to the top cylinder, is the arm/club system of the previously discussed two-lever model. There may be a

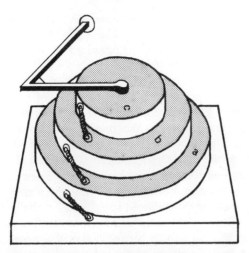

Figure 10.2 A mechanical model driven by springs which illustrates the principles of body rotation, and the importance of maintaining tension during the downswing in golf. From the 'wound-up' position, with all springs fully stretched, the top-most cylinder (C) can ultimately be given the greatest speed of rotation if the springs are released in sequence from the bottom upwards. Adding an 'arm' and a 'club' completes the analogy with the golf swing, and the principle of maintaining the tension can be continued. The hinge between arm and club should not be released until all the springs driving the cylinders have done their work

spring to power the hinge of this. The model is 'wound up' by turning each cylinder from the bottom upwards clockwise as far as it will go (30° to 40°) against the spring below it, and locking the system in that position; and the 'club' is likewise drawn back and locked at about 90° to the 'arm'. This. would correspond to the golfer's top of the swing position. We can imagine the cylinder, C, to be the golfer's shoulders, B his torso, and A his legs and hips.

The question then, is: if we want the clubhead to possess the greatest possible speed when it passes through the impact position, in what order, indeed, at what precise times, should the springs be released? This is a question that can be answered by computation; and, of course, the precise answer depends on the inertias of the cylinders and the characteristics of the springs. Broadly speaking, though, the answer is that they should operate in sequence from the bottom upwards. The spring joining cylinder A to the base is released first, driving the whole system (A + B + C + club) together as a single unit. When all, or most, of the energy of the first spring has been imparted to the system, the next spring is released. This drives the unit (B + C + club) faster, and, at the same time, reaction slows down A. When all, or most, of the energy in the second spring has been used up, the third spring, that joining B and C, is released, further speeding C and slowing down B. We are left with C rotating rapidly; B and A slowly. Finally, the hinge between arm and club is released. Even without a spring in the hinge, centrifugal force throws the clubhead out, thus speeding it up still further with the reaction slowing down cylinder C.

There are many complications which indicate that this model is a considerable oversimplification but the basic message seems valid: to produce the power needed (and achieved) by the expert golfer, some such sequence is needed in order that the power from the big muscles of the legs is channelled efficiently to the club. Every part of the rotating, swinging system should be pulled round by the part nearer to the ground until that part can no longer apply useful effort. That is, the legs pull round the hips, the hips pull round the trunk, the trunk the upper chest and shoulders, the shoulders the arms, the arms the hands and the hands the club. This is essentially what is meant by 'timing'; and, in practice, it seems that if timing is wrong, especially early in the downswing, not only is clubhead speed lost, but the clubhead is usually also thrown out of the desired plane and needs corrective action to return it. There is thus at least a connection between some of the conditions to achieve greatest clubhead speed, and those needed to achieve accuracy and consistency.

In practical playing terms, the sequence of actions described in the last few paragraphs sounds extremely complicated, and virtually impossible to execute consciously. In fact, it is both easier and more difficult to execute than to describe. It is easier insofar as it is, to a large extent, natural. Human beings (and animals) are well adapted to physical activities with their limbs and bodies; and many of these involve striking, throwing or moving extremities fast. The construction of the body, with large muscles near the centre moving large loads slowly, and smaller muscles near the extremities moving lighter loads rapidly, is well suited to golf. Also, the 'programs' which arrange muscular activities in the best sequences and combinations are either innate or learnt from early childhood. The golf swing is not, in one sense, a 'natural action', but it has some of the gross features of these basic actions. On the other hand, the sequence of muscular activity is very difficult to carry out in the sense that it would be virtually impossible to follow by consciously, step by step, trying to do so. This, of course, is the complete beginner's problem.

All this discussion of models would, of course, only amount to a plausible mechanical argument, were there no evidence that it actually happens. As with the simpler, two-lever model, evidence comes in several forms, none of it conclusive, but together, amounting to considerably more than mere plausibility. Many golf teachers and skilled performers talk, for example, of "getting the left side (or hip) out of the way", which in model terms means driving the lowest cylinder as far as possible before activating those above it. The first movement of the downswing is described in many ways, but the most common ones refer to movement of some part of the left leg – foot, heel, knee, hip. Photography affords a chance of more objective evidence, though less capable of making fine distinctions than the impressions and feelings of expert players and teachers. For example, high-speed cine-photography can be used to show the swing in slow motion and so give a better chance of directly observing whether the sequence of activity suggested by the model actually occurs; and whether it is planar and pivots about a fixed point.

The general sequence for the skilled golfer is fairly clear: the 'downswing' is not a simultaneous event for all parts of the system, but begins earlier from the lower parts of the body. At first sight this might seem to contradict the basic principle of the co-axial cylinder model, which would lead us to expect all parts to start down together. But, in the discussion of this model, the backswing was only briefly referred to; we spoke of 'winding up' the system, but considered the possible sequences of movement only from the fully wound-up position (or top-of-the-backswing position in golfing parlance) onwards. We regarded this as a static *position*. In fact, one of the purposes of having a backswing is to get wound-up into the fully stretched position, and it seems that this can best be accomplished by having the parts of the system farthest from the ground still going back, when the parts nearest the ground have come to rest and started moving forward. This also partially explains the surprisingly large amounts of power calculated earlier for the downswing. Momentum is produced and 'stored' in the legs and lower body before the clubhead starts its downswing, and is later transferred to the clubhead. In effect, this means that the swing is really not two separable movements, backswing and forward swing, but that these merge into one; and 'timing' is not just connected with a correctly timed sequence of actions in the forward swing, but also with the earlier actions needed to facilitate the correct sequence.

Again, this is consistent with golfing adages: "slow backswing" is one of the most common, and it warns against the difficulties caused by too much speed on the backswing. It certainly seems borne out in practice that a fast or jerky backswing, besides causing problems in control of the club (and hence in accuracy), also nearly always causes mistiming of the downswing, with maximum clubhead speed being achieved too soon, that is before the clubhead reaches the ball.

In recent years, 'tempo' has been something of a vogue word among top-class golfers. The term embraces all the desirable features illustrated by the model; it also implies something of a pendulum-type rhythm. The analogy is not too appropriate, at least for the backswing, which, unlike a pendulum, starts off from rest at the bottom point in the arc; yet many good golfers find it a helpful idea.

When ordinary club golfers watch professionals play, it is common for them to come away with an overall impression of rhythm and smoothness which they can retain in their minds and apply to their own swings for a short time. During both backswing and downswing, the expert golfer gives the impression of aiding, adding to, getting the best out of some natural periodic motion of his own particular, club–arm–body system; with additional forces he applies being properly synchronized with the natural movement. The inexpert golfer often appears to be fighting against such natural movements – perhaps partly because he is consciously trying to do so many things, and avoid doing so many others.

The last few paragraphs have been written mainly with timing and achievement of maximum clubhead speed in mind, but they apply also to the direction of the swing. A swinging system, with the clubhead being thrown outwards by centrifugal force, will tend to move in a plane, unless other forces move it out of plane. Conversely, once the clubhead has moved out of plane it requires correcting forces to move it back in. In practice, it is hardly ever possible to correct the plane itself. The best that can be done is to modify something else such as the clubface position, in order that the consequences of swinging in the wrong plane – i.e. approaching the ball from the wrong direction – will not be too serious. It is therefore of great importance that the backswing not only winds up the body in the best possible way to generate clubhead speed, but that it positions the club and arms correctly; and that the initial stages of the downswing establish the correct plane. While discussing the backswing, it should be noted that, mechanically, it is not necessary that the backswing plane, if it *is* a plane, should be the same as the downswing plane. Indeed, observation of the best players suggests that the two planes very rarely are the same. If a backswing plane exists it is usually 'inside' that of the downswing; that is, it intersects the horizontal plane along a line which points to the right of the target (for a right-handed golfer).

The sequence of rotations on the downswing suggested by the co-axial cylinder model has to incorporate at least one further major movement (in addition to the swing up and down of the arms already mentioned). This is a sideways thrust of the hips towards the target, while keeping the head and shoulders stationary. It is a powerful movement, driven by the leg muscles, which, in effect, rotates the upper part of the body about a *horizontal* axis. Combined with the previously analysed rotations about the near-vertical axis of the spine, this produces rotation about an inclined axis. Of course, this combined movement, together with the downward swing of the arms, needs not only to channel momentum efficiently to the clubhead, but also to set clubhead and hands off in a correctly aligned plane (i.e. about the correctly inclined axis). The great simplification in the models, in representing the hands on the club shaft as a single pivot, gives rise to a number of complications in timing and accuracy. We shall mention only one. Geometrical and anatomical considerations require that, as the arms are swung up and the body rotates to an in-plane top-of-backswing position, rotation of the arms and the club about a longitudinal axis takes place. It is easiest to picture this by concentrating on the left hand and forearm; the right hand fits into the pattern set by the left. The left forearm rotates during the backswing through an angle of 60° to 90° – equivalent to starting with the thumb upwards and finishing with the back of the hand upwards. This means that at the top of the swing, the back of the left hand (and with it the clubface) lies approximately in the plane of the swing and not at right-angles to it, as it is at address and at impact. Further, in the downswing, because of the need to delay the uncocking of the wrists – i.e. the release of the hinge in the model – these orientations are preserved until a later stage – around the position X in Figure 10.1.

Thus, in order to 'square-up' the clubface at impact, the hands must not only 'release' the club – i.e. allow the lower lever of the model to fly outwards – but they must also rapidly rotate the clubface through about 90° over a very short time interval. The timing of this rotation back to the square position, to an extent, happens naturally, provided the golfer has gripped the club correctly, but it is still remarkable that expert golfers succeed in doing it to within the $\pm \frac{1}{2}°$ necessary to strike the ball as accurately as they do.

EXECUTION SKILLS

Earlier we noted that the whole series of movements which together make up a good golf swing is easier to carry out than their detailed description might suggest, because many of the sequences are, to an extent, natural. But it goes further than this; at least for a skilled golfer, the whole thing becomes so integrated that he makes no conscious attempt to carry out any component movement, but merely sets his 'swing' in motion. The golf club becomes an extension of the golfer and responds in the same way as the limbs do. Furthermore, each individual's overall action becomes not only repetitive, but characteristic of him and recognizably different from that of others. It is, therefore, meaningful to talk, as golfers do, of "my swing" or "your swing", or "Jack Nicklaus's swing".

In a sense, this is perhaps surprising. All highly skilled players must (and do) achieve very similar clubhead conditions at impact, and since these conditions lie near the limits of available power, they must result from swings which are similar in overall pattern. However, variations in certain features seem to be allowed, without adversely affecting the result – for example, the angle of the downswing plane, the way in which the hands and wrists act as a pivot between the club, and the path the backswing takes relative to the downswing. In addition to these, there are a number of other movements which do not directly contribute either to producing great clubhead speed, or to conditions likely to facilitate accuracy. In some cases they are mannerisms rather than movements, and, in a sense, are unnecessary. Many of them are associated with initiating the backswing, or with finally bringing the club to rest in the follow-through. But, though they may be unnecessary in the mechanical sense, they are often important for the particular golfer, to help him accomplish the mechanically essential movements. Jack Nicklaus's slight turn of the head just before commencing the backswing, and Gary Player's inward press of the right knee at the same time, are both triggering mechan isms which help them to start the swing proper, smoothly and correctly.

To talk in this way of 'triggering mechanisms', which many good golfers employ, suggests that the swing is some kind of programmed sequence of events. There are two senses in which this is a useful idea.

First of all, the *downswing* is a ballistic movement: it is not guided. Once committed to it, the golfer cannot alter it. That is not to say that golfers cannot make corrections to swings that have gone wrong; but to do so they must have received the information and decided how to act on it during the backswing. Since the downswing lasts for only 0.2 to 0.25 seconds inability to react to information received after it starts is not surprising, and is consistent with human reaction times. Direct experiments have confirmed this with golfers.

In another sense, the whole swing, backswing and downswing, has the characteristics of being programmed. As mentioned above, it *can* be altered in response to information received during the early stages; but a good swing can function without this information – or at least, without some of it. This view is not only consistent with the expressed feelings of expert players, but at least for visual information, it has been confirmed experimentally by Noble (1967). The experiment was done by having golfers hit shots into a net in a room whose only source of light could be switched off (with rapid decay) at various stages of the swing. Most of the golfers tested could strike the ball with normal speed and accuracy if the light remained on for only a few inches of the clubhead movement on the backswing, with the rest of the backswing and the whole of the downswing taking place in complete darkness. Very few of them could, however, strike the ball accurately, or even at all, if the light went out before the backswing began, i.e. before the clubhead was moved away from the ball.

These results are consistent with the idea of the golf swing's being a pro grammed event, in which visual information at least is unnecessary beyond an early stage. The same may not be true of information received via the proprioceptors, but it is a plausible hypothesis to say that successful golfers succeed in programming their swings in such a way that no interruption or correction is needed. The idea of a programmed swing suggests that, once triggered, it will happen without further thought. This may be true for a few golfers, but the vast majority need something to think about, some positive aim to achieve during the swing. Nearly all good golfers can, and do, take trouble and care to set themselves up correctly and consistently before com mencing the swing; and, as mentioned earlier, many then have one conscious triggering mechanism which sets the swing in motion. But during the swing itself, it is really not practicable to think of more than one, or possibly two, things – which is of course, one reason why beginners find the game so difficult. It seems that nearly all good golfers have one key thought, usually the mental impression of some feeling they wish to experience during the swing

These key thoughts can be related to almost anything and may change from time to time, sometimes quite frequently. Indeed, it may be that they *must* change, otherwise they result in exaggerated movements which actually change the swing. Properly applied, key thoughts help *retain* the swing.

On this question, we should note the words of Jack Nicklaus, the best golfer of modern times, and, many would argue, of all time, speaking of his own swing: "I still rarely get through one tournament using the same swing thoughts or feels that got me through the last one. The basics of my swing don't change, but the mental pictures I need to keep it oiled and running smoothly certainly do . . . Sometimes my key thoughts will change from round to round, or even in mid-round if something about my game dissatisfies me . . . The point I want to make as emphatically as possible is that you cannot automate the golf swing", (Nicklaus, 1974).

It is worth adding that completely identical successive swings are neither possible nor desirable. From what we know of the way the nervous system controls the muscle groups that cause body movements like the golf swing, complete replication time after time would be impossible. In any case, a completely replicating swing in every detail is not what is wanted by a golfer, otherwise he would not make proper contact with the ball if the external or internal circumstances changed even slightly from those in which he had perfected his swing. External changes might be caused by having to play off sloping ground; internal changes might occur if he changed his stance or posture, or even felt cold or hot. There is evidence that skilled golfers *do*, whenever possible, succeed in setting themselves up more consistently than the unskilled do − for example, in positioning their feet − but the skilled golfer's swing, or programme, is such that, even if forced to make changes in his set-up, he can still reproduce nearly identical club movements.

JUDGEMENT SKILLS

Up to this point we have limited the discussion to the full-power swing. We now consider the mechanics, and more particularly the mental processes involved in playing a shot to a target which lies at less than the maximum possible range from the golfer. As mentioned earlier, we should distinguish, in this context, two kinds of shot − those in which the reduction of range can be achieved by using a less powerful (more lofted) club and swinging at more or less full power, and those that do not require a full power swing, even using the most lofted club.

For the former type of shot, the mechanics of the swing are, in essence, the mechanics we have already discussed − and we need not go into minor variations of swing plane and length of swing here. The important new element in hitting a given distance using a full-power swing lies in judging how far off the target is, and translating that into correct club selection. The mental process by which this is most commonly done is easy to describe in layman's terms, but difficult to analyse in any detail. The golfer looks at the target (nearly always a green with a flag in it), relates the picture he sees to a store of similar pictures, and shots he has played, and selects a club accordingly. Specifically, he can use the apparent size of known features such as the flag-stick, other golfers on or leaving the green, bunkers around the green, trees to the side of it, even the green size itself. On a strange course, judgement can be upset by unusual size features – small greens, large bunkers beside the green. If a golfer is used to playing on a hilly course, he finds distance judgement (among other things) difficult on a very flat course, and vice versa. On a familiar course, other aids to judging distance are available; the golfer will know that from a particular landmark, for example a bunker or a tree at the side of the fairway, he needs, say, a 6-iron to reach the green.

This approach is carried to its logical extreme by most of today's top professional golfers, who pace out (or have paced out) beforehand the distances in yards to the green from a number of landmarks, such as bunkers, trees etc., on each hole. During play, they then only have to count a few paces forward or backward from their ball to one of these reference points, and they know to within one or two yards the distance their next shot must travel. They know, also to within one or two yards, how far they hit the ball with each club; thus, club selection becomes a matter of measurement and arithmetic. Adjustments can, of course, be made for wind, slopes and extra hard ground. This method is of most value to players who hit the ball consistently the same distance each time with a given club.

However it is done, judgement of distance tends to be better in good players because the information that is fed back to them as the result of a shot is more reliable than it is to poor players. If a shot finishes 15 yards short of its target, a consistent and accurate striker can correctly deduce that his judgement of distance was wrong by 15 yards; an inconsistent striker may not be able to tell how much of the 15 yards was a result of bad judgement, and how much a result of bad striking. This crops up in all parts of the game where assessment of distance, and on the putting green of slopes also, is involved. Poor performers find it difficult to separate errors in judgement from errors in execution; better players find it easier. They therefore learn more rapidly and can perfect their judgement. There is a further complication in taking account of the roll of the ball, particularly before it reaches the green. This is less predictable than flight through the air.

The next question we have to consider is the judgement of distance when a full-power swing is not possible, that is, when the distance is less than 100 yards or so. Here, although the modern professional golfer may well know the distance in yards, it is difficult to see how it can help him much. The situation is akin to judging how hard to throw and what trajectory to use when throwing a ball to another person some distance away. It is related to the judgement of roll to the extent that inevitably, whatever the ground conditions, the shorter the shot becomes, the larger proportion of the distance has to be allowed for roll.

In this length of shot, since the constraint of achieving maximum clubhead speed is removed, a greater variety of techniques may be used, with each of which the expert golfer can produce a slightly different kind of shot which he will use depending on the conditions, the precise nature of the terrain, the position of the hole, the lie of the ball and, generally, his ability to visualize the path he wishes the ball to take. Expert players who utilize variety in shots of this kind, as with other aspects of the game, tend simply to convert the wish to play a specific kind of shot directly into the production of it. Thus, for example, a player who visualizes a 50 yard pitch over a bunker to a green a little above the level from which he is playing, as being a high lofted shot, landing 'softly' and running on a few yards, does not have to reason that this will require the clubhead to be at least level with the hands at impact, and travelling horizontally rather than slightly downwards, and that to achieve this, the ball should not be placed too far back in the stance, and the swing should be long and slow. He simply visualizes the shot and plays it: either without much conscious thought, or perhaps with one single, key thought in his mind which he knows from experience helps him play the particular shot in mind. The subject of key thoughts is discussed on page 210.

The mechanism that tells the golfer how hard to hit is not easy to analyse further. Certainly there seems to be no conscious effort to take a $\frac{3}{4}$ length backswing, or to swing down at $\frac{2}{3}$ speed, for example, though it sometimes helps beginners to be given this kind of advice. It seems that a golfer must build up in his memory a very large store of shots attempted and their outcomes before he can reliably decide what shot to play and how hard to hit it. And, of course, as we discussed earlier, the more consistently he strikes the ball, the more reliable the feedback information.

Nearly all the remarks made about short approaches are relevant, with perhaps even more force, to putting; and there are a few additional considerations peculiar to putting. Because of the low clubhead speed involved – anything from virtually zero up to 20 ft/sec. – a wide range of styles and methods of swing are possible – not to mention an equally wide range of putter designs. The putting performance of professional golfers has been analysed at tournaments both in the United Kingdom and USA. Results vary, depending chiefly on the difficulty of the greens, but overall typical success rates are 90% holed at 3 ft, 52% at 6 ft, 20% at 15 ft and 6% at 30 ft (Cochran and Stobbs, 1968).

The drop-off in success rate is to be expected, but, since the object is always to put the ball into the hole, it is of interest to ask why some putts miss. There are errors of judgement and errors of execution and combinations. It is useful to think of two categories of error: those made before the putter is swung back involving assessment of the putt, and those made during the stroke itself. Is it possible to tell which type of error is more important?

Common sense suggests that errors of judgement, though swamped by random effects in long putts, are more important the longer the putt, and errors of execution become important for the very short putts. Putts of 2 ft, for example, are sometimes missed − surely rarely through failing to assess the correct line. In one test (Cochran and Stobbs, 1968) carried out to try to separate the relative contributions of the two basic types of error, about 4000 golfers of all abilities had five attempts at the same 6 ft putt across a slightly sloping (artificial) surface. It was reasoned that if the only cause of missing was errors of judgement, a big improvement in the number of putts holed would be seen with successive putts, since the subjects would learn about the slope and speed of the surface. On the other hand, if the only cause of missing were errors in executing the stroke, little or no improvement would be likely. (It was assumed that execution would not itself improve with successive strokes.) In the event, the results were inconclusive. There *was* an improvement in the results of successive putts, but not a very marked one: 33% of first putts were holed, 38% of second putts, with the rise continuing more slowly, finally reaching 43% at the fifth attempt. These results were typical of other similar tests.

EXPERT GOLF

Perhaps the only conclusion that can be reached is that the skills of judgement and execution are less separable than might be imagined. Models and hypotheses can be put forward which are, however, difficult to test, not least because many of them depend on the activity being carried out in the real competitive situation. Improbably, short putts are quite frequently missed when something perceived as important by the player is at stake.

It is, for example, plausible to argue that it helps in the execution of an accurate stroke to have confidence in the line selected. This, of course, happens when the golfer has, on the previous green, succeeded with a putt, and there seems little doubt that success breeds confidence, and confidence breeds success. Conversely, failure breeds uncertainty of mind; uncertainty of mind breeds uncertainty of stroke. Indeed, one might construct a model (Figure 10.3) of the mental and mechanical processes, the basic abilities, and the interactions between them. Like all models, it does not give a complete representation; on the other hand, with one or two minor modifications, it probably applies to most golf shots as well as to putting, though perhaps with different emphasis. The model highlights the importance of the inputs which represent the player's basic abilities: 'green-reading', mental attitude and technique. They are the qualities which enable the player to break in to the two positive feedback loops which otherwise tend to make failure follow failure.

There is little question that expert golfers build sound putting techniques, but they do vary considerably from one to another. Generally, they keep their heads very still, with their eyes directly above the ball, keep the putter head close to the ground on the backswing and, at least at the present day, keep wrist movement to a minimum. But many additional features are said

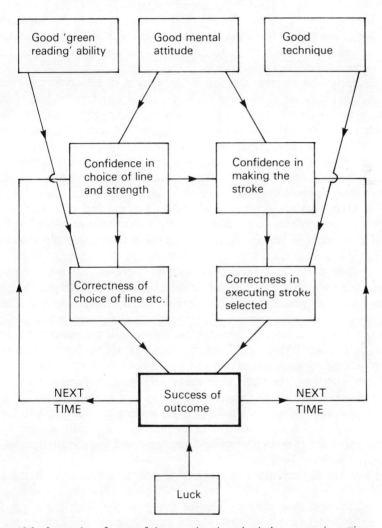

Figure 10.3 Interaction of some of the mental and mechanical processes in putting

to be essential by some and not by others – and simply adopting all the above precepts does not guarantee a sound method.

"Good mental attitude" in the diagram refers to the ability, possessed by some and not by others, to concentrate on the stroke being played, rather than look forward to the one after, or dwell on the one before; to think positively rather than negatively; to be clear what one is trying to do rather than what one is trying to avoid doing; and, once the line and strength of hit have been decided, to believe wholeheartedly in the decision.

Positive thinking is aided if the golfer can actually visualize the path the ball takes across the surface of the green. The ability to do this successfully constitutes the third basic input: 'green-reading'. This develops with experience as the golfer builds up in his memory a store of greens, slopes, putts, green speeds, successes and failures.

It is fairly obvious that the use of the eyes is of importance in 'green-reading', but it is not at all clear whether there is any best method of using them. Prior to taking their stance for a putt, expert golfers nearly always crouch behind the ball and examine the line of the putt from ball to hole, with their eyes perhaps 2 ft above the surface of the green. But many also do the same looking from hole to ball, and some stand well back from either side of the line, and examine it from there. Some even dangle the putter between their fingers like a plumb line whilst looking along the line of the putt.

It is likely that the sometimes quite lengthy 'stalking' of a putt in this fashion is more related to general mental preparation than it is to a direct visual assessment of the line of the putt. Mental preparation also manifests itself in the routine that many top performers go through prior to actually striking their putts. This varies from player to player, but might typically begin during the final stages of the 'stalking' phase. For example, the golfer might finish this phase by standing upright directly behind the ball looking towards the hole, have two practice swings with the putter in that position, then move towards his ball, but take his stance with the putter head a few inches to one side of the ball. There, he may take one further practice swing before edging forward and laying the putter head directly behind the ball, and finally striking the putt. With many golfers, a routine of this kind is repeated in exactly the same manner with every putt, except perhaps for those of a few inches. Some golfers have a pre-striking routine like this for all shots, though it is not so common as for putting, and usually shorter. Some golfers carry out their routine quite deliberately and consciously; others are unaware that they have one.

One of the slightly puzzling features of golf at a high level is the high degree of skill at putting which the top players exhibit. Since neither great physical strength, nor superbly precise timing are required in putting, it is difficult to understand why there should be any strong correlation between putting skill and the ability to hit the ball 250 yards consistently straight. And yet the top players are, or become, highly accomplished at both.

Of course, there may be no paradox in this. Maybe you cannot *be* a top player *unless* you are accomplished at both putting and driving; but general observation suggests there is more to it than that. If it were so, one would expect to see in most golf clubs, a few golfers who were as good at putting as the best professionals. It is very difficult to collect reliable observations on this, but such as do exist – partly subjective, partly from results of putting competitions (which are rarely recorded) – suggest that few, if any, club golfers putt anything like as well as professionals. The reason might, of course, simply lie in practice; or in the competitive environment in which professional golfers play; but perhaps, after all, putting and driving have more in common than might appear.

Competitive strategy and tactics play a part in all sports. The extent to which they do so is related to the degree to which each player's actions are dependent upon those of other players. The golfer responds to the shot presented to him, and plays 'against the course' rather than against an opponent. There *are* exceptions to this and the psychological interaction between the two players in 'match-play' golf should not be underestimated; but there is nothing that corresponds to the direct interaction between, say, two tennis players. In the jargon of sports psychology, golf, and certainly the execution of the full-power golf swing, is a less 'open' skill than other games (Knapp, 1963). In these games, deficiencies in the basic techniques ('closed' skills) can often be partially redeemed by good tactics – or, conversely, good techniques can be impaired by poor tactics.

In golf, the opportunities for employing good or bad tactics arise mainly in deciding what shot to attempt in situations where a choice exists. In practice, this usually means assessing the likelihood of bringing off a risky shot, and the consequences of success and failure; and weighing these against the likely outcomes of a more conservative shot. Because of the large shot-to-shot variation of a poor player, the gains to be made by good tactics are probably greater for him than for the expert. Nevertheless, leading professionals do quite consciously bring tactical considerations into their play; and indeed, have coined the term "playing percentage golf" to describe conservative tactics such as aiming for the middle of the green rather than for the flagstick when the hole is cut to one side of the green and close to a deep bunker.

In any given situation where a choice is to be made, it will depend on a number of things: on the state of the game or the whole tournament; on how well the golfer himself is playing on the day, particularly over the last few shots; and, in match-play, on his assessment of his opponent's chances. It depends also on the temperament of the individual. Some by nature are attacking players who take risks in seeking high rewards. Others are defensive and feel that good scores will come without a reckless assault on the golf course. Incidentally, a well-designed golf course is one which, among other things, presents challenges like these: offering to those willing to take risks, large rewards for success and severe penalties for failure.

Sometimes, also a player gets a 'feeling' about a shot; something about the lie of the ball, the contours of the course, the background, or a similar shot recently played, enables him to picture the shot very clearly, and he may attempt a shot that, viewed more objectively, seems unwise. The reverse also happens at times, when there seems to be no way of playing the shot.

One danger of consciously employing attacking or defensive tactics is that they may influence actual striking technique. It is common, for example, on a hole where the penalty for inaccuracy is especially severe, for golfers to try to 'steer' the ball, the idea being to produce a shorter, slower, more carefully controlled swing. In practice, this often results in a restricted backswing which doesn't give the proper timing sequence a chance to occur. The result is a shot worse than the normal swing would produce. Yet another golfing adage covers this: in tight situations "trust your swing". Thus, deciding on what to attempt with a shot which offers some alternatives is not simply a matter of correctly assessing the probabilities and acting accordingly, but of assessing a number of internal psychological factors as well as external factors related to opponents or the state of the competition.

Having said all that, it seems doubtful that good strategy or tactics play a big part in separating the highly skilled performer from the rest; at least, not to the extent that it contributes in tennis, squash, badminton or team games.

At the very highest level of performance it is fairly generally agreed that the difference between those who win important tournaments and those who do not does not lie mainly in technique. Anyone watching top-class tournament professionals hitting balls on the practice ground is impressed by two things. First, how consistently long and accurate their shots are; but second, how very similar to each other they are in this respect. From the results of the shots it would be impossible to distiguish the champions from hundreds of other professional golfers.

This might, at first sight, seem to confirm the view sometimes voiced that, at this level, everything depends on putting. There must, of course, be an element of truth in this; the player who has a 'hot' week on the putting greens may be 8 or 10 strokes lower on a four-round tournament than he otherwise would have been, which must increase his chance of winning. But even casual observation strongly suggests there is more to it than this; and the few occasions on which play in tournaments has been analysed in greater detail than simply counting strokes suggest that people who win tournaments, or for that matter finish high in the prize list, do everything just a little better than those who do not: their drives, long approach shots, short approach shots and their putting are all marginally better (Cochran and Stobbs, 1968).

It is difficult to escape the conclusion, therefore, that some aspect of personality is decisive: something which enables the winners to play as well under stress as they do on the practice ground – or, conceivably, even better. It is possible to describe superficially what some of these attributes are: for example, the ability to shut out completely any anger or elation over the shot or shots just recently played; to avoid thinking too far ahead; to concentrate on the next shot in a positive way – that is, to think about what one is trying to do rather than what one is trying to avoid doing.

It is also said that champions have the ability not just to maintain their standard of shot-making when in a winning position, but to improve it; to bring off one or more 'super-shots'. The evidence for this seems a little doubtful. Certainly it seems true that players can get 'charged up' in the closing stages of a tournament (and indeed at other times) and play a succession of superb strokes; and precisely how and why this happens is difficult to explain. But these occasions usually occur when a player is a few strokes behind the leader. When there is little to lose and everything to gain, positive thinking becomes much easier. The problem of playing the last five holes can look very different to the man who is leading by two strokes than to the man who is two strokes behind.

There can be little doubt that the feelings and thoughts experienced by the golfer can affect his performance. The champion either schools himself not to have the wrong kinds of thoughts, or not to allow them to affect his performance. The ability to do this may be partially innate, but cannot be entirely so, since experience helps to develop it. It is often said, for example, that before a golfer can win a major championship, he must, on one or more previous occasions, have been in a winning position and failed. In principle it would be feasible, though to the writer's knowledge it has not been done, to collect evidence on this. A few attempts (e.g. Whiting, 1969) have been made to collect evidence on the personality and attitude of golfers, but they have been inconclusive – perhaps because they failed to make the distinction between high-class performers and winners.

Golf, of course, is not unique in the 'test of nerve' imposed on winners; but it could be argued that the test is more severe than in most other games on account, basically of one thing: the ball is stationary when hit. This has two effects: first, starting from a static position makes the golf swing liable to be affected by any jerkiness caused by nervous tension. Secondly, and much more important, the fact that it is, for all practical purposes, entirely up to the golfer to decide when to make his stroke gives him plenty of time, both as he walks up to his ball from his previous shot, and as he stands over it about to play, to think about the shot to be played, the consequence of success or failure, the things to be attempted, the things to be avoided.

In most other sports the player reacts to the play of an opponent or a team-mate and has not time, in tennis, for example, to think about anything except playing the next stroke. It is relevant that the situation in other games when tension most obviously affects performance, are just those in which the player *has* time to think – for example, the double-faulted tennis serve on match point. Of course, the special problems posed by having plenty of time to play the shot apply at any time in golf, but they are particularly acute when a player is in a winning position.

CONCLUSION

Let us now try to sum up what we have said about highly skilled golf. It makes extreme demands on both power and accuracy; and we can analyse in simple qualitative terms the mechanics of how this is done. The mental processes which effect the required mechanical movements can be described, but are not really understood in that they cannot be explained as the outcomes of more basic psycho-motor mechanisms. It seems fairly clear, however, that the golf swing is a programmed sequence which it is difficult to break into; though events and thoughts experienced before it is initiated can shape it. Champion golfers have programmes of this kind which are not only more efficient, but are less affected by extraneous thoughts.

With such wide areas of ignorance there is clearly plenty of scope for further study of the skill involved in golf. Whether there is any point in doing so is not so clear. There is, of course, the point made early in this chapter, that golf is quite a good vehicle to use for a study of human skill, in that measures of performance are readily obtained. But if research on golfing skill is to have any real purpose, it must be to bring about ultimately an improvement in performance. There are two grounds for at least questioning the desirability of research for this reason.

Firstly, it might not be effective. Top performers in golf, and other games, have only a limited awareness of how they carry out their skilled actions; and, conversely, those with the greatest knowledge are seldom among the top performers. "Paralysis by analysis" is the phrase used by golfers for this state. It is fairly clear, therefore, that if the results of research into skills such as golf are to be useful, they are likely to be so to coaches rather than performers. If that is so, then perhaps the most fruitful aspects to study would be those involved in teaching and learning – for example, to assess the effectiveness of different teaching methods or artificial aids; to determine what words, gestures or demonstrations created the impressions in the mind, and the feelings in the muscles, which would enable individual golfers to carry out the sequence of movements desired. The methods of assessment used in educational technology could be applied.

The second reason for questioning the desirability of further scientific study of golf is a more philosophical one. Golf is a game; and the satisfaction derived from playing it depends on meeting a challenge that is neither too ridiculously easy nor too impossibly difficult. If the result of scientific study were *too* effective and improved overall standards too much, the game would, in effect, become too easy, and would either be less satisfying, or would require some changes in the basic ground rules to restore things (such as expensive lengthening of golf courses). It is of relevance that the game's ruling authorities, the Royal and Ancient Golf Club of St. Andrew's, and the United States Golf Association, have elaborate rules and specifications which prevent further improvement in the performance of golf *equipment,* for just this reason.

We are, of course, a long way from this state of affairs when we talk about the performance of most of the world's golfers – for whom the game is still too difficult – and it would be absurd to suggest that any amount of increased understanding of the swing would, in the near future, bring such improved overall standards that the game could be said to have become too easy. Nevertheless, some would argue the case in principle against even trying to do so by research and scientific investigation.

The somewhat paradoxical conclusion, then, is that further research would be thought pointless by some people because it is ineffective, and undesirable by others because it might be too effective.

References

Cochran, A. J. and Stobbs, J. (1968). *The Search for the Perfect Swing*. (London: Heinemann)
Knapp, B. (1963). *Skill in Sport*. (London: Routledge and Kegan Paul)
Nicklaus, J. (1974). *Golf My Way*. (London: Heinemann)
Noble, D. T. (1967). Unpublished – described in Whiting (1969) below
Whiting, H. T. A. (1969). *Acquiring Ball Skill*. (London: G. Bell and Sons)

11

The Expert Pilot

E. EDWARDS

WHAT IS A PILOT?

Even today, when flying enjoys almost universal acceptance as a means of transport, there remains a certain aura of glamour surrounding the role of the aircraft captain. He may be visualized as performing an enormously skilled job, not without an element of danger, for which many are called but few are chosen. He has at his command power and speed, and he exerts absolute authority over his ship. His equipment represents the vanguard of current technology, and his off-duty periods may be spent in the exotic corners of the globe. Financial rewards are known to be amongst the highest available.

Whilst there may be some elements of truth in the various aspects of the popular image, there are, too, large disparities between the image and the reality. Nowhere is this more evident than in the case of the display pilot. Here the apparent ease and grace of the manoeuvres belie the intense concentration required to achieve accurate heights, speeds and attitudes, and the spectator readily overlooks the physical and mental distortions effected by high accelerative forces. Similarly, the airline passenger, whilst easily impressed by the array of switches and instruments on the flight-deck, probably appreciates very little of the real difficulties which must be overcome to ensure the safe and expeditious progress of the flight. These might include, at different phases of the flight, both the extremes of high information throughput during take-off and landing, and underload during a long cruise. Both these conditions must often be met whilst the crew is suffering the effects of sleep disturbance.

The popular misconceptions concerning the nature of the piloting task probably give rise to misleading notions concerning the characteristics of the outstanding performer, particularly since the real expertise resides most especially in those facets of the job which often escape notice.

It is important to recognize that the term 'pilot' does not adequately describe a single job function. We may differentiate several types of operator including the military combat pilot, the airline transport pilot, the engineering test pilot, the executive pilot and the flying instructor. Whilst the characteristics which differentiate the professional pilot from the rest of the population probably display a good deal of commonality across the types, it seems likely that the abilities which distinguish the outstanding performers within each group differ considerably one from another. These differences may encompass temperamental variables, such as attitudes towards the assessment and acceptance of risks, as well as variations in technical skills.

THE PILOT'S TASK

The manual control of aircraft comprises a multi-axis tracking task in which the variables are highly interactive. The system being controlled exhibits complex dynamic characteristics which require a considerable amount of anticipation on the part of the human pilot in order to achieve acceptable standards of control. These basic skills of visual and instrument flight are learned early in the pilot's training and require only minor modifications associated with the transition from one aircraft type to another.

These skills must be performed simultaneously with such other tasks as consulting documents, monitoring and adjusting various aircraft systems, or carrying out verbal communications. Normal control performance is subject to interruption in the face of new incoming information, such as evidence of equipment malfunction or some new instructions involving a change in tactics. During the critical phases of flight the pilot must be prepared to make dramatic changes in his immediate goals such as aborting a take-off or deciding to abandon an approach to land. Such decisions might be based upon signals which call for accurate diagnosis of the prevailing situation, and need to be made swiftly since such factors as the limiting length of runways demand that decisions are reached almost instantaneously if the flight is to be conducted safely without the erosion of quite narrow safety margins.

Once the take-off roll has commenced, the pilot is committed within a very narrow range of options. Having attained a certain critical speed on the runway (V_1) he is no longer able to abort, and must become airborne. Once there, he cannot stop whatever difficulty might arise but must continue to maintain control, within the performance envelope of his aircraft and taking due account of such external features as high terrain or air traffic restrictions, until a safe landing can be achieved.

Certain critical elements of the pilot's task have, then, been identified. He must have acquired the basic control skills necessary for the guidance of his vehicle. Additionally and simultaneously he must cope with supplementary tasks and with interruptions. He may be called upon to make swift decisions some of which may comprise substantial changes to his goals. Because of his inability to stop or even slow down the operation, the timing elements of his skill are central to its nature. There seems no doubt that the expert performer must have outstanding aptitudes to excel at this multi-dimensional task, with all the facets of receiving and processing information which the task demands.

It is often remarked that the successful pilot is one who is able to carry out several tasks simultaneously. This view is, on the face of things, contrary to the widely accepted 'single-channel hypothesis' which describes the mechanism of human information processing. One route out of this dilemma is to postulate that the apparent performance of 'simultaneous' tasks involves the swift shift of attention from task to task in order that each may have its due appropriate share of the central processing capability. Whilst this distinction is of considerable theoretical import, the difference between multi-channel and time-shared single channel operation may be of little consequence in the understanding of real skills. The pilot must be able to deal with several simultaneous inputs and outputs and must, in addition, be able to organize his own 'brought forward' items at the correct point in the sequence of events.

A computer analogy may be helpful here. Each separate task may be regarded as a sub-routine which has been learned and practised and thus facilitates the performance of individual sub-tasks. All the sub-routines are under the overall control of an executive program, with its associated priorities and interrupt facilities, characterized by smoothness, anticipation, consistency and versatility.

The acquisition of skill almost certainly proceeds by way of the development of each individual sub-routine in relative isolation under the crude overall control of a primitive executive program. Only after the sub-routines are well-rehearsed is it possible for the executive to develop. Conversely, in the face of fatigue or other stresses, it is probably the executive which first deteriorates, leading to a lack of co-ordination in the total skill.

There has been some tendency for psychological research to proceed by attempting to analyse skills into their component parts, and to investigate these – whether for selection, training or other purpose – individually. Such a procedure diverts attention from the executive program, and in so doing excludes from study the most essential characteristic of complex performance.

It may well be virtually impossible to distinguish the expert from the relative novice in terms of the assessment of individual sub-routines. The hall-mark of the expert is his ability to 'put it all together' and produce a co-ordinated total performance, appropriate to the particular prevailing circumstances. Furthermore, the expert is likely to have developed an executive which is highly resistant to deterioration, resulting in the maintenance of the integrated skill in the face of stress. Whilst the skilled observer will recognize this highly developed executive program, he will find it a difficult facet of performance to assess objectively.

It seems beyond doubt that the high informational throughputs which typify the performance of many complex skills can be achieved only by means of the prior development of sub-routines which are capable of execution with little or no monitoring once they have been called up. The penalty for this means of operation is, of course, the difficulty of inhibiting a pattern of response once the series has been triggered. Again, the expert is distinguished by the ability of his executive to initiate an interrupt, or at least to make a quick change at the termination of an inappropriate sub-routine. (Over thirty years ago it was clear to Bartlett that an expert does not necessarily make fewer mistakes than a novice. His skill resides in the ability to detect and correct the errors.)

AUTOMATION

In recent years, particularly in the case of military and transport aircraft, something of an automation revolution has taken place. As a result of this, pilots are much less occupied with manual control tasks, which can be performed reliably and accurately by means of electronic, electrical and mechanical hardware.

The provision of sophisticated automatic equipment does not necessarily lead to a reduction in piloting skill or in work-load. The primary change effected is an increase in the operational efficiency of the system. The role of automatic equipment must be evaluated in the context of increases in aircraft speeds and in traffic density, coupled with reductions in crew complement, in separation standards and in permissible weather minima for take-off and landing. Additional problems are created by the need for constant monitoring of the automatics, and the requirement to revert to manual control in the event of major equipment failures. This latter problem is exacerbated by the lack of regular practice at manual control tasks and the necessity to enter 'cold' into the control loop.

Some idea of the extent of the complexity of contemporary equipment may be derived from consideration of alerting systems. These are designed to bring to the attention of crew members information regarding the malfunction of equipment or the existence of any other untoward circumstances. A contemporary transport aircraft may be equipped with over 400 visual alerting devices on the flight-deck. Some of these will serve more than one purpose with the result that the number of alert conditions which might be signalled may exceed 600. Obviously a considerable monitoring load is thereby generated, and in the event of major equipment failure or of inadvertent procedural errors on the part of the crew, the diagnostic problems might assume gigantic proportions.

Flight guidance, navigational, and thrust control systems tend now to be computer-driven. The military pilot may, in addition, be obliged to manage highly sophisticated weapon control systems. All these devices call for considerable expertise if they are to be exploited to the full. The older pilot might well feel that his job is very different from that which he was initially selected to perform and that much of his earlier operational experience bears little relationship to his current day-to-day activities.

This is not to say that no problems remain in aircraft handling. Visual landings, particularly at night, at airports lacking full ground radio facilities present a continuing source of difficulty and, indeed, of disasters. Similarly the problems associated with the negotiation of low-level wind-shear may tax to the full the ability of a crew to cope with a particular type of problem in vehicle guidance.

Automation, then, introduces its own problems. The expert pilot must possess the ability to interact effectively with highly complex computer-driven systems, whilst at the same time maintaining readiness to revert to a more primitive mode of operation.

SELECTION, TRAINING AND ASSESSMENT

Pilot selection tests have engaged research workers for several decades but even now remain at a fairly crude level of reliability and validity. Ideally the employers of pilots, whether in a test function, in an airline or in the military, would wish to have a procedure by which they could predict with some precision the rate of progress of a pilot through his training course and his subsequent performance throughout the rest of his career. In most cases, the employer would wish to know not only the potential of the individual as a pilot but whether he will eventually be able to assume command and function successfully as a leader of a crew and possibly as an instructor or a group manager. This demands, of course, prediction of the capabilities of the individual some 15 or 20 years after his initial selection. The problems of prediction are exacerbated by the difficulty that the selector is concerned with assessing temperamental characteristics as much as those of technical ability and perceptual–motor skill.

In the years following World War II most pilots were initially selected for military training and, having demonstrated their ability in that function, transferred to other posts. The results were not always successful, demonstrating the significant differences between the requirements of varying pilot roles. The expert combat pilot is not necessarily an expert, or even a successful performer, in civil aviation.

One of the most sophisticated selection procedures within European airlines was that developed by SAS (Scandinavian Airlines System) beginning in the late 1940s. In its developed form, the SAS scheme makes extensive use of specially trained psychologists in addition to assessors from the medical and personnel departments. Each applicant is examined independently by two psychologists whose assessments include:

(1) Measures of previous education and experience
(2) Measures of technical, inductive, and verbal intelligence
(3) Measures of personality traits, including maturity, self-confidence, social adjustments, etc.
(4) Measures of performance and behaviour, including motor ability, resistance to panic, ability to co-operate, tact, etc.

All this information is examined and integrated into a recommendation regarding employability. Any substantial discrepancies between the two examining psychologists must be resolved by the introduction of a third examiner. Evidence shows a high degree of predictive power in the relationship between scores on a nine-point rating scale by the selectors, and the division of pilots into the categories "still in service" or "left service" over the 15-year period of the investigation.

Few, if any, other professional people are so subjected to training and to performance assessment throughout their careers. An airline pilot at 50 years of age may well be called upon to learn to fly a new aircraft, possibly one in which the technology is some 15 years in advance of his previous machine. This represents a considerable demand upon the individual's capacity to absorb new information and acquire new skills, and is exacerbated by the necessity to meet the set standards within fairly tightly fixed time limits.

Professional pilots are required by law to demonstrate their proficiency either in a simulator or in the air at six-monthly intervals. This examination will cover both normal and emergency operating procedures. In addition, the pilot may be accompanied on any flight by either a company route check captain or an inspector from the controlling agency, who will report upon his proficiency. Annual renewal of the instrument rating is also required, and medical examinations must be completed every six months. Poor ratings in any of these assessments might lead to removal from duty and ultimately to the loss of licence. It is interesting to speculate upon the effects such rigorous examinations might introduce into other professions!

The assessment of pilot performance is normally conducted in subjective terms, albeit by highly experienced observers using reasonably well-standardized criteria. Typically an assessment form is first sub-divided into phases of flight, comprising pre-flight preparation, ground handling, take-off, climb, cruise, descent, approach and landing. Further categories will cover aspects relevant to the whole operation, such as R/T discipline or flight-deck management. The assessment of each phase will be further sub-divided, highlighting the aspects which are considered to be of most significance. The examining pilot will assess each category, probably using a 4- or 5-point scale, and in addition will make an overall rating of performance. Scale points will be defined verbally using such terms as "Very good standard" at one end and "Requires considerable further training" at the other.

Two features of this assessment system will be apparent. Firstly, performance is rated largely in relation to the achievement of system goals rather than in terms of behaviour per se – although marked departures from standard operating procedures will certainly attract severe penalties. Secondly, ample opportunity is provided for the assessor to rate the integrated levels of the skill (the 'executive program') as well as individual sub-routines.

The outstanding pilot will emerge from this process of frequent assessment by virtue of his constantly high ratings. As a consequence, he is likely to be offered additional responsibilities, particularly in a training and assessing function. Only as a result of assessment does this emergence take place, since – with a few exceptions in the military and sporting sectors of flying – a pilot is not in direct competition with his peers. Neither is he subject to any effective form of acclamation or censure from his clients.

COMMAND

The military pilot is likely to have gained a good deal of experience in the role of commander of his aircraft quite early in his flying career. Indeed, he may have no experience other than flying dual as a student pilot under training or as a solo pilot in a single-seat vehicle.

The airline pilot, on the other hand, may spend as much as fifteen years after his basic training before being again in command of his aircraft. During this period he may have spent some years away from the two front seats, being engaged, instead, in the management of aircraft systems (a role sometimes performed not by a pilot but by a professional flight engineer) or in navigational duties. Policies vary considerably concerning the allocation of duties amongst multi-pilot crews. Some companies utilize operating procedures whereby each crew member performs pre-defined functions at every phase of the flight. Others operate such that the captain and first officer alternate as 'pilot flying' on each successive sector with the other pilot carrying out the supportive duties. Such a procedure may involve exchanging seats for the sussessive sectors, in order to facilitate the performance of the respective duties. Obviously, the captain retains his overall command function whatever allocation system is in operation. Thus the kind of flying experience which has been gained by a pilot before he achieves command will vary greatly dependent upon the type of aircraft flown, and the crewing policy of his company.

The role of the commander, whilst presenting no problems in legalistic terms, comprises many subtleties in leadership skills in addition to the technical problems of command. Again, considerable variety is to be seen in the policies' adopted by different airlines in selecting and training for command. In part, eligibility for consideration will be based upon seniority (in some instances this could be the only criterion). Other factors which may be taken into account include the levels of competency assessed during the recurrent proficiency checks and line checks, and assessments of the pilot's temperamental characteristics including 'maturity', 'keenness', 'stability' or 'self-confidence'. Such assessments may occur before, during, or after command training courses. In most cases the assessments are made by senior training captains.

After initial selection, or possibly as part of a selection process, the pilot is then likely to undergo further training in technical skills, and within those organizations using a 'fixed seat' policy will gain his first experience of flying from the coveted left-hand seat. Some companies limit both training and assessment to the technical aspects of aircraft operation. Others provide courses on leadership, company policies, personnel management and other topics considered to be of relevance to the aircraft commander.

The skilled observer will recognize certain features of the outstanding commander, although such features may defy objective measurement. The captain will establish a 'tone' of operation on the flight-deck which is associated largely with what has been called the "trans-cockpit authority gradient". This defines the social relationship between crew members. The gradient is too steep when there is a reluctance to bring certain matters to the captain's attention; it is too shallow when the flight-deck is being run by a committee or by an individual not in command. Either of these situations is potentially dangerous. The expert commander is able to lead without driving his crew, and thus obtains the highest possible standards of team performance. On long-haul operations, it is the captain's responsibility to maintain the proper standards of performance throughout a flight of up to 8 or 9 hours duration and often in the face of severe problems arising from sleep disturbance and deprivation.

It is doubtful whether really outstanding handling skills are an essential part of the command role. Obviously, a high degree of competency is essential, but it has sometimes been thought that there might be an inverse relationship between the outstandingly skilful 'airframe handler' and the expert aircraft captain.

JOB STRESSES

Every pilot must be aware of the extent to which the safety of human lives and the security of expensive equipment are directly dependent upon the execution of his judgement and skill. It is rare for errors in the performance of professional duties to provide the potential for such drastic consequences.

During different phases of flight, problems either of information overload or underload may occur. The test pilot or the military pilot may operate almost entirely with fairly high workloads, and the transport pilot may well be hard-pressed whilst operating in a terminal area. Few tasks are more onerous than that of the executive pilot when approaching a busy and perhaps unfamiliar airport during a single-handed operation. During a long cruise on a sophisticated transport aircraft, the converse problem may arise due to an extremely low work-load but with the necessity to remain vigilant in monitoring the automatic guidance systems.

The disturbance of sleep and other diurnal rhythms constitutes one of the most significant stressors of the long-haul pilot. He may well be called upon to begin a duty period at the point at which body-time is demanding the commencement of sleep, and then to fly through the whole period of biological 'night'. The problem is confounded by time-zone changes and the associated difficulties of attempting to sleep during local daytime.

Scheduling systems make it difficult for pilots to plan their periods of social and recreational activities in line with conventional norms. Such disruption of activities combined with frequent and sometimes lengthy absences from home do seem to place abnormal stresses upon marital and other personal relationships. Proficiency checks and medical examinations occur at six-monthly intervals throughout a pilot's career. Since failure might lead to a loss of livelihood, it is inevitable that a certain amount of anxiety is generated as these hurdles approach.

To a large extent, the expert pilot is one displaying a high level of resistance to the stressors associated with his particular task. Differences between individuals in this respect appear to be largely determined by constitutional factors, although education and training play their part in the production of mechanisms of defence.

CONCLUSION

In common with all complex skills, that of the aircraft pilot comprises a set of well-developed sub-tasks integrated together to form an ability to react in a co-ordinated and versatile fashion in response to a variety of circumstances. The hall-mark of the expert resides essentially within his ability to maintain this overall co-ordination in the face of internal and external stressors.

Different types of piloting call for differing types of expertise. The combat pilot operates near the biological limits of human endurance, and therefore requires the exceptional levels of fundamental abilities associated with youth. The test pilot needs, in addition to his technical knowledge and skill, an unusual degree of excellence in handling ability and sensitivity to performance characteristics. The transport pilot must possess the ability to maintain high levels of compliance with standard operating procedures and at the same time be ready to deal with unusual and unforeseen circumstances. He must, too, have a high level of resistance to stress factors resulting from his life style and be able at some stage in his career to assume the leadership of his crew.

The profession of flying is not one in which the expert readily and clearly emerges from his peers, partly because of the technical difficulties associated with assessing piloting skill, and partly through the lack of any need to establish and recognize a small elite of champions amongst a group for which the penalties for inadequate performance are liable to be catastrophic.

12

The Musician

W. G. BROWN

The writer is not a musician but an occupational psychologist with a wide-ranging interest in music who is often surrounded by professional musicians. Faced with the problem of what to leave out in a chapter of this length the alternatives eventually became clear and settled down to two: abandon the task or opt for selectivity on the basis that, in musical skill, *excellence* carries with it special considerations. In Volume I the frame of reference was "the average skilled operator" and this description signals the first difficulty when trying to apply standard psychological jargon to musical ability. The leader of the National Youth Orchestra could be a better violin player than a new arrival in the second violins of a professional symphony orchestra. Such is the wide appeal of music that it is possible to obtain tuition and work up through the Associated Board's* graded examinations, eventually playing regularly in local amateur orchestras or groups. Professional players would usually develop from full-time studies at one of the Royal Schools or schools of music in larger cities. From this population would come the soloists working full-time as a solo pianist or violinist, or part-time solo concerto performers who also work regularly with top-line orchestras as, say, a French horn player. A third category must be mentioned commonly called *prodigies* where musical ability appears at a very young age and possibly in some cases the routine described above is by-passed. There is a good deal of journal literature linking music and psychology beginning in the early 1900s. Carl Seashore in the USA studied music analytically using a laboratory-based experimental approach and distinguishing between the psychological experience of the listener and the physical characteristics of sounds. His group tests *Measures of Musical Talent* were first available in 1919 and revised in 1939. As

---

*Associated Board of the Four Royal Schools of Music

Wing and Bentley (1966) point out, the inevitable criticism of the Seashore *Measures* was principally levelled at his analytical approach which destroys the unity of music (a whole can have a quality which is additional to the sum of its component parts). Additionally, behaviourists were unhappy about his theory of *innate* talent. Such tests, and others developed since – Lundin (1953), Bentley (1966) and Davies (1971) – have widened our understanding of musical abilities.

More recently Barrett and Barker (1973) surveyed research studies and concluded that no test or battery of tests in current use measures the composite of musical aptitude, and studied several aspects of musical performance relating a musical performance to five measures of pattern perception. Subjects were 51 children between 8 and 12 years old who had completed between one and three years of private instrumental study. Using Barrett's Musical Performance Test (which called for actual musical responses involving vocal duplication of pitch and reproduction of melodic and rhythmic patterns), the children were classified into three musical ability groups regarded as "differing in critical aural and perceptual motor skills required for successful pursuit of musical performance". Five perceptual measures were selected from the Princeton Kit of Reference Tests for Cognitive Factors (revised 1963) and focussed on four distinct perceptual factors chosen as representing pattern perception: the ability to keep specific configurations in mind in the face of perceptual distractions (flexibility of closure); the ability to combine apparently disconnected visual stimuli into a single percept (speed of closure); speed of symbol discrimination (perceptual speed); perception of configuration and position of objects in space (spatial orientation). A statistically significant relationship between the averages of ability groups was established for the first three of the five perceptual variables described above. The authors were guardedly optimistic about the prospect of finding significant correlations between music performance and other cognitive and perceptual abilities in future research.

Attempts to relate tests of musical talent to the highly talented are under-standably thin on the ground. The obvious difficulty is persuading busy musicians of international repute to sit down and do objective tests willingly and well. This was done in 1969 by Bruton-Simmonds (25 musicians over a period of eight years), who wanted to find out which acoustic abilities, if any, as measured by the Seashore Test of Musical Talents, are essential to high musicality and to test whether basic weaknesses can be revealed in groups not as highly musical but which have had as much training as the 'highly musical' group. He points out that a scientific definition of 'high musicality' is impossible because most of its elements are immeasurable but quotes Revesz (1953); "High musicality is evidenced by an emotional and intellectual need to experience music, together with a creative or interpretive talent for it that it is capable of giving a wide range of intense pleasure to another who has high musicality." Seashore's test covers pitch, loudness, rhythm, time, timbre and tonal memory and Bruton-Simmonds was also interested in whether pitch, rhythm and intensity are essential abilities for only certain instrumentalists, such as pianists, or for all kinds of musicians, such as violinists and singers, as well. The 15 "classical musicians of international renown" (the criterion group for high musicality) had high scores (75th percentile or above) for rhythm, relative pitch, intensity discriminations and tonal memory, whereas the other 10 had basic weaknesses in pitch, rhythm and intensity discrimination. Excellent sense of time and timbre, as measured by the Seashore test, do not seem necessary for high musicality and at this level of skill the pianist requires a sense of pitch as acute as the violinist's, and the violinist a sense of intensity (loudness) as acute as the pianist's.

Bruton-Simmonds (1969) was well aware of the limitations of his study which illustrates the difficulty in obtaining samples from the world of work, but if skills of 'excellence' are to be explored this would seem an obvious approach. The alternative might be a longitudinal study over many years of a cohort group (or groups) of the careers of musicians after leaving full-time training. In the field of occupational information attractive alternatives to 'dry', objective descriptions are highly personal accounts from able, verbal operators, who can put over the essence of their work with balance and feeling. When describing examples of skills of excellence an obvious approach is to ask a practitioner to analyse what he does and how he does it. The writer has no such frame of reference and for this short chapter has relied on a small number of semi-structured, taped interviews with professional musicians purposely mixed in terms of level of professional standing and operation, a good deal of anecdotal evidence collected over fifteen years, a selective reading of the background literature including autobiographical works by Menuhin (1976), Moore (1959), Neuhaus (1973), and, particularly, reference to Shuter (1968).

Most writers on the subject of the psychology of music agree that there is a chain of activity which comprises a musical event. Firstly the *composer* (who may or may not be a highly skilled instrumentalist) who creates original works (the score), the *performer* who recreates the music from a printed page of abstract symbols (or after memorizing it), and the 'passive' *listener* who hears with understanding and enjoyment (or the opposite). This communication (usually one-way, though the listener may tell the performer that the composer intended something else) is fairly well understood in physical terms, and the instrument–player interface can also be studied ergonomically; the difficulties begin when 'emotional reactions' and 'experiences' are studied. The listener may, for example, have a completely different emotive response from the emotions experienced by the composer when he was composing. Also, the emotions aroused in any two people listening to the same piece of music are not necessarily the same. As Wing and Bentley (1966) point out there is no doubt that music communicates but only *how* it communicates (methods of composition, the tonal materials used, etc.) is amenable to study and analysis; *what* it communicates is by no means fully understood or definable in words. Both 'musicality' and the musical event have important implications for discussing musical skill at a high level of excellence. Could one implication of Bruton-Simmonds' findings mean that the performer with high musicality can take liberties with time (rubato) and produce a highly individual *interpretation* which is pleasing to more listeners in any given audience than the reverse? The other measure he claimed could be less than excellent in high musicality was timbre; defined as the ability to discriminate between complex sounds which differ only in harmonic structure. One aspect of musical skill at a high level is the ability to play very quickly and accurately at the same time. Could the visual–aural feedback loop be inadequate in physio-psychological terms to cope in this context and the top class performer has to learn to compensate for this?

A first look at the list of skills of excellence suggests that in some cases (e.g. rock climber and pilot) environmental dominance can be so important as to blur the separation between the categories of compliance and excellence. A pilot or rock climber may not survive a particular event however much he applied his excellent skills; a young concert pianist would certainly survive his first major concert in public and would, without asking, be able to read assessments of his performance the next day. A well-known concert pianist told the writer that he is less anxious walking out onto the stage of the Royal Albert Hall before several thousand people than he is appearing at a meeting of a north-country music club. Assuming that the piece has been effectively prepared, a live performance can produce in the player a keyed-up, heightened awareness with the right amount of anxiety to enhance rather than limit the display of skill. A small audience can mean, for the performer, a feeling of closer scrutiny and judgement; a large one that it is joining in to share the player's enjoyment. After a concerto the soloist will receive the applause of the audience; he may also notice the reactions of the members of the orchestra. If they are also applauding they tap their music stands *and* smile; if they look straight ahead and tap they are being polite. It is almost always the case that highly skilled solo players display their talents before an audience but this does not mean that they could not produce, to their own satisfaction, a particularly good performance whilst practising.

Musical ability seems, at first, to repond to analysis. The player must make a motor response with timing related to printed symbols representing movements of tones in time. The printed symbols (conveniently applicable to all instruments) indicate pitch, note values, melodic patterns, chords, keys, scales and intervals. Motor response involves control to produce complete finger independence; hands, and sometimes feet, must synchronize with the feedback loop involving vision and hearing, as the player hears what he has just played and relates this to the next passage in the score. Such a description would apply to an eleven-year-old child playing a set piece for the examiner at an Associated Board Grade 4 examination. It would also apply to the four string players of a world-famous chamber group playing, in public, one of Beethoven's last quartets, but the analysis falls far short of a full description of what is happening in the latter example. Each player has attained a level of excellence in his musical skill to be able to cope with the demands of this particular kind of music, particularly the importance of playing together in a very 'exposed' situation. The technical requirements have been substantially raised to cope with legato and staccato, variations from fortissimo to pianissimo, phrasing, etc.

The Associated Board examiner allocates marks for set pieces, scales and arpeggios, playing at sight and aural tests, the total of which produces a level from pass, merit to distinction. The quartet's performance evades such objective analysis but is communicated to members of the audience. Some, perhaps musicians themselves, may be following the same score for the purposes of study and analysis, but the majority, including the analysts, are likely to find the music emotively appealing. Furthermore, as stated earlier, the emotions aroused in one person by the particular piece of music may be quite different from the emotions it arouses in another. Though top athletes and rock climbers have individual styles, one could turn to the Olympic Games records and times, and to photographic evidence of conquests, not-withstanding the dangers and emotional and physical efforts involved. For musicians there are no objective criteria and the complicated player–listener interaction must also be seen against a context of a wide spread of types of music and individual difference. Music can differ in type (jazz, swing, rock, brass band, classical, etc.) and listeners in their state (oral efficiency, musical training, mood, expectations). It may be handed down (Indian sitar) or written down (Beethoven string quartet) or improvized at the time (traditional jazz). It may be listened to live at a one-off performance in a concert hall, or from a recording which resulted from several 'takes' thus preserving the particular skilled performance for future generations of listeners. Listeners may be keen parents at school concerts, Associated Board examiners, good amateur players listening to top professionals, critics attending concerts. Any listener is entitled to his or her opinion and example of the highest level of musical skill whether it is a clarinet solo at a jazz festival, a cornet solo at the National Brass Band competition, or the solo violin part in Tchaikovsky's concerto. In recent years the increasing availability of good quality equipment for home listening has meant that listeners to live performances are probably far outweighed by those who hear music from records or a radio. The former have a very complicated sound field with reflections from walls and ceiling which is very difficult to record and playback. The latter hear sound recorded in a studio which has gone through many processes before it reaches their sitting room. Indeed, one hi-fi enthusiast said, after his first attendance at a symphony concert, that there was "no bass response"! As Shuter (1968) has said, "a musical event may be described as consisting of a *score* that is permanent and unchanging, *executants* who may hold genuinely different opinions on the manner of performance, and a *listener* who has the privilege of ultimate interpretation whether he comes in knowledge or ignorance, enthusiasm or boredom."

The accepted and most common method of developing an aptitude for playing a musical instrument into ability and perhaps to skill, is to prepare, via lessons from a qualified music teacher, for the Associated Board graded examinations. The Board provides an independent national examining system and reference point for the rating of musical ability, and provides information on its development. The populations examined are large; a total of 244 492 candidates was examined in 1976 with wide differences in numbers between the sixteen instrumental sub-groups. Piano 110 994 (eight grades); violin 26 473 (eight grades); clarinet 14 792 (six grades); violoncello 6 523 (eight grades); trumpet 5378 (five grades); guitar 1905 (five grades); bassoon 711; harp 73 (both five grades), out of sixteen instrument categories. Unfortunately, the Board does not ask for the ages of candidates but anecdotal evidence from experienced examiners suggests that about 98% of them are of school age. (As a physiological aside, it is interesting to note that whereas in athletics it is the oxygen intake rate – rated per kilogram of body weight and reaching a peak by twelve to fourteen for girls and eighteen to nineteen for boys – which decides the development – through training – of available 'power' output, no such considerations apply to musical activity). A child prodigy could be playing a violin concerto in public at the age of ten; Rubenstein was giving concerts at the age of 80. Today, many children develop an interest in and begin to learn an instrument through the considerable musical activity in schools which have regular peripatetic teachers and local orchestras, the National Youth Orchestra representing the highest level of young amateur skills in the 'classical' area. Domestic influence is important whether as background support financially (for an expensive instrument), or providing help through a knowledge of music. Parental support, hopes and expectations, as musicians or not, sometimes clash with the child's uneven application to the learning task. Where there is high motivation, time available and a more mature approach it is possible, in exceptional cases, to start learning the violin at the age of fifteen and reach grade 5 with distinction within one year.

An analysis of the Associated Board's summary of results for 1976 (87th Annual Report) show that pianoforte (59%), violin (14%) and clarinet (8%) account for over 80% of all candidates examined. When analysed by pass levels and failures (percentages) over the eight grades for all instruments there is a rise in the number of distinctions after grade five and a fall in failure rate. When this treatment is applied to the above-named instruments the results are as in Table 12.1.

These figures suggest that there is a 'break point' or 'plateau' of some kind at which the development of musical skill levels out (or fizzles out) and that those who pass through this 'barrier' are capable of lifting their skill to a

TABLE 12.1 Summary of Associated Board results for 1976 for piano, violin and clarinet

Grade	Number examined	Distinction (%)	Merit (%)	Pass (%)	Fail (%)
Pianoforte					
8	2 927	12·4	22·7	41·7	23·2
7	4 228	11·5	24·9	47·4	16·2
6	5 994	6·6	18·5	50·8	24·1
5	13 750	6·6	21·0	55·4	17·0
4	13 473	5·1	18·4	58·3	18·2
3	20 917	6·7	23·1	59·2	11·1
2	23 294	8·7	26·7	56·5	8·1
1	26 411	11·8	28·2	53·4	6·6
Total	110 994	8·5	24·1	55·3	12·1
Violin					
8	556	30·2	32·4	28·6	8·8
7	1 013	22·8	28·8	38·7	9·7
6	1 077	16·1	27·4	45·0	11·5
5	2 646	11·6	26·7	48·0	13·7
4	2 689	9·6	26·1	53·8	10·5
3	4 816	10·0	26·6	54·6	8·8
2	6 039	9·1	25·5	55·5	9·9
1	7 637	8·4	25·0	57·3	9·3
Total	26 473	10·6	26·1	53·3	10·0
Clarinet					
8	595	17·3	27·1	41·2	14·4
6	1 080	8·8	25·6	47·8	17·8
5	3 055	7·4	23·3	56·2	13·1
4	3 871	5·5	23·3	62·0	9·2
3	6 191	7·1	25·4	59·0	8·5
Total	14 792	7·3	24·5	57·6	10·6

'player' level either as a basis for amateur music making or beginning full-time studies at a school of music. The figures for the violin are particularly interesting and suggest that those who manage to get beyond Grade 6 are capable of developing their skill level significantly better than either pianoforte or clarinet on an instrument which is accepted as difficult to learn to play. Other factors may of course intrude. In addition to dropping out because the limit of ability has been reached, the person may have become occupied with preparation for GCE 'O' and 'A' level exams; occasionally the one reason is made an excuse for the other. Also, a larger percentage of learners on a particular instrument may take examinations than on another. Experienced teachers may have their own special views, for example, that there are 'keyboard' people, 'string' and 'wind' people. Also that, simply put, physical co-ordination plays a very big part in acquiring musical skill. If a child is not physically dexterous *and* co-ordinated no amount of intelligence, motivation, or capability for rapid learning will achieve results. The reverse is also thought by some teachers to be true but the phenomenon of the so-called 'idiot savant', an individual of very low intelligence who shows some special aptitude, such as musical ability, contradicts this view. As Shuter (*ibid*) points out, "the typical musical accomplishments of idiot savants show some similarities to those of infant prodigies. They can often play a tune by ear after hearing it only once or twice. Some learn to read music. But their lack of general ability and of emotional stability prevents them from developing their talent normally." Musical ability has a tendency to emerge at a relatively early age and, in a small number of children, has a precocity which develops into a conspicuous musical skill. The public performances of musical prodigies (not necessarily their first appearance in public) was in one study shown to be at an age a little over thirteen. Much evidence is available in the history of music with Mozart accepted as one of the greatest of musical prodigies. Shuter has six chapters on the development of musical ability followed by a thorough treatment of heredity and environmental factors. Her book has the merit of being interesting, informative and readable and is well referenced and indexed. The writer, very much aware of the impossibility of describing "the musician's skill" in one chapter, strongly recommends readers to refer to Shuter's book for a wider frame of reference, particularly the assessment of musical ability by objective tests. The penultimate section of her book looks at theories of musical abilities and includes a short part on 'musicality' (aesthetic appreciation of music).

A cursory examination by an ergonomist of a violinist in action would produce enduring sympathy for the player and perhaps surprise that no radical alterations to the shape of the instrument and the playing position had taken place over the last couple of centuries. Two features which immediately impress are the lack of width of the finger board for a large male hand and the awkward holding position. To make life even more difficult there are no useful frets as with a guitar to predetermine the length of string which is vibrating. It is therefore possible to play the instrument perfectly in tune (another challenge). Naturally enough, it is also very easy (particularly in the early stages) to play it out of tune and so the auditory–kinaesthetic (muscle sense) feedback loop, whereby the player listens and adjusts, becomes a key component of his skill. It is also important that the strings are bowed into life by about 150 stretched hairs from the tail of a Siberian stallion.* Given the right combination of player and instrument it is possible to produce a

---

*Male because the cross-sectional nature of the hair acts better on the strings. Today, Western bows tend to have Canadian horse hair, the two locations having in common a dry climate.

breathtaking exhibition of skill, sometimes to the point where the observation of such technique in action can detract from the potential enjoyment of the music in a wider sense. Paradoxically, some listeners when faced with such a situation find that they have to close their eyes, thus shutting off the visual aspect of the skill of excellence to be able to listen fully and effectively. For performers, there may be ·individual differences particularly a facility for memorizing scores. Some are able to exploit a 'photographic' memory and others find difficulty in committing a score to memory (say a solo concerto part). Playing from memory can help the player to reallocate his or her attention priorities, switching from the reading mode to a more visual over-view of his own playing and, perhaps, a greater concentration on inter-pretation. Yehudi Menuhin has described the string quartet as "the highest form of musical activity" and the demands at the highest levels of excellence, placed on such a small number of string players, are unusually difficult. The sheer 'exposure' of their playing requires co-ordination, timing and sensitivity of the highest order.

If the chamber group is playing one of Beethoven's late quartets before an audience at a music festival, the musical event could attract both musicians and non-musicians; it may be a demanding experience, it most probably would not suit or satisfy or move all of the listeners. The performance could not possibly be exactly the same as the group's recording of the piece and the recording may have been compared (on a radio programme) with others of the same work. Such an analysis can enrich the non-musician–listener's knowledge or disturb the mystery of his overall experience, or annoy a professional string player who has his own very definite ideas on how the particular piece should be played. At least one well-known virtuoso recom-mends that musicians should listen to and judge themselves critically and objectively and never worry about what critics may say or allow them to influence their approach to music or their state of mind. To return to the musical event (score–executant–listener), it will be evident from the previous paragraph that the second and third components provide the basis for infinite variability. Menuhin argues that "the greater the artist the greater the know-ledge of his own maximum capacity, and of the gap between his actual achievements at concerts and that supreme conception which he carries in his mind and heart." To stretch the analogy towards occupational psychology; the difference between the immediate and ultimate criteria in job performance.

If excellent musical skill consisted only of the technical mastery of an instrument so as to be able to play (with near perfection) the most difficult scores, there is much that could be objectively described and measured. Playing in tune could be checked from a standard reference note by suitable recording and analysis with scientific apparatus.* Mistakes could be counted

---

*In the 1950s a popular singer called Eartha Kitt developed to an attractively high level of skill being able to sing just *out* of tune.

by an expert playing back a recording and comparing it with the score, optimum fingering techniques could be compared. Thus, through regular practice and feedback from such analyses, the development of skill could be encouraged and monitored. The player, perhaps a violinist or pianist, would reach the stage where he or she could read a demanding score at first sight and change the notes into sounds which were accurate in terms of pitch, timing, and intensity; this is called *technique*. An accurate reading and playing of an unaccompanied piece for violin by Bach (there are, of course, many other good examples) is a demonstration of high level technique and, if heard by naive listeners, as well as those with skills and experience in music, would probably lead to a good level of agreement that this was technically satisfactory, component, acceptable, admirable, etc. There is, however, another component of musical skill which is much more subjective, much less easy to define and certainly connected with the emotive appeal of music. Shuter, quoting Revesz (1953), explains 'musicality' as primarily denoting the ability to enjoy music aesthetically and goes on to distinguish it from creative or interpretive talent, aural abilities (for example, discriminating rhythmical and tonal relationships) and affective response to, love of, or interest in music. This use of the word 'musicality' differs from that of Bruton-Simmonds mentioned earlier in that it applies also to the listener. Revesz recognizes various degrees of musicality from the very pronouncedly musical downwards and states that, to be considered musical, a person must possess several of the following characteristics: ability to contemplate a piece of music as a work of art, to assimilate and co-ordinate it as a whole, to be sensitive to composition and performance in terms of artistic quality, to understand the structure of the work, to follow or even to anticipate the composer's intentions, and to become so absorbed in the emotions expressed that he feels as if he were creating it.

This concept of musicality adds an important dimension to the score–executant–listener linkage but is focussed almost entirely on the last link in the chain: the listener. 'Technique', as explained, certainly links the score and the executant; this is the objective/cognitive/physiological aspect. There is another factor which can profoundly influence the musical event as far as the listener is concerned and this is really connected with how the executant, from the vehicle of his technique, *interprets* the score or piece. One very frequent comment heard when professional musicians are discussing the playing of another professional musician, usually but not always a solo artist, is that they are or are not 'musical'. The word is very similar to 'musicality' but the two should not be confused. It may also be possible that more musically naive listeners, happy with the overall effect of what they are hearing and unable or unwilling (perhaps to their benefit) to be analytical are also affected by a particularly 'musical' interpretation. Attempts to get a definition from a small sample of professional musicians including a concert pianist, a leader of an orchestra and two orchestral string players were only partially satisfying and the impression is that we must accept 'being musical' as a quality which certainly has its effect but, on the whole, cannot be defined:

"Successful use of the language of music"

"Understanding, appreciating and interpreting the structure of a piece"

"The score gives overall form but every musician has an individual language"

"An intuitive feeling for musical expression"

"Some very able musicians are competent, tremendously co-ordinated, self-confident, highly skilled technically but not musical"

"An understanding of the work being performed, its style, structure and emotional content, and the ability to project so that all those things are immediately recognizable to the audience. To translate for the listener the requirements of the composer. You have to take yourself back on an instrument he didn't write it for"

"Where playing is logical and natural. In a musical soloist, one is not aware of technique, the instrument is only an excursion of him or her. How they would sing it"

"Any instrument can be mechanized, the truly musical player makes it sing with the give and take of a phrase, a certain rise and fall, how he treats the sound"

On Sunday 9 April 1978 a seventeen-year-old trombonist Michael Hext won the BBC TV Young Musician of the Year award. Each of the four finalists ('cellist aged thirteen, clarinettist and pianist aged sixteen) played a concerto with a professional symphony orchestra, having won heats in their instrument class playing solo or piano-accompanied pieces. During the finals each player was interviewed immediately after performing and asked to introspect on his performance. This was followed by an assessment from a professional musician who was not a member of the panel of judges. The girl 'cellist had given a confident, sensitive, delicately phrased and highly musical performance of the Elgar concerto with a technique limited by the size of her hand (the length of the finger board requires an adult-sized hand span to produce adequate linking of notes, particularly at speed). Clearly, she demonstrated a high level of ability and assuming continuing motivation has a great deal of potential as a performer. Both the clarinettist and pianist had produced confident, technically competent, thoughtful performances. The trombonist, clearly nervous when playing said he found the heat troublesome and was obviously unhappy with part of his performance – he came unstuck in a very tricky passage which included a high F. The interviewer said that his was a very good performance of a rarely-heard trombone concerto and that he made more mistakes than any of the others. The trombonist won and the result illustrates the importance of looking beyond technical mastery when judging musical skill and supports the notion that when built up to a level of excellence the capacity for a special, individual quality of interpretation is perhaps the component which most affects a musical event.

In musical skill there is a hierarchy of excellence from the casual amateur through to professional musicians and on to individual solo performers, a number of whom are known world-wide. There are also a very small number of musicians, including Heifetz, Richter and Holliger, who are regarded even by some of the international solo performers as occupying some special pinnacle of perfection as performers on their particular instrument (violin, piano, oboe). Such a hierarchy seen against a context of contemporary recording standards and playback availability has an obvious motivational element. It also has a built-in assessment factor upwards and downwards. The excellent *performer* could be a child in a school. The excellent *performance* must have as a basis a flawless technique, but the acceptability of the interpretation by the listener seems to depend on another, extra factor – being *musical* – which may or may not develop in the musician.

References

Barrett, H. C. and Barker, H. R. (1973). Cognitive pattern perception and musical performance. *Perceptual and Motor Skills*, **36**, 1187

Bentley, A. (1966). *Musical Ability in Children, and its Measurement*. (London: Harrap)

Bruton-Simmonds, I. V. (1969). A critical note on the value of the Seashore measures of musical talent. *Psychologia Africana*, **13**, 50

Davies, J. B. (1971). New tests of musical aptitude. *Br. J. Psychol.*, **62** (4), 557

Lundin, R. W. (1953). *An Objective Psychology of Music*. (New York: Ronald)

Menuhin, Y. and Primrose, W. (1976). *Violin and Viola*. (London: Macdonald and Jones)

Moore, G. (1959). *The Unashamed Accompanist*. (London: Methuen)

Neuhaus, H. (1973). *The Art of Piano Playing*. (London: Constable)

Revesz, G. (1953). *Introduction to the Psychology of Music*. (London: Longmans, Green)

Shuter, R. (1968). *The Psychology of Musical Ability*. (Methuen)

Wing, H. D. and Bentley, A. (1966). The mystery of music. *New Scientist, Nov. 66*

13

The Research Scientist

P. BRANTON

MATERIAL AND METHOD

Introduction

It is at least as difficult to formulate the right questions in this area as it is to try and answer them. On that point all the sources consulted for the material in this chapter agree. Two of those interviewed expressed scepticism about the feasibility of probing at all into such mental activity as skilled thinking. They seemed to think it might spoil spontaneity and, as it were, take the gilt off the gingerbread. There is no answer to this except that since there does not seem to be too much known about the skill aspect of thinking, this study is likely to be more heuristic than explanatory. It should therefore be no surprise that the evidence presented here is slender, not quantitative, and cannot lay claim to being statistically representative. Much of the effort is given over to examining critically the assumptions behind the views collected from and about successful scientists. From this a rough canvas may emerge of what they did to achieve their undoubted successes, and only then more testable propositions might be evolved about "what makes a good research worker?"

The sources drawn on were of three kinds: books, depth interviews and extended discussions. Firstly, biographies and autobiographies of distinguished scientists were searched in order to identify what it was that distinguished these individuals from the ordinary run of scientific worker. This meant scanning notes kept over many years, re-reading descriptions by psychologists of findings about creative thinking, e.g. Bartlett (1958), Wertheimer (1959), as well as currently reading through life histories of ten eminent physicists, astronomers and biologists. The author has had interviews in considerable depth with two Nobel Laureates, Professor Sir Andrew Huxley and Professor Ragnar Granit (Stockholm), with Professor H. Düker (Marburg) and Professor O. Edholm, and numerous other interviews and conversations with scientific researchers.

The choice of those interviewed was largely dictated by the desire to ask persons who had led and administered research teams and who were willing to respond. The opening question was usually: If you are to select among researchers, can you distinguish a good one from an indifferent one? This was unfailingly answered in the affirmative. However, the answers to the next question – as to how this was done – were strikingly more hesitant and vague. One Fellow of the Royal Society said, "I can smell it".

The method of approach to all this material was seminally influenced by five days of intensive (philosophical) discussion with a group of teachers on the relation between language and thought. Two basic insights emerged from this: firstly, that thought processes without the use of words seemed possible, and, secondly, that all scientific thinking inevitably involves application of some principle for the selection of facts. These were used as criteria in extracting from the material that which may be special about the successful and distinguished scientific researcher and which prompts the attribution of excellence.

Excellence and skill

Psychologically speaking, there is an unresolved puzzle in the act of achieving something which one has never done before in quite the same way and which has not yet existed in one's own experience. In that sense, scientific research is a blind date, a rendezvous with a stranger. We say of a tennis champion that she 'excelled herself'. The excellence seems to reside in the Self, and if we knew the workings and the limits of this Self, we might be nearer to understanding the phenomenon. There are probably many elements in the champion's strivings. One of these, the competitive element, would need to be discounted, because that would only mean that she strives to excel others, rather than herself, and she was already champion in the previous round. Even if they puzzle us, new achievements in scientific research are not thought inexplicable, as witness Medawar's phrase "The Art of the Soluble".

What follows is restricted to work in the natural and biological sciences, rather than in history, economics or the social sciences. The task is difficult enough in these more established and formally exact disciplines, without having to jump in at the deep end of the pool. The focus is more on the researcher rather than on the practical, applied scientist.

SKILLED THOUGHT

Anyone expecting to find here a do-it-yourself guide on how to be a good researcher should be disabused right away; no nostrums will be offered and no short-cuts mapped. The only thing put forward in the face of all the efforts, anecdotal, descriptive and self-descriptive – from famous practitioners like Einstein to writers like Koestler – is a small, systematic contribution towards making research less of a lottery and more of a controlled and concerted activity, reducing the accidental element in the accretion of new knowledge and understanding. From the start the usual concern with originality, creativity and any somewhat mystical, somehow sensational description of discovery was avoided. The distinction was clearly seen by Granit (1972) when he entitled an essay *Discovery and Understanding*. This is not to diminish any of the findings of the proponents of 'originality' but merely to add some points to the syntax of research. In doing so, skill in research is treated as an ultimately rational and methodical quest for a kind of trans-subjective truth.

Skilled labour has been defined as "a combination of manual dexterity and acquired knowledge, command over materials and tools and a high degree of control over the quality of the finished product". (Burnett, 1977). Substitute 'mental flexibility' for manual dexterity and this is a reasonable working definition of research work. These then were the preliminary criteria of skilled thinking:

Controlled behaviour, as distinct from purely impulsive, spontaneous entering into the 'stream of consciousness';

Activity, as distinct from a passive waiting for inspiration;

Overcoming the element of chance, by systematic application of techniques and deliberate exposure to experience.

One informant explicitly stated that he did not consider originality a prime requirement of a good researcher. Another called for a "capacity to analyse and integrate, which requires mastery of the topic". William Herschel was said to have had "the ability to organize vast masses of observational material and far reaching, but never uncontrolled, imaginative power" (Sidgwick, 1953).

Coming to modern psychologists, there is among the many books and papers one by Mackworth (1965) who assembled a mass of useful hints on the discovery and development of talented persons. Treating a topic as being a skill has an advantage which Bartlett (1958) pointed out – it cannot be treated as a stimulus–response matter without doing it violence. Purely behaviouristic treatment is therefore ruled out. Bartlett's implicit definition of skill – behaviour capable of internal modification – centres our attention right inside the head, rather than outside or at the periphery, of the scientific performer. It would also seem to exclude a simple gestalt interpretation, such that the novel pattern discerned by the researcher resided in some 'objective' stimulus property, there all the time and just waiting to be picked out. Scientific research thinking should, however, not be taken as wholly divorced from a reality outside. "Skill, whether bodily or mental, has from the beginning the character of being in touch with demands which come from the outside world, or in a wider sense, from evidence that is treated as objective." (Bartlett, 1958). Perhaps the thought process consists of a continuous revision of implicit judgements and updating adjustments to perceived reality? A scientist could then be characterized as one who actively controls his implicit judgements by interaction with the world around him. Good scientists are engaged in perfecting their combinations of imagination with realism. Excellence, in this field, is the farthest reaching yet most realistic flight of fancy.

However, fancy does not seem to fly entirely free over this field and the restraint comes not only from selectively perceived reality. Thinking must also be to some purpose or directed to a goal of which the scientist must have some kind of internal representation, however vague. How else could he conclude that the outcome of the process was not just a random event?

SKILL OR ACCIDENT

Strangely enough, if one were to take the various descriptions and self-reports of scientists purely at their face value, the evidence would be strongly in favour of it all having happened by chance. "The creative scientist often appears to stumble across new problems" (Mackworth, *ibid.*). "The approach in which you take up a theory and test it by experiment has high prestige, but a very great deal of the advance happens in a much less systematic way . . . by looking with a new method and with an open mind at some problem and finding something quite unexpected . . . As soon as we stretched the muscle fibres and looked through the new interference microscope, it was obvious . . . This was totally unexpected. It wasn't what we were looking for. I had built the microscope to investigate another 19th century phenomenon . . . In a recent lecture on astronomy, Professor Wilson showed a number of advances since the war and everyone of them had been a total surprise . . ." (Huxley, 1978, personal communication). So much for a typical account of appearances. Only when one probes for the skill does one realise that modesty and indeed a certain humility come into play. Another distinguished colleague put it thus: "In biology one must be alert to what happens in living material. If you are just intent on shooting a hare that comes out of a particular bush you may miss him. But to be prepared for the chance observation one must first be doing something systematic. Most . . . other . . . people don't see the relevance of their own observations." (Granit, 1978, personal communication). The systematic preoccupation with a topic itself, to which Granit refers as leading up to the threshold of understanding, is not pure chance. A noteworthy difference appears between the views taken from the researcher's own angle or from that of his director. "There is a gradual progression from A to B to C to D in a majestic sort of way; suddenly you realize that they got to Z and are there. Most people go zig-zag. The really efficient person, even though he cannot see, goes straight for it" (Edholm, 1977, personal communication). Niels Bohr described himself as a "dillettante" and "explained how he had to approach every new question 'from a starting point of total ignorance'. It is perhaps better to say Bohr's strength lay in his formidable intuition and insight, not at all in erudition". (Pais, in Rozental, 1967). Sometimes, the modesty of the person may hide what is in fact a subtlety of the process. It appears that Bohr used a critical simplicity to force complexity into new moulds. "He was a practitioner in the application of sets of ideas from one field into others in which, at first sight, they appear quite foreign." (Crowther, 1970). Thus the simplicity of the successful scientist is more apparent than real. "Take the Gamma System – the small nerve fibres in the motor inner-vation of muscle spindles. I offered the subject to several people for PhD work. They laughed and thought it was not worth while. So I did it myself, here in this very room." (Granit, *ibid.*). The 'it' in this case led to the description of a nervous system with functions of far-reaching significance.

As another director of researchers put it: "One of the greatest difficulties . . . is to build up your observational experience . . . and to develop concepts that have never entered any human mind before. They may even appear to contradict long-established principles, as when Einstein proposed the equivalence of mass and energy, or when de Broglie postulated that material particles could also behave as waves, or when Bohr had to conclude that the radial acceleration of electrons in his orbits did not make them radiate." (Jones, 1978). Did Bohr have to conclude as he did, perhaps because this was somehow conditioned by historical trends? Does the time have to be ripe? Not necessarily. "I once asked Dirac which he thought was the greatest discovery of recent times. He pondered, and then replied: 'The General Theory of Relativity, because it did not follow from what had gone before. It came out of the blue . . .' 'Out-of-the-blueness' was, of course, a very characteristic feature of Dirac's own greatest discoveries. Their combination of intellectual boldness and elegance took the breath away." (Crowther, *ibid.*).

If there is a skill element even in so spontaneous a quality as originality, it appears to lie in the direction of the combinations of ideas scientists make. The intentionality of the combinatorial process shows something other than the operation of chance, happy or otherwise.

THINKING WITH THE HANDS

To recapitulate, the objective is to describe and explain an activity, which is definitely carried out 'in the head', deals with abstract concepts and is con-sciously mental or cognitive. It was interesting that none of those whose biographies were read, or who were interviewed, could be considered really clumsy with their hands. Indeed, most of them were positively and outstandingly dexterous. (In passing, the same may be inferred about Einstein from reports that he played music to a high standard.) Edholm considered manual dexterity essential to his description of the good researcher. "He handles things in the laboratory with confidence and reassurance and there is a feedback from this. Medawar once said to me, 'I can only think with my hands!'" As he spoke about team work, Edholm spontaneously illustrated point upon point by hand movements: "Often (Henry) Barcroft and I complemented each other as well as supplementing. We interdigitated like this – [The fingers of one hand intercalated with those of the other] – rather than this, adding this to that – [One fist put on top of the other]". Crowther (*ibid.*) describes a lunch at Harvard in 1937 with James B. Connant and other academics. "Among my remarks I repeated my ideas about the influence of ball-games on experimental science, especially in particle physics. Shapley commented that he could tell from the way a student played ping-pong whether he would make a good observational astronomer."

Apparently even the more basic perceptual–motor functions contribute to the scientist's exercise of his potential. Herschel had "hawklike observational acuity combined with bold exercise of imagination in interpretation" (Sidwick, *ibid.*). Bohr was good at woodwork, metalwork, crafts with strict demands on accuracy giving him particular satisfaction. From a skill point of view, these crafts involve close eye–hand co-ordination and detailed muscle control. "To know where to look, as much as how to look, is a necessary step in experiment . . . The identification of problem sites of outstanding concentration and importance has over and over again played a very great part in directing experimental research." (Bartlett, 1958). Could it be that the formation of habits of accurate control over oneself and matter eases the transfer from the concrete to the abstract? As to manual dexterity, according to Clark (1968), T. H. Huxley had the native ability to draw "which would have provided many a Huxley with a second profession". His grandson, when interviewed, did not directly refer to this, but led off in an even more important direction: tools and technology.

New techniques and better instruments

"Rather little of what has been done with the electron microscope has been of thinking: is there something there to be seen? It has been a matter of looking and seeing and improving fixation techniques, and having got embedding techniques under control, staining as well . . ." (Huxley, 1978). Is it really true that discoveries are made when the technology is ready? "Instrumentation and new technology were just becoming available when Watson and Crick looked at DNA" (Edholm, *ibid.*). Gauss is said to have gone to the limit of the technology of his time by building a Heliotrope, an instrument using mirrors and sun rays which extended land survey trigonometry to about 85 km, the visual limit imposed by the earth's curvature.

It seems to be typical rather than exceptional that good scientists do not sit and wait for advancing technology to present them with their instruments. Herschel himself made telescopes with magnifications of 6000 times when those of others gave only about 100 times. His advances exceeded the contemporary state of craft and knowledge by orders of magnitude and this, it is now suggested, is what creates the 'quantum jump'. ". . . the experimenter must, . . . more and more as knowledge develops, be able to think with instruments . . . practise a technique and handle a technology . . . There is something about experimenting, sometimes even in its routine forms, which demands a variety of interests." (Bartlett, 1958). That active extension of the Self includes an extension of one's body — if necessary with tools and apparatus.

Linking the practical handling of artefacts with the nimbleness of operating in the abstract, it seems that scientific giants have their own ways of handling numbers. Gauss was said to have calculated the orbit of the asteroid Ceres in 3 hours, while Euler took three weeks and others would take months for the same calculations. Moreover, Gauss' work was distinguished not only by speed but also by its accuracy. He systematized and expressed in exact mathematical terms the experimental results of others. What is exceptional about this mathematical ability is not accuracy of itself — any pedant can chase that hare without distinguishing himself. Two collaborators of Bohr remark on "his skill to obtain qualitative results without detailed calculations" (Casimir); "His analysis was partly based on an amazing skill in separating effects according to orders of magnitude." (Rozental, *ibid.*). While these quotations testify to an undoubted grasp and overview of the problem in hand, what they really mean in psychological terms is that there is no necessary conflict between a scientific researcher being exact and being approximately right. Either way, his methods must be good enough to understand and operate upon his internal constructs of the outer world.

The evidence cited above, scant and tentative as it may be, points to the existence of thoughts which are at first unspoken and neither in the mould of pictures, nor of words or other symbols. Yet the thinker himself is not only conscious of these thoughts, he actually uses them to further his ends. After 'reflection', some are expressed in writing and speech, others through the hands and their extensions through instruments. Any thoughts of the creative scientist which may remain unexpressed — and inexpressible? — are not at present of interest to us here; we do not know them and they do not fall within skill or system categories. Those thought acts which are expressed, we can speak about. For their expression, much would depend on how they are represented in the head. In a previous discussion of that problem, in relation to other skills, Branton (1978) referred to a categorization by Bruner (1964) into enactive, iconic and symbolic information processing. The enactive mode of internal operations may be an important and feasible bridge from concrete experience to the formation of abstract concepts. Empirical evidence on the influence of handling physical objects on concept formation in children is familiar since Piaget. From a somewhat different quarter, experimental evidence of the critical importance of sensory–motor involvement in the acquisition of basic skills comes from R. Held and his associates. In all these cases, the mode of operation is enactive, whether it is called thinking or not.

What relation has manual skill to the researcher's experience? There is no doubt that he experiences the object when he handles it but when he looks through a telescope, especially one he has built himself, he does not 'handle' the stars. Nor does he when he looks through a microscope handle the cell body in the preparation that he himself has stained and sliced. The evidence justifies the provisional conclusion that objects are manipulated vicariously and that dexterity in using the hands and their instrumental extensions contributes to success.

EXPERIENCE AND ITS SKILFUL USE

There is a virtue in a concentrated analysis of the excellence of great scientific thinkers: it forces certain basic problems to the surface for scrutiny, which in ordinary people would escape attention just because they are so basic. One of the most taxing of these is to determine the role of experience in all perceptual motor skills, as well as in thinking and, by extension, in scientific research. Most researchers interviewed strongly stressed empiricist views: "There is no substitute for experiment. The only basis for making any progress on whether an idea is right or wrong, is experimental evidence. You mustn't rely on pre-existing generalizations or wishful thinking about your own theories or anything else, in deciding whether an idea is right or wrong . . . Of course, there are other aspects, very intangible and difficult to define . . ." (A. Huxley, 1978).

This may seem a forceful affirmation of empiricism – to rely only on observation as evidence. Alternatively, however, it is a warning to be critical of one's pre-conceived notions. Or, again, it may be read as a plea for realism in research, to restrain fanciful proliferation of theories. All three interpretations are necessary if one is to remain within a framework of reality. But they are insufficient to explain successful scientific research, let alone guide future scientists to "grind out general laws from collections of facts" (Darwin, 1902). The trouble is that empirical scientists are too modest. Excellence is not to be achieved by merely following the precedents of past experience.

Intuition

The evidence shows that choices are most often explained by resort to intuition as the ultimate source of understanding of empirical evidence or insight into abstract connections. To take Thomas Huxley's own recorded reaction to Darwin's *Origin of Species*: "It had the effect of the flash of light which, to a man who has lost himself on a dark night, suddenly reveals a road which, whether it takes him straight home or not, certainly goes his way." The biographer (Clark, *ibid.*) adds, "Huxley, like many others at the time, intuitively wanted to reject the 'creation hypothesis' but had so far seen no feasible alternative . . . to give a reason for many apparent anomalies in the distribution of living beings in space and time . . ." A strikingly similar description is given by Heisenberg of Bohr's situation: "I understand that his insight into the structure of the theory was not a result of a mathematical analysis of the basic assumptions, but rather of an intense pre-occupation with the actual phenomena such that it was possible for him to sense the relationships intuitively rather than derive them formally." (Rozental, *ibid.*).

That Huxley saw the alternative as "feasible" and confidently knew "the road which certainly goes his way", and Bohr's "intense pre-occupation with the actual phenomena", are evidence of more explanatory value than the label of intuition. These instances indicate that some principle of selection of so-called facts must operate before or whilst they present themselves to be experienced. "It would be very difficult to judge intuitively what weight to put on some observation or idea, or whether to follow it up or to disregard it. There are no rules about this and I could not put this in words, no more than I could write instructions for composing music." (A. Huxley, 1978). "The value of a clue is in suggesting lines to follow up. If given too much weight it can prevent other (valuable) research." (A. Huxley, 1977). Or as Edholm put it, "the good researcher just has the capacity for judgement of what is a good idea." The question is whether such intuition is discursive or dissoluble, or whether it must remain mystical, and insolubly irrational. The evidence suggests an originally dark, vague, qualitative, feeling-like event, to which the sensitive person listens and which self-sought exposure to facts resolves by reflection, bringing the feeling to the objective clarity of reason and communication. If we relied on intuition for the answer to what is true or false, or right or wrong, we could find ourselves in an infinite regress. For how does the scientist know which of his (sometimes contradictory) intuitions is right?

It is therefore another of his skills that he uses experience in either of two ways: one is to build up piecemeal a description of his goal – Bohr's "intense pre-occupation with the actual phenomena". The other is to seek confirmation of his conjectures by experiment. To understand the specific role of experience in research, we have first to realize that the scientist as experimenter has gone out of his way deliberately to experience something – he has set up an experiment; i.e. with the help of past experience he exposed himself to a self-created experience in the present. It is, of course, a fact well known but inexplicable in purely empirical terms, that 'to learn from experience' is a lengthy process in which something is left behind from every occasion of exposure. In mental, as in all other skills, any contribution which required storage in the past and which in turn is put into storage presently is experience. It is well established that to look through a microscope or at an X-ray picture, *and extract meaning,* requires extended practice.

Mackworth, who takes visual pattern recognition as his paradigm of the research problem, speaks of the scientist's "relating the customary facts to his existing set of categories; in this way he finds that these are not adequate to cover some new way of looking at the usual evidence. The crux of the experimental approach would therefore be to discover how people set up rules for visual pattern recognition." It seems reasonable to go along with Mackworth in that it is critical to discover how people set up rules. Indeed, the search is for the rules for "grinding out general laws from collections of facts". But before seeking the self-created experience of experimentation, another orientation is needed. To avoid the trap of the infinite regress of pure empiricism, psychologists may be better advised to develop systematically first an epistemic approach to gain a little greater clarity on the scientist's judgements and intuitions and their sources.

Thus, it seems that while scientists appear to depend on their accumulated experience and their intuitions, this does not provide satisfying explanations for their findings in the first place. However, it is clear that, once they have 'intuited', they can use experiments very skilfully to confirm or refute their theories.

THE HEURISTIC PROCESS

Psychological descriptions by Helmholtz, Wallas, Wertheimer, Granit, Bruner, Bartlett, Mackworth and others suggest steps in a process common to most of scientific research. A start is usually made either from "happy coincidences and fancies" (Helmholtz) or from problems set by someone else. Certain differences are detected between present observation and past experience, certain illogicalities, incompatibilities, incongruences or contradictions appear to inhere in traditional descriptions of a particular state of affairs, and this dissonance or dissatisfaction creates an inner tension in the researcher. There follows a period of preparation, sometimes prolonged over years, in which a network of facts and ideas are tested, some rejected as unfit and others incorporated into a system. "I don't know what I'm looking for, but I know what does not fit when I come across it", as one informant put it. "Overlap and agreement is discovered where formerly isolation and difference was recognised." (Bartlett, 1958). "It is more important to realise that something is possible, than to know how it is possible." (Singleton, 1978, personal communication). Sometimes there appears to be a period of "incubation" (Wallas), "the endless journey round a single skull" (Mackworth), which produces insight, often only fleeting, into the tacit assumptions underlying former constructions of the problem. Sometimes, by striving to make these assumptions explicit, the accepted connections are disrupted and the way is opened to new connections. Sometimes, there is a moment of "illumination" (Wallas), 'Eureka', the 'Aha Erlebnis'. And then comes the point when "the owner of the idea propounds it as a definite, well formulated hypothesis, capable of being tested". (Granit).

Majestic though this progression may appear to the outsider, in practice it is mostly by fits and starts, some of them obviously false starts, and if it is seen as progression in retrospect, this probably expresses the notion that a certain unity or continuity had been created, a coherent system of abstract ideas.

The epistemic approach

It is no digression to ask at this point whether we, as ordinary outsiders or observing psychologists, can at all enter into the thought processes of the extraordinary scientists. "The brain struggling to understand the brain is society trying to understand itself." (Blakemore, 1976). Two outstanding modern scientists who had such epistemic clarity – and expressed it consistently – were Bohr and Heisenberg. They questioned: How do I know this? What can I know at all? What are the proper questions to ask? What methods to use? What is the appropriate terminology in which an answer should be formulated? "Thinking about one's thinking represents a singularity of the consciousness" (Bohr). His major problem in life was said to be "Man's position as an observer of that nature of which he himself is part . . . the reciprocal interaction between the object of investigation and what one might call the instrument of measurement, whether a piece of apparatus or a human observer." (Rozental, *ibid.*). Gauss, to judge from his diaries, was profoundly influenced by Kant and a contemporary, Fries, in regard to the distinction between the act of thinking and the object of thought.

The fact is that we – and the scientists – are all in the same boat when it comes to understanding each other. The heuristic process of constructing a conceptual system for the first time ever may be very complex, but it does not remain for ever uniquely difficult. If it were, other less gifted people could not follow it later and re-enact it for themselves as they clearly do after Newton, Galileo, and will do after Einstein. The truly psychological problem of research skill is to describe how scientists know when they have got 'it'. If 'it' is the goal, the stranger with whom the rendezvous was arranged, how does the researcher *know* that he has met her, him or it? This is what we mean by the *epistemic* approach to heuristics. And the strangely exciting thought is that the same questions can be asked with equal force and justification about the perceptual and cognitive processes of normal, ordinary persons. In ordinary every-day life, how does one attend to certain facts and environmental features selectively and how do we know what is 'relevant', or 'important'?

Those who would refer back to past experience as a long process of cumulative development of selection have still to show how an experience we had long ago, say, even in childhood, is actually recalled and judged 'relevant' at the 'appropriate moment' in the here and now.

A thought experiment

To clarify these conjectures, assume for the purpose of a 'thought experiment' that, all through our wakeful lives, an indwelling principle of selection is at work, without which past and present experience is meaningless. This principle not merely selects some facts from among the in-streaming mass, it also simultaneously assigns 'values' by giving an event or fact the qualities of relevance, adequacy, appropriateness, significance and fitness for a purpose. This active principle is the process of abstraction. It is both a principle because it functions as a rule or criterion for choice, and a process because it is an active transformation of objects given.

Of course, there is no Cartesian homunculus sitting at the threshold of experience, saying 'Admit this fact', 'Reject that one'. Neither is it a rule with a fixed content. 'Admit all green facts, reject all blue ones.' More likely it is a method, a formal rule without a specific content, a bottomless vessel into which experience sifts its grain all the time. At the same time, this vessel is so plastic that any new observation or concept could change its shape. If an input affects the shape of that internal construct, that input is provisionally labelled 'relevant'. Thus it is the consequences which a new fact or concept may have for the conceptual system, say, of the scientist, which make that newcomer accepted or rejected.

The process of abstraction

In his *Grammar of Science,* Karl Pearson expresses "the idea that geometrical conceptions, such as Euclid's perfect points, lines and angles are the ultimate products of a process which starts in perceptions of the actual world. The mind abstracts qualities from the perceptions until pure conceptions only are left. The notion of a point is the result of abstracting colour and the three dimensions of space from solid objects." (Crowther, *ibid*). How is abstraction possibly carried out? Have we got the equipment? How does it function?

Modern experimental research into perception leaves no doubt about its complex, hierarchical nature, its speed and ubiquity (cf. Haber, 1970). Consider in particular the discoveries by Hubel and Wiesel (1968), by Blakemore and Nachmias (1971) and others, of single nerve cells operating as 'feature analysers' in the midbrain and cortex. They open up a new interpretation of much older evidence that had not fitted in anywhere. It could mean that each cell or part of the brain extracts (or abstracts?) from the incoming stream of signals those of special interest to itself: colour, brightness, straightness, skewness, roughness, etc. The preferences of, say, certain visual neurons to respond to lines in specific orientations, or even to binocular equivalence, can be interpreted as evidence of structures being used in an abstracting process. A great deal more than we are aware of is turned into generalizations (and used to update the experiential store) (cf. Bartlett, 1958; MacKay, 1965; Bach-y-Rita, 1972). This would be a continuous internal reconstruction of our representation of the external world. The postulated existence of feature analysers for each attribute of the input from the environment does not of itself provide the principle by which some rather than other 'facts' are selected for abstraction from the continuous stream of signals. But the assumption leads further: H. Düker, the doyen of German experimental psychology, expressed the following thoughts in a delightful interview: "In the old school they spoke of introspection and self-observation, as if I could observe my Self. But we can speak only of our Selves as experiencing something, and those experiences do not hang in the air. This requires a postulate: Experiences must have a Bearer. This bearer can be my Self. My hearing, my seeing, are activities of this Self. But if I see a table, I merely perceive a patch of colour and assert it is a table. That is to say, we attribute the features – colour, extent, etc. – to another bearer. Attributes cannot exist without such a bearer, (carrier, vehicle or subject). When I observe features, I must necessarily postulate someone or something behind them." If neither the general thing-itself nor the specific thing-out-there exist in our heads, but only its attributes are stored in them, it is a short – but very important – step to propose that the combination or collective of activated neurones, 'representing' the features observed, is that thing for us. Hence, whatever is stored and represented inside us, is already an abstraction. As speculations go, this is no new thought at all. Indeed, with variations it has been put forward perennially as explanation of deep-rooted experience. It reflects Plato's Theory of Forms. We may appreciate the aptness and simplicity of language of the following quotation when we realize that 'predicate' stands for feature or attribute: "It is the 'presence' of the form in a thing that makes anything beautiful or whatever else we say it is. The predicate of a proposition is always a form, and a particular sensible thing is nothing else but the common meeting-place of a number of predicates, each of which is an intelligible form . . . On the other hand none of the forms we predicate of a thing is present in it completely, . . . Apart from these . . . predicates, the thing . . . has no independent reality, and if we know all the forms in which anything participates, there is nothing more to know about it." (Burnet, 1914). The literal translation of the Greek for "forms of predication" is "schemata tes kategorias" and this is much the same notion of "schemata" as Head and Bartlett used.

That no form we give to a thing as predicate is present in it completely, suggests two notions: the open-endedness of scientific systems as much as of any skilful construction, and the ideal nature of internal representations. These notions need elaboration.

Open-endedness of scientific excellence

Joliot-Curie, asked for his opinion on Rutherford's published papers, said, "One had to remember that an experimenter probably had a hundred times as much supporting material as he actually published. A great deal of this might be imperfect and incomplete and unsuitable for publication, but its total effect on the judgement might be decisive. The experimenter who has worked for years in the laboratory on a problem acquires many impressions of its nature which are not sufficiently definite to be put into words, but create an intuition of what kind of conception or explanation is probable or improbable." (Crowther, 1970). Overlooking the use of 'intuition' this quotation is chosen because it so aptly marks the qualities of 'ideality'. Rutherford, like Joliot-Curie and others, had some inner yardstick of perfection or completeness of material, even if it was expressed in the dissatisfaction with the opposites – imperfection and incompleteness. Of course, science is open-ended, asymptotic, never finite or perfect. Just as modern science speaks of the statistically probable rather than of the absolutely true.

Idealized representation

It has been suggested that whatever is stored inside the head is already the resultant of a process, an abstraction. This notion implies that representations are characteristically incomplete, imperfect, we could always improve on them, describe them more fittingly and more precisely than they were. Our internal representations must be capable of approaching a better state than we experienced in the past. They are idealized in the sense that what is beyond experience is ideal. Otherwise, how could we explain improvement or indeed any qualitative change? What we do with these representations is essentially a bootstrap process, Baron Münchhausen's trick of pulling himself out of a mire by his own pigtail. But it is also one of the fundamental (apparent) contradictions of real life – the truly open end of knowledge.

Manipulation of time

In abstraction, if a predicate can at all be detached from its subject, the detachment can only be from a specific location in space and time. The perceiving organism reports, as it were: 'out there now exists a shiny, brown, square, four-legged, inanimate thing, a metre high with horizontal flat top of smooth texture'. In fact, to analyse and abstract is to break up the space/time unity of the thing, in this case the table. It is just this break-up which allows us to store the percept as an experience. We disconnect the specificity of the feature from the feature-bearer and thereby assign the bearer to a class of things-bearing-this-feature. The elevation of the thing to a class is the critical stage in the process of abstraction, because at this point a potential generalization and re-combination becomes possible, even though there may at the time be only one exemplar in the class. To generalize is then to assert the potential that there could be more than one member of that class. It is this re-combination of features into prospective events which is a manipulation of time and which constitutes the creative aspect of abstraction.

The 'game of consequences'

'Vicarious manipulation' of percepts and concepts has already been discussed. Also at the beginning of the thought experiment, reference was made to the dual nature of the active principle: that it evaluated at the same time as selecting material for thought. Any selection is an investment, an assigning of values. The two are inseparable. When faced with real-life ambiguities, we select figure from background or the goblet rather than Peter and Paul. We express what we are interested in at the moment, what we 'value'. The alternative is very deep indecision or paralysis of thought. Yet the facts of normal life are that decisions are made and carried out. Does our information from scientists help us to describe the vicarious manipulations more closely?

"The really skilled man looks at the possible answer to that and the next questions, like in a game of chess. Most of us can only see one move ahead. The best see three." (Edholm). It seems that, in abstraction, a game of consequences is enacted. 'What if this or that state of affairs were generally true? What would follow from this generalization or that combination?' Thus the scientist compiles a list of particular consequences which the ideal solution of his problem must entail. This, however imperfect and limited, becomes his 'warrant of apprehension', his list of attributes of 'It', that stranger, with which he can compare each experience and experiment. Note here that this process is not the same as the hypothetico-deductive one, so often imputed into scientific thinking.

The 'ideal solution' to his problem is the common meeting place (in the scientist's head) of those accumulated predicates and attributes as they are apprehended, abstracted and their consequences reviewed. There is one aspect of abstraction so far not accounted for: scientists have the additional problem of explaining or justifying the new connections between, say, two imaginary events, such as the casual connection. If concepts are idealized percepts, what about such connective concepts? Strictly speaking, while we may have perceived with the senses any two events, we never perceive the connection between them. (The Gestalt theories and Michotte's experiments have never seemed to the author to be adequate explanations, since proximity of time and place, and even the meaning of 'event', have been brought into question by the revision of physics due to Bohr and others.)

There is no doubt that abstraction, generalization and connection are mental operations performed as much by non-scientists in normal life as by scientists and therefore are the proper concern of psychological investigation. The researcher uses much the same processes, only more so. He deals almost wholly in abstract concepts and constantly probes the boundaries of logic-ality. And, of course, he uses his experience to devise experiments, refining his predicates more exactly in the process. The anticipatory quality of a concern with consequences is open to investigation and experimentation. The practical implications of the statement that every thing stored is already an abstraction are considerable, especially for laboratory psychology. The use of the term memory for stored information has been deliberately avoided. If any representation, probably committed to a long-term store, is already processed and generalized, a present manifestation of the past would have to be, as it were, reconstituted in recall by reversing the process.

COMMUNICATIVE SKILL

Perhaps the most difficult task of the researcher is to transform his abstractions into symbolic and yet unambiguous and unequivocal communication. Without that the best theories are not worth being thought. The scientist's skill in communication has two aspects of interest: one is the interaction between the different levels within the thought process itself, the other is about the inter-action with his peers either in team work or as critics. If there are indeed such different levels of the thought process as the transition from thinking with the hands to abstraction and hence to symbolization, then it seems to be the need to communicate which forces the process along.

On the problems of interpersonal skills and team work a great deal of anecdotal and literary evidence is available. That these skills are necessary underlined by one research director's remarks that mathemati-cians, statisticians and theoretical physicists can work alone nowadays, whereas biologists, biochemists and physiologists need to be in teams. This is presumably due to the extreme specialization required in these fields. As regards the 'challenge by publication', all those whom we consulted agree on the need for scrutiny by peer referees as the fairest available method of adjudication, although many are well aware of the shortcomings of the 'intuitive' approach it often involves. Doubtless, publication has consequences for the researcher and, as the reference to Joliot-Curie showed, is therefore an important aspect of scientific skill.

SOME PSYCHOLOGICAL CHARACTERISTICS

In the literature there are certain allusions to personal characteristics of those famous men which should be mentioned for completeness' sake as they may throw further light on their peculiar thought processes. The first recurring feature mentioned in a number of cases is their self-reported hypnopompic thinking and imagining. Gauss not only mentions his own experiences in this respect; an entry in his diary, formulating the laws of magnetic induction, is headed '7 a.m., before getting up'. He also draws attention to others, 'Descartes and Helmholtz also testified to the great value of such early morning thoughts'. Another remarkable trait seems to be the abiding curiosity of some scientists. Sidgwick *(ibid)* speaks of Herschel's "lust to know" which urged him on. Edholm likes to think that "the good researcher must have a 'bump of inquisitiveness'". Moreover, he asks "are they cranks or just individualists?" The successful scientists whose careers we reviewed here did often meet with incredulity and even ridicule. What probably differentiates them from cranks is that the latter live in a certain closed system whereas the scientist remains aware of the essential open-endedness of his system. He thus tolerates a high degree of uncertainty about the completeness of his achievement. It is doubtful whether cranks have similar tolerances.

CAN RESEARCH SKILLS BE TAUGHT?

"Many people who have written about science and originality, often popularizing very effectively, miss the point of skill if they have not themselves researched. To know the flavour of an act of creation one has to experience it oneself. Also, you can only assess a man really well when you have worked with him". (Edholm). It seems that the successful exercise of the skill is an essential pre-requisite for the judgement of it in others. Only if one has actually ridden a bicycle or driven a train can one judge the degree of skill of another practitioner. Is it so in science too?

The perceptual-motor aspects of skilled thinking seem susceptible to practice. ". . . the aberration of one star will efface the other star or make them appear as one . . . Seeing is in some respect an art which must be learnt. To make a person see with such a power is nearly the same as if I were asked to make him play one of Handel's fugues upon the organ. Many a night have I been practising to see, and it would be strange if one did not acquire a certain dexterity by such constant practice." (Herschel, quoted by Sidgwick, *ibid*).

Recent reports by the Department of Education and Science expressed the conviction that bright children can be spotted and brought on in abstract subjects like mathematics. "In mathematics, the regular run of pupils feels insecure when the way forward is obscure and prefers solutions by standard methods: gifted children welcome an unknown outcome and a variety of approaches." (HMSO, 1977a). " . . . young eagles may reveal themselves by the unexpected question, a leap to the abstract and a desire for perfection . . . Mathematical potential may be revealed by beautifully precise communication." (HMSO, 1977b).

It remains to be seen whether practice improves the process of abstraction and the reach of awareness of consequences which seem to be at the centre of thinking, whether ordinary or scientific. Only by practice are those background assumptions and axioms acquired which we all use every moment of the day, whether we verify them consciously or not. But one cannot be made to practise against one's will. Thus we come to the paradoxical conclusion that, while it may not be possible to *teach* research thinking, it must be possible to *learn* it.

References

Bach-y-Rita, P. (1972). *Brain Mechanisms in Sensory Substitution* (New York: Academic Press)

Bartlett, F. C. (1958). *Thinking.* (London: G. Allen and Unwin)

Blakemore, C. (1976). *Mechanics of the Mind,* The Reith Lectures. *The Listener.* **96,** 782

Blakemore, C. and Nachmias, J. (1971). The orientation specificity of two visual after-effects. *J. Physiol.,* **23,** 178

Branton, P. (1978). The train driver. *In* Singleton, W. T. (ed.). *The Study of Real Skills I.* (Lancaster: MTP Press)

Bruner, J. S. (1964). The course of cognitive growth. *Am. Psychol.,* **19,** 1

Burnet, J. (1914). *Greek Philosophy: Thales to Plato.* (London: Macmillan)

Burnett, J. (1977). *Useful Toil.* (Harmondsworth: Pelican)

Clark, R. W. (1968). *The Huxleys.* (London: Heinemann)

Crowther, J. G. (1970). *Fifty Years with Science.* (London: Barrie and Jenkins)

Darwin, C. (1902). *The Origin of Species.* (London: Watts and Co.)

Granit, R. (1972). Discovery and understanding. *Ann. Rev. Physiol.,* **34**

HMSO (1977a). Ashbrook, A. HMI in *Trends.* (Dept. of Education and Science, Aug, 1977)

HMSO (1977b). *Gifted Children in Middle and Comprehensive Schools.* (Dept. of Education and Science, London)

Haber, R. N. (ed.). (1970). *Contemporary Theory and Research in Visual Perception* (London: Holt, Rinehart and Winston)

Hubel, D. H. and Wiesel, T. N. (1968). Receptive fields and functional architecture of monkey striate cortex. *J. Physiol.,* **195,** 215

Huxley, Sir A. (1977). *Evidence, Clues and Motive in Science.* Presidential Address to Annual Meeting, British Assoc. for the Advancement of Science

Jones, R. V. (1978). *Most Secret War.* (London: Hamish Hamilton)

MacKay, D. M. (1965). A mind's eye view of the brain. *Prog. Brain Res.,* **7,** 321

Mackworth, N. H. (1965). Originality. *Am. Psychol.,* **51**

Pearson, K. (1928). *Grammar of Science.* (London: Everyman Edition)

Rozental, S. (1967). *Niels Bohr: His Life and Work.* (Amsterdam: North-Holland)

Sidgwick, J. B. (1953). *William Herschel: Explorer of the Heavens.* (London: Faber)

Wallas, G. (1926). *The Art of Thought.* (New York: Harcourt Brace)

Wertheimer, M. (1959). *Productive Thinking.* (London: Tavistock)

14

Perceptual Skills

J. WIRSTAD

INTRODUCTION

Perceptual skills cover the domain of human inputs from the outer world. It is obvious that these skills are important and are involved in many contexts of our waking life. For example, in the morning we drive to our jobs or perhaps even go there by bicycle and the success of arriving safely and in time can be traced back to how we registered other vehicles, traffic signals, the road and so on along the way. At work we are involved in different activities and many of them demand adequate and precise perceptions, e.g. in process operation or decision making. We spend some of our spare time in games like tennis, football, squash, golf, badminton or ping pong where the perception of the ball and the other player or players are necessary conditions for success. In our life together with other people we are very much dependent on how we are able to detect and identify their reactions, the degree to which we are accepted by other people is dependent on our social perception. Perception is obviously important in our everyday life. Furthermore, we realize that in many activities which involve perception we have to develop some kind of qualified behaviour; the fact that we are talking about qualified behaviour indicates that we are dealing with an area of human skills.

In this chapter the intention is to go further than looking into the psychology of perception and perceptual skills. The question is what constitutes the extraordinary skills, i.e. the skills which stand out in comparison to other perceptual skills. The chapter has been arranged so that the first part gives examples of extraordinary perceptual skills primarily in the visual field. The examples are described in phenomenologically oriented terms. In the second part some of the main theoretical areas are described. In the third part some methodological aspects are covered according to the type of analysis needed for training design or equipment design. Finally in the fourth part the implications of the above aspects for the state of knowledge and for research are discussed.

Some observations of learning in perceptual skills

In one early study on development of human perception it was found that a person who was born blind and later acquired vision following an operation had an unorganized visual perception (von Senden, 1932). It took some time to learn to perceive in an organized way. When an egg was presented to the patient after the operation he had to learn to connect the idea of an egg with his visual stimulus. The object was familiar to him through his tactile and taste senses and after some learning he could also identify it visually. During the process to reach the stage of the visual identification the perceptual field became organized in the sense that the form, the colour and the surface structure of the egg formed a distinct meaningful object which stood out from the surroundings. There are some indications from this and other related studies that the human being's first visual field is chaotic, in which some colours and perhaps some forms can be detected. Through learning the visual field gets organized. The degree of organization is a matter of experiences of the individual and is related to characteristics such as use and meaning of the objects in the visual field.

In these contexts some intercultural studies of human beings living under different conditions are of interest. Turnbull (1961) reports an observation of a pygmy who had always lived in a large forest and who was taken out on the open plain for the first time in his life. There was a herd of buffalo which could be seen at a distance of a couple of kilometres. The pygmy perceived the big animals as insects and he did not want to accept the declaration that they were buffalo about twice as big as the buffalo he was used to in the forest. The forest-man had no experiences of objects at long distances and his perceptual mechanism of size constancy had not been developed under such conditions.

Anthropologists have reported large variation in the 'resolution' of words related to living conditions. If something is important there are normally more specific words available to describe the phenomenon. The classical example is the number of words for snow among Eskimos. They had more than ten words with different meanings to describe what in everyday language is called snow. There is probably a positive relationship between linguistic resolution and perceptual resolution.

The examples above indicate some interesting aspects of perceptual skills. Perceptual learning starts early in human life and the learning concerns fundamental characteristics of objects. Furthermore what is learned can follow different paths depending on cultural and living conditions. The demands and the type of stimulation which are dominant in given living conditions are very important. These observations might be important for the understanding of perceptual skills in general and should be kept in mind when we now look into some examples of outstanding perceptual performance closer to everyday life.

CLASSIFYING PERCEPTUAL SKILLS

In general perceptual skills are associated with the ability of the observer to attend to relevant input information, to register this information economically, to decode the registered information by means of effective decision rules and finally to utilize the decoded information with a high degree of efficiency in performing a certain task. This chain of activities is well integrated, and focusing on the input side of the chain, as when perceptual skills are studied, is partly artificial.

Depending on characteristics of the chain of information, perceptual skills can be divided into the following main categories:

Perceptual–motor skills – The input information is used for discrete or continuous motor responses. Typical examples within the category are found in sports like golf or tasks like rifle aiming. Some manoeuvring tasks in process control can also be included in this group.

Perceptual–locomotor skills – The chain in these types of task normally includes substantial motor responses. The primary aim of the activity is to move oneself through the environment, on land, at sea, in the air or in space. Examples are cycling, driving a car or flying an aircraft.

Perceptual–cognitive skills – This is a large category of skills in which there is a greater emphasis on the perceptual side of the individual's chain of activities mentioned above. The input information is used for decision purposes or for judgements. The type of output can vary between different kinds of actions involving quantitative or qualitative expression. These types of skills are found in tasks like identification of aircraft, photo-interpreting and in certain process and quality control operations.

There are no clear boundaries between the above mentioned categories. Most tasks include sub-tasks which fall under different headings. For instance flying an aircraft includes not only manoeuvring (perceptual–loco-motion) it also includes navigation (primarily perceptual–cognitive). High altitude flying is also, through the use of aids like the autopilot, more perceptual –cognitive although with a strong emphasis on the perceptual input.

Perceptual–motor skill

A classical perceptual motor skill is birdhunting, in which the hunter aims the rifle towards the flying bird before firing. In choosing the firing point he has to take into consideration the speed of the bird and its flying direction. He cannot point directly at the bird as it will fly some distance during the time taken for the round to move from the rifle to the bird. The hunter thus has to predict the hit point in front of the bird; to be able to do so he must in some way estimate speed and flying path. Classically the hunter makes these estimations as a whole task combined with precise and well timed motor activities. The hunter is performing a completely integrated task without any clearly distinguishable part actions. It is also interesting to notice the degree of precision reached in the task; he has accepted that he sometimes misses. He is helped by the fact that he is normally not firing just one round which has to hit the bird directly, but each cartridge contains a charge of shots spreading out over an area. This makes it possible to hit the bird without the highest degree of precision in performance.

What skills does the hunter need to be extremely good at birdhunting? Let us look at the rifle before trying to answer the question. As an instrument it has developed and has been modified over years of use. Technical innovations, e.g. in material, in production techniques, in ammunition, in sights etc., have improved the precision of the instrument as such. It is fairly well adapted to man's physical and physiological conditions. Improvements can still be made in the design, as demonstrated by weapons being used in competitions like the Olympic games, but on the whole we can take the rifle as given. The high degree of skill of the hunter is reached through an integrated knowledge of the static and dynamic characteristics of the situation. First he has to know the weight of the rifle and its dynamic characteristics and to relate these to his muscular co-ordination. Second his visual input of the flying bird must be co-ordinated with his motor actions; he has to physically relate the track of the round to the bird. He uses the tube of the rifle and some sight on it to establish the relationship. Finally he has to estimate the point ahead in the direction of the bird's flying path to fire at. In doing this he has to know about the speed, direction and flying characteristics of the bird.

The words 'know' and 'knowledge' have been used here although it is perhaps not exact to talk about knowledge by which normally is meant something conscious and analysable for the performer himself. It may be that the hunter has some use for discrete and conscious 'knowledge' when he starts training and perhaps also during the early phases of training but he will never become a good hunter through just knowing or being able to describe what to do. He has to learn through doing the task. Extensive training which can go on over years is normally needed to build up the advanced skill.

In this context it is interesting to notice that there is at least one alternative way to organize the task of shooting towards a moving target which in principle could be adopted by the birdhunter. In some types of sight the rifleman chooses one point among several points within the sight area and then points directly at the target, the choice depends on the speed and direction of the target. The sight in this case is constructed so that a certain point in the sight aligns the tube of the rifle ahead of the target, thus taking into consideration the time required for the round to move through the air. To make the choice the rifleman has to make an estimate of speed, distance and direction. The sight is constructed more or less to force the rifleman to make a discrete estimate of distance expressed in a certain number of metres and in similar estimates of speed and direction. In this case the birdhunting task is not carried out as the whole perceptual–motor operation described previously. Analysis into discrete steps makes the task easier to teach. It will be possible to get practically all riflemen to a decent performance level within a rather short period but the brilliant rifleman or hunter will not emerge as long as he loyally follows the analytical way in estimating and applying distance, speed and direction of the target before he chooses his sighting point and fires.

One explanation for the differences in performance level and precision between the two ways to shoot at moving targets is that man is not very good at reporting his estimates in terms of an absolute scale (e.g. Gibson, 1950 Gibson, 1955). His errors in these types of reported estimates influence directly the rifleman's shooting precision in the latter alternative. Man is better at relating distance and probably also speed of a target to himself as an observer and as a participator in the situation. In classical birdhunting the distance, speed and direction estimates are not separated out and handled discretely, they are handled as parts in an integrated whole task. The estimates are all related to the observer, the instrument and its use. The integration is all the time being done unconsciously by the hunter.

Perceptual–locomotor skills

This type of skill is found in the driving or controlling of a car, a bicycle, an aircraft, a boat and even a submarine. The inputs to the driver, the controller or the operator come from the moving vehicle and its surroundings. Visual inputs are normally dominant but they can be supported by auditory, tactile and kinaesthetic inputs. In cycling and in flying aircraft the non-visual inputs such as kinaesthesis play an important role. In car driving this type of input plays a less important although not a negligible role.

Let us look at the task of an attack pilot which comprises extremely high perceptual demands. When he is given his attack mission at the base he has to make certain preparations, which are of both a technical and a tactical nature. He uses certain aids such as a navigation system, display systems and an auto-pilot which automatically regulate the speed, course and altitude of the aircraft. He also gets support from combat direction centres. When he is approaching his target he is flying about 30 metres above the ground with a speed which can be close to the speed of sound, thus he is covering between 250 and 300 metres per second. To be able to do this his navigation system helps him in keeping his course but the orientation of the aircraft has to be checked at certain points by the pilot. When he is flying over land the check is done against distinct points in the terrain such as a church, a cross-road, a railway, a river, a bridge, etc. The physical visibility of such objects from an altitude of 30 metres is normally no more than 2000 metres, so the aircraft must not be very far out from its planned course to give the pilot a chance to detect his check points, and he has just a few seconds to decide whether he is right or wrong. The pilot is working within severe time constraints and ten seconds for decisions in these contexts must be regarded as plenty of time.

As he approaches his target he reaches a point where he has to rise to a somewhat higher altitude to be able to acquire the target. Now, he has to carry out target detection, identification and some kind of decision-making depending on his aids for target search and sensing, e.g. TV or FLIR (Forward Looking Infra-Red Sensor). The tasks after delivering his missiles can vary. This is described through his alternative behaviour 'launch and leave' or 'fire and forget'. Because of the risk of counteractions he must as soon as possible go back to his low altitude. Some characteristics of the last phase of an attack mission are illustrated in Figure 14.1.

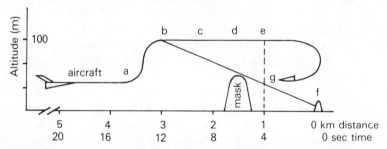

Figure 14.1   The behaviour of an attack aircraft near the target – a: rising from lowest altitude; b: limit for target acquisition; c: detection, identification or decision making is carried out; d: missile firing; e: inner firing limit; f: target; g: back to lowest altitude

The visual search task carried out by the pilot has been studied, e.g. Senders (1966), as also has the process of visual input of the human operator, e.g. Russo (1977). There are discrete fixations of short duration; times down to about a quarter of a second up to a second and more have been registered depending on the type of task. Extrafoveal vision also contributes in the process of information input. Currently there is considerable interest in analysing the more specific role of extrafoveal vision, e.g. Williams (1973).

Perceptual–cognitive skills

In perceptual–cognitive skills the visual input can vary in extent, complexity, in timing demands and also in importance. The input will be used in some kind of decision or human judgement included in the task and representing the cognitive part of the skill process.

Photo-interpreting is an axample of a task in which the visual input is dominant; it is used, for example, to get information about enemy positions from photos taken from the air over a terrain area. The skill of the photo-interpreter is related to the fact that objects on the photo are very small and can be camouflaged. The object itself may give very little information and the interpreter must use secondary cues, e.g. a well camouflaged object will not stand out at all from the surroundings but there may be a shadow which indicates that there is an object. If you know the time of day when the photo was taken and the distance to the ground you can also calculate the height of the object from the size of the shadow. Photo-interpreting is normally carried out on a negative film. On the negative film the picture is normally organized in space analogous to the real world under observation by the human eye, but there may also be parts of the picture which reproduce the real world in a distorted way, e.g. the optical conditions or the resolution of the film may not allow any form or size characteristics to come out on the film. The user of the picture has to learn the meaning of the distortion and how it works and influences the picture. Quite a lot of the photo-interpreter's work is a recoding of the picture in comparison to the coding which is learned from everyday visual experience.

The picture can be blurred and it will not be easy to distinguish a meaningful object; the meaning can in this case be connected with certain patterns in the picture and these patterns can also be more or less clear. Thus there is a degree of uncertainty in the relevance of a cue or a pattern. The degree of uncertainty is reduced through checking and re-checking against other cues, which can be based also on other sources than the photo. The perceptual skill is associated with the photo-interpreter's ability to utilize these more and less clear cues and patterns in the picture and systematically to build up his interpretation. One characteristic which distinguishes the outstanding skilled performance from more ordinary skilled behaviour is the certainty in or the reliability of the judgement, i.e. the stability of a person's judgement when stimuli are the same or similar. The very skilled observer can develop a surprisingly high degree of stability in his judgement in spite of uncertainties in individual cues. In analogous tasks such as wine classification there is also a surprising stability among several experts in their judgements. This indicates that rules for stimuli utilization, strategies and decision rules can be shared after extensive training and retraining.

The operator in process industries, e.g. electrical power generation, chemical plants and paper mills, also relies on perceptual–cognitive skills. The skilled process operator is dependent on visual inputs from the process, most of which are mediated from a control room where there are many instruments and alarms. Today's control engineering, however, has changed the task of the operator so that there is less demand for rapid discriminations of states in process variables. Discriminations in individual variables and related control actions have been taken over to a large extent by automatic control loops. For example in a nuclear power station the whole system is closed down automatically when the process is moving towards states which are unwanted from a safety point of view, including reactor cooling, turbine operations and auxiliary engine states. Thus there are very few if any situations where there is a demand for quick and precise perceptions and control actions as in flying an aircraft. There is a tendency to conclude from this that the human operator has no or little importance for process availability, based on the fact that he is not involved in the immediate operation of the process. This is not true and Bainbridge (1978) has formulated elegantly the task of the process operation. "An experienced controller uses his process behaviour and takes anticipatory action rather than controlling by feedback." The timing – although normally in a different time scale from flying an aeroplane – and the adequacy of the operator's predictions have consequences not only for process variables but also for the function of sub-systems and components. These predictions represent skilled behaviour which can be developed by the operator to a very sophisticated level, if he is given adequate process instrumentation in combination with possibilities to check physically in the station, if he is given good training and retraining possibilities and if motivational and organizational conditions are fulfilled.

THEORIES RELATED TO PERCEPTUAL SKILLS

Theoretical constructions in general perception related to perceptual skills can be divided along two main lines: *information transfer and processing approaches* and *higher order psychophysics*. There are also social, psychological and personality theories which cover human perception. One personality theory will be described: *percept-genetic theory*. The purpose of the present description is to cover briefly some dominant theoretical approaches; there is no claim to completeness. For more thorough presentations of each one of the approaches mentioned, the references given can be consulted.

Information transfer and processing

These approaches are inspired by information theory and its very strict definition of information as the number of binary digits – bits – needed to define the transfer of a message. Its aim is to find transfer functions between information input and output of the human being. In its most strict form the human being is looked upon as a black box.

One of the classical studies within this frame of reference is "The magical number seven plus or minus two: Some limits on our capacity for processing information" by Miller (1956). He found that the number of absolute discriminations in a unidimensional discriminatory task tended to centre around the number seven. Thus he found that the human being could discriminate between four levels of saltness representing an information transfer of 1·9 bits and six absolute pitch levels representing 2·5 bits. A line could be divided into ten discriminated parts representing 3·25 bits. Presenting more than one dimension of the object increases the number of levels discriminated. Furthermore a combination of individual ability and learning can improve the discrimination extensively. A musician can for instance report about 45 absolute pitch levels which represents an information transfer of 5·5 bits (Sheridan and Ferrell, 1974). The largest information transfer for the human being is found in reading silently which represents about 50 bits per second. A skilled piano-player reaches a speed of up to 22 bits per second A very skilled typist reaches an information transfer of about 15 bits per second, while the performance of an average typist represents about 10 bits per second.

The information transfer approach has similarities with classical S–R and behaviouristic theories in psychology. If focuses on the stimuli of the human being and on human responses and neglects the intervening variables, i.e. how the information is processed. Undoubtedly the information transfer approach, which is used extensively in engineering, has an attraction in the study and understanding of human behaviour. It is a positive answer to the demand for bridging the gap between engineering and psychology which is required in ergonomics or human engineering. But it can also be objected – in the same way that S–R and behaviouristic theories were criticized – that the information transfer approach oversimplifies the relation between information input and output. There is a risk that the simplification represents a model for human behaviour which cannot be used for generating any fruitful hypotheses for further research and which still less can be used for any practical predictions.

One answer to the critique of oversimplification of the information transfer approach is developments which can be called the information processing approaches. These have largely been inspired by computer sciences and technology, and they look at the intervening processes between information input and output using computer analogy concepts. The information processing approaches resolve the human being as one black box into a number of smaller black boxes. One consequence of the interest in the intervening variables is that the original, binary information concept tends to be turned into an information concept which is less precise and more general and similar to our everyday use of the information concept. A classical work within the human information processes approach is that of Newell and Simon (1972). Within the frame of reference of human information processing, perception is looked upon as a digital data acquisition system built up by a large number of components or information units interconnected by programmes and buffering memories. From the smaller units larger units are formed which can perform complex tasks. Perceptual skills are understood through analogies of programming, programme operations and memory storage.

Higher order psychophysics

A different theoretical approach is the so-called higher order psychophysics. Contemporary theories within this tradition (see for instance Gibson, 1966, and Johansson, 1974) assume higher order properties of the stimulation, i.e. complex patterns of light impinging on the retina as a basis for perception. The perceptual system registers higher order relations, such as motion vectors, texture gradients and expansion patterns. The perceptual system is looked upon as an active, exploring instrument which is designed to detect relevant properties of the stimulation. Runesson (1977) has demonstrated the possibilities for such an instrument by comparing the perceptual system with the polar planimeter which measures the area of irregular shapes by tracing the boundary line of a figure.

Using the approach of higher order psychophysics as a frame of reference, car driving has been explained as a perceptual skill by Lee (1974). He has shown that a driver can avoid a collision by predicting the potential course of his own car and a meeting car following the registering of the relations between the optical images.

The theory of percept-genesis

This is a quite different theoretical construction for perception, on an assumption that there is a close relationship between perception and personality (Kragh and Smith, 1970). It postulates that one has to take the past of the individual as represented by personality into consideration to understand certain important aspects of perception. Important characteristics of the personality have been formed during childhood, such as the so called "defence mechansims". These were originally Freudian concepts related to anxiety such as denial of threat or repression. The general meaning of these concepts is that when a person is exposed to something which is felt to be dangerous he responds with anxiety which is followed by a defence against this anxiety. The defence is set up differently and varies from individual to individual. Thus each individual has a set of defence mechanisms whose primary aims are to reduce anxiety in threatening or, to use another term, in stressing situations. The defence mechanisms influence our perception of the outer world especially when there is something threatening in it.

Kragh (1959) has developed a technique, the Defence Mechanism Test (DMT), which can be used to discover the set of defence mechanisms of an individual. Kragh also makes predictions about how a certain set of defence mechanisms influences the person's ability to cope with threat or stress from the surroundings. DMT has been tried out on pilots in the Swedish Air Force. Pilots and particularly fighter and attack pilots are very dependent on a quick and adequate perception of dangers, i.e. threats. The predictions of success in flying made on DMT have been followed up by actual records of success from flight training and also success later as active fighter or attack pilots. It has been shown through normal validation and cross-validation that there is a clear relationship between the prediction of success based on the set of defence mechanisms found by DMT and success as a pilot both in flight training and actual flight operations. Certain sets of defence mechanisms are more likely to result in inadequate behaviour in stressful situations (Neuman, 1978). According to the theory of percept-genesis the inadequacy of the behaviour can be traced back to distortions in the perception of the threat. Furthermore the perceptual distortion is related to the organization of the defence mechanisms. The Defense Mechanism Test has been used since 1970 in the Swedish Air Force for the selection of trainees for pilot training.

Some comparisons and criticism

Quite a lot of empirical data has been collected within the three mentioned theoretical approaches. A basic problem seems to be that communication between them is not easily established. This may partly be due to differences in emphasising theory and empiricism. The information transfer and processing approaches seem to be more empirical and pragmatic and on the whole more oriented to the real world in comparison to higher order psychophysics which strongly emphasises theory supported by laboratory experiments.

The percept–genetic approach is based on sophisticated theoretical constructions and has an empiricism which emphasises real world relevance although it also uses laboratory experiments. The information processing approaches have been criticized for splitting complex processes into separate entities which may make it difficult for integrated concepts to emerge. On the other hand higher order psychophysics has been criticized for focussing on stimulation and also for neglecting percept-to-percept dependency and heuristic characteristics of perception, which puts constraints on the perceptual world especially when the input information is incomplete (Epstein, 1977).

The theory of percept–genesis has been criticized especially by higher order psychophysics representatives for vagueness in its theoretical construction. This criticism can be traced back to differences in very basic ideas of science. Higher order psychophysics traditionally bases its ideals and roots in the classical sciences while percept–genesis as a theory is based to a large extent on philosophical and humanistic traditions in psychology.

METHODOLOGICAL ASPECTS

Let us consider on one side real world observations of advanced human performance in the area of perceptual skills, as in the examples of birdhunting, flying an attack aircraft and photo-interpreting. The quality of the performance stands out when we compare a very experienced person with a less experienced one. The difference in performance is perhaps even clearer when we for example look at piano-playing and compare a beginner with a student who has been playing for a year with a couple of hours of training per week, and further compare this student with a concert pianist who has been training several hours a day for perhaps 10 to 15 years. Consider also psychological theory on perception and perceptual skills. To what extent does current theory cover extraordinary human performance? Are there concepts and relations within the theories which are relevant and contribute to the understanding of advanced skills?

Higher order psychophysics has been dealing with and is still dealing with basic functions in human perception like contrasts, movements and size constancy. Today so-called smart functions are also investigated. It is still very much an open question whether research on these perceptual functions, basic or smart, will contribute to the understanding of advanced human performance in the perceptual skill area.

Within the information processing approaches there are theory-based or model-based concepts like long-term memory, sequential processor, parallel processor, foveal perception and extrafoveal perception. These concepts and the relations between them may have potential for the understanding of advanced human performance but to a large extent they still represent analogies which have to be developed further before they can be characterized as knowledge or even hypotheses which may contribute to this understanding.

The percept–genetic theory recognizes the advanced behaviour in flying an aircraft in terms of defence mechanism configurations. The relationship between behaviour and these theoretical concepts has also been supported by empirical data in the form of pilot performance in stressful situations, e.g. accidents and near-accidents where there is a demand for quick and adequate perception. This relationship, which is surprisingly stable, is interesting and promising. It contributes to the understanding of advanced perceptual skills when there are load and time constraints on the individual, but it is questionable whether it has any relevance for other types of perceptual demands, e.g. in situations where there are no severe time constraints.

The conclusion from a brief examination of contemporary perceptual theories seems to be that there is no theory or theoretical approach which can offer a complete framework for the understanding or for the development of understanding in advanced perceptual skills. This statement indicates that one should perhaps look at real skills, and particularly at advanced perceptual skills, without any theoretical or methodological assumptions, as there is no approach which seems to be closer to the understanding of advanced human performance than any other.

Let us, with this discussion as a background, consider, as an example of an exploratory approach, the systematic study of birdhunting. The aim within such a study could be to define factors which may be significantly related to advanced performance levels in connection with the hunter, his rifle, his procedures in handling the rifle and his surroundings. Subjects for the study can probably be found in a rifle association, whose members normally have access to a shooting range and training and testing facilities. It is important to introduce the study to the subjects thoroughly; they must feel an interest in co-operating in it. It is probably not necessary to promise any specific results which can be applied but the hunters should understand the intentions of the study. There should be possibilities for the subjects to discuss the study with the investigator when the study is carried out. Subject acceptance and positive co-operation can further be facilitated if the investigator happens to be a hunter or rifleman himself.

In the planning of the study a number of questions will be formulated, e.g.:

Are there any performance measures on the shooting range which are generally accepted by hunters, e.g. percentage hits in a series of shoots?

Can the hunters be divided into performance levels based on this measure?

Are there any easily detected relationships between possible performance levels and degree of training or years of experience?

How is the training carried out for the hunters, concerning basic training and continuous training?

Are there any performance difficulties for the hunter during the training and if so what is difficult?

What kind of training aids are there and how are they used in the training?

How is the feedback of hunter performance given to the trainer?

Are there any extra feedback or feedback amplifications to the learner working during the training?

Are instructors being used during training and what do they do?

The next step in the planning of the study is to find data and other material which can be used for answering or exploring the study questions. Some questions may be answered through investigating available performance records from testing and training sessions in the rifle association. If there are no records available or if some additions to the records are needed a procedure for taking performance records during testing sessions can be set up. One has to be careful when deciding what should be recorded and when. The recording of performance during test sessions may be accepted as something self-evident but recording during training sessions may be felt as a load on the hunter and the instructor and may have negative influences. In a study like this it is important to find methods which do not result in load or stress on the trainer and the instructor. Observations of the performer can, for instance, be problematic from this point of view.

Interviewing is a method which can be very useful and which does not normally load the subject. The interviews can start with experienced instructors who are training hunters, they can talk about what they are doing during training sessions, they can describe about the training aids and how they are used, they probably have a good picture of the difficulties during training and what they and the trainers are doing to face the difficulties. They may also have quite a lot of ideas about what contributes to the development of advanced performance in birdhunting. Interviews with hunters of different skill levels may be more difficult to carry out because of the fact that a skilled person may not be aware of what he is doing, but this problem should not be over-emphasised. An interview study similar to the one described here on advanced shots with a pistol gave much information on behaviour and on factors which influence the performance levels. A person who is strongly interested in his performance, e.g. because he is taking part in competitions, seems often to have good insight into his behaviour even on factors which are not directly conscious. Thus there is a good chance that interviews with hunters at different performance levels can give substantial information about factors which influence the performance level and the possibilities of reaching an advanced level.

The data which are collected in an exploratory study like the one described here should be used to re-formulate questions and to formulate new ones related to the advanced performance. The new questions can be tested out in further studies on hunters.

There are practical difficulties in carrying out traditional learning experiments because of the time and the amount of training which is needed to reach good performance levels. Furthermore one cannot assume that it is just learning which builds up the advanced levels. There may be, for instance, motivational and personality factors, and the significance of these factors must be explored. However, it can be useful to follow a group of learners, e.g. 4 to 6 hunters, over a longer period and register their performance and interview them and their instructors on certain occasions or at certain intervals. Experiments which fulfil treatment and control group demands as well as statistical demands can be carried out to test and investigate limited questions. But a condition for such methods is that the investigator has an adequate overview, e.g. through an exploratory approach described above. The overview should include a tentative description of factors which significantly contribute to the advanced human performance.

Equipment and training design

In the earlier sections of this chapter an alternative procedure for shooting at moving targets was described. In this procedure the task was divided into some delimited steps, such as estimations of target distance, speed and course. These estimations were used by the rifleman to choose one point among several possible points in his sight which he aligns with the target. This step procedure can be compared with the holistic procedure in birdhunting. The hunter aligns his rifle to a point in front of the bird and fires thus taking the speed, course and distance into consideration without consciously thinking of it.

Both these procedures can be analysed for equipment and training demands through the approach suggested above. Although very time consuming and costly a comparative study between the two procedures would be very interesting. Each procedure could be evaluated against specified criteria, e.g. number of subjects above certain performance levels (expressed for instance as number of hits in a series of shots) and amount of training needed to reach a certain performance level. Subjective criteria could be used too. Each subject will get an opportunity to try just one procedure. A subject who has been trained thoroughly on one procedure is spoiled for training on another, as there may be negative and/or positive transfer of learning between the procedures.

For the attack pilot's tasks, the time constraints are so severe that his behaviour must be registered with technical aids. Eye movement recordings have been used for the pilot's visual fixations when he is carrying out a flight mission (normally in a flight simulator because of safety reasons and of space available for the extra equipment). The visual fixations have been related to mission conditions. It is assumed that a fixation also represents a demand for information which the pilot will need for his actions. Analysis of fixation points has been used to suggest placement and configurations of instruments and displays in the cockpit.

Eye movement recordings have been used extensively in other visual tasks such as car driving. This method gets less useful with decreasing time constraint in the task. When the operator gets less involved in direct feedback loops to the machine the usefulness of eye movement recording is also reduced. In process controlling where automatic procedures tend to handle the direct feedback and the important operator task is to predict dangerous or otherwise unwanted states in the process, eye movement recordings will be of limited value. Interviews with operators and 'think aloud' methods when the operator carried out his task will be more useful. In a recent study interviews with experienced operators in nuclear power stations were used among other methods for training development and evaluation (Sjölin *et al.*, 1978).

Personnel selection

The defence mechanisms as they are defined in the percept–genetic theoretical frame have been used as a basis for the selection of pilot trainees. The idea behind this personnel selection is that the defence mechanism configuration of the individual influences his perception of threat in the physical world. The perception will be slower and less adequate with certain defence mechanism configurations, which raises the risk of accidental behaviour when flying. Thus through the screening of those individuals who carry 'risky' defence mechanisms the accident rate will be influenced.

An interesting question in this context is whether a certain defence mechanism configuration of an individual can be changed. According to the psychoanalytical theory the defence mechanisms are formed in early childhood and will thus be more or less stable, unless the individual takes part in a psychoanalysis. A preliminary study is being carried out among pilots to investigate to what extent psychotherapy will influence the defence mechanisms, particularly those which make the perception of threat in flying more difficult.

CONCLUDING REMARKS

Extraordinary human performance is largely an unexplored area within the human sciences. The present state of knowledge of human perception and perceptual skills offers important but fragmentary contributions to the understanding and to the further development of understanding of advanced skills. It seems clear that advanced visual or perceptual performance is not just built up of what we know about perception and human learning. There are other aspects which are very important, such as motivational, emotional and social factors which in some way have to be considered in the development of a better understanding in this field. A theoretical framework is needed and this probably has to be organized on a higher level than the traditional perceptual framework, e.g. as in higher order psychophysics.

There are also some important philosophical aspects. What values are connected with advanced human performance, values connected with the skilled individual and values connected with the surrounding society? In industry, mechanization and automation have influenced the demands of advanced skill levels. Are there any relations between skill demands and job satisfaction, self-esteem or self confidence? It is not unrealistic to hypothesise that in jobs with high skill demands there is also higher job satisfaction. If we accept the developed industrialized society and do not think that we should strive towards going back to a society based on craftsmen, we should find ways to influence the industrial job so that it will demand more skill. When one looks into today's procedures in industry, or rather lack of procedures, for an active job design, one will find that jobs can be made more skill-demanding if one is conscious of the possibilities and if there is a will to use these possibilities. A will can be mobilized perhaps within unions. Laws and national regulations on work environment and job content can facilitate its realization.

There is a tendency today to attack competition within society because it causes stress, anxiety and unhappiness. It could be argued that demands on advanced skills amplify the competing tendencies which are very strong in some 'authorized' skill areas such as sports and arts. A solution to the problem of competition could be a widening of the field of advanced skills or rather a widening of the idea of advanced skills. A working hypothesis could be that an advanced performance level can be developed in practically any human activity and every human being can reach an advanced skill level in at least one activity.

Another objection may be that the rapid social and technical change of the society makes it impossible to develop advanced performance levels simply because the instrumental and social stability is not sufficient to allow the time for development. This statement cannot be true concerning instrumental stability; it is not necessary to freeze the instrument as for instance in music (e.g. the violin). A good example of the new instrument which has resulted in very advanced performance levels is the skateboard.

Acknowledgement

I would like to thank Hans Marmolin at the Swedish National Defence Research Institute for valuable discussions during the writing of this chapter.

References

Bainbridge, L. (1978). The process controller. In W. T. Singleton (ed.). *The Study of Real Skills I*. (Lancaster: MTP Press)

Epstein, W. (1977). What are the prospects for a higher-order stimulus theory of perception? *Scand. J. Psychol.,* **18,** 164

Gibson, E. J. (1955). The effect of prior training with a scale of distance on absolute judgements of distance over ground. *J. Exp. Psychol.,* **50**

Gibson, J. J. (1950). *The Perception of the Visual World*. (Cambridge, Mass: Riverside Press)

Gibson, J. J. (1966). *The Senses Considered as Perceptual Systems*. (Boston: Houghton Mifflin)

Johansson, G. (1974). Projective transformations as determining visual space perception. In R. B. MacLeod and H. L. Picks (eds.). *Perception: Essays in Honor of James J. Gibson*. (Ithaca: Cornell University Press)

Kragh, U. (1959). Types of pre-cognitive defensive organization in a tachistoscopic experiment, *J. Proj. Techn.,* **23,** 315

Kragh, U. and Smith, G. (1970). *Percept–Genetic Analysis*. (Lund: Gleerup)

Lee, D. N. (1974). Visual information during locomotion. In R. B. MacLeod and H. L. Picks (eds.). *Perception: Essays in Honor of James J. Gibson*. (Ithaca: Cornell University Press)

Miller, G. A. (1956). The magical number seven plus or minus two: Some limits on our capacity for processing information. *Psychol. Rev.,* **63,** 81

Neuman, T. (1978). Dimensionering och validering av percept–genesens försvarsmekanismer. En hierarkisk–geneteisk analys mot pilotens stressbeteende. FOA Report (in preparation). Stockholm

Newell, A. and Simon, H. A. (1972). *Human Problem Solving*. (Englewood Cliffs N. J: Prentice-Hall)

Runesson, S. (1977). On the possibility of 'smart' perceptual mechanisms. *Scand. J. Psychol.*, **18**, 172

Russo, J. E. (1977). Adaptation of cognitive processes to the eye movement system. In J. W. Senders, D. F. Fisher and R. A. Monty (eds.). *Eye Movement and Higher Psychological Functions*. (Hillsdale, N. J: Lawrence Erlbaum)

von Senden, M. (1932). *Raum- und Gestaltauffassung bei operierten Blindgeborenen vor und nach der Operation*. (Leipzig: Barth)

Senders, J. W. (1966). A reanalysis of pilot eye-movement data. *IEEE Trans. Hum. Factors Electron.*, **7**, 103

Sheridan, T. B. and Ferrell, W. R. (1974). *Man-Machine Systems: Information, Control and Decision Models of Human Performance*. (Cambridge, Mass: MIT Press)

Sjölin, P. G., Wahlström, B. and Wirstad, J. (1978). A task analysis for the planning of operator training in nuclear power plants. Paper presented at the OECD Halden Reactor Project Programme Meeting in June 1978, Loen.

Turnbull, C. M. (1961). Some observations regarding the experiences and behaviour of the Bambuti Pygmies. *Am. J. Psychol.* **74**, 304

Williams, L. G. (1973). Studies of extrafoveal discrimination and detection. Visual Search. (Washington D.C: National Academy of Sciences)

15
Creative Thinking

A. HEDGE AND B. R. LAWSON

INTRODUCTION

Of all the skills we may possess, none have more frequently eluded description than those underlying creative thinking. This is not because of any dearth of examples of creative endeavour, but rather it is a reflection of the extraordinary difficulty of systematically dissecting the "act of creation". At its most fundamental level it seems that this can be decomposed into at least two classes of skills, those of problem solving and those of problem finding. That is to say, man not only has the skills to create solutions to problems, but he also has the skills to create the problems themselves. This important distinction will be repeatedly discussed throughout the chapter. Furthermore, as with any feature of human behaviour, there are marked individual differences in the degree of competence with which these skills are exercised. It is axiomatic that not everyone possesses the ability to achieve the excellence of Newton or Einstein, Mozart or Beethoven, Turner or Picasso, but a better understanding of creative thinking skills should facilitate the development of training programmes which may assist particular individuals to improve their own performance. If we are to try to promote excellence in "creation" then we must ask questions about how we may further assist those who already appear competent at creative thinking. Moreover if we are to ensure competence we must ask questions concerning the development of creative potential within an individual. In short, is it possible to define the critical factors which determine the success or failure of creative thinking?

We shall attempt to do this initially by examining a wide variety of studies of creative behaviour within the traditional framework of products, processes, persons and situations, and then finally, in keeping with the theme of this book, we shall attempt to integrate these various perspectives beneath a common conceptual umbrella and consider creative thinking from a skills viewpoint.

THE CREATIVE PRODUCT

At the outset we appear to be faced with an almost insurmountable obstacle – what will be our measure of creative thinking? This criterion problem has frequently been avoided by studies of creativity, yet it remains a central issue. Basically we have only one measure of creative thinking and that is the outcome of this activity, the creative product. But this in itself is dependent on many variables. First of all we have a problem of level; for example, if we consider the evolution of any product then who should we call "creative": only the inventor or should we also include all others involved in the subsequent refinement of his product? Secondly we have the perennial problem of quality versus quantity of output. How should we compare a person who may occasionally have "highly creative" thoughts with someone who may have frequent but somewhat "less creative" thoughts? Indeed we may question whether such differences exist or whether highly creative people are also prolific? Shapiro (1968) adds to our dilemma by pointing to a further problem which concerns the use of ultimate versus concurrent criteria. From an individual's viewpoint the ultimate criterion of his creative performance is based on his life's output, but unfortunately this can only be assessed retrospectively. History is littered with outstanding people who failed to gain recognition in their own lifetimes. The timescale of ultimate criteria clearly preclude their use for most practical purposes and therefore in general we must rely solely on concurrent criteria. The two concurrent criteria most frequently used are those of persons and products. Should we choose to use, say, psychometric instruments to measure the creative potential of individuals we still cannot assess whether this potential is ever likely to be realized. Consequently we seem to have little choice but to rely primarily on assessing the products of creation. However as we have already seen this involves the problems of level, quality versus quantity etc. Furthermore our assessment of the "creativity" of a product will not be objective but will depend upon our values, beliefs, attitudes, current social norms etc. De Bono (1976) elegantly summarizes this problem thus: "Creativity is a value word and represents a value judgement – no one ever calls creative something new which he dislikes."

Thus any form of assessment must also call into question the nature of the assessor; for example, should we accept the views of a majority of the lay public or those of a panel of 'experts', given that a disagreement exists between these?

Unfortunately there appears to be no concise and satisfactory solution to these dilemmas, and any comprehensive consideration of their philosophical implications would greatly exceed the space available in this chapter. We therefore propose that while we must acknowledge the fundamental importance of the criterion issue, progress in the discussion of creative thinking is still possible in the absence of any rigorous measure of the products of creation.

Although not entirely satisfactory, Bruner (1962) has proposed an elegantly simple solution to the problem by suggesting that we merely define creativity as "an act that produces effective surprise". So with bated breath let us proceed to examine what we know of the characteristics of such acts.

THE CREATIVE PROCESS

As with many other types of problem solving, psychologists have conceptualized creative thinking as a process which may be functionally divided into a series of phases or stages. Perhaps the earliest attempt at this was made by Helmholtz (1896, cited in Vinacke, 1974). Based on introspective evidence, he proposed that the creative process began with a period of initial investigation of the problem, and when further progress towards a solution was impossible, there ensued a period of rest and recovery. Then, in an apparently sudden and unexpected manner, a solution would occur to him. The French mathematician, Poincaré, agrees with Helmholtz's analysis but emphasises the need for an additional phase, a second period of conscious work following the "inspired" thought. He claims that such a phase is necessary "to put in shape the results of this inspiration, to deduce from them the immediate consequences, to arrange them, to word the demonstrations, but above all verification is necessary" (Poincaré, 1924).

Largely as a result of such anecdotal descriptions of creative thinking, Wallas (1926) attempted to classify the stages of the creative process. He concluded that a four-stage classification would suffice to cover both scientific and artistic creativity. These stages occur in the following sequence: *preparation, incubation, illumination* and *verification*. His classification, with minor modifications, has since been widely adopted. The first phase, *preparation*, is the period during which the creator acquires knowledge, skills, techniques and experimental information which allow him to formulate the problem. The creative thinker cannot commence work without this repertoire of experience and skills. It is entirely erroneous to think that any creative person, whether artist, musician, mathematician or scientist, did not first undertake long and patient training in his discipline before exhibiting his creative talent. Although competence at this stage depends upon the individual's entire life history, of paramount interest to psychologists are those immediate experiences which lead the person to perceive and formulate specific problems, and the motivational factors which lead him to search for their solution. Kneller (1965) has argued for a sub-division at this point into a period of "first insight", that is, the apprehension of an idea or of a problem, and a subsequent period of "preparation" during which the creator explores the possibilities of his germinal idea. This proposal is similar to Mackinnon's distinction between "preparation" and "effort" (see below). There is clearly a case for separating the skills associated with problem finding from those of problem solving, but we shall postpone a more thorough discussion of this until later in the chapter.

Once the problem has initially been crystallized there follows a period during which the person concentrates his effort on generating a solution to the problem. Mackinnon (1976) calls this the period of "effort", while Kneller prefers the term "period of preparation". Indeed, as Kneller notes: "One of the paradoxes of creativity is that, in order to think originally, we must familiarize ourselves with the ideas of others . . . These ideas can then form a springboard from which the creator's ideas can be launched." The crucial role of this initial period of "effort" is similarly emphasized by Thomson (1959) who asserts that "no intuitions will come without prior hard work".

The nature of the problem will determine the length of this preparatory phase. If the problem is relatively simple then the period of "effort" will be comparatively short. Unfortunately the types of problem which usually require one to indulge in creative thinking before a solution is produced tend to be extremely difficult. Symphonies are not composed or buildings designed without considerable "effort" or "preparation".

It is during the phase of *preparation* that the problem may itself be revised or even completely re-defined. Then what generally appears to happen is that after extensive grappling with the problem without success, the creator becomes so frustrated by his failure that he relieves the pressure by turning to some other activity. Wallas terms this period of withdrawal from the problem *incubation,* because it is a period during which there appears to be no conscious effort expended toward solving the problem. Several authors (for example Mackinnon, 1976) have outlined two possible processes which may operate during this period. One suggestion is that the individual is engaged in unconscious cerebration, that is, he is expending effort in subconsciously processing the problem. The other suggestion is that the creator, having been away from the problem, returns refreshed and thus adopts different attitudes and approaches to it. Whatever the processes involved, this stage is terminated when a solution to the problem suddenly springs to mind. This unexpected appearance of a solution is termed "insight" or, as Wallas proposes, the moment of inspiration. This is a familiar but tantalizing elusive experience, the point when all becomes clear, when the pieces fall into place, the "Eureka" syndrome. Characteristically we afterwards wonder why we had any trouble in seeing the solution in the first place. The moment of inspiration is generally held to be very exhilarating and one feels excited, proud and frequently elated at achieving success.

The final phase proposed in this taxonomy is again one of intense effort where attempts are made to confirm the validity of the solution. This period of *verification* also includes the time spent in evaluating, modifying, and elaborating the solution. It may even involve selecting between a variety of possible solutions.

A slightly different taxonomy of the creative process has been proposed by Stein (1974). He acknowledges the need for a preparatory or educational phase, but proceeds to argue that creative thinking really only comprises three overlapping stages: *hypothesis formulation, hypothesis testing,* and *communication of results.* This latter phase has generally been omitted by other workers, but it is clearly crucial if one is to implement ideas successfully such that creative products will be realized. During this time other people have the opportunity to appraise the solution and this may lead to its subsequent modification. Winning recognition for and approval of their achievements is a gauntlet which all creators must run.

Although it appears possible to classify the creative process into functionally discrete phases, this approach can be rather misleading because the activities associated with each of these generally are not temporally discrete. Vinacke (1974) reiterates Wertheimer's suggestion that it is more appropriate to conceptualize creative thinking in holistic terms, as a total behavioural pattern in which there is considerable interweaving and overlapping of the various processes which mediate between the original stimulus and the formation of the final product (Wertheimer, 1945). In all fairness, most authors have emphasized that the various stages are not temporally discrete, yet they still favour conceiving of creative thinking in phasic terms rather than as Vinacke suggests, "in terms of dynamic, interplaying activities". Perhaps in part the reasons for this lie in the romantic ideas which customarily are associated with terms such as "flashes of insight" or "moments of inspiration". In reality, the truth frequently seems a little harsher. One of Britain's most "creative" engineers, Barnes Wallis, has this to say about his work: "There has always been a problem first. I have never had a novel idea in my life. My achievements have been solutions to problems . . . things have never come in a flash: they come only as a result of months, even years, of very heavy work." (Whitfield, 1975).

An attempt at reconciling these two viewpoints is possible by a diagrammatic summary of both the functional stages of creative thinking and the various conscious and unconscious activities which might be supposed to operate for each of these (see Figure 15.1). The result is a description of an interactive cycle of creative activity which eventually may result in a solution being found for any given problem. However such a diagram must necessarily be read very loosely. In different problem situations the functions take on varying degrees of significance. In some cases the majority of time might be spent in solution generation while in others problem identification may be the dominant activity and so on. Nor should the diagram be read too rigidly in terms of sequence. Certainly the cycle of creative activity begins with a problem and ends with a solution but in between the model must allow for loops within the cycle as a whole.

What becomes abundantly clear from careful consideration of any approach which attempts to partition the creative process solely into discrete stages is that it actually tells us very little about the kinds of skills which are essential

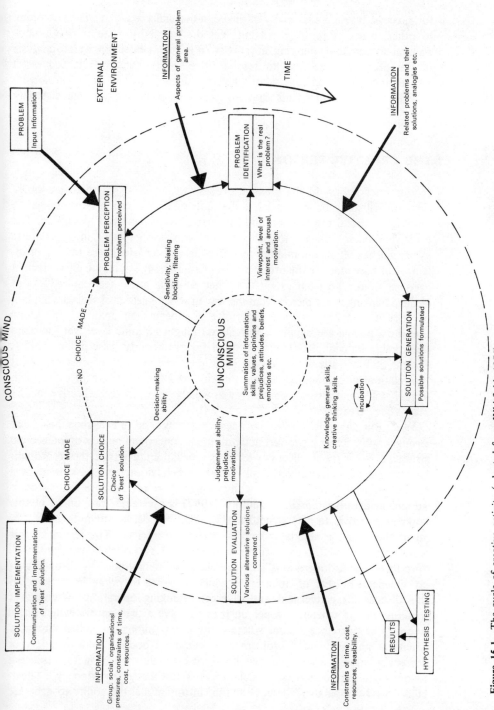

Figure 15.1 The cycle of creative activity (adapted from Whitfield, 1975)

for success. It seems that many of the cognitive skills required will be common to other forms of problem solving. Yet the possibilty remains that unique abilities for creative thinking may exist. We face a dilemma which analysis of the process alone fails to resolve. Are we to construe the successful creator merely as someone who is better trained and more skilled at solving a wide variety of problems that his peers, or is he really some distinctly special kind of person?

THE CREATIVE PERSON

In our brief review of the creative process we have suggested that creative thinking will only be successful if the individual in question is motivated to undertake careful preparation and to pursue his original idea to fruition. The creative thinker appears to be someone who is competent in appropriate skills, yet flexible in the manner in which he can transfer these to new problems. But how much is the product of such thinking the outcome of intellectual exercise alone? To what extent are other personal attributes required? Does creative thinking result merely from the way in which intellectual skills are applied, or does it lean heavily on a repertoire of independent abilities? We know that most people are capable of creative thought at some level, yet there are remarkable individual differences. What factors underly these differences? It is clear that any attempt to answer such questions requires information about the relationships between creative thinking and the operation of other intellectual skills, and also about the way in which various non-intellective factors may affect creativity.

Work on the relationship between creativity and intelligence has been strongly influenced by two distinctly different conceptual models of intellectual structure: either the intellect is viewed as a broad unitary trait, the co-ordinating aspects of which underlie all intelligent behaviour, or it is viewed as a constellation of specific factors within which there reside those factors operational in creative thinking. Guilford (1967) is the major proponent of this latter perspective. In his "Structure of Intellect" model he attempts to identify all of the separate abilities which comprise the intellect. The results of this work have led Guilford to postulate three major classes of abilities: "contents", "products", and "operations". In the class of "operations" he distinguishes six independent sets of abilities of which two are of prime importance to this discussion: convergent and divergent thinking operations. Convergent thinking occurs whenever a person tries to solve a problem for which there is only one correct solution, whereas divergent thinking is called into play whenever an open-ended problem is encountered because here a variety of correct solutions may be possible. Guilford lists three sets of factors essential to divergent production (see Table 15.1). These he terms "fluency", "flexibility", and "originality". It is clear that in this model the ability to generate a creative idea rests on these divergent thinking skills which may operate quite independently of other intellectual skills.

Table 15.1   A summary of the factors associated with divergent production in Guilford's "Structure of Intellect" (Guilford, 1967)

Factors	Ability
A. *Fluency Factors*	
1. Word fluency	To produce words, each containing a specified letter or combination of letters
2. Associational fluency	To produce as many synonyms as possible for a given word in a given time
3. Expressional fluency	To produce phrases and sentences
4. Ideational fluency	To produce ideas
B. *Flexibility Factors*	
1. Spontaneous flexibility	To produce a great variety of ideas
2. Adaptive flexibility	To change solution strategies when a problem is not solved
C. *Originality Factors*	
1. Originality	To produce unusual responses

Based on this assumption, Getzels and Jackson (1962) attempted to distinguish between adolescents who scored high on conventional intelligence tests (tests of convergent thinking) but low on creativity tests (tests of divergent thinking), and those who scored highly on creative tests but less on conventional IQ tests. They claimed to have demonstrated a variety of differences between such individuals. A major difference was apparently related to the person's self-image; the high IQ pupils held a self-image consistent with what they felt would meet with approval from their teachers, whereas the highly creative pupils held a self-image consistent with their own projected values. What is more teachers preferred the high IQ children to the highly creative ones. We shall return to these points later in this discussion.

However, despite some support for their views (for example Torrance, 1962), Getzels and Jackson's work has been severely criticized, especially by those who favour the "broad unitary trait" model of intelligence (Freeman *et al.*, 1971). Burt (1962), Ripple and May (1962), Vernon (1964) and Edwards and Tyler (1965) have all detailed problems with this work. Among these are the facts that the children tested were a restricted sample (the average IQ was 130), adminstration of the IQ tests was not standardized, creativity scores were not corrected for variations in children's age, and the inter-test correlations between the tests of creativity were almost as low as between these and the IQ scores. In a re-analysis of their data, taking some account of these problems. Marsh (1964) concludes that for a heterogenous population "the conventional IQ score is the best single criterion for creative potential".

In a more sophisticated replication of Getzels and Jackson's work, Wallach and Kogan (1965) found that although their measures of creativity (from a variety of associational procedures) were fairly highly correlated they were largely independent of IQ scores. Wallach and Kogan emphasized that in considering the child's behaviour, his joint position on both of these variables needed to be assessed. When they classified children on the basis of their IQ/creativity scores four groups emerged, high/high; high/low; low/high; low/low. Of these Wallach and Kogan found that it was the children in the low/high group (low on IQ but high on creativity) who suffered most problems, for they displayed a lack of self-confidence, hesitancy and unsociability. However, how far their associational measures were adequate measures of the total creative potential of each child is questionable.

Studies by Cropley (1966) and Lovell and Shields (1967) have shown that if the scores from a representative selection of tests of intelligence and of creativity are factor analysed then the two major factors which emerge are those of convergent and divergent thinking. Although "creativity" emerged as the separate divergent thinking factor, it was significantly correlated with "intelligence" (convergent thinking). Thus a high score on the tests of divergent thinking was strongly associated with a high score on tests of convergent thinking, and vice versa. Cropley concludes that although the two styles of thinking are not identical "it is unacceptable to think of creativity as a separate basic intellective mode".

Mackinnon (1976) admirably summarizes the evidence for the relationship between intelligence and creative thinking. He says, "it is simply not true that the more intelligent person is necessarily the more creative person"; however, he points out that "no feeble-minded person turned up in any of our samples, where our samples of creative individuals had been nominated by experts". This is an important point for, as originally proposed by Meer and Stein (1955) and Mackinnon (1962), above a certain level of intelligence, being more intelligent does not seem to guarantee that one will be more creative. Hasan and Butcher (1966) obtained results which are explicable by such a "threshold" hypothesis, and similarly Yamamoto (1965) failed to demonstrate any corresponding increase in creativity with increased intelligence above a certain level. In reviewing the evidence, Dellas and Gaier (1970) and Mackinnon place this "threshold" around the IQ range 115–120.

It seems appropriate at this point further to consider Guilford's work, for although he makes a distiction between convergent and divergent thinking, he also emphasizes that the creative product is only realized when both modes of thought are employed. It is not a sufficient end in itself to merely generate a creative idea, it must be refined, tested, elaborated and eventually implemented. There must, therefore, be a continual interplay between these two modes of thought as the creative process progresses. Within this framework the "threshold" hypothesis implies that a person must first be competent in applying his convergent thinking skills to solving problems, because only then can he translate his "creative" thoughts into reality. Perhaps this is why in Wallach and Kogan's study, the low IQ/high creativity group apparently experienced such pronounced emotional problems.

Intellectual skills apart, there is considerable evidence that a variety of non-intellective factors influence the progress of creative thinking, although there seems to be little systematic evidence about those factors which initially motivate creators to create. Anecdotal reports suggest that perhaps artists are motivated by a "desire to show", whereas scientists are motivated by a "desire to know". However, it has generally been assumed that regardless of what stimulates the creator to produce, the underlying process and the factors influencing it do not systematically vary between professions.

In support of this view characteristic personality traits have been reported in several studies. Roe (1951, 1952, 1953) presents details of these in her studies of a variety of scientists judged to have made creative contributions to their respective disciplines. Her main conclusions are that in general such people are very highly motivated, very persistent, and very intelligent. Furthermore, they show considerable self-sufficiency, autonomy of judgement and stubbornness. Persistence and dedication to work appear to be almost universal characteristics among such creative individuals, indeed Barron (1955) says "voluminous productivity is the rule and not the exception among individuals who have made some noteworthy contribution". Shapiro (1966, 1968) has reviewed numerous studies of the relationship between creativity and personality in creative scientists, Mackinnon (1962) and Lawson (1978) detail the personality characteristics of creative architects, and McPherson (1967) has summarized the main traits of creative engineers.

In addition to the influence of personality variables there is also evidence for differences in perceptual ability. Lang and Ryba (1976) have shown that creative artists and musicians apparently share a heightened perceptual discriminatory ability across all sensory modalities.

Overall, then, the most essential characteristics of the creative thinker appear to be possession of a flexible mind, non-conformity, and self-confidence. Mackinnon particularly emphasizes the importance of "flexible" thinking, and he summarizes the creative person's abilities thus: "he is discerning, observant in a differentiated fashion, he is alert and concentrates attention readily and shifts it appropriately, and he is fluent in scanning thoughts and producing those which meet some problem solving criteria".

Non-conformity in his attitudes and behaviour appears to assist the creator's flexibility of thought. Barron (1955) says "the pervasive and unstereotyped unconventionality of thought which one finds consistently in creative individuals is related to a tendency to resist acculturation, where acculturation is seen as demanding of one's personal, unique and fundamental nature". Of course any rejection of normal standards of behaviour leads to many problems for the creator. We have already noted how, in Getzels and Jackson's study, teachers favoured those pupils who held conformist attitudes. The creator is frequently caught in a dilemma between what he believes and does, and what is expected of him. Whitfield again provides a summary of these problems: "being the odd man out is an uncomfortable feeling. Most of us avoid challenging the *status quo* . . . We find it very difficult to overcome the values and habits that have been implanted in us from childhood . . . Unable to break out ourselves, we seek to pull others into captivity with us. The odd-ball somehow must be brought in line. His non-conformity in habits or attitudes can blind us to the possession of his unique personal resources . . . he is not likely to be welcome in the normal industrial organization". Life can be very uncomfortable for the highly creative person. How then can he survive intact when he may frequently be rejected by others?

In the light of these problems it is not surprising that perhaps the most salient feature which appears to characterize the creative person is his self-image. He must retain faith in his own ability first of all to generate a feasible solution to an open-ended problem, he must be prepared to accept failure but persevere until he is successful, and he must be committed to convincing others of the utility of his solution, even if it is frequently criticized and rejected. The need for this strength of personal commitment is emphasized by the American poet Spender (1946), who says that to be creative is "to be what one is with all one's faculties and perceptions, strengthened by all the skill which one can acquire". So universal is this characteristic that Mackinnon (1976) summarizes all of his work on creative individuals by saying: "In our studies, one of the most valuable non-intellective indicators of creative potential has proved to be a person's concept of himself, that is, his self-image or self-percept. If I had no other way to measure an individual's creativity (i.e. I couldn't interview him, I was limited to one question in order to determine how creative he is) the simple question that I would ask the individual is 'Are you, or are you not, creative?'".

It might seem that, from the work reviewed, there is sufficient information to compile a fairly detailed profile of a disposition towards creativity. However, there are numerous problems which prevent this. We tend to overlook the fact that it is not possible simply to aggregate many of the research findings because invariably workers have neither used the same instruments nor the same factors in summarizing their results. Furthermore, different researchers have used different criteria of creativity, e.g. patent applications, nomination by experts etc. Such methodological discrepancies preclude meaningful direct comparisons. It is also lamentable that almost all of the studies have questioned only creative males. Does this really mean that we should suppose some biological predisposition toward creative thinking in favour of the male sex? As far as "creative potential" is concerned there appears to be no evidence to favour superiority of either sex (Kogan, 1974). Clearly, any account of creative thinking as it applies to real world problems must also consider the role played by environmental variables, for, as Hinton (1970) points out, "creative potential" only becomes "creative behaviour" under favourable circumstances.

THE CREATIVE SITUATION

We have seen how certain personality traits typically can be associated with individuals judged to be unusually creative, and we have also seen how morphological studies have suggested some apparently fundamental stages in the creative process. At this stage in the investigation of creativity it would be easy to conclude that by combining these two contributory factors one could obtain the complete picture. Person plus process describes the cognitive phenomenon. Nothing could be further from the truth, indeed such a conclusion would lead the investigator to miss an extremely important body of knowledge about creativity.

Above all, creativity is about context: the situation within which the person perceives the problem and performs the process. This context embraces such matters as the experience of the person or people involved, their familiarity with the type of problem and the attitudes which they are predisposed to adopt. In group situations the relations and communications between individuals have considerable influence on the creative powers of the group. Similarly the sense of urgency or the cost of failure can either inhibit or release creative potential.

All of this is "known" to the student of the creative applied arts who has experienced the pains of being creative on demand, but regrettably this situational aspect of creativity has been left relatively untouched by experimental psychology. This is hardly surprising considering the extraordinarily intractable nature of the problem and the consequent difficulties of devising controlled experiments. It is obviously easier to design experiments where the solution to a problem can be judged either right or wrong, or alternatively optimal in some pre-defined sense, since the criteria of success are easily rendered objective. Perhaps for this reason much of the early work in this field is now usually to be found in books about "thinking", "reasoning" and "problem-solving" rather than "creativity". However, classic among these is a treatise on *Productive Thinking* by Wertheimer (1945). Although Wertheimer's work has had a lasting effect it unfortunately is either frankly anecdotal or, at best, very sketchily described in terms of experimental procedure. Wertheimer's pupil, Karl Duncker, in his own classic paper "On problem-solving" (1945), reports rather more rigorous experiments in which subjects were required to solve both practical and mathematical problems, and some of the former are remarkably similar in style to current day creativity test questions. Probably the greatest importance of this early work by Wertheimer, Duncker and also Maier (1931) is that the results show the universal tendency of experience to have a mechanizing effect on individual thinking, and this frequently impairs rather than promotes creativity.

Many experimentalists have provided further evidence of these not always beneficial effects of experience. However, some workers have taken matters a step further towards the real world outside the psychologist's laboratory by attempting to uncover situational factors which could possibly prevent this mechanizing effect. Luchins and Luchins (1950), who see such mechanization as the establishment of a habitual mental set or "Einstellung", report their attempts to reduce this effect by concretizing abstract problems or introducing counter mental sets in the task description. In their tasks numbers representing volume were replaced by subjects actually pouring water from one jar to another. This concretizing of the problems was unfortunately not successful in preventing the Einstellung phenomenon, and Luchins and Luchins conclude that: "It appears that a tendency towards mechanization can occur both on the concrete and abstract levels . . . the major factor in determining whether or not an Einstellung developed seemed to be the attitude with which the S viewed the tasks".

From all these studies the evidence is clear that experience of similar problems all too readily leads to a mechanization of thought whereby we attempt to fit old solutions to new problems. This is the very antithesis of creativity, and it has always been a matter of considerable concern for designers. Since few design problems are completely novel how can a designer avoid the mechanizing effect of being familiar with so many previous solutions? Thus in design schools considerable emphasis is frequently laid on techniques of destroying these "preconceptions". In industry itself the need to improve perhaps already successful products provides the ultimate real world test of creative thinking. Such mechanical channelized thinking as discovered by the Gestalt psychologists is the very opposite of what is required here. Thus to learn more about how to generate potentially creative situations we must move our investigation from the psychologist's laboratory to the designer's studio.

From this rather more commercial work come two highly influential books: Alex Osborn's (1963) *Applied Imagination* and William J. J. Gordon's (1961) *Synectics*. Neither book could fairly be described as scientific and yet both have interested psychologists and designers alike. Amongst Osborn's ideas on creativity is his invention of brainstorming which together with synectics form the basis of many group problem solving techniques still in current use. Both these techniques "trick a group of problem-solvers into playful thinking by promulgating very tight rules of conduct" (Adams, 1974). Participants are reprimanded by the chairman for adopting judgemental attitudes but encouraged to build on the ideas of the members of the group. Participants are also encouraged to generate as many different ideas as possible to prevent internal criticism, and to assist in this even the widest ideas are welcomed.

Meadow and Parnes (1959a, b) found that subjects trained with Osborn's method did indeed generate more, and what were judged to be better, ideas.

However brainstorming has received much criticism for leading to superficial results through lack of a provision for analysing the problem. Synectics by comparison is a more elaborate technique having a number of separate stages beginning with an investigation and reformulation of the problem and moving on to solution generation. Synectics like brainstorming depends upon the temporary suspension of criticism, but there are many more positive techniques for encouraging a wide variety of ideas. Participants are encouraged to "make the strange familiar", or "make the familiar seem strange". However the central theme of synectics is one we shall return to again in this paper, that is the deliberate use of analogy. The four types of analogy employed in synectics are personal, direct, symbolic and fantasy analogy. When using personal analogy the problem solver identifies personally with some part of the problem or solution; that is he acts it out. Direct analogy is the direct use of parallel facts or systems as in the use of a water flow model of electricity. Symbolic analogy allows for the use of analogous objects (as opposed to people or ideas), and finally fantasy analogy allows for the generation of totally fantastic ideas. Synectics is rather more complex than this brief description can portray, and perhaps it is this complexity, and thus the rather extensive training required, which makes it less popular for the casual user than brainstorming. However this complexity would also seem to indicate that teasing the human mind into creative thinking is no simple matter.

Many other writers have published their ideas on how to be creative, but perhaps none has been so influential in recent times as Edward de Bono. De Bono treats creativity not as a gift but rather as skill. This is very much in line with the tradition of the great British psychologists such as Ryle (1949) ("thought is very much a matter of drills and skills") and Bartlett (1958) who considered thinking to be a "complex and high level kind of skill". However lest this be thought a rather mechanistic attitude it is only fair to add that de Bono also sees the human mind not so much as an information handling machine, but rather a special environment which allows information to organize itself into patterns.

It is with this concept of information patterns that de Bono (1970) comes close to the central theme of this section. De Bono's thesis is best summarized by his own words: "The self-organizing, self-maximizing memory system is very good at creating patterns and that is the effectiveness of mind. But inseparable from the great usefulness of a patterning system are certain limitations. In such a system it is easy to combine patterns or to add to them but it is extremely difficult to restructure them for the patterns control attention. Insight and humour both involve the restructuring of patterns. Creativity also involves the restructuring of patterns but with more emphasis on the escape from restricting patterns. Lateral thinking involves restructuring, escape and the provocation of new patterns".

Most of de Bono's writing is devoted to explaining techniques for facilitating this restructuring process, to allow the problem to be viewed differently, to overcome what James Adams calls perceptual blocks. Such techniques of "conscious blockbusting" (Adams, 1974) involve reversing established procedures, challenging assumptions, random stimulation and the use of analogies. Adams also suggests the use of "alternative thinking languages" which describe the problem differently.

It is easy to see the link between these techniques for liberating personal creativity and the group based systems already discussed; all involve manipulating the context within which the problem is handled and the separation of idea generation from evaluation. However, although we have evidence that creativity may be encouraged by situational factors, regrettably it cannot be guaranteed.

CREATIVE SKILLS

So far we have examined the various components of the creative act separately. We have discussed aspects of the product, the process, the person and the situation which have been identified as associated with creativity. This structure has been used for the convenience of authors and, it is hoped, readers alike, but we are convinced that the interaction between the three components of process, person and situation, is at least as important as the components themselves. Even the most highly gifted individuals are not always creative. Artists cannot always paint or designers always design. Similarly, following a prescribed pattern of behaviour associated with creativity will not necessarily achieve a creative result. Design methods can only be as good as the designers who employ them, and both are totally impotent without a problem. This then brings us to examine creativity in its professional context: the creative skill exercised by those whose job it is to be creative, whether they be scientists, designers or artists. Such people are all too easily imaged as back room boffins or artists in garretts from whose minds flows a ceaseless stream of original answers to perplexing and tantalizing problems. Of course the reality is rather more prosaic. Indeed it is important to identify yet another major difference between reality and image, for in a professional context creativity does not just involve producing solutions, but also finding problems. This distinction between problem solving and problem finding is of central importance in understanding the activity of a research scientist or that of a designer (Getzels, 1975).

Mackworth (1965) in his discussion of originality in science argues that there are good reasons for pursuing the distinction. He suggests that problem finders are more valuable to science than problem solvers since they are more scarce and that the supreme solver in science is now the computer. "The rate at which discoveries are made now depends more than ever on the number of people who can formulate important research problems". Mackworth argues that until input and output of computers is at a much higher (more human) level, computers can do little to help find problems. This suggests to Mackworth that we should concentrate our efforts on understanding more about the skills exhibited by excellent finders of problems. It is interesting to compare this argument with that advanced in a paper issued by the Board of Education of the Royal Institute of British Architects (1969): "In practical terms the schools (of architecture) must produce, and the RIBA must welcome those whose excellence is towards 'problem understanding' as well as those whose excellence is towards the design of solutions. These two types are not divided by a sharp line, but have tendencies towards either end of a spectrum. Both have a great deal in common, and both to some extent can do the other job".

More recent writers on design methodology have taken this argument even further. Cross (1975) insists that one of the characteristics of design is that "the resolution of design problems entails finding as well as solving problems." Cross also summarizes Rittel's argument that design problems are "wicked" in the sense that they are vicious and tricky. By this Cross means that, in design, there can be no objective formulation of the problem. "The boundaries and causes of any 'wicked' problem are inevitably hazy, ill defined, subjective and solution dependent. Many current manuals on design methodology exhort their readers to perceive their problems as hierarchially organized and thus each problem can be viewed as symptomatic of a higher level problem."

However, the sequence of problem finding is quite different in science and design. In science the task is to piece together available evidence from possibly diverse areas and compress these findings into a precise formulation of a new problem capable of being tested. In design by contrast the aim is not to be precise but rather to shake loose from a possibly rigidly defined problem, to a more general description which may embrace many other previously unforeseen problems. Thus being creative at problem finding in design and science may well not require the same skills. These differences may be reflected in the route taken through the creative cycle shown in Figure 15.1. Since, as we have seen, design problems cannot be comprehensively stated, it is traditional for designers to explore their problems through attempting solutions (Lawson, 1975) resulting in frequent returns from solution generation and evaluation to problem identification.

Mackworth urges investigation of problem finding skills but he warns that since they are so complex and intricate "such processes are likely to be too involved to permit adequate analysis by direct study". Agabani and Lawson are currently examining the way in which architectural students modify their perceptions of design problems as they develop solutions (Mackworth's warning has been well heeded!). Difficult though it may be, it seems to the authors that research into problem perception is likely to be one of the most productive directions in further understanding creativity. However it is necessary simultaneously to consider art, science and design since they differ so markedly in the way their problems are formulated.

Murphy (1947) in his biosocial approach to personality is helpful here for he suggests that mental processes are bipolar, being influenced both by external works and by inner needs. Murphy is interested in the individual's susceptibility to these influences and the resultant predominance of certain kinds of thinking observed in any one individual. However he emphasizes that behaviour is also situation dependent. For example science is directed towards solving real world problems while art is self-motivated and centres on the expression of inner thoughts. In this sense design comes between the two and occupies a whole spectrum of balance from chemical engineering to fashion design. Clearly, the individuals with high needs for self examination and expression may become creative in art but are unlikely to make productive scientists, while those who are fascinated by external problems may become creative research scientists but are unlikely to find sufficient inspiration to make great painters.

This argument tends to sound similar to C. P. Snow's (1964) "two cultures" or Hudson's (1966) "contrary imaginations". One of the great values of studying scientists and artists simultaneously is that of easily perceiving the error of Getzels and Jackson (1962) in identifying creativeness only with divergence. As previously described, in their development study Getzels and Jackson identified two types of child, those who excelled at conventional IQ tests and those who performed better at what they referred to as creativity tests. The conventional IQ test sets problems to which there is objectively one correct answer and clearly calls for what Hudson has since called convergent ability. By contrast what Getzels and Jackson call creativity tests set problems requiring divergence such as "how many functions can you think of for a paper clip?". Hudson has shown that boys who show convergent abilities tend to be drawn towards the sciences while divergers tend to be drawn towards the arts. Thus unless we are to abandon the notion of a creative scientist we must reject Getzels and Jackson's implicit conclusion that creativity is exclusively the result of divergent behaviour as they measured it. Hudson (1968) himself best summarizes this point: "Each field has its own waveband of emotional openness; only within this range of openness which each waveband affords are certain degrees of openness or restriction more conducive to good work than others."

Some artists work in a manner which is entirely original and creative, while others may follow and develop traditions without substantially breaking new ground. Turner must surely rank as one of the most creative English painters. He not only recorded scenes and events extraordinarily prolifically but also showed how to control paint in a completely new way, enabling us to appreciate light and colour as never before. His contribution to painting is unique. It is this essential creativity that singles him out in our admiration above the many in English painting.

But this creative quality can be seen in science as well as in art. Einstein, in arriving at his theory of relativity, connected the two previously well developed but unrelated concepts of mass and energy. James Watson in *The Double*

Helix (1968) describes how he and his colleague Francis Crick discovered the structure of DNA. The process that Watson describes is certainly not our conventional image of the convergent reasoning employed by scientists. At least one great leap into the unknown was required. The structure of DNA could not be deduced solely from previously gathered evidence. That precious and vital spark of divergent reasoning was to provide a new insight leading to many subsequent convergent trains of thought. Einstein's ideas were not the evolutionary result of a deductive process but rather the revolutionary outcome of a divergent leap. Kuhn's (1962) analysis of scientific revolutions shows how great advances in science are made when the two forces of traditional development and innovatory revolution are held in tension.

Creativity, then is not simply the ability for divergent thought but rather a balance of ability for divergent and convergent thought that is appropriate to the activity. The truly creative scientist is one who can bring to bear on his problem some of the artists' divergent thinking skill; while the creative artist needs to be able to apply the single-minded perseverance of the scientist to drive home his ideas, and what makes design such a challenging psychological task is the very even balance of these two sets of thinking skills that comprise the essential prerequisites of creative work.

THINKING ABOUT CREATIVE THINKING

In this chapter we have attempted to present a coherent overview of the current state of our knowledge of creativity. Unfortunately the resulting picture is all too frequently imprecise and incomplete. However, in spite of all the difficulties there remains a considerable body of research, much of it still continuing, devoted to promoting creativity. The majority of the studies we have discussed have been conducted on the basis that the promotion of creative talent is a desirable objective. If we readily accept this then we must face two consequences. Firstly, as has already been pointed out, creative individuals tend to be non-conformist and disruptive. We must therefore ensure that any organizational setting has the flexibility to cope with this (Taylor, 1972). Secondly, the kind of environmental setting which appears to foster creativity is frequently the very antithesis of that which already exists, especially within our educational system where settings may be highly structured. Of course if we conceptualize creative thinking as the cyclical operation of both divergent and convergent skills then we obviously need structured settings to enable the development of our convergent abilities. The question is to what extent continual exposure to such environments stifles the development of creative thinking skills?

We have already stated that one problem with the dissection of the creative act into temporally discrete stages is that this actually tells us very little about the skills involved. Furthermore, while we strongly favour a possible distinction between problem finding skills and problem solving skills, the paucity of empirical evidence precludes any detailed description of the differences or similarity between these. By now it should be apparent that there is one feature which we believe gains prominence over all others and that is that the creative thinker is extraordinarily competent at re-patterning information. What is more, the degree of competence shown is dependent on the particular combination of intellectual, personality and situational factors that gives rise to the possibility of a creative act taking place.

At this point it is worthwhile considering the work of three prominent psychologists, Piaget, Kelly and Bruner. Piaget (Flavell, 1963) views the adaptiveness of human beings as the result of the operation of two processes, accommodation and assimilation. Simply expressed, assimilation refers to the process of integrating new information into our existing cognitive frame of reference (or schema). We may take functional fixedness as an example of this, i.e. we attempt to integrate information about a new problem into our existing schema which itself is based on our solutions of previous yet similar problems. Such assimilation is essential, for without it we could never establish functional cognitive invariants and hence never learn to cope with our world. Conversely, accommodation is the process whereby we are able to restructure our cognitive schema in accordance with new information which fails to fit the existing schema. Is this not what happens when we suddenly see an old problem from a new perspective which may ultimately afford its solution? Perhaps what we are really talking about when we discuss creative thinking is our ability to accommodate?

In support of this viewpoint let us consider Kelly's (1955) proposed cycle of creativity, that is, creativity proceeds through an alternating cycle of loose and tight construing. He suggests that we may initially approach a problem with our tightly defined construct system only to find that we are unable to successfully formulate a solution, i.e. we are unable to assimilate the problem information into our existing cognitive schema which in the past afforded successful solutions. Consequently we must loosen our constructs such that they can be restructured, i.e. accommodation. It is this re-alignment which gives birth to the creative idea. Once an appropriate construct system (or schema) has been found we then begin to tighten our constructs as we realize the solution. Thus the creative cycle is terminated by tightened and validated construing. Following this we may then attempt to generalize our solution to other problems. Thus we can conceptualize creative thinking as a dynamic activity, a cycle of tight and loose construing, of assimilation and accommodation, of convergence and divergence.

From this viewpoint we can begin to formulate proposals for training creative thinking. The crucial role of contextual factors in facilitating creativity has previously been discussed in our brief review of some of the main training techniques which have been developed. An evaluative summary of these techniques is presented in Table 15.2. What most of them have in common is that they attempt to use the situation to force the person to reconstruct the problem, to accommodate new information. Thus individuals are encouraged to loosen their constructs by shifting the context of their perceptions, e.g. the use of analogies in synectics, or by generating ideas in uninhibiting situations, e.g. brainstorming. Once ideas have been generated they must eventually be evaluated and elaborated and the best solution selected and translated into practical reality.

This dynamic view of creative thinking also emphasizes that the ultimate expression of creativity will depend on the nature of the information being repatterned. Bruner *et al.,* (1966) have proposed that as our cognitive abilities develop so we change the kind of information which we use to represent the world. Basically they suggest a tripartite taxonomy into enactive, iconic and symbolic representation. Each level of representation reflects a progressive sophistication of our cognitive schemata. At the enactive level we develop our sensori-motor schemata, at the iconic level our visuo-spatial schemata, and finally at the symbolic level our linguistic and mathematical schemata emerge. Applying this view to our dynamic model provides a possible description of both the unity and variation in creative expression. The unity is the creative process, the cycle of events. However, the variation may reflect the operation of this cycle at varying levels of representation. Thus the creative athlete or ballet dancer may be recombining enactive information, the creative artist may be re-organizing iconic information, whereas the creative writer, poet, scientist or mathematician may be re-patterning symbolic information. Certain kinds of individuals may even need to operate at more than one level, e.g. the creative architect may need to manipulate both iconic and symbolic information.

Of course this is not a rigorous and flawless analysis of creative behaviour; it is obviously simplistic and yet it holds a certain intuitive appeal because it distinguishes between the kind of information being used and the processes which may re-pattern this, i.e. creative thinking skills. If accepted it does, however, have profound training implications, for if we are to successfully teach "patterning" skills we must first of all ensure the possession of a degree of competence in other cognitive skills. Laxton (1969), in discussing design education in schools, has suggested that children cannot be expected to be creative in design until they have what he calls a reservoir of visual ideas. Thus he suggests that the early years of design education should concentrate on providing the child with as great a range of novel experiences as possible. Only later should the child be expected to draw on these experiences and initiate new ideas by drawing on and combining previously unrelated ideas. This then seems to be almost the paradox of creative thinking: to achieve excellence in divergent skills we must first attain competence in convergent skills.

To summarize, it has been the aim of our argument to show that it is essentially the combination of intellectual, personality and situational factors

Table 15.2   An evaluative summary of the main techniques for enhancing creativity

Level of operation	Psychological processes affected	Technique	Evaluation
Individual	Personality	(a) Role playing	Techniques attempt to reverse or remove blocks, distortions or inhibitions to creative thinking. Evidence in favour is mainly anecdotal. No systematic evidence for real-life changes in quality or quantity of creative output
		(b) Hypnosis	
		(c) Psychotherapy	
Individual	Cognitive	(a) Level of consciousness: (i) relaxation, reflection, biofeedback, meditation (ii) dreams (iii) depressants – alcohol etc. (iv) stimulants – caffeine etc. (v) "mind-expanding" drugs – marijuana, morphine, LSD, mescaline, amphetamines, psilocybin, etc. (b) Personal focussing of attention on self and on particular features of stages of creative	Techniques attempt to enhance understanding, perception etc. of self and of world. Evidence for increased breadth of consciousness is anecdotal. No systematic evidence for changes in quality or quantity of creative output. Long term drug effects unknown

			more creative. Some evidence for an increased quantity of ideas but not an increased quality Some evidence that nominal groups, where individuals work alone and then present ideas to the group, generate more ideas than real groups where individuals work on ideas in the group, but no evidence for qualitative differences. No systematic evidence of real-life improvements in output
Group	Cognitive	Creative problem solving (Parnes, 1967)	Attempts to train a person to pass through following stages of creative thinking — fact finding, problem finding, idea finding, solution finding, acceptance finding. Training program uses many techniques including brainstorming. No systematic evidence for real-life improvements
Group	Cognitive	Synectics (Gordon, 1961)	Attempts to make the strange seem familiar and then make the familiar seem strange using operational mechanisms, e.g. metaphors, analogies etc. Evidence to date suggests possible improvements in real-life situations
Group	Cognitive, personality	Insight training (James et al., 1962)	Attempts to train individuals to develop an awareness of how cognitive and personality factors influence creative thinking. Evidence to date suggests that changes in attitude need to occur as a result of personality insight prior to changes in problem solving skills. Thus for maximum effectiveness both kinds of training are required. Some evidence for differential effects of training depending on personality of participant. No systematic evidence of real-life improvements in creative output

that gives rise to the possibility if a creative act taking place. Indeed, it could be argued that, if we use the word creativity in its broadest sense, we are all potentially creative. However, whether that potential can be realized may well depend on our ability to accurately perceive our own intellectual strengths and weaknesses, and having done so, to seek out suitable employment.

SQUARE PEGS IN ROUND HOLES: APPLYING CREATIVE THINKING TECHNIQUES

In concluding this chapter it is perhaps fitting that, having outlined what we feel to be the fundamental skills of creative thinking and having summarized several of the training methods which attempt to develop these skills, we end on a cautionary note. Between 1973 and 1974 two surveys of the awareness and use of various idea-generation methods in 500 industrial companies in Germany were conducted (Geschka, 1977). The main findings were that, firstly, the first survey showed that there was little general awareness of the variety of methods available (see Table 15.2 for several of these), in fact only brainstorming was widely known (although there was no check that all companies used this term to refer to the same method and Geschka points out that often free discussion is called "brainstorming").

Secondly in this survey many firms reported unforeseen difficulties in actually practising any kind of idea-generation method. Furthermore the success of these techniques varied with the kind of industry, e.g. they were more successful in mechanical than chemical industries. Finally, the second survey examined companies which had been using idea-generation methods and this showed that only when these were used with active interest and commitment by the firm was there any marked degree of success. Fowles (1977), in reviewing the literature on design methods, has shown how, after a sudden burst of publications in the early nineteen sixties, there have been no published reports on the actual application of design methods in architectural education during the last ten years. Green (1971) has warned that educational philosophies and attitudes are generally rather slow to change, and that new design methods may not easily be assimilated into existing curricula. Although there are undoubtedly many limitations to the kinds of study reported by Geschka and Fowles, if we take their findings as a general guide it does seem that in future we must not solely focus attention on developing techniques for enhancing creative thinking, but we must also devote considerable effort to examining the many problems which may be encountered with the organizational integration of such techniques.

References

Adams, J. L. (1974). *Conceptual Blockbusting.* (San Francisco: Freeman)

Barron, F. (1955). The disposition towards originality. *J. Abnorm. Soc. Psychol.,* **51,** 478

Bartlett, F. C. (1958). *Thinking: An Experimental and Social Study.* (London: Allen and Unwin)

de Bono, E. (1970). *Lateral Thinking: A Textbook of Creativity.* (London: Ward Lock)

de Bono, E. (1976). *Teaching Thinking.* (London: Temple Smith)

Bruner, J. S. (1962). The conditions of creativity. In Bruner, J. S. (1974). *Beyond The Information Given: Studies In the Psychology Of Knowing.* Ch. 12, pp. 208–217. (Surrey: Unwin Brothers Ltd)

Bruner, J. S., Olver, R. R. and Greenfield, P. M. (1966). *Studies in Cognitive Growth.* (London: Wiley and Sons)

Burt, C. (1962). Critical notice of 'Creativity and Intelligence' by Getzels and Jackson. *Br. J. Ed. Psychol.,* **32,** 292

Cropley, A. J. (1966). Creativity and intelligence. *Br. J. Ed. Psychol.,* **36,** 259

Cross, N. (1975). *Design and Technology.* Open University (T262 9)

Dellas, M. and Gaier, E. L. (1970). Identification of creativity: The individual. *Psychol. Bull.,* **73,** 55

Duncker, K. (1945). On problem solving. *Psychol. Monographs,* **62**(5), whole no. 270.

Edwards, M. P. and Tyler, L. E. (1965). Intelligence, creativity and achievement in a non-selective public junior high school. *J. Ed. Psychol.,* **56,** 96

Flavell, J. H. (1963). *The Developmental Psychology of Jean Piaget.* (London: van Nostrand)

Fowles, B. (1977). What happened to design methods in architectural education? *Design Methods and Theories,* **II,** 1, 17

Freeman, J., Butcher, H. J. and Christie, T. (1971). Creativity: A selective range of research (2nd ed.) *Research into Higher Education Monographs.* (London: Soc. Res. Into Higher Education Ltd.)

Geschka, H. (1977). Idea generation methods in industry: Part I. *Creativity Network,* **3** (2), 3

Getzels, J. W. (1975). Problem-finding and the inventiveness of solutions. *J. Creative Behaviour,* **9,** 12

Getzels, J. W. and Jackson, P. W. (1962). *Creativity and Intelligence: Explorations With Gifted Children.* (New York: Wiley)

Gordon, W. J. J. (1961). *Synectics: The Development of Creative Capacity.* (New York: Harper and Row)

Green, C. W. B. (1971). Learning to design. *Archit. Res. Teach.,* **2** (1), 40

Guilford, J. P. (1967). *The Nature of Human Intelligence.* (London: McGraw-Hill)

Hasan, P. and Butcher, H. J. (1966). Creativity and intelligence. A partial replication with Scottish children of Getzels and Jackson's study. *Br. J. Psychol.,* **57,** 129

Hinton, B. L. (1970). Personality variables and creative potential. *J. Creative Behaviour,* **4,** 210

Hudson, L. (1966). *Contrary Imaginations: A Psychological Study of the English Schoolboy.* (London: Methuen)

Hudson, L. (1968). *Frames of Mind: Ability, Perception and Self-perception in the Arts and Sciences.* (London: Methuen)

James, B. J., Guetzkow, H., Forehand, G. A. and Libby, W. L. (1962). *Education for Innovative Behaviour in Executives.* Co-operative Res. Proj. No. 975 Washington D.C.: Office of Ed., U.S. Dept. Health Ed. and Welfare. August

Kelly, G. A. (1955). *The Psychology of Personal Constructs* (2 vols.) (New York: Norton)

Kneller, G. F. (1965). *The Art and Science of Creativity.* (London: Holt, Rinehart and Winston)

Kogan, N. (1974). Creativity and sex differences. *J. Creative Behaviour,* **8,** 1

Kuhn, T. S. (1962). *The Structure of Scientific Revolutions.* (Chicago Univ. Press)

Lang, R. J. and Ryba, K. A. (1976). The identification of some creative thinking parameters common to the artisitic and musical personality. *Br. J. Ed. Psychol.,* **46,** 267

Lawson, B. R. (1975). Upside down and back to front. *RIBA J.* **82** (4), 25

Lawson, B. R. (1978). The architect as designer. In Singleton, W. T. (ed.). *The Study of Real Skills 1*. (Lancaster: MTP Press)

Laxton, M. (1969). Design education in practice. In Baynes K. (ed.). *Attitudes in Design Education*. (London: Lund Humphries)

Lovell, K. and Shields, J. B. (1967). Some aspects of a study of the gifted child. *Br. J. Ed. Psychol.*, **37**, 201

Luchins, A. S. and Luchins, E. H. (1950). New experimental attempts at preventing mechanization in problem solving. *J. Gen Psychol.*, **42**, 279

Mackinnon, D. W. (1962). The nature and nurture of creative talent. *Amer. Psych.*, **17**, 484

Mackinnon, D. W. (1976). The assessment and development of managerial creativity. *Creativity Network*, **2** (3), 3

Mackworth, N. H. (1965). Originality. *Am. Psychol.*, **20**, 51

Maier, N. R. F. D. (1931). Reasoning in humans. II. The solution of a problem and its appearance in consciousness. *J. Comp. Psychol.*, **12**, 181

Marsh, R. W. (1964). A statistical re-analysis of Getzels and Jackson's data. *Br. J. Ed. Psychol.*, **34**, 91

Matchett, E. (1968). Control of thought in creative work. *The Chartered Mechanical Engineer*, **15**, 163

McPherson, J. H. (1965). How to manage creative engineers. *Mech. Eng.*, **87** (2), 32

Meadow, A. and Parnes, S. J. (1959a). Evaluation of training in creative problem solving. *J. App. Psychol.*, **43** (3), 189

Meadow, A. and Parnes, S. J. (1959b). Influence of brainstorming instructions and problem sequence on a creative problem solving test. *J. App. Psychol.*, **43** (3), 413

Meer, B. and Stein, M. I. (1955). Measures of intelligence and creativity. *J. Psychol.*, **39**, 117

Murphy, G. (1947). *Personality: A Biological Approach to Origins and Structure*. (New York: Harper)

Osborn, A. F. (1963). *Applied Imagination*. 3rd Ed. (New York: Scribner)

Parnes, S. J. (1967). *Creative Behaviour Guidebook*. (New York: Scribner)

Poincaré, H. (1924). Mathematical creation. In Vernon, P. E. (ed.). (1970). *Creativity*. Ch. 7, pp. 78–88. (Harmondsworth: Penguin)

RIBA (1969). Strategies for architectural research. *RIBA Board of Education Paper*

Ripple, R. E. and May, F. B. (1962). Caution in comparing creativity and IQ. *Psychol. Rep.*, **10**, 229

Roe, A. (1951). A psychological study of eminent biologists. *Psychol. Monographs*, **65** (14), whole no. 331

Roe, A. (1952). A psychologist examines sixty-four eminent scientists. *Sci. Am.*, **187**, 21

Roe, A. (1953). A psychological study of eminent psychologists and anthropologists and a comparison with biological and physical scientists. *Psychol. Monographs*, **67** (2), whole no. 352

Ryle, G. (1949). *The Concept of Mind*. (London: Hutchinson)

Shapiro, R. J. (1966). The identification of creative research scientists. *Psychologia Africana*, **2**, 99

Shapiro, R. J. (1968). Creative research scientists. *Psychologia Africana Monograph Supplement*, **4**

Snow, C. P. (1964). *The Two Cultures: and a Second Look*. (New York: Mentor)

Spender, S. (1946). The making of a poem. In Vernon, P. E. (ed.). (1970). *Creativity*, Ch. 6, pp. 61–76. (Harmondsworth: Penguin)

Stein, M. I. (1974). *Stimulating Creativity*. 2 vols. (London: Academic Press)

Taylor, C. W. (1972). *Climate for Creativity*. (Oxford: Pergamon Press)

Thomson, R. (1959). *The Psychology of Thinking*. (Harmondsworth: Penguin)

Torrance, E. P. (1962). *Guiding Creative Talent*. (New Jersey: Prentice-Hall)

Vernon, P. E. (1964). Creativity and intelligence. *Educ. Res.*, **6**, 163

Vinacke, W. E. (1974). *The Psychology of Thinking*. 2nd ed. (London: McGraw-Hill)

Wallach, M. A. and Kogan, N. (1965). A new look at the creativity–intelligence distinction. *J. Person.*, **33**, 348

Wallas, G. (1926). *The Art of Thought*. (London: Jonathon Cape)

Watson, J. D. (1968). *The Double Helix: A Personal Account of the Discovery of the*

Structure of DNA. (London: Wiedenfield and Nicolson)

Wertheimer, M. (1945). *Productive Thinking*. (New York: Harper)

Whitfield, P. R. (1975). *Creativity in Industry*. (Harmondsworth: Penguin)

Yamomoto, K. (1965). Effects of restriction of range and test unreliability on correlation between measures of intelligence and creative thinking. *Br. J. Ed. Psychol.*, **35**, 300

16
Final Discussion

W. T. SINGLETON

VARIETY

The intention, in selecting the studies in this book, was to illustrate the enormous variety of skilled performance. This stems partly from variations in objectives and partly from variations in procedures; the two are linked of course but not completely, since procedures change not only with objectives but also with the capacities, training, experience and temperament of the individual skilled performer. The skills analyst must match this variety with a corresponding range and flexibility in his procedures. There are also changes with his objectives; the purposes of skills analysis range from an academic need to know which may be conceptualized in terms of any one or any combination of the human sciences, through to all the operational activity associated with human resources: education, selection, guidance, placement, training, work design, system design and manpower studies.

This variety of approach and interest can be demonstrated by a precis of just one or two aspects of each of the preceding papers.

Singleton – Skills link person attributes and jobs which is the problem of occupational disability. There are at present no skill taxonomies adequate for this purpose but it is possible to enumerate a relevant Job Demands/Human Factors taxonomy.

Nettelbeck – To describe the mentally retarded effectively an assessment with greater relevance than that provided by traditional psychometrics is needed – one which incorporates the wide spectrum of potentially relevant attributes and which relates more clearly to training deficits and potential occupations.

Kyle – For hearing-impaired children a more sensitive description of their attributes is needed which is not so dependent on 'normal' standards. Education and job choice should relate person attributes to the societal situation. The deaf would thereby be less underestimated and underemployed.

Welford – Human performance results from the interaction of three sets of factors: demands, capacities and strategies; this last is the skills domain. In aging, demands and capacities change so that strategies must change correspondingly.

Spurgeon and Thomson – There are conflicts of goals and strategies between the various parties involved in an institution but there must be some resolution because the system will not function without at least tacit consent of all parties. For an inmate there is a switch of life plan made up of events, people and activities accompanied by a drastic change in the significance of time.

Singleton – The designer 'with safety in mind' brings into focus on one problem a very wide and not obviously related range of information from data, incidents, history, folklore and knowledge. Input and output processes proceed almost independently within a wide-band window related but not locked fixedly on to real time.

Godden and Baddeley – Human skills are extraordinarily resistant to stress, at least for these selected and experienced commercial divers. Compensation for or adaptation to these stresses involves slowing down and intelligent adaptability in job design and conduct. Advanced technology and adequate finance still cannot provide a substitute for direct human performance.

Drasdo – The rock climber is exploring himself and in particular his physical and nervous resources. These two resources are different but both are limited.

Cochran – During the swing itself golfers have one key thought, usually the mental impression of some feeling they wish to experience during the swing. These key thoughts change from time to time; perhaps they must change to retain the overall pattern of the swing and to avoid exaggerating one element of it. Expert players who utilize a variety of shots tend simply to convert the wish to play a particular kind of shot directly into the production of it.

Edwards – Excellence is in the 'executive programme' demonstrated by the ability to 'put it all together' and to keep it together in conditions of stress. The executive programme and the balance of sub-routines, i.e. the expertise, changes with kinds of pilot: military, airline, engineering-test, executive and instructor.

Brown – There are at least three distinguishable if not entirely separate aspects of the skills of the musician: 'technique' which depends on mastery of the instrument, 'musicality' which is to do with structure and artistic quality and 'being musical' which describes success in interpretation and communication.

Branton – For the research worker, discovery is "a common meeting place of predicates", which is "a rendezvous with a stranger". Since it is a stranger how does the discoverer know when they have met?

Wirstad – It is difficult in academic discussion and impossible in operational terms to isolate perceptual processes from sensory activity, broader cognitive activity and even the resultant outputs in motor and locomotor terms. Different theories about perception differ in their relative attention to the associated processes.

Hedge and Lawson – Creative thinking is accommodation – restructuring of cognitive schema in accordance with new information, but this must proceed in parallel with assimilation – the integrating of relevant information into existing schema (in Kelly's terms the alternating cycle of tight and loose construing). Unity and variation in creative expression originate respectively from the process (the cycle of events) and from representational switching between enactive, iconic and symbolic modes.

COMPLIANCE AND EXCELLENCE

The variety of skilled performance was deliberately emphasised by concentrating on what were seen to be two extremes of compliance and excellence. It was hoped also that there would be some contrast between compliant performance and excellent performance which would illuminate the principles of skilled performance. It seems fair to conclude that although the variety of skilled performance has been demonstrated the differences between compliance and excellence are not clear and consistent. One source of obscurity is that neither persons nor occupations are readily classifiable in these terms. It is true that the disabled, the aged and the institutionalized are, on average and at a given time, very different in both physiological and psychological terms from rock climbers, golfers and pilots but, as a person, a rock climber can become disabled in the time it takes for a fall, and all skilled practitioners are subject to ageing at a rate where about a decade makes an appreciable difference to performance. Excellent musicians seem to be least affected by age – this is true for the young and the old. There is a group exemplified by the diver who must be compliant in that the environment is extremely hostile but in coping with his environment there can be indications of excellence. In terms of the dominance of safety and risk aspects, diving, climbing and flying have much in common. The rock climber differs from the others as described in this book because he has no commercial objectives, he is exploring his own temperament rather than serving a societal need, but there are equivalents to this in the other activities, respectively the speleologist, the underwater sportsman and the private pilot. The musician and the research worker may be disabled in other functional contexts and visual detection is an aspect of skill common to almost all skilled performance. For creative thinking there do seem to be thresholds of intelligence respectively below which the concept has not been explored and above which there is no obvious relationship between the two. As often happens in the skill context we have a taxonomy, in this case compliance/excellence which has some value but it is by no means universally useful or applicable.

Compliance is a surface phenomenon beneath which these are active positive processes. Nettelbeck reminds us that the traditional "dull work for dull minds" dictum has little evidence to support it. It is negative in that it discourages the positive approach of more adaptive training methods which can elevate considerably the level of performance of the retarded. The characteristic of perseveration may originate in the need to gain attention and respect rather than being a consequence of a limited breadth of interest. In institutions the inmates do not have a diminished need for information, there is merely a change in the styles of acquiring it.

Excellence also has some superficial characteristics which are not sustained by detailed analysis. In diving and climbing the excellent performer is not the 'cowboy' dashing into risky situations without fear, nor the cool pilot, golfer or musician performing unemotionally and impeccably. All these skilled performers are aware of and are subject to all kinds of anxieties and stresses but they achieve their goals by technical excellence and drive which override and even utilize the stress rather than avoid it. Excellence remains difficult to identify because it takes different forms even within the same task but it is more frequently centred in perceptual and integrating skills rather than in motor skills. Cochran considers that the prize winning golfer does everything a little bit better, but an aspect of personality which indicates resistance to stress is decisive. Wirstad suggests that although the ordinary rifle aimer can be assisted, certainly during training, by separating out the factors affecting anticipation of target position, the excellent aimer integrates all the factors unconsciously and his performance may diminish if he is persuaded to analyse it. For the climber, Drasdo describes it as imagination which can appear as 'an eye for a line", and determination which is the overt expression of motivation. Branton asks the interesting question "how does one excel oneself?" and emphasises what he calls "the open-endedness of excellence". Hedge and Lawson make a similar point in mentioning Bruner's graphic description of "an act that produces effective surprise". They also emphasise that creativity is expressed in problem finding as well as problem solving.

CONCEPTS OF SKILL

Corresponding to the variety in skilled performance related to different tasks there is variety in individual capacities and strategies ostensibly in relation to the same demand. As Nettlebeck (p. 63) puts it, "Retarded persons should not be regarded as constituting a homogeneous population". Kyle points out (p. 82) that "It is meaningless to talk about 'the deaf child' as a single entity". Welford (p. 99) writes that "Individuals differ greatly in the rates at which their various capacities change: a man or woman of say forty may be typical of his or her age in some respects but resembles the average of those many years younger or older in others". Spurgeon and Thomson mention the considerable difference between individuals in adaptation to the institution which in the case of the prison at least justifies a taxonomy of personality styles. Singleton emphasises that the situation of an impaired person differs greatly in terms of supporting skills depending on whether the impairment is congenital or traumatic in origin. Kyle encompasses this point within his description of handicap as a function of degree of loss, age of onset and intelligence; in particular the deaf child who was able to learn to read before the onset of deafness is in a very different position or context from one who could not do so.

The importance of the environment or context is emphasised consistently. Branton quotes Bartlett's view that skill is behaviour capable of internal modification, but it has the second characteristic of being in touch with the real world. Singleton describes the distinction which has become necessary in the world of disablement between impairment which is person-centred through disability, which is the activity context, to handicap which is a function of the physical, economic and social environments as well as the disability. In Welford's account of ageing the different demands on particular age groups are just as relevant as the changing capacities. The dramatic change in demands as a person enters an institution is seen by Spurgeon and Thomson as the essence of the problem of institutionalization. The same is true in a mainly physical sense for the diver in that he has to cope with physiological stressors, neutral bouyancy, water viscosity and unchanged inertia, although Godden and Baddeley note also that these are informational aspects to do with visibility underwater and surface–undersea communication. Singleton suggests that safety problems can usefully be considered under the three headings of the safe situation, the safe operator and the safe climate. Hedge and Lawson emphasise quite strongly that "it would be easy to conclude that . . . person plus process describes the cognitive phenomenon. Nothing could be further from the truth . . . above all creativity is about context". Within context they include the relevant experience and attitudes of the individual, group relationships and the sense of urgency and the cost of failure. It is worth noting once more that the difficulty, almost the impossibility, of simulating context is a fundamental limitation on the application of experimental methods to the study of skill.

In addition in Persons, Processes and Situations, Hedge and Lawson also identify key aspects of creative thinking in Products and Skills which has close similarities to Singleton's subdivision of Person-, Job-, Skill- and Operational-centred issues on the very different topic of disablement. Another interesting similarity in relation to two different topics is in Branton's emphasis on the good research worker as the man who can concentrate on one objective and yet not miss the unexpected while Edwards discussed the expert pilot's ability to reel off perceptual–motor skills and also have the ability to swiftly interrupt when subtle indications appear that this is necessary. The reverse of this is noted as one of the basic sources of human error – namely what Singleton refers to as preoccupation and Godden and Baddeley call perceptual narrowing. On the other hand Cochran suggests that the expert golfer concentrates on the stroke being played – he looks neither forward at the next one nor backwards at the previous one. The close integration of perceptual and motor skills described in the introduction is exemplified in a number of papers. Wirstad classifies kinds of perception in terms of the related peripheral activity. Godden and Baddeley mention in relation to the skill of the diver that his carrying out of activities with reliance on touch probably needs to be sustained by good visual/spatial memory. Cochran concludes that judgement and execution in putting are less separable than might be imagined. Drasdo mentions the climbing phenomenon of dealing with a problem "on the auto-pilot" which means solving it without conscious intervention as the actions are taking place. Nettelbeck describes the limited psychomotor performance so often associated with mental retardation while Branton notes the comple-mentary effect that gifted research workers are often physically highly dexterous – he sees an interesting aspect of thinking in vicarious manipulation. There is some contrast here with the Hedge and Lawson emphasis on incubation as a key phase in the creative process. They suggest that experience can have a mechanizing effect which impairs creativity and this coincides with Branton's point that originality is often in the direction of combination and in getting the order right after selecting the essentials. Identifying the essentials can be described in other terms as selective attention and Nettelbeck mentions that the retarded are poor in this respect and also in anticipation.

The concept of the objective defining the boundary of a skill inevitably raises the complex issue of motivation. This crops up in many different guises in the various chapters. Spurgeon and Thomson comment mildly that the exact nature of motives and distinctions between primary and secondary desires is rather hazy in psychology. They introduce the Berger, Berger and Kellner notion of a life-plan with time and motive parameters in a context of events and people. Welford and Nettlebeck, as academic colleagues, have a common view of the importance of understanding motives and motivation particularly in relation to feedback. As Welford puts it if feedback is to be an incentive it must indicate a favourable cost–benefit ratio for the action taken. Welford also reminds us of Woodworth's principle that activity, and in particular results from action, is a fundamental human need or motive. This matches Drasdo's view that people climb rocks in spite of the obvious dangers because they enjoy the self-appraisal of expending energy resources, physical and nervous. Throughout the descriptions of and comments about excellence there runs a common theme of the importance of drive which manifests itself in the overcoming of obstacles and resistance to stress. Hedge and Lawson point out that the creative individual is, in one sense, at odds with society where conservation is endemic, so that he must have security of self.

Singleton emphasises that risks are inseparable from purposes. The orthodox assessment of risks in terms of probabilities is inadequate for the maintenance of safety because even highly improbable events do happen occasionally. The concept of the fair risk looks very different after the disastrous event. One value of the skilled man is that his dynamic appraisal of events and behaviour as they develop on the spot and at the time can result in the remote possibility becoming even more remote. This is the converse of his adaptive behaviour in the creative context where the objective is to make the remote possibility less remote.

Not surprisingly in a book concentrating on non-average human behaviour the importance of individual differences is another common theme. In the education and training context both Nettelbeck and Kyle point out that different systems suit different children. This has wide research implications; it is no use attempting to determine whether disadvantaged children should be educated separately or in company with their peers. We can be fairly sure that one system will be best for some children and the other for others. Similarly, it is no use attempting to generate the best training methods; some methods are best for some children, others for other children.

In relation to excellence also it seems clear that it may be achieved to the same level by very different combinations of procedures and individual attributes. It follows that means are a dubious source of assessment if ends are the important criterion. Edwards mentions that pilot assessors rely on effective achievement as the main criterion but with some reference to procedures.

SKILLS APPRAISAL

The possibility of a straightforward universal technique for the analysis of skills diminishes even further in the light of the case studies in this book. Edwards points out that the key to skilled performance is in the overall control or the 'executive programme' and that skills analysis in the sense of studies of component skills diverts attention from this. Singleton suggests that great flexibility in methods of analysis of accidents is required and the method is mainly a function of the analyst's objective. In this respect the skills analyst is the same as any other skilled performer, his objectives determine his procedures or behaviour. This is one aspect of the complexity of institutionalization as described by Spurgeon and Thomson in that the different groups of participating people – society, staff and inmates – often have quite different and sometimes conflicting objectives.

In almost all the chapters there is some mix of evidence based on academic or laboratory experiment and evidence based on operational or field observation. Cochran is perhaps the most fundamental with a strong foundation in the physics of the golf swing, but models constructed on mechanical arguments are checked by observation of and discussion with expert performers and experienced teachers. Godden and Baddeley necessarily begin with the physiological aspects of the diver's artificial environment; they have in common with Welford a strong reliance on human performance experiments supplemented by field studies including skilled observation. Wirstad and Hedge and Lawson's papers also have a foundation in experiments but they place more reliance on the study of the problem solver in action in the real situation because of the importance of the context parameter. This also is true of Branton who relies on a mix of biographies, interviews and broader discussion. Kyle also starts from physics and moves through psychometrics to the overall situation review. Nettelbeck and Brown would probably have liked to rely more on psychometrics but, as Nettelbeck points out, the classical measurement of human abilities is not comprehensive enough to describe the retarded in the context of planning either education or employment. There is a widening of the range of required skills analysis for the retarded, in that training cannot be only job-related, it must also include the need for independent functioning of the person. Brown suggests that although tests may indicate some structure for musical 'technique' there is no corresponding way of analysing the equally important attribute of 'musicality'. Edwards and Singleton (safety) rely mainly on the distillation of extensive experience in human factors problem solving in their areas of interest. Singleton (disability), Brown, Spurgeon and Thomson and Drasdo have used as the main source discussion with those who have practised, including themselves, in their respective fields of interest supplemented of course by the writings of specialists. In relation to the disabled Singleton emphasises the confusion in practice between assessment and guidance on the one hand and therapy and rehabilitation on the other. It is apparently convenient for practitioners not to concern themselves with any such distinction but it does make the analysis and description of what is happening that much more difficult. Edwards describes two different ways of making an assessment of pilots – one devised and used by psychologists which depends on a taxonomy of education, experience, technical ability, personality and performance under stress, and one devised and used by peer pilots who rely mainly on observing degree of success in achieving different sub-system or task goals. These two different methods appear implicitly in the Godden and Baddeley study of the diver. The achievement method would be particularly difficult to apply to the climber who, as Drasdo points out, is engaged in deliberately maintaining a degree of uncertainty about the outcome of his activities. Nonetheless, Brown suggests that relatively speaking climbing ought to be much easier to assess than musical achievement, which depends on the complicated player–listener interaction. Cochran has no problem in measuring achievement at golf. Hedge and Lawson have a difficult criterion problem in that, as they point out, the assessment of creativity is highly dependent on the assessors values. With Branton, Cochran, Brown, Wirstad and Edwards they are wary about what they call "the difficulty of systematically dissecting the creative act" and the possibility of losing what is sought during the process of dissection.

The conclusion of the first book is supported, namely that the analytical or investigatory procedure changes partly with the personality of the investigator but mainly with the topic of study. The skills analyst is a skilled operator who varies his method with his objectives and with his experience of previous and current success in progressing towards objectives.

RESEARCH NEEDS

In common with other kinds of psychology we could benefit greatly from the clarification of the whole mix of constructs including self-actualization, motivation, drive and need. Self is a very old psychological and philosophical issue. The studies in this book re-emphasise that even when the skilled operator is ostensibly coping only with the physical world he must also cope with himself. This is the most complex part of the context in which he is operating. As a biological entity he has a variety of potent attributes but these have their own consequences for behaviour. He can generate, store and release energy and although these mechanisms can operate at different rates they cannot be switched on and off. Thus the organism must necessarily be active most of the time to disperse the energy. As a matter of survival or safety this energy release must be monitored and controlled by the elaborate sensory and control systems and these are designed to function in relation to sequences and hierarchies of self-organized objectives. From this point of view introspection leading to the postulate of a motivational hierarchy is a gross rationalization. Such behaviour is a necessary consequence of the structure and function of the energy generation and control systems which must operate if the organism is to survive. From this point of view the concepts of need and drive are closer to the fundamentals of what is happening than is motivation. Motivation may belong in a category with other terms such as stress, health and safety which are useful in lay conversation but have no value in systematic investigations for two reasons. Firstly they are an inextricable mix of too many parameters and secondly they orient the research worker in the opposite direction to that in which he might make progress; the reverse terms are the ones which can be approached positively, respectively needs, strain, disease and danger. However this is highly speculative and any research progress on these matters would be most welcome. Specifically the concept of risk in relation to purpose is worthy of extensive investigation.

Another topic which has emerged is individual differences. There are differences in attributes which relates back to self discussed above and there are differences in demands but these are not independent. Attributes include capacities and skills; the skills are developed to match capacities to demands but the demands themselves are interactions between the external parameters of the world and other people in it and internal parameters which are detected by self-appraisal. While this is a relevant cautionary context which reminds the research worker of the complexities of the matters he is dealing with, it need not detract from more mundane but important detailed problems such as the assessment of disabled young people. If individual differences can be structured and methods of measuring some of the parameters can be provided, then assessors and trainers can be better equipped with the tools and skills needed to guide the individual child into and through the most appropriate educational and work systems.

It was suggested in Volume I that the experimental psychologists have fallen into the trap of overemphasising those aspects of human behaviour which are most readily manipulable and measurable in the laboratory. Correspondingly it emerges from these studies that the psychometrists have been obsessed by one attribute of the person, namely intelligence, presumably because it is important in the educational world which is the context most familiar to academics. In other worlds where ordinary people live and work, intelligence is relatively much less important and it would be more relevant if the academics could structure and measure human characteristics on which life and work skills are based.

For problems as apparently different as the concept of motivation and improving techniques for disability assessment there are underlying similarities in the potentially useful method of study. One such method is the one exemplified in these two books. Namely creative investigation of particular cases, and comparison and contrast of such investigations in the hope that generalizations will emerge. The fact that the skills analyst bases his studies on practical problems does not diminish his interest in and respect for good theories about human behaviour. Behind every analysis there is some structure and this structure is determined equally by the operational objectives and by at least an implicit model of the functioning of the human operator. It is usually, although not always, helpful to make his modelling as explicit as possible.

OPERATIONAL UTILITY

The material in the various chapters of this book is less directly useful in practice than that in the previous book, perhaps because the emphasis has extended from industry to include also education and leisure. Thus we enter the more elusive area of quality of life as well as gainful employment. Drasdo for the climber and Cochran for the golfer are ambivalent about the benefits of research because it is essential to enjoyment of these activities that some match is maintained between the difficulty of the task and the ability of the performer. Research and innovations can disturb this equilibrium. The chapters concerned with disablement consistently emphasise the importance of an occupation which simultaneously utilizes, even stretches, the capacities of the individual and makes some contribution to society. Even for the very old, Welford suggests that the proper strategy is to optimize rather than minimize external demands and to maintain an appropriate variety of stimulation. Kyle and Nettelbeck are clearly dissatisfied with a situation in which their respective concerns, the hearing-impaired and the retarded, are not realizing their full potential in society. Their remedy, suggested also by Singleton in relation to the disabled generally, is that we need more comprehensive accurate and work-related descriptions of the impairments so that we can facilitate the progress towards adequate employment. At present it does seem feasible that application of principles of skill will help attain this. Spurgeon and Thomson point out that sensitivity to the less obvious needs of inmates including greater skills in intercommunication will not only serve a humane purpose but may well make a contribution to the more concrete achievements of institutions, such as effective containment and eventual transfer back into society of prisoners and more rapid recovery of health for hospital patients. For the higher levels of human endeavour Branton and Hedge and Lawson share the modest aim of improving the probability of creativity by providing the individual with a more facilitatory environment or context. These things cannot be made to happen but they can marginally be persuaded if one understands more about the processes involved. Similarly, for the chapters about particular occupations, the grasp of the human factors in what is happening provides a foundation for suggestions about improved training and task design as well as the context in which suggestions which arise from this or other sources can be evaluated.

CONCLUSION

1. Principles of human skill

The first volume concluded with the propositions that man is conceptually a model builder and categorizer and operationally a map-maker and navigator. The overall control system is dominated by objectives of widely differing degrees of immediacy and determinacy and operates through a hierarchy of self-monitoring systems from immediate kinaesthetic feedback to a conscious management-type control.

This still seems an appropriate although not a sufficient description of his behaviour. Even when he is restricted to coping with the physical world he must also cope with himself. The concept of skills bounded by particular aspirations requires an understanding of the aspirations as well as the procedures outlined above. Both arise from the nature of the internal mechanisms, particularly the continuous energy generating system and the monitoring and control systems which modulate the output of energy.

In addition to the general human operator we must also consider the particular operations – the individual is unique in his array of capacities, in his previous experience and in the ways in which these are manifested in his skilled performance.

2. General procedure for skill appraisal

If the task involved is relatively straightforward then follow the prescription given at the end of the first book and in the introduction to this book. For more complex skills widen the flexibility of approach within a structure where there are three sources of evidence:

  (i) The performance of the skilled operator

  (ii) His introspections about what he is doing and how he is doing it

  (iii) Empathy from the skills analyst who is himself a skilled operator.

Design the analysis with relative emphasis on these sources determined by the particular problem, the resources available and personal inclination. Proceed on the basis that the observer and observed are not independent but are partners in the shared enterprise of interpreting their joint skilled performance. Acknowledge the fallibility of this method by including checks of validity as an essential part of the implementation.

Author Index

Bold numerals refer to names cited in reference list at chapter ends

Subject Index